THE MAKING OF
MASCULINITIES

THE MAKING OF MASCULINITIES

The New Men's Studies

Edited by
HARRY BROD

ROUTLEDGE
New York   London

Published in 1987 by Unwin Hyman

4th printing in 1992 by
Routledge, an imprint of
Routledge, Chapman and Hall, Inc.
29 West 35 Street
New York, NY 10001

Published in Great Britain by
Routledge
11 New Fetter Lane
London EC4P 4EE

Library of Congress Cataloging-in-Publication Data

The Making of masculinities.

   Includes bibliographies and index.
   1. Mens studies.   2. Men.   3. Masculinity (Psychology)
4. Sex role.   I. Brod, Harry, 1951–
HQ1088.M35   1986   305.5′1   86-28796
ISBN 0-04-497035-8
ISBN 0-415-90702-0 (PB)

British Library Cataloguing in Publication Data

The Making of masculinities: the new men's
   studies.
   1. Men   2. Masculinity (Psychology)
   I. Brod, Harry
   305.3′1   HQ1067
   ISBN 0-04-497035-8
   ISBN 0-415-90702-0

In remembrance of the past,
appreciation of the present,
and anticipation of the future,
this book is dedicated to
Srulek Brod and Lieselotte Schüfftan,
my parents before they were my parents,
to Maria Papacostaki, with love and thanks,
and to our children, Artemis Leah and Alexandros Zev,
when they shall no longer be children.

Contents

Foreword

"Man": the word seems as easy to define as "dog" or "stick." Everyone can conjure up a picture of a man. He is an adult, human male. Everyone knows at least one man — at home, school, work, or in the mirror. However, we often do not know what we think we do. This is one of the lessons of the detective stories in which neighbors in a sleepy village suddenly discover a corpse in the church yard and a murderer next door. "Man" is complicated.

Signs of this complexity are pervasive. Look, to take only one example, at a standard reference work, *The Penguin Dictionary of Quotations*. Though it has no entries for "masculinity," it has 18 entries for "mankind," over 175 for "men," and nearly 200 for "man." The first of these is a ballad about a banished man who goes into the green-wood alone. The last is the famous, even notorious, paternal injunction from Kipling's *Gunga Din*:

> *If you can fill the unforgiving minute*
> *With sixty seconds' worth of distance run,*
> *Yours is the Earth and everything that's in it,*
> *And — which is more — you'll be a Man, my son!*

In part, the word "man" is perplexing because each historical period, every society, and each group within a society interprets the raw materials of existence in its own way. Its interpretative practices help to distinguish a period, a society, a group. A turkey for contemporary Boston is not the same bird as it was for the Massachusetts Bay Colony. The more anthropologists, sociologists, and historians explore the meanings of being "a man," the more inconsistent, contradictory, and varied they become. A Harvard graduate in contemporary Cambridge is not the same "man" as he would have been in a seventeenth-century American colony. Today, a Harvard graduate might even be a woman.

In part, the word "man" is manifold because of the work of a new intellectual enterprise, "men's studies," a complement to women's studies. Taking shape in the 1960s, women's studies is now a rich body of theory, ideas, and facts. Women's studies argues that our narratives about "mankind" are exactly that, narratives about a kind of man. Deliberately or carelessly, they have excluded women. When we think about women, we realize that their experiences tend to be different, not only from each other, but from those of men. Odysseus has his story, Penelope hers. What, women's studies asks, would Penelope say, about herself, about Odysseus, about ship-building, about Ithaca, if she were to speak by herself? For herself? Of herself? Yet, women's studies goes on. Even if the stories of Odysseus and Penelope do flow through separate channels, they are a part of the same network of social relations, the same social landscape. That terrain has taught Odysseus how to be "manly," Penelope how to be "womanly."

As women's studies brought women into history, men's studies began to ask how men had experienced history *as men*, as carriers of masculinity. To be "masculine" is to have a particular psychological identity, social role, cultural script, place in the labor force, and sense of the sacred. In secular, modern industrial cultures, "real men" should define themselves in at least three ways. First, they earn money in the public labor force and support their families through that effort. Next, they have formal power over women and the children in those families. Being a man means being stronger than women and children. Finally, they are heterosexual. They sleep with the women whom they dominate and bully the homosexuals whose desires openly surge elsewhere.

Postindustrial cultures undercut such a definition of masculinity. They are heedlessly destructive of the industrial jobs that men have traditionally filled; heedlessly generative of the lower-paying service jobs that women frequently occupy. Less problematically, postindustrial cultures also tend to accept the values of egalitarianism within the family and sexual variety. One of the current tensions in the United States is between those who are fighting to retain the older pattern of masculinity and those who are struggling to permit newer forms to emerge.

Like women's studies, men's studies assumes that "masculinity" and "femininity" are the products, not of God, not of nature, but of historical processes. To be sure, both women's studies and men's studies have some practitioners who believe that nature demands that males become masculine; females feminine. For them, the wiring of the brain and the plugging away of the hormones, especially those old warhorses "testosterone" and "estrogen," carry out nature's orders. However, most scholars in men's studies have concluded that gender, our sense of being masculine or feminine, is as much a human construct as the pyramids or pewter. Like all human constructs, gender systems can change.

Believing in the possibilities of change, men's studies wants the future to be more generous than the present. Explicitly or implicitly, men's studies asks the future to embody certain values. One is that of fatherhood, in which men will nurture both sons and daughters with tender wisdom. Another is that of friendship, in which men will seek affectionate bonds with both other men and women. Still another is that of flexibility. Boys will grow up to be men, but no boy will think that being a man demands marching in lockstep with other men while women cheer them on from the sidelines.

The Making of Masculinities: The New Men's Studies: its dogged, imaginative scholarship, sticking to its task, is rewriting that deceptively simple word, "man."

CATHARINE R. STIMPSON

Acknowledgments

I could not have formed the conception of men's studies this book embodies without the support of two particular groups of friends and colleagues. I would first like to thank my colleagues on the faculty of the Program for the Study of Women and Men in Society at the University of Southern California for ongoing intelligent, critical, and committed dialogue regarding the issues raised in this volume. In the chronological order in which I came to have the privilege of working with them, they are: Gloria Orenstein, Joelle Juillard, Judith Stiehm, Mark Kann, Lois Banner, Carol Jacklin, Walter Williams, and Helen Horowitz. I also had the great fortune to feel I had a support community spread out over the nation in the persons of the men and women of the National Organization for Changing Men (NOCM). I am particularly appreciative of the work of NOCM's Men's Studies Task Group, in which Joseph Pleck, Sam Femiano, Martin Acker, James Doyle, and Shepherd Bliss have played particularly important roles in creating and nurturing a community of scholars and activists that continues to nourish and challenge me. I have felt a special kinship in the men's movement with Tom Mosmiller, with whom I share a sense of the rightness of certain things.

Maria Papacostaki remains the first and foremost reader of all my writing. As the person who knows me best, she has on numerous occasions saved me from speaking against myself. She and our children, Artemis and Alexandros, have also immeasurably increased my understanding of men's issues related to fathering.

The contributors to this volume deserve special thanks. They committed themselves to this project before I could guarantee any rewards. The Introduction to the volume has been improved by comments several of them made, and the brief introductions that precede each section are in most cases simply compiled and edited by me from abstracts written by the authors themselves.

The entire manuscript has benefited from comments by James Doyle, Martin Acker, and anonymous reviewers. The enthusiasm and support for the book shown by Lisa Freeman-Miller, my editor at Allen & Unwin, have also contributed greatly to what success I hope this volume may have, and certainly to my peace of mind in assembling it.

Introduction:
Themes and Theses of Men's Studies

Harry Brod

DELINEATING THE FIELD

In the call for papers that led to this anthology, I described it as one "designed to analyze the depths of and exemplify the best of the deconstruction and reconstruction of masculinity emerging from the new men's studies." This purpose has been achieved. The essays in this volume can legitimately claim to demonstrate the state of the art in men's studies. They are wide ranging in scope and finely nuanced in detail. They appropriate useful insights and methodologies from existing literature, as well as initiate innovative directions. Using the essays collected here as exemplars, in this introductory essay I articulate some of the principal characteristic themes and findings in men's studies. I do not summarize each article individually; instead, I highlight salient connections among them. Men's studies is a recent and, by comparison with more established fields, still relatively small addition to the academy. Nonetheless, it is a growing field, and it has matured sufficiently to allow for some evaluation.

Throughout the essays in this collection is a shared sense of the project of men's studies, a sense that men have been seen "through a glass darkly," a sense that there is a need for men to be re-cognized in some fundamental way. James Riemer, in "Rereading American Literature from a Men's Studies Perspective: Some Implications," writes: "To borrow a term from feminist criticism, the aim of a men's studies approach to American literature is re-vision: a revision of the way we read literature and a revision of the way we perceive men and manly ideals." Peter Filene, in "The Secrets of Men's History," writes that the distinctiveness of men's history "has to do with *how* more than with *what*," and speaks of early men's historians as

1

"(literally) reconnaissance men." One finds, throughout, a sensibility that combines two strains of thought: an acceptance of the obvious fact that most scholarship, in the conventional sense, has been about men, and the contention that such scholarship, in perhaps a more significant sense, has not really been about men at all. In my attempt to make "The Case for Men's Studies," I offer the following formulation:

> While *seemingly* about men, traditional scholarship's treatment of generic man as the human norm in fact systematically excludes from consideration what is unique to men *qua* men. The overgeneralization from male to generic human experience not only distorts our understanding of what, if anything, is truly generic to humanity but also precludes the study of masculinity as a *specific male* experience, rather than a universal paradigm for *human* experience. The most general definition of men's studies is that it is the study of masculinities and male experiences as specific and varying social–historical–cultural formations. Such studies situate masculinities as objects of study on a par with femininities, instead of elevating them to universal norms.

Men's studies questions assumptions that have passed beyond the horizons of usual scholarly inquiry to bring them back under critical purview. These assumptions about masculinity are so widely shared that they cease to appear as assumptions. Much of Joseph Pleck's "The Theory of Male Sex-Role Identity," for example, traces the historical processes by which the seemingly simple idea (but, as Pleck demonstrates, actually a complex conglomeration of distinct ideas) that a sense of masculinity is a positive desideratum of male personal identity entered into and came to dominate professional and popular discourse, thereby obscuring fundamental difficulties with this view and hiding its pernicious effects.

PROBLEMATICS OF SEX ROLES

Men's studies scholars repeatedly face a problem in explaining their task. Many people find readily understandable and intuitively congenial the accurate claim that the necessity for women's studies lies, in large part, in the need to rectify the injustices done to women in having been "written out of history" and systematically ignored by traditional scholarship. Women's lives have been so privatized that they have been pushed outside the range of public discourse, outside the mainstream — some feminists call it the "male-stream" — tradition. Men's studies has no such immediately appealing claim to make, since men have clearly been the subjects of scholarship. Yet, men's studies has a task corollary to that of women's studies. The nineteenth-century German philosopher Hegel wrote that what is familiar *(bekannt)* was often not really known *(erkannt)* precisely because it was so seemingly familiar. One is reminded of Edgar Allan Poe's "The Purloined Letter," in which a particularly clever thief realizes that the best way to hide something is to keep it in plain view. Paradoxical as it may seem, some of the essays in this collection argue that men's public lives in an important sense represent a retreat and escape from their personal lives, a shrinkage rather than an enlargement of their spheres. More significantly, at least in terms of the potential influence of men's studies in the academy, they argue that the concepts and methodologies of traditional scholarship have perpetuated these misunderstandings of masculinity precisely because they share the same male biases. Filene argues that, in their criteria of significance, "the histories that men have written about themselves, then, contain the same bias as the histories they have written about one another." Public events and achievements, not personal feelings and experiences, are what count. Riemer cites criticism of Ernest Hemingway as an example of how a fundamental acceptance of patriarchal values can influence the interpretation of a text in which ideals of manhood are a central concern.

In much the same vein, Richard Ochberg, in "The Male Career Code and the Ideology of Role," demonstrates how the concept of sex roles, a core concept that "might serve as a shorthand description" of both women's and men's studies, can aid in denying the subjectivity of the experience ostensibly under study, a denial crucial to the pretensions to objectivity of the male construction of experience. Ochberg writes: "Men may attempt to escape their private troubles by migrating — like souls fleeing diseased bodies — from their private lives into public ones." He argues that in viewing and experiencing themselves as acting in a role, men lose the ability to experience *themselves* outside the role. He cautions: "Men's studies, which takes as part of its disciplinary mandate the critique of cultural forms that deprecate male subjectivity, should be careful not to find itself passively acquiescing in this deprecation by an uncritical acceptance of pure role theory."

Ochberg's point illustrates the finely nuanced character of many of the analyses presented here, and the enormous debt men's studies owes to the women's studies scholarship of the past two decades. While acknowledging the importance and centrality of sex roles, a concept introduced by Talcott Parsons and developed by women's studies, several essays take up criticisms of sex-role frameworks, criticisms also developed by women's studies scholars. Thus, in addition to Ochberg's criticism, we find Michael Kimmel, in "The Contemporary 'Crisis' of Masculinity in Historical Perspective," arguing that simplistic formulations of sex roles "posit masculinity as a fixed and definable set of behavioral norms, a static and universal box into which all men must fit." He writes:

Not only does the male sex-role paradigm ignore historical and cross-cultural dimensions to the social construction of masculinity, but it ignores how much of masculinity is a product of the interaction between men and women, that is, how much of the normative behaviors of both women and men has more to do with gender relations than either does with a fixed and isolated role to which individuals are socialized to adopt. Further, the focus on sex roles minimizes our analytic ability to specify the ways in which relations between men and women are derived from the power men as a group maintain over women as a group.[1]

Kimmel's "interactionist" perspective, in which men and women "negotiate" changes in gender relations, emerges from recent trends in women's and men's studies toward deeper examinations of the social processes of engenderment, whereby gender dichotomies are first created, instead of simply assuming gender differentiation and then proceeding to analyze its ramifications on each gender in isolation. Such trends are historically situated and analyzed in my essay, which in this regard complements Pleck's historical account of the development of the theory of male sex role identity. Kimmel's essay attempts to rectify the deficiencies he perceives in the sex-role paradigm by comparative analysis of three periods during which a "crisis of masculinity" was discerned by contemporaries: England in the late seventeenth and early eighteenth centuries, the United States in the late nineteenth and early twentieth centuries, and the present. Significant parallels emerge in "transformations in the social organization of work, the structure of social mobility, and changes in family and gender relations . . . in which the meaning of masculinity is itself brought into question." Significant parallels also emerge in male reactions to these changes, which Kimmel analyzes as falling into three categories: antifeminist backlash, promale backlash, and profeminist men. The most strident criticisms of the sex-role model are in Tim Carrigan, Bob Connell, and John Lee's "Toward a New Sociology of Masculinity." They speak not of inadequacies or misdirections in the sex role model but of the "theoretical incoherence built into the 'sex role' paradigm," flatly stating that "the 'male sex role' does not exist." They criticize the ahistorical, conservative functionalism of sex-role theory and remind the reader that "we do not speak of 'race roles' or 'class roles' because the exercise of power in these areas of social relations is more immediately evident."

---

1. An extended version of Kimmel's argument may be found in his Introduction to the special issue he edited on Researching Male Roles, *American Behavioral Scientist* 29, no. 5 (May/June 1986): 517–529. For a similar criticism of the sex-role paradigm, see Liz Stanley and Sue Wise, *Breaking Out: Feminist Consciousness and Feminist Research* (London: Routledge & Kegan Paul, 1983), pp 97–105.

Michael Messner's "The Meaning of Success: The Athletic Experience and the Development of Male Identity" also stresses the historical nature of questions about masculinity in its exploration of the rise and role of organized sports. Moreover, Messner attempts to answer a question he argues is not raised by a simplistic or mechanistic employment of socialization theory. The perspectives he criticizes consider solely the effects of sports on men, with some praising sports for their alleged character-building function and others condemning sports for their alleged character-debilitating function. Missing from such analyses, argues Messner, is the logically prior question: What is it about masculine identity that first attracts young males to sports? His answer meshes well with the analysis of male friendships given by Drury Sherrod in "The Bonds of Men: Problems and Possibilities in Close Male Relationships," as well as with Ochberg's analysis of the male career code. They point to a male need to construct relationships of intimacy and friendship bounded and defined by articulated rules. Examples would be what Ochberg refers to as the need to achieve a "detached collegiality" in relationships with coworkers in hierarchical settings, and what Messner refers to as the need to establish "work-related (or sports-related) positional identity" before "exploring close friendships and intimate relationships."

In their work, one sees emerging an important men's studies methodological strain that incorporates into studies of men critical examinations of the nascent gender identities with which men come to many traditional socializing institutions. This creates more dynamic, multidimensional frameworks for understanding the relationships between men's selves and men's roles than exists in much gender scholarship.

BEYOND ONE-DIMENSIONALITY

One finds repeated calls throughout this volume not simply to substitute one reductionist understanding of masculinity for another, as when Filene writes that the investigation of the personal dimensions (i.e., the "secrets") of men's lives is not a matter of "digging up skeletons in heroes' closets. . . . The point is not the secret but the interplay between the secret and the rest of his behavior and attitudes"; or when Riemer argues that the men's studies rereading of American literature he proposes does not commit one to the flaw of "reducing literature to sociological resource." One also finds a determination to listen to the voices of men themselves, whether they be friends (Sherrod), businessmen (Ochberg), or athletes (Messner), to capture the "ephemeral side" (Sherrod), "subjecti-vity" (Ochberg), and "personal–existential level" (Messner) of masculin-ity. In inverse fashion to the struggle in women's studies to establish the *objectivity* of women's experiences and thereby validate the legitimacy of women's experiences *as women,* much of men's studies struggles to estab-lish the *subjectivity* of men's experiences and thereby validate the legiti-macy of men's experiences *as men.*

This difference follows logically from the differential and complemen-tary effects of the public–private dichotomy on women and men. The commitment to take as one's point of departure and legitimize men's experiences as men leads in some cases to a critique of the use of female norms to categorize male experience, a critique analogous to the women's studies critique of the generic use of male norms. For example, Sherrod questions the equation of intimacy and verbal self-revelation, arguing that although on this measure of intimacy men are judged to have less intimate relationships than women, this judgment may result from an inappropri-ate imposition of female norms on males. On this line of argument, per-haps men are not quantitatively less intimate but qualitatively differently intimate, in nonverbal ways.[2] Perhaps male intimacy is not face-to-face intimacy, but occurs side by side, as when engaged in some joint activity, or even back to back, as when backing each other up.[3] Such a contention has mixed implications. Its validating attitude toward men's experiences in their own terms may well be more effective in encouraging men to develop their own styles of intimacy than simply berating them for failing to meet female norms. But if one extends the idea to the point where it posits the existence of incommensurable modes of intimacy by gender, it suggests a kind of separatism that augurs poorly for the possibility of cross-gender intimacy. In other cases, the commitment to reexamine male experiences may lead to a call for greater attention to informally structured relation-ships, such as Dorothy Hammond and Alta Jablow's examination of "Gil-gamesh and the Sundance Kid: The Myth of Male Friendship." Their argument suggests that in its inattention to the study of male friendships in our society, the tradition of male anthropology incorporates and is limited by the same male needs for clearly bounded relationships addressed by others in this volume.

2. In *Intimate Strangers: Men and Women Together* (New York: Harper & Row, 1984), Lillian Rubin differentiates intimacy from male bonding largely by this criterion. The ex-plicit argument that intimacy requires self-disclosure is one of the virtues of her treatment; often this is simply assumed.

3. The imagery is from Shepherd Bliss, "Men Are Such Interesting Creatures," *Twin Cities Men's Center News* (Minneapolis) 10, no. 4 (August and September 1986): 13–15.

In the name of achieving a different kind of multidimensional under-standing of masculinity, Perry Treadwell characterizes his "Biologic Influences on Masculinity" as "a plea that the biosociology of gender be an integral part of men's studies," in full awareness that many, if not most, scholars working in the area of gender might see such a plea as an argument for biological determinism, a position with which he takes care to say he does not align himself.

DIVERSITIES OF MEN'S LIVES

One of the criticisms of the early stage of men's studies voiced in my and others' articles in this volume is that, all too often, scholars have tended to write too simplistically of *the* male sex role, rather than the multiplicity of male roles. Steps in the right direction on this issue are taken by several contributors to this volume. Clyde Franklin's "Surviving the Institutional Decimation of Black Males" looks at conflicting role pressures exerted on black men by multiple levels of the societies in which they live — their immediate male peer group, the wider subculture of the black community as a whole, and the larger white society — and concludes that the conflicts engendered in black men by competing prescriptions for masculinity issued by these groups are devastating and tragic. Pleck notes the misapplication of theories of masculinity from the dominant culture to shift the blame for the black community's problems from white racism to "black men's frustrated masculinity," a theory that played an important role in the social policy formulated in the so-called Moynihan Report. Riemer studies "notions of manhood and masculinity that exist among southern rural blacks" in works by Ernest Gaines. But blacks are clearly not the only subgroup requiring greater attention. Filene notes the emergence of regional and generational studies in men's history, as well as studies focused on differences relating to homosexuality and class. Riemer argues:

> Through studies of works such as Henry Roth's *Call It Sleep* and Pietro DiDonato's *Christ in Concrete*, we could gain insight into how masculine roles and ideals from various ethnic backgrounds and the ability to achieve a sense of masculine identity were affected by the immigrant experience.[4]

4. The work of revisionist women historians on immigration will doubtless influence and refine our understanding of male immigrant experiences. See, for example, Elizabeth Ewen, *Immigrant Women in the Land of Dollars: Life and Culture on the Lower East Side, 1890–1925* (New York: Monthly Review Press, 1985).

Sensitivity to diversity and an understanding of the interplay between dominant and marginalized modes of masculinity are well integrated in Louis Crompton's "Byron and Male Love: The Classical Tradition" and John Crowley's "Howells, Stoddard, and Male Homosocial Attachment in Victorian America." Crowley notes the historical genesis of the concept of homosexuality as a distinct type, as well as the existence of distinct homosexual-homosocial "styles," which vary by class and nationality. Crompton's analysis of divergent Greek and Latin classical models of male love and the effects of homophobia on Byron's life and work dispels myths of monolithic homosexual norms. Crowley invokes the concept of homosociality explored by Eve Kosofsky Sedgwick to analyze "the entire spectrum of same-sex bonds . . . reserving 'homosexual' for those parts of the homosocial spectrum that seem most marked by genital sexuality," while also acknowledging that the boundaries between homosociality and homosexuality are sometimes blurred.[5] Much of the analytic originality and strength of Crowley's essay lies in his demonstration of how these boundaries are blurred in a case of literary fatherhood whereby male authority figures confer "something like the apostolic succession" on one another. Crowley argues that the family, usually conceived of as the locus par excellence of intimacy, has also served as a retreat and defense against a threatening kind of male homosociality. The contemporary analogue is visible in heterosexual men's use of the pictures of their children they carry in their wallets to project a secure identity.

THE POLITICS OF MEN'S STUDIES

Crowley's discussion of "the generation of male authority in a patriarchal culture" exemplifies a perspective I attempt to establish in my essay. I argue that a feminist men's studies perspective must go beyond simply demonstrating, for example, "how male role constraints on emotional display inhibit and repress men" to show "how male emotional restraint also confers power on men, in large part by effectively withholding information about oneself." The point is also implicit in the critiques of the male sex-role paradigm discussed earlier. In its explorations of the debilitating effects of various codes of masculinity on men's lives, men's studies must take care not to ignore or obscure the questions of power raised by feminism. Instead, men's studies, at least in its exemplary mode, demon-

5. Eve Kosofsky Sedgwick, *Between Men: English Literature and Male Homosocial Desire* (New York: Columbia University Press, 1985).

strates the connections between the pursuit of patriarchal power and various sorts of male self-denials.[6]

The question of the relationship between women's and men's studies, or, more generally, the question of the relationship between feminism and the critique of masculinity, is taken up most explicitly in my essay, but figures in others as well. Pleck credits feminism for certain advances in men's studies because it "challenged the traditional patterns of sex roles for which the theory of male identity provided ideological justification." My essay attempts to articulate and justify the component parts of men's studies' pro-feminist standpoint. The authors here seem to assume that their analyses are complementary rather than contradictory to essential tenets of feminist scholarship. The articles are critical of masculinity and at the same time sympathetic to men. One is reminded of Marx's characterization of his standpoint as one that, even as it condemns capitalists, "can less than any other make the individual responsible for relations whose creature he socially remains."[7]

Disagreements about other aspects of the politics of men's studies emerge in these pages. While my essay stresses the connections between men's studies and the men's movement, Filene writes that the results of men's political activism "hardly measured up to announcements of 'our own birth as a movement.' A network is closer to the truth." Carrigan, Connell, and Lee register their agreement with this verdict.[8] Elsewhere, in what is more an issue of focus than disagreement, the difference between a sociological and a psychological orientation emerges in tracing the history of conceptualizations of masculinity in the 1950s, as Carrigan *et al.* emphasize the problem of social deviance, notably "juvenile delinquency and

---

6. For a skeptical analysis of men's studies' ability to retain this perspective, see Mark Kann, "The Costs of Being on Top," in a special issue on men's studies, *Journal of the National Association for Women Deans, Administrators, and Counselors* 49, no. 4 (Summer 1986).

7. Karl Marx, Preface to the first German edition of *Capital*, in Robert C. Tucker, ed., *The Marx-Engels Reader*, 2d ed. (New York: Norton, 1972), p. 297.

8. Though it can be inferred from the sections included here, the point is made most clearly in a section of the essay omitted from this volume. I would also argue that while the assertion that the men's movement ignored gay liberation arguments is correct when applied to "men's rights" groups, this cannot be said of the feminist men's movement. Robert Brannon has argued that the men's rights and feminist men's groups should not be conceptualized as different right and left wings of the same movement, but as opposing movements. See "Are the 'Free Men' a Faction of Our Movement?" *M.: Gentle Men for Gender Justice* 7 (Winter 1981–1982). The most recent comprehensive overview of the men's movement is in Anthony Astrachan's *How Men Feel: Their Responses to Women's Demands for Equality and Power* (Garden City, N.Y.: Anchor, 1986). A good earlier, but by now somewhat dated, account is Joe Interrante's "Dancing Along the Precipice: The Men's Movement in the 80's," *Radical America* 15, no. 5 (September–October 1981): 53–71.

educational underachievement," while Pleck emphasizes the problems of postwar mainstream breadwinners as the underlying social motivations for scholarly research. Other disagreements in these pages perhaps center principally on the extent to which masculinity may be said to be socially constructed. Crowley and Treadwell would seem to be at odds over the social or biological construction of homosexuality. Although they take pains to show the malleability of men's behavior as a function of cultural experience, many scholars and activists (myself among them) would be suspicious of Treadwell's and Sherrod's seeming flirtations with biological explanations of various aspects of masculinity, however qualified they are. Finally, several essays seem to invoke the sex-role paradigm criticized by others.

A MEN'S STUDIES CANON?

To speak of a men's studies canon is premature. The field is still too new for such grandiose claims. Yet the collection of these essays in one volume makes clearly visible for the first time the initial components of what such a canon might look like.

The emergence of certain figures at the core of men's studies was predictable. Two of the authors included here, Joseph Pleck and Peter Filene, have already emerged as key figures in the field. Pleck's *The Myth of Masculinity* and the anthology he coedited with Elizabeth Pleck, *The American Man,* are repeatedly cited as having made definitive contributions to establishing the parameters of men's studies. Filene's *Him / Her / Self: Sex Roles in Modern America* has also established itself as a fundamental work, sometimes being cited in these pages in conjunction with another survey of American history, Joe L. Dubbert's *A Man's Place: Masculinity in Transition.* Several authors rely on Daniel Levinson's *The Seasons of a Man's Life.* Also somewhat predictably, what emerges from an examination of this volume is that the women feminist theorists who seem to have influenced most significantly the direction of men's studies are Nancy Chodorow, Dorothy Dinnerstein, Barbara Ehrenreich, and Carol Gilligan.

What is more unexpected is the emergence of specific literary works as in some sense representative of contemporary dilemmas of masculinity. There has been no single book as influential in establishing a common frame of reference for men's studies literary criticism as was Kate Millett's *Sexual Politics* in the early stages of women's studies. Yet more than one of the authors here turns to John Updike's novel *Rabbit Run* and Sam Shepard's play *True West* for insights on masculinity. In addition, Kimmel writes: "Nowhere is the male antifeminist backlash [in the late-nineteenth-century United States] better expressed than in Henry James's novel *The Bostonians*," and I cite Arthur Miller's *Death of a Salesman* as "still the most eloquently profound single statement of mainstream contemporary American male dilemmas."

A consensus is emerging that, in American history, the late nineteenth and early twentieth centuries are particularly significant. In much the same way that a revision of our understanding of the Renaissance has become one of the paradigmatic examples of the fundamental historical reconceptualizations necessitated by new women's studies scholarship (influenced in large part by Joan Kelly-Gadol's classic essay, "Did Women Have a Renaissance?"), it appears that men's history's examination of this period may become paradigmatic of the necessity to incorporate men's studies perspectives into historical scholarship.[9] Filene and Dubbert highlight this period in their books, it is one of the periods examined by Kimmel, and other essays in this volume also describe as pivotal such phenomena in this period as the rise of Teddy Roosevelt, organized sports, and organizations such as the Boy Scouts. There remain other areas where common references have yet to emerge. For example, Messner, Filene, and Treadwell all cite literature on sports and masculinity, yet even in the rare case where more than one author cites the same work, it is in a different context, as when the references are to different articles in Donald Sabo and Ross Runfola's anthology *Jock: Sports and Male Identity*.

What may well be the beginning of a trend to claim certain texts as precursors of men's studies is also discernible and of significance in these pages. In this regard, William Whyte's *Organization Man* and C. Wright Mills's *White Collar* are particularly noteworthy.[10] Words written by Herbert Marcuse in 1964, not about men's studies but about analyses of advanced industrial civilizations, seem remarkably apropos and prescient if applied to men's studies:

> I should like to emphasize the vital importance of the work of C. Wright Mills, and of studies which are frequently frowned upon because of simplification, overstatement, or journalistic ease — Vance Packard's *The Hidden Persuaders*, *The Status Seekers*, and *The Waste Makers*, William H. Whyte's *The Organization Man*, Fred J. Cook's *The Warfare State* belong in this category. To be sure, the lack of theoretical analysis in

9. Joan Kelly-Gadol, "Did Women Have a Renaissance?" in *Becoming Visible: Women in European History*, ed. Renate Bridenthal and Claudia Koonz (Boston: Houghton Mifflin, 1977).

10. I criticize the omission of these books in my review of Eugene R. August's *Men's Studies: A Selected and Annotated Interdisciplinary Bibliography* (Littleton, Colo.: Libraries Unlimited, 1985), in *Changing Men: Issues in Gender, Sex, and Politics* 16 (Summer 1986).

these works leaves the roots of the described conditions covered and protected, but left to speak for themselves, the conditions speak loudly enough. Perhaps the most telling evidence can be obtained by simply looking at television or listening to the AM radio for one consecutive hour for a couple of days, not shutting off the commercials, and now and then switching the station.[11]

FUTURE DIRECTIONS

In the concluding section of this introduction to men's studies, I am both descriptive and prescriptive. I also broaden my focus from the essays in this collection to the field as a whole. Without claiming to predict the future, I attempt to extrapolate new directions for men's studies from currently emerging trends, as well as argue for the need to forge new paths. I also take the opportunity to voice some criticisms of certain trends in men's studies.

The title of this volume was chosen to highlight the need for greater attention to two areas. The pluralized "Masculinities" is intended to call attention to the need for men's studies to move beyond race and class biases. Franklin's essay is the only sustained analysis of men of color in this collection, despite references to Third World men in several essays, and even Franklin deals only with black men. This deficiency reflects the general lack of such work in the field, which must move beyond its parochialism.[12] The privileging of U.S. white middle-class men's concerns, from which overgeneralizations are sometimes made, makes it impossible for men's studies to gain the needed critical distance on "hegemonic masculinity." This is Carrigan, Connell, and Lee's term for the institutionalized codes that embody these concerns, govern and restrict all men's lives, and give some men power over others.

The title phrase "The Making of" alludes to E. P. Thompson's seminal *The Making of the English Working Class*, and highlights my belief that we need more social constructionist accounts of masculinities.[13] Many of the early writers on men, especially those who wrote for the popular press, tended to describe men as passive victims of impersonal socializing forces,

11. Herbert Marcuse, *One-Dimensional Man: Studies in the Ideology of Advanced Industrial Society* (Boston: Beacon Press, 1964), xvii.

12. Two collections partially filling the gap are Doris Y. Wilkinson and Ronald L. Taylor, eds., *The Black Male in America* (Chicago: Nelson-Hall, 1977); and Lawrence E. Gary, ed. *Black Men* (Beverly Hills, Calif.: Sage, 1981).

13. E. P. Thompson, *The Making of the English Working Class* (New York: Random House, 1966). The same strategy of invocation by titular allusion is evident in Kenneth Plummer's *The Making of the Modern Homosexual* (Stroudsberg, Penn.: Hutchinson, 1981).

often in defensive reaction against overly voluntarist interpretations they found in some feminist writings. The male victimization thesis seemed to provide an escape from blaming men for the evils feminists identified. But with the denial of blameworthiness often went the denial of responsibility. Consequently, the political and scholarly aspirations of these writers remained unfulfilled. Politically, the image of men as victims too sharply contradicted the in-charge image men had of themselves and therefore led to popular criticisms of writers on men, as well as the "new men" themselves, as complaining "wimps." Academically, lacking a complementary group to identify as victimizers, the analysis was vague and glossed over too many issues, particularly issues of power. What was and is needed are analyses that show how men both form and are formed by their conditions, or, as Marx put it, how men make their own history, but not in circumstances of their own choosing.

Valid social constructionist accounts of masculinities will most likely come from a conjunction of two specific intellectual traditions: socialist feminism and developmental psychology, most notably Freudian theory. I cite these not simply because they are my own intellectual affinities, and because much of the most innovative feminist theory in recent years has emerged from the synthesis of psychoanalysis and Marxism, but also because of the four women's studies scholars already cited as currently being most influential in men's studies — Chodorow, Dinnerstein, Ehrenreich, and Gilligan — the first three explicitly speak from psychoanalytic and socialist perspectives, while Gilligan works in the nonpsychoanalytic branch of developmental psychology.

Since my own background is in political theory rather than psychology, the potential impact of socialist feminism on men's studies is clearer to me than that of psychoanalysis. I would like to begin a sketch of a distinctive men's studies socialist feminist analysis of capitalist patriarchal masculinity.

The starting point for any socialist feminist conceptualization of masculinity lies in the distinction between precapitalist and capitalist patriarchy. A transfer of power from the hands of individual patriarchs to the institutions of capitalist patriarchy is an essential component of this shift. This transfer is part of the widening depersonalization and bureacratization of human relationships in the development of capitalism, which individuals experience in and as various forms of alienation. Capitalism increasingly creates a gap between institutional and personal power.[14] For men, this

---

14. See Carol Brown, "Mothers, Fathers, and Children: From Private to Public Patriarchy," in *Women and Revolution: A Discussion of the Unhappy Marriage of Marxism and Feminism*, ed. Lydia Sargent (Boston: South End Press, 1981).

creates a disjunction between the facts of public male power and the feelings of men's private powerlessness. Certain changes in male personality traits, for example from authoritarian to nurturing traits, can be increasingly tolerated by the system because interpersonal relations are no longer the locus of male power, especially when these changes concern men as fathers rather than bosses.[15] Men may even be encouraged to draw personal rewards from fatherhood, and the market may respond in its own inimitable fashion to new demands for fathers' consumer goods (e.g., less frilly diapers and longer baby-carriage handles), but, in the final analysis, capitalist and patriarchal institutions retain their imperatives of power.

This public–private split in masculinity creates contradictory tensions within capitalist patriarchy. On the one hand, certain changes are encouraged by a system aiming to modernize masculinity, such as a more cooperative rather then competitive masculinity required by a more corporate rather than entrepreneurial capitalism. On the other hand, there is incentive to retain certain traditional aspects of masculinity insofar as they interact with the dynamics of advanced capitalist patriarchy in ways functional to the system. For example, persisting images of masculinity hold that "real men" are physically strong, aggressive, and in control of their work. Yet the structural dichotomy between manual and mental labor under capitalism means that no one's work fulfills all these conditions. Manual laborers work for others at the low end of the class spectrum, while management sits at a desk. Consequently, while the insecurities generated by these contradictions are personally dissatisfying to men, these insecurities also impel them to cling all the more tightly to sources of masculine identity validation offered by the system. This makes them its more willing and efficient servants.[16] Capitalism and patriarchy are at times complementary and at times contradictory for men.[17] The interplay between psychological, economic, and political advantages and disadvantages is

15. See Ross Wetzsteon, "The Feminist Man?" in *The Women Say, The Men Say: Issues in Politics, Work, Family, Sexuality, and Power*, ed. Evelyn Shapiro and Barry M. Shapiro (New York: Dell, 1979), pp. 25–29.

16. See Cynthia Cockburn's *Brothers: Male Dominance and Technological Change* (London: Pluto Press, 1983), esp. chap. 5, "A Man among Men"; and *Machinery of Dominance: Women, Men, and Technical Know-How* (London: Pluto Press, 1985). As members of one of a vanishing breed of male craft industries, printers of the kind Cockburn investigates are particularly illustrative cases of occupationally related aspects of masculinity in transition. Studies that shed light on this but lack explicit focus on masculinity are Robert Blauner, *Alienation and Freedom: The Factory Worker and His Industry* (Chicago: University of Chicago Press 1964); and Theresa F. Rogers and Nathalie S. Friedman, *Printers Face Automation* (Lexington, Ky.: Heath, 1980).

17. This conceptualization is greatly indebted to Heidi Hartmann's "The Unhappy Marriage of Marxism and Feminism: Towards A More Progressive Union," in Sargent, ed., *Women and Revolution*.

fertile ground for the development of psychosociological analyses of masculinity. Consider the significance of delayed gratification in the work ethic of capitalism's early development and the Oedipal phase of male identity development, the common subordination of present desire to future power. Such structural analyses would complement in materialist, social historical terms analyses by intellectual historians of the isomorphism of values between patriarchal and capitalist masculinities broadly conceived, such as are evident in those traits marking Weber's ideal-typical puritan, or between instrumental masculine and scientific rationalities, evoked in feminist philosophy of science and ecofeminist writings.[18]

While the cliché that white middle-class men are less sexist than Third World or working-class men abounds in the culture, the perspective outlined here can be developed to suggest that these latter masculinities may instead be conceptualized as cultures of resistance, as counterweights to the leveling of differences essential to hegemonic masculinity. The cliché is perpetuated by a failure to distinguish personal from institutional power. Institutional power is camouflaged, so it does not appear to be exercised by any one individual. Thus men may appear more personally congenial farther up the economic ladder, even as they exercise the institutional power responsible for women's lower status. In contrast, men who have but their personal power are more conspicuous but actually less efficacious when exercising their power in patriarchy's service. Here the radical feminist emphasis on theories of difference can be applied in innovative ways as an important source of reconceptualizations of race, class, and ethnic differences in men's studies.[19]

Since one important source of current interest in men's studies is the belief that our present historical period is particularly tumultuous for men, it is understandable that much of men's studies currently focuses on crises and contradictions in men's lives. Part of the focus on changes was also motivated by a desire to demonstrate the untenability of naturalistic as-

18. On Weber, see David Morgan, "Men, Masculinity and the Process of Sociological Enquiry," in *Doing Feminist Research,* ed. Helen Roberts (London: Routledge & Kegan Paul, 1981). Important texts on gender and science include Evelyn Fox Keller, *Reflections on Gender and Science* (New Haven: Yale University Press, 1985); Carolyn Merchant, *The Death of Nature: Women, Ecology and the Scientific Revolution* (New York: Harper & Row, 1980); Genevieve Lloyd, *The Man of Reason: "Male" and "Female" in Western Philosophy* (Minneapolis: University of Minnesota Press, 1984); Sandra Harding and Merill B. Hintikka, eds., *Discovering Reality: Feminist Perspectives in Epistemology, Metaphysics, Methodology, and Philosophy of Science* (Dordrecht: Riedel, 1983); and Sandra Harding, *The Science Question in Feminism* (Ithaca: Cornell University Press, 1986). The most recent statement I have seen is Susan Bordo, "The Cartesian Masculinization of Thought," *Signs* 11, no. 3 (1986): 439–456.

19. See the chapter on "Men: Comrades in Struggle" in Bell Hooks, *Feminist Theory: From Margin to Center* (Boston: South End Press, 1984).

sumptions about masculinity. Despite the support given to such changes in most of the literature, such an approach nonetheless contains an important conservative strain. In emphasizing that such changes require explanation, it perpetuates the notion that the seemingly unremarkable daily transmission and perpetuation of masculinities through time and space is somehow less problematic. But unless one accepts deeply conservative assumptions, social and historical continuity requires analysis and explanation just as much as discontinuity does. As we learn more about the reproduction of masculinities, the focus of men's studies will inevitably shift from periods and situations of strain and conflict to the superficially unremarkable, mundane realities of most men's lives.

Men's studies would also benefit from a greater skepticism about current male role changes. Ehrenreich's work is one example of such skepticism. She asks the classic *cui bono* question of men's liberation, and concludes that much of it is inimical to women's interests. Invoked by name only in the conclusion, the feminization of poverty clearly underlies Ehrenreich's concerns about men fleeing from their commitments to support women and their families. Such skepticism could also be generated were cross-cultural comparisons made more central to men's studies. For example, there are numerous anthropological studies of the couvade phenomenon, where men in prestate societies ritually simulate bearing and giving birth to children, often including appropriate cramps and pains. There is considerable debate whether such rituals are supportive or subversive of women's procreative powers. From a comparative anthropological perspective, much of the "new fathers'" childbirth involvement, usually unquestioningly accepted as a benefit to women, appears suspiciously like a couvade ritual, down to the laborious panting and the counterfactual "we're pregnant" announcement.[20] It remains unclear how much of the "new fathering" ethos is an attempt to surrender or reestablish male power in the face of feminist gains for women.

Another line of investigation often appreciated on its own terms but not yet fully integrated with other areas in men's studies is the sort of life-cycle development research carried on by Daniel Levinson and his colleagues, among many others. For example, as one moves from soft to hardcore pornography, the average age of the male consumer increases from adolescence to midlife. Is this simply a case of overexposure leading to the need for greater doses to reach satiation, or are other factors involved,

20. I am indebted to Maria Papacostaki for this insight. She reminded me that while people say "we" are pregnant, they also say "she" had the miscarriage or Caesarean delivery. The question is also raised in Carol Tavris and Carole Wade, *The Longest War: Sex Differences in Perspective*, 2d ed. (New York: Harcourt Brace Jovanovich, 1984), pp. 189–190.

relating to the waxing and waning of the power of both the physical and social self?

Carrigan, Connell, and Lee's "Toward a New Sociology of Masculinity" is, as its title indicates, the essay in this volume most explicitly concerned with new directions for the field. Much of what I advocate is eloquently expressed in the latter sections of this piece, and I shall not repeat it here. A particular virtue of their analysis is the way the concept of "hegemonic masculinity" connects the themes of pluralities of masculinities and the power imbalance between men and women by understanding both as contested, interactive historical practices. In addition to mounting the strongest critique of the sex-role paradigm, they also make the strongest case for integrating gay and men's studies.

Toward the beginning of this introduction I used the Hegelian distinction between what is familiar and what is known to make a point about the present intentions of men's studies. Let me close these speculations on the future of men's studies by invoking another Hegelian metaphor, that "the owl of Minerva spreads its wings only with the falling of the dusk."[21] The point here is that one can truly come to know something only after it has fully developed, philosophical knowledge being in some sense retrospective. It follows that if the field of men's studies has reached the point where it is possible fully to articulate and analyze its initial achievements and possibilities, both positive and negative, then this initial stage must now be over. I believe we are just now on the verge of an exciting second stage in the development of men's studies, I hope along lines outlined here. My greatest hope for this volume of essays in the new men's studies is that it be a stepping-stone for a newer men's studies.

21. G. W. F. Hegel, *Philosophy of Right*, trans. T. M. Knox (New York, Oxford University Press, 1967), p. 13.

I
Overviews

The three essays in this part, by Joseph Pleck, a social psychologist, Harry Brod, a philosopher, and co-authors and sociologists Tim Carrigan, Bob Connell, and John Lee, address the past, present, and future of the study of men.

"The Theory of Male Sex-Role Identity: Its Rise and Fall, 1936 to the Present" analyzes psychology's construction of the theory of male sex-role identity. This theory dominated the social scientific study of sex roles in the 1950s and 1960s. It evolved from cultural concerns about American men's adequacy that began in the 1930s and was first operationalized by masculinity–femininity tests, rooted in the early-twentieth-century psychometric tradition. Fueled by wartime concerns about draft disqualifications and battle breakdowns, and postwar economic trends threatening male provider roles, as the paradigm developed it incorporated certain psychoanalytic concepts and began to be applied to social phenomena such as father absence and delinquency. Anomalous research results and new conceptions of sex roles initiated by feminism led to its demise beginning in the 1970s.

"The Case for Men's Studies" articulates paradigmatic questions and perspectives of men's studies, particularly in problems of male violence and history, and attempts to determine its niche in the academic curriculum. It views men's studies as an extension of feminist scholarship and analyzes differing feminist perspectives on the politics of men's studies.

"Toward a New Sociology of Masculinity" traces research on men from its prehistory in sex-difference research and functionalist sex role theory to current feminist and gay liberation perspectives that see contested power rather than complementary roles at issue between the sexes. The concept of hegemonic masculinity incorporates into the sociology of masculinity a dynamic sense of the construction of gender and relations of power within each gender. For example, from this perspective male violence emerges not as a manifestation of some essence of masculinity but as testimony to the bitterness of the struggle to forge dominating identities. New research must situate current male role changes in the context of the ongoing modernization of masculinity in response to structural changes in advanced capitalism, and relate the sociology of masculinity to recent feminist scholarship on the division of labor, patterns of emotional attachment and detachment, and the unconscious as a field of politics.

1

The Theory of Male Sex-Role Identity: Its Rise and Fall, 1936 to the Present

Joseph H. Pleck

The theory of male sex-role identity (MSRI) has been the dominant paradigm in American psychology for understanding male experience.[1] In brief, this theory holds that for individuals to become psychologically mature as members of their sex, they must acquire male or female "sex-role identity," manifested by having the sex-appropriate traits, attitudes, and interests that psychologically "validate" or "affirm" their biological sex. However, many factors conspire to thwart the attainment of healthy sex-role identity, especially for males (e.g., the actual or relative absence of male role models, and women's changing roles). The resulting problems for males include effeminacy and homosexuality (too little masculinity), as well as hypermasculinity (too much masculinity). This theory provides the underlying basis for many well-known lines of research and theory on diverse topics such as the effects of the absence of the father, male crime and violence, male attitudes toward women, boys' problems in elementary schools, adolescent initiation rites, and black males. Only recently, as we step back from the conventional social scientific wisdom of the 1950s and 1960s on sex roles, has it become clear how thoroughly dominated the social sciences have been by this highly explicit and detailed theory of the male role.

This chapter was originally published in *In The Shadow of the Past*, edited by Miriam Lewin (New York: Columbia University Press), 1983. Copyright © 1984 Columbia University Press. By permission.

1. J. Pleck, *The Myth of Masculinity* (Cambridge: MIT Press, 1981).

BACKGROUND

From the 1930s to the recent present, the study of sex roles was preoccu-pied with, as much as with any other single question, "What makes men less masculine than they should be, and what can we do about it?" To understand why, it is necessary to place the theory of male sex-role identity that psychologists began to construct in the 1930s in the context of the cultural concerns about masculinity that had developed earlier.

During the century before the explicit emergence of the theory, men were increasingly perceived as not measuring up to the new and more stringent demands placed on them by a changing society. Changes in women's role in the nineteenth and twentieth centuries seemed to threaten women's mental and physical well-being. Recent research brings to light how men seemed to face profound risk as well. To give only a few examples, Jessie Bernard reminds us of De Toqueville's observation in the 1830s that America's equality of opportunity imposed a subtle demand on men not simply to be family providers but also to be *good* family providers through success in a competitive economy.[2] Demos notes the rise of the "tramp" in the nineteenth century, the large and growing number of men who gave up, often fled, the male provider role.[3] Peter Filene recounts the cultural shock that occurred when nearly half of World War I recruits were physically or mentally disqualified for military service.[4] In these and other ways, American men in the nineteenth and early twentieth centuries gave indications that they were having trouble meeting male role demands.[5]

Over the same period, women were seen as taking a larger role with children, particularly sons. In the early nineteenth century, the mother was considered to be a far less significant figure in the childrearing of sons (and to some extent daughters as well) than she is today. Examination of correspondence between parents and children suggests sons' relationships with their fathers were actually closer than those with their mothers.[6] But

2. J. Bernard, "The Good-Provider Role: Its Rise and Fall," *American Psychologist* 36 (1981):1-12.

3. J. Demos, "The American Family in Past Time," *American Scholar* 43(1974): 422-446.

4. P. Filene, *Him/Her/Self: Sex Roles in Modern America* (New York: Harcourt Brace Jovanovich, 1975).

5. See also E. H. Pleck and J. H. Pleck, eds., *The American Man* (Englewood Cliffs, N.J.: Prentice-Hall, 1980).

6. J. Demos, "The Changing Faces of Fatherhood: A New Exploration in Family History," in *Father and Child Development and Clinical Perspectives*, ed. S. Cath, A. Gurwitt, and J. Ross (Boston: Little, Brown, 1982); and E. A. Rotundo, "Manhood in America, 1770-1910" (Ph.D. dissertation, Brandeis University, 1982).

during the mid and late nineteenth century, mothers were encouraged to take the dominant emotional role in childrearing. Notions of women's moral "purity" arose, which elevated women above men and made them particularly suited for "rearing" the young. The increasing involvement of women in childrearing was also manifested in early education. Educational reformers like Horace Mann greatly increased the numbers of women teachers in the schools, departing from the earlier pattern of male elementary teachers.[7]

Women's influence on boys and men's difficulties in their role came to be formulated in terms of "feminization." Articles with titles like "The Effeminization of Men" appeared in popular magazines as early as 1893.[8] In 1909, the prominent psychologist J. McKeen Cattell argued that the new confinement of the boy in elementary schools exposed him to the ministrations of a "vast horde of female teachers" who tended to "subvert both the school and the family" because of their spinsterish attitudes.[9] Concerns about feminization were a major factor in the rapid rise of the Boy Scouts, which received a federal charter in 1911. As Hantover emphasizes, scouting served to relieve the masculine anxieties of the scoutmasters at least as much as those of the boys they worked with.[10] Altogether, such concerns set the stage for the emergence of the theory of male sex-role identity.

INITIAL FORMULATION, 1936–1945

The first step in the explicit development of the theory of male sex-role identity was taken by Lewis Terman and Catherine Miles in *Sex and Personality*.[11] They formulated a notion that gave previously existing cultural concerns about men's (and women's) roles more precise intellectual focus: for each sex, there is a psychologically normative or ideal configuration of traits, attitudes, and interests that members of that sex demonstrate to varying degrees. Men (and women) are psychologically normal to the extent that they possess these sex-appropriate characteristics and psycho-

7. R. Suggs, *Motherteacher: The Feminization of American Education* (Charlottesville: University of Virginia Press, 1978).

8. J. Dubbert, "Progressivism and the Masculinity Crisis," *Psychoanalytic Review* 61(1974):433–455.

9. Quoted in W. L. O'Neill, *Divorce in the Progressive Era* (New Haven: Yale University Press, 1967).

10. J. Hantover, "The Boy Scouts and the Validation of Masculinity," *Journal of Social Issues* 34, no. 1 (1978):184–195.

11. L. Terman and C. Miles, *Sex and Personality* (New York: McGraw-Hill, 1936).

logically deficient or abnormal to the extent that they do not. Terman and Miles introduced the term "masculinity – femininity" (MF) for the personality dimension on which members of each sex varied, and the first of what soon became many psychological tests to assess it.

In Terman and Miles's words:

> The belief is all but universal that men and women as contrasting groups display characteristic sex differences in their behavior, and that these differences are so deep and pervasive as to lend distinctive character to the entire personality. That masculine and feminine types are a reality in all our highly developed cultures can hardly be questioned. . . . But along with the acceptance of M-F types of the sort we have delineated, there is an explicit recognition of the existence of individual variants from type: the effeminate man and the masculine woman. Grades of deviates are recognized ranging from the slightly variant to the genuine invert who is capable of romantic attachment only to members of his or her own sex. . . . It is highly desirable that our concepts of the M-F types . . . be given a more factual basis. . . . A measure is needed which can be applied to the individual and scored so as to locate the subject, with a fair degree of approximation, in terms of deviation from the mean of either sex.[12]

And again:

> Masculinity and femininity are important aspects of human personality. They are not to be thought of as lending to it merely a superficial coloring and flavor; rather they are one of a small number of cores around which the structure of personality gradually takes shape. . . . The M-F dichotomy, in various patterns, has existed throughout history, and is still firmly established in our mores. In a considerable fraction of the population it is the source of many acute difficulties in the individual's social and psychological adjustment.[13]

Terman and Miles's notion of normative personality styles for each sex, whose presence (or absence) reflects psychological health (or deficit), was widely adopted in American psychology. Its popularity is attested by the many other MF tests that rapidly proliferated in the late 1930s and 1940s.[14] Particularly important were the MF measures included as component scales in a new kind of psychological instrument, the omnibus personality inventory. The MF scales of the Strong Vocational Interest Blank,[15] Guilford's Temperament Survey,[16] and the Minnesota Multiphasic Per-

12. Ibid., pp. 1 – 2.
13. Ibid., p. 451.
14. See M. Lewin, ed., *In the Shadow of the Past: Psychology Protrays the Sexes* (New York: Columbia University Press, 1983).
15. E. K. Strong, *Vocational Interests of Men and Women* (Stanford: Stanford University Press, 1943).
16. J. Guilford and R. Guilford, "Personality Factors S. E. and M and Their Measurement," *Journal of Psychology* 2(1936):109 – 127.

sonality Inventory[17] are among the most important examples, together with the slightly later California Psychological Inventory.[18] These machine-scorable tests met the growing needs of "people-processing" institutions of increasing social importance: the military, the modern firm, prisons, and mental hospitals.

Terman and Miles's idea of normative, sex-linked personality patterns that are essential for psychological health applied equally to both sexes and did not give any special attention to the male role. The conceptual developments necessary to elaborate this notion into a theory concerned primarily with the male role came only later. The work of Terman and Miles (and their successors) had as yet too simple a theoretical basis. Its immediate intellectual context was the successful scientific operationalization of intelligence in the early twentieth century, the event that, as much as any other, established psychology as a modern science. Terman himself had been senior author of the Americanized revision of Binet's classic children's intelligence scale, and a milestone in its own right, the Stanford–Binet Intelligence Scale.[19] After this triumph, psychologists began to look to other domains of personality that were socially important, the object of confusion and disagreement, but that might likewise yield up their true nature when subjected to the scientific psychological method. They first turned in the 1920s to moral behavior, which, like intelligence, was of great concern to a society that felt itself flooded by foreign immigrants of possibly deficient character. But here psychology faltered: Hartshorne and May's classic *Studies in the Nature of Character* failed to reveal any commonality of association between prosocial moral behaviors across a variety of settings and circumstances.[20]

Led by Terman and Miles, the field of psychology turned next to sex typing, or within-sex variation in sex-role-related traits, attitudes, and interests. The study of intelligence provided a direct model. Binet and his successors had, in effect, defined intelligence as the capacity to answer correctly those items that older children answered correctly more often than younger children. In like fashion, masculinity–femininity was operationalized as having those characteristics that one sex said they had more often than the other sex did. Having sex-appropriate traits was, thus, like having intelligence. Terman and Miles included in their scale such then-

17. W. G. Dahlstrom, G. S. Welsh, and L. E. Dahlstrom, *An MMPI Handbook*, vol. 1, *Clinical Interpretation* (Minneapolis: University of Minnesota Press, 1972).

18. H. Gough, "An Interpreter's Syllabus for the CPI," in *Advances in Psychological Assessment*, ed. P. McReynolds, vol. 1 (Palo Alto: Science and Behavior Publications, 1964).

19. L. Terman, *Stanford–Binet Intelligence Scale* (Boston: Houghton Mifflin, 1916).

20. M. Hartshorne and M. May, *Studies in the Nature of Character*, vol. 1, *Studies in Deceit*, vol. 2, *Studies in Self-Control*, vol. 3, *Studies in the Organization of Character* (New York: Macmillan, 1928–1930).

contemporary psychometic methods as word associations and perceptions of inkblots but interpreted them in a strictly empirical way, not in the psychodynamic context in which they are seen today.

One respect in which Terman and Miles and their followers were theoretically bolder was their postulation of homosexuality as the extreme end of the continuum of the "grades of deviates" who depart from the normative male and female patterns. Homosexuality was of great concern to both the developers and users of MF tests. Nearly 20% of *Sex and Personality* is devoted to various studies of homosexuality. (There is a foretaste of the theory's later focus in males in that nearly all of these are studies of male homosexuals.) The MMPI MF test is based on comparisons of 54 male soldiers, 67 women airline employees, and 13 male homosexuals.[21] Harrison Gough writes that the goal of this MF scale (later integrated into the California Psychological Inventory) "has been to develop an instrument which is brief, easy to administer, relatively subtle and unthreatening in content, and which will, at the same time, differentiate men from women and sexual deviates from normals."[22] The critical assumption: Male homosexuals differ from male heterosexuals in the same respects as women differ from men.[23] These tests were in fact considered effective to screen male populations for homosexuals.

Giving homosexuality such central attention as a departure from the personality structure considered psychologically normative for each sex was an important conceptual step, and it was later to be elaborated much further. But even here, Terman and Miles's theoretical simplicity is evident. They interpret homosexuality not from the perspective of psychoanalysis but from that of the early twentieth-century "sexology," which classified and described homosexuality and other sexual deviations in an elaborate taxonomy. If Terman and Miles have another intellectual forerunner besides Alfred Binet, it is Havelock Ellis, not Sigmund Freud.

There was some contemporary opposition to Terman and Miles's concept of psychologically normative personality styles that are inherently related to psychological health. The most notable was Margaret Mead's *Sex and Temperament in Three Primitive Societies*.[24] Mead's book is invariably cited only as providing disconfirming exceptions to Western stereotypes about cultural patterns of sex differences (i.e., Arapesh men are gentle and artistic; Mundugumor women are aggressive). In reality, Mead did not see her contribution primarily as showing that the *actual* characteristics of the

21. Dahlstrom, Welsh, and Dahlstrom, *Clinical Interpretation*, pp. 201–202.

22. H. Gough, "Identifying Psychological Femininity," *Educational and Psychological Measurement* 12(1952):427–439.

23. See also Lewin, *In the Shadow of the Past*.

24. M. Mead, *Sex and Temperament in Three Primitive Societies* (New York: Morrow, 1935).

sexes differed across the three cultures she studied. Rather, it was showing that the temperaments considered *ideal* for men and women, and therefore the characteristics of those who deviated from these ideals, varied. Since individuals differ in their personality characteristics within each sex, not everyone can conform to any particular ideal, and a subgroup of each sex in each society is perceived by both others and themselves as deviating from the prescribed temperament. But since societies vary in their ideals for the sexes, those viewed as deviant will be different subgroups in each one. The titles of the final chapters on each society convey Mead's focus on sex-role deviants: "The Arapesh Ideal and Those Who Deviate from It," "Deviants from the Mundugumor Ideal," and "The Unplaced Tchambuli Man and Woman." Mead's real point was that a man or woman perfectly adapted to the sex-role norms of one culture could be a misfit (a term Mead used repeatedly) in another.

Mead's cultural relativism directly challenged Terman and Miles's interpretation of masculinity and femininity as universal psychological ideals or norms like intelligence. But Terman and Miles's view prevailed. It is perhaps not a coincidence that *Sex and Personality* was published in 1936, in the midst of the Great Depression, clearly the greatest single historical crisis in the institutional basis of the traditional male role: the breadwinning job. As the conventional social arrangements underlying traditional roles eroded so dramatically, the culture sought to reestablish them on a hypothetical inner psychological basis. In short, if holding a job could no longer be counted on to define masculinity, a masculinity–femininity test could.

THEORETICAL MATURATION AND DEVELOPMENT, 1945–1970

In the postwar period, Terman and Miles's masculinity–femininity conception, which had equal application to both sexes, evolved into a theory primarily focusing on males. Several trends in men's experience and how it was socially perceived helped set the stage for this theoretical development.

In some respects, World War II caused a temporary reversal in the long-term historical decline of the traditional male role and of the shorter-term, more specific crisis of the depression. The economic boom that anticipated World War II put many men back to work. In the war itself, men lived by themselves, away from women, in a war perceived as brutal but morally justified, and emerged victorious. But these effects were short-lived compared to other social anxieties and social changes the war stimulated. Repeating the experience of World War I, there was great concern about the large number of males who had been physically or mentally disqualified for the draft, and particularly about the high incidence of male emotional breakdowns in battle. Not everyone interpreted these as failings of masculinity (e.g., Grinker and Spiegel's *Men Under Stress*, a milestone work in stress research[25]). But others, like psychiatrist Edward Strecker in *Their Mothers' Sons*, did.[26]

During the war and after, male–female relationships underwent a transformation. During the wartime boom, women had been drawn into the labor force, and particularly in previously male blue-collar work. They also developed a new degree of psychological independence from men by virtue of having to live without them. When men returned, they found that their wives and girl friends had changed. Negotiating new relationships with women posed a real challenge to men; the spurt of postwar divorces provided testimony. Altered equally by the war was men's economic role. Wartime technological advances had transformed the economy. A good job now required levels of education and training previously unprecedented. Severe postwar inflation caused by war-deferred consumer demand undermined men's family provider role even more.

Social analysts noticed that the new occupational roles and associated life styles emerging as dominant for men in the 1950s in response to these changes were discordant with what they saw as men's traditional self-image and might have negative effects on men's identities. This was actually one of the main themes in two major sociological studies not usually interpreted in this light, C. Wright Mills's *White Collar: The American Middle Classes*, and W. F. Whyte's *The Organization Man*.[27] Ehrenberg, extending Mills' views further, explicitly argued that the new, impulse-restraining male role was damaging to men's mental health.[28] The title of Whyte's book became a widely used term for the bureaucratically domesticated male. Popular culture in the 1950s also expressed these concerns. As Ehrenreich and English note:

> In cartoons, the average male was shorter than his wife, who habitually entered the frame in curlers, wielding a rolling pin over her cowering husband. TV squeezed the American male's diminished sense of manhood for whatever laughs—or thrills—were left. The domesticated Dad, who was most hilarious when he tried to be manly

25. R. Grinker and J. Spiegel, *Men under Stress* (Philadelphia: Blakiston, 1948).

26. E. Strecker, *Their Mothers' Sons* (Philadelphia: Lippincott, 1946).

27. C. W. Mills, *White Collar: The American Middle Classes* (New York: York: Oxford University Press, 1956); and W. H. Whyte, *The Organization Man* (New York: Simon and Schuster, 1956).

28. O. Ehrenberg, "Concepts of Masculinity: A Study of Discrepancies between Men's Self-Concepts and Their Relationships to Mental Health" (Ph.D. dissertation, New York University, 1960).

and enterprising, was the butt of all the situation comedies. Danny Thomas, Ozzie Nelson, Robert Young, and (though not a father) Jackie Gleason in "The Honeymooners," were funny only as pint-sized caricatures of the patriarchs, frontiersmen, and adventurers who once defined American manhood.[29]

A particularly dramatic example occurs in still the most popular of James Dean's films, *Rebel without a Cause*. In the film's psychologically most powerful scene, Dean seeks out his father for advice but recoils in disgust after finding him wearing an apron while washing dishes. World War II's respected returning war hero had been transformed into a henpecked husband whose son holds him in contempt.

New Theoretical Conceptions: Identification

The theoretical development that led to a special focus on males was the introduction of the psychodynamic concept of identification to the study of masculinity–femininity. The basic notion is that the developmental origin of MF is the individual's psychological identification with the mother or father. The acquisition of MF is, in fact, a process of "sex-role identification." But since mothers are such central figures in the lives of children of both sexes, this means that boys initially identity with a female and therefore develop a feminine identity. Thus, males have far more difficulty than females in acquiring an appropriate sex-role identity. In turn, overcoming their initial feminine identification is hypothesized to be the central problem in males' psychological development. This argument is the essence of the theory of male sex-role identity.

The first clear statement of this view appears to be Talcott Parsons's essay "Age and Sex in the Social Structure of the United States," and it was a major argument in Parsons and Bales's influential *Family Socialization and Interaction Process*.[30] Franck and Rosen are apparently the first to conceptualize an MF measure as revealing sex-role identification.[31] This expression and its variants soon supplanted MF itself as the term for within-sex differences in sex-role-related traits, attitudes, and interests. Developmental psychologists began to study sex-role development in children. Through the work of Brown, Lynn, Kagan, and Biller, the theory of

29. B. Ehrenreich and D. English, *For Her Own Good: One Hundred Fifty Years of the Experts' Advice to Women* (New York: Doubleday Anchor, 1979), p. 240.

30. T. Parsons and R. F. Bales, *Family Socialization and Interaction Process* (Glencoe, Ill.: Free Press, 1955).

31. R. Franck and E. Rosen, "A Projective Test of Masculinity–Femininity," *Journal of Consulting Psychology* 13(1948):247–256.

male sex-role identity became the reigning interpretation of sex-role development in American psychology.[32]

Although this core argument in the theory of male identity used the psychoanalytic concept of identification, it was never a mainstream view within psychoanalysis itself. To the early Freud, the father was the towering figure in the life of the son. He gave a role to the mother, but only as the object of the son's libidinous drives. To the early Freud at least, the mother was psychologically important primarily because the male child's love for her brought him into competition with his father in an Oedipal drama whose outcome — identification with the father and the resulting consolidation of the superego — would shape the boy's character structure. Freud saw the girl — not the boy — as facing special problems in psychosexual development.

Led by Freud himself, psychoanalysis in the 1920s began to focus on pre-Oedipal issues. "Pre-Oedipal" is, in fact, the psychoanalytic codeword denoting the mother. Within the variant formulations, the overall theme was: The Oedipal conflict is the key to the clinically less serious neurotic disorders, but the more severe forms of psychopathology (the psychoses and personality disorders) result from far earlier and more fundamental problems in the pre-Oedipal period. As developed by theorists like Bowlby, Mahler, Winnicott, Klein, and Benedek, the problem of the pre-Oedipal relationship is that the mother is rejecting or otherwise inadequate as an attachment figure, or at the other extreme, the mother facilitates the child's attachment but then refuses to permit the child to individuate. To these theorists, the idea that the male child might *identify with* the mother, leading to a cross-sex identification, would have seemed quite novel.

Hypermasculinity

The notions that an individual's sex typing derives from parental identification and that the boy's initial identification with his mother could therefore be a source of difficulty, combined with the psychoanalytic idea of the

---

32. D. Brown, "Sex-Role Preference in Young Children," *Psychological Monographs* 70, no. 4(1956):421; D. Brown, "Sex-Role Development in a Changing Culture," *Psychological Bulletin* 55(1958):232–242; D. Lynn, "Sex Differences in Identification Development, *Sociometry* 24(1961):373–383; D. Lynn, *Parental and Sex Role Identification: A Theoretical Formulation* (Berkeley: McCutchan, 1969); J. Kagan, "Acquisition and Significance of Sex Typing and Sex-Role Identity," in *Review of Child Development Research*, ed. M. L. Hoffman and L. W. Hoffman, vol. 1 (New York: Russell Sage, 1964); H. Biller, *Father, Child, and Sex Role* (Lexington, Mass.: Heath Lexington, 1974); and H. Biller and L. Borstelmann, "Masculine Development: An Integrative Review," *Merrill-Palmer Quarterly* 13(1967):253–294.

unconscious, stimulated another theoretical development of great importance: the concept of *hypermasculinity* (exaggerated, extreme masculine behavior) as a defense against the male's unconscious feminine identification. In Terman and Miles's earlier conception, the potential problem for males was only in not having enough masculinity. With this new concept, too *much* masculinity could be viewed as a psychological problem as well. Because of the many behaviors that could be interpreted as expressions of hypermasculinity, this conceptual advance considerably broadened the range of phenomena that the theory of male sex-role identity addressed.

While this concept had been foreshadowed in such European psychodynamic writings as Adler's "masculine protest" and Boehm's "femininity complex in men",[33] it caught on in the American social sciences only during and after World War II. We earlier noted cultural concerns about draft disqualifications and battle breakdowns as showing widespread masculine inadequacy during the war, and about the apparent domestication of masculinity in the 1950s. But the war and postwar period simultaneously seemed to reveal, perhaps more starkly than before, another side of masculinity that called out for explanation: first, wartime male aggression (and the blind obedience that could make them the tools of a fascist state), and, later, male juvenile delinquency in the 1950s.

The wartime roots of the hypermasculinity concept are evident in its early history. In "Certain Primary Sources and Patterns of Aggression in the Social Structure of the Western World," Talcott Parsons interpreted male violence as due to the male's need to disengage himself from the inner feminine identification caused by the Western pattern of close mother–child relations.[34] In what is now recognized as the pioneering work of "psychohistory," psychoanalyst Walter Langer prepared a case study of Adolf Hitler for the OSS.[35] Langer concluded that the dictator was a divided personality who masked a timid side with an exaggerated and sadistic version of masculinity.

In Adorno *et al.*'s *The Authoritarian Personality* (the first two of whose four authors were European refugees from Hitler) one of the study's principal interpretive hypotheses concerned defenses against unconscious cross-sex identity. As Adorno *et al.* put it:

> One might expect high-scoring [i.e., authoritarian] men to think of themselves as very masculine, and that this claim would be the more insistent the greater the underlying

33. A. Adler, *The Practice and Theory of Individual Psychology* (New York: Harcourt, 1927); and F. Boehm, "The Femininity Complex in Men," *International Journal of Psychoanalysis* 11(1932):444–469.

34. T. Parsons, "Certain Primary Sources and Patterns of Aggression in the Social Structure of the Western World," *Psychiatry* 10(1947): 167–181.

35. W. Langer, *The Mind of Adolf Hitler* (New York: Basic Books, 1972).

feelings of weakness. . . . There seems to be, in the high-scoring men, more of what may be called psuedo-masculinity—as defined by boastfulness about such traits as determination, energy, industry, independence, decisiveness, and will power—and less admission of passivity.[36]

As Nevitt Sanford, one of the study's investigators, recounted later, "The authors of *The Authoritarian Personality* became convinced that one of the sources of this personality syndrome was ego-alien femininity—that is to say, underlying femininity that had to be countered by whatever defenses the subject had at his disposal."[37]

Sanford was the only one of *The Authoritarian Personality's* investigators to follow up the hypermasculinity hypothesis. In an utterly intriguing article originally prepared in 1950, Sanford brilliantly perceived the opportunity provided by combining the older questionnaire MF scales with the newer, projective tests (then just starting to appear) aspiring to tap unconscious sex-role identification.[38] By interpreting the questionnaire scales as assessing superficial, conscious-level sex-role identity and the projective tests as tapping the unconscious level, he could sort subjects into a fourfold classification representing the various combinations of conscious and unconscious masculine and feminine sex-role identity. Sanford's study concerned the correlates of the various sex-role identity patterns on intellectual productivity and creativity in a sample of postwar male Berkeley graduate students. He chose these dependent variables apparently because, in his ego-psychological persepctive, he expected the unconscious-feminine/conscious-masculine (FM) pattern in men to have a great potential cost in the cognitive rigidity necessitated by the repression of inner femininity. But the main conclusion of his study was, interestingly, not the problems of the FM males, but the unusual creativity and intellectual strength of the reverse male pattern: unconscious-masculine/conscious-feminine (MF).

Sanford's conclusion harked back to Jung's notion that the mature personality requires the integration of the unconscious cross-sex self, men's *anima* and women's *animus*. But such an idea could not be incorporated in 1950s thinking. Sanford dropped this research, not even publishing his results until 1966. However, Daniel Miller and Guy Swanson's *Inner Conflict and Defense* turned Sanford's methodological breakthrough into a line of research more consistent with the cultural concerns of the

36. T. W. Adorno, E. Frenkel-Brunswick, D. J. Levinson, and R. N. Sanford, *The Authoritarian Personality* (New York: Wiley, 1950), pt. 1, pp. 428, 405.

37. R. Sanford, "Masculinity–Femininity in the Structure of Personality," in his *Self and Society* (New York: Atherton, 1966), p. 196.

38. Sanford, *Self and Society*.

period.[39] They adopted some of Sanford's measures (the Franck Drawing Completion Test as the unconscious measure and the Gough MF scale as the conscious one) and arranged his sex-role identity categories as a series of stages in male development. Males start as FFs (unconscious and conscious feminine identity) totally identified with the mother, then progress to the FM stage acquiring superficial masculine traits but maintaining their deep feminine identity, and complete their maturation as MMs, developing inner masculine identification to match the surface behavior they earlier acquired. At the MM stage, argue Miller and Swanson, male development is complete. Miller and Swanson simply omitted Sanford's fourth type, the MF, whom he regarded as the most mature and creative.

The studies in *Inner Conflict and Defense* that used this revised, threefold typology of sex-role identity examined arousal of guilt and defenses against aggression, viewed as ego-psychological personality processes, as hypothetical correlates of the FM pattern. This line of research then passed to Fred Strodtbeck and his students at the University of Chicago.[40] Like Sanford, and Miller and Swanson, Strodtbeck and his students focused on cognitive, ego-psychological variables as dependent measures. One study in the series, however, got closer to sex-role issues.[41] In this study, subjects heard what was purported to be a naval court-martial about an event modeled loosely after Melville's *Billy Budd,* in which a handsome young sailor accidentally kills an officer. Under one experimental condition, evidence is included implying that the defendant is homosexual. The prediction was that in this condition, the FM males would more often find the defendant guilty and recommend the death sentence. (The prediction was not clearly supported.[42])

The unconscious feminine identity hypothesis became an extremely popular one and began to extend in many directions. McClelland and

39. D. Miller and G. Swanson, *Inner Conflict and Defense* (New York: Holt, 1960).

40. F. Strodtbeck and P. Creelan, "Interaction Linkage between Family Size, Intelligence, and Sex-Role Identity," *Journal of Marriage and the Family* 30(1968):301–307; F. Strodtbeck, W. Bezdek, and W. Goldhammer, "Male Sex Role and Response to a Community Problem," *Sociological Quarterly* 11(1970):291–306; W. Bezdek and F. Strodtbeck, "Sex-Role Identity and Pragmatic Action," *American Sociological Review* 35(1970):491–502; P. Lipsitt and F. Strodtbeck, "Defensiveness in Decision-Making as a Function of Sex-Role Identification," *Journal of Personality and Social Psychology* 6(1967):10–15; T. Cottle, "Family Perceptions, Sex Role Identity and the Prediction of School Performance," *Educational and Psychological Measurement* 28(1968):861–886; and T. Cottle, C. N. Edwards, and J. H. Pleck, "The Relationship of Sex Identity and Social and Political Attitudes," *Journal of Personality* 38(1970):435–452.

41. Lipsitt and Strodtbeck, "Defensiveness in Decision-Making."

42. Pleck, *Myth of Masculinity*, pp. 105–106.

Watt, and others applied it to psychopathology more generally.[43] Burton
and Whiting applied it to male initiation rites by establishing an association, in a sample of world cultures, between "exclusive mother–child
sleeping arrangements" (the father sleeps in a different room, and often in
a different building, than the mother and young child) and male initiation
ceremonies.[44] Robert and Ruth Munroe studied both the couvade (a practice in many cultures in which husbands of pregnant wives engage in
symbolic birth ceremonies of their own) and psychosomatic symptoms in
expectant fathers in the United States in the light of the unconscious
cross-sex identity hypothesis.[45] But the topic studied by far most frequently in the light of the hypermasaculinity hypothesis was male juvenile
delinquency. Walter Miller introduced hypermasculinity as a leading interpretation in his "Lower Class Culture as a Generating Milieu of Gang
Delinquency."[46]

Absent Fathers and Black Males

The consequences of the fathers' absence on sons and the sex role problems of black males each became important new substantive areas in which
the theory of male sex-role identity was applied in the 1950s and 1960s. To
some degree, these substantive issues were theoretically linked to hypermasculinity: The model study of this period was an investigation of delinquency as a consequence of the sex-role identity problems resulting from
the father's absence in black males.[47] Studies of hypermasculinity, paternal
absence, and black males all reinforced each other.

In many senses, the father's absence as a large-scale social problem had
been created by World War II. The war had, of course, directly taken
fathers away from their children (for many, permanently), and the earliest
studies concern these wartime separations. But more indirectly, the

43. D. McClelland and N. Watt, "Sex-Role Alienation in Schizophrenia," *Journal of
Abnormal Psychology* 73(1968):226–239; and Pleck, *Myth of Masculinity.*

44. R. Burton and J. Whiting, "The Absent Father and Cross-Sex Identity," *Merrill-
Palmer Quarterly* 7(1961):85–95.

45. R. L. Munroe and R. H. Munroe, "Male Pregnancy and Cross-Sex Identity Symptoms," *Journal of Social Psychology* 84(1971):11–25; R. L. Munroe and R. H. Munroe, "Psychological Interpretation of Male Initiation Rites: The Case of Male Pregnancy Symptoms,"
Ethos 1(1973):490–498; and R. L. Munroe, R. H. Munroe, and J. W. M. Whiting, "The
Couvade: A Psychological Analysis," *Ethos* 1(1973):30–74.

46. W. Miller, "Lower-Class Culture as a Generating Milieu for Gang Delinquency,"
Journal of Social Issues 14(1958):5–19.

47. E.g., J. Rohrer and M. Edmonson, *The Eighth Generation Grows Up* (New York:
Harper, 1960); and I. J. Silverman and S. Dinitz, "Compulsive Masculinity and Delinquency," *Criminology* 11(1974):499–515.

changes in male – female relations resulting from war had led to a spurt of postwar divorces, creating more absent fathers. The war also greatly stimulated the migration of rural dwellers, particularly blacks, to cities, where many factors led to the breakdown of their traditional two-parent family structure. Male identity theory proved a convenient and convincing explanation of the delinquency and other social problems that resulted. The effects of paternal absence on sons quickly became one of the most frequently studied topics in the sex-role field. The contrast with the earlier period is striking. In the psychological theories of Freud and Jung, the father is the towering figure in the psychological development of the child.[48] In the 1950s and 1960s, he became a dominating figure, not by his presence, but by his absence.

When social science began to pay serious attention to blacks in the 1960s, male identity theory was prominent among the conceptual perspectives it employed. On the basis of MF studies of a sample of Alabama convicts and working-class veterans in Wisconsin, social psychologist Thomas Pettigrew in *A Profile of the Negro American* interpreted black males as suffering from sex role identity problems.[49] To Pettigrew, common to all black males' problems — from the father-absent, mother-dominated home to their overrepresentation in low-paying service jobs occupied by females — is the underlying theme of threat to male sex-role identity. As Pettigrew put it, "The sex-identity problems created by the fatherless home are perpetuated in adulthood."[50] In the following year, Daniel Patrick Moynihan leaned heavily on this hypothesis in "The Negro Family: The Case for National Action," the so-called Moynihan Report.[51] He argued that the humiliations suffered by blacks during Reconstruction had a particularly devastating effect on black males because "the very essence of the male animal, from the bantam rooster to the four-star general, is to strut."[52] As American mobilization in Vietnam grew, he also praised military service as an almost ideal solution to black men's frustrated masculinity, which he saw as having such destructive consequences for them and the whole society: "Given the strains of the disorganized and matrifocal family life in which so many negro youth come of age, the Armed Forces are a dramatic and desperately needed change: a world away from women, a world run by strong men of unquestioned author-

---

48. M. Lewin, personal communication, 1980.

49. T. Pettigrew, *A Profile of the Negro American* (Princeton, N.J.: Van Nostrand, 1964).

50. Ibid., p. 21.

51. D. Moynihan, "The Negro Family: The Case for National Action," in *The Moynihan Report and the Politics of Controversy*, ed. L. Rainwater and W. Yancey (Cambridge: MIT Press, 1967).

52. Ibid., p. 62.

ity."[53] In a somewhat later expression of liberal concern in the same vein, Biller and Meredith's *Father Power*, a popular guide for fathering, includes material on black fathers only in a chapter titled "Fathers with Special Problems," of which the other examples are the physically handicapped and elderly father.[54]

DECLINE, 1970 TO THE PRESENT

Starting in the 1970s, the dominance of the male role identity paradigm in sex-role research began to wane. I have recounted in detail elsewhere major theoretical and empirical problems accumulated in its component lines of research.[55] For example, it became apparent that research failed to support the bipolar conception of masculinity – femininity so essential to interpreting MF tests as measures of sex-role identity.[56] Measures of sex typing did not have the relationships predicted with psychological adjustment and well-being.[57] Father absence did not prove to have the effects it was so widely believed to have on boys' sex typing, school performance, and delinquency.[58]

Male identity theory declined, however, not so much because of a detailed critique of its internal problems as because of new conceptual and research developments and new social attitudes about sex roles. One such research development was Money and Ehrhardt's distinction between "gender identity" (the individual's awareness of and satisfaction with being a male or female) and "gender role" (the extent to which individuals have the traits, attitudes, and interests culturally expected for their sex — i.e., what is measured by MF scales).[59] They argued that once gender

53. Ibid., p. 42.

54. H. Biller and D. Meredith, *Father Power* (New York: Doubleday, 1975).

55. Pleck, *Myth of Masculinity;* and J. Pleck, "Prisoners of Manliness," *Psychology Today,* 1981, pp. 69–83.

56. A. Edwards and R. Abbott, "Measurement of Personality: Theory and Technique," *Annual Review of Psychology* 24(1973):241–278; L. Tyler, "Individual Differences: Sex Differences," in *International Encyclopedia of the Social Sciences*, ed. D. Sills (New York: Macmillan, 1968); and A. Constantinople, "Masculinity – Femininity: An Exception to the Famous Dictum?" *Psychological Bulletin* 80(1973):389–407.

57. P. Mussen, "Long-Term Consequents of Masculinity in Adolescence," *Journal of Consulting Psychology* 26(1962):435–440.

58. E. Herzog and C. Sudia, *Boys in Fatherless Families*, HEW Publication No. OCD (Washington, D.C.: GPO, 1971), pp. 72–73; and E. Herzog and C. Sudia, "Children in Fatherless Families," in *Review of Child Development*, vol. 3, ed. B. Caldwell and P. Ricciuti (Chicago: University of Chicago Press, 1973).

59. J. Money and A. Ehrhardt, *Man and Woman, Boy and Girl* (Baltimore: Johns Hopkins University Press, 1972).

identity is established (as it is without difficulty for all but the tiniest minority), variations in gender role do not cause psychological problems.

A second research development was Bem's and Spence and Helmreich's studies of psychological androgyny.[60] Actually, mainstream sex-role identity researchers had somewhat earlier first proposed assessing masculinity and femininity as separate dimensions as a way of solving the problems that had become evident in sex-role identity research concerning the relationship between sex typing and psychological adjustment.[61] But Bem, Spence, and Helmreich used this new conceptualization to challenge in a more fundamental way the then-dominant prediction that traditional sex typing was necessary for good adjustment. This research legitimated individuals' having traits associated with the other sex.

At a broader social level, feminism challenged the traditional patterns of sex roles for which the theory of male identity provided ideological justification. Initially, though, feminists appropriated certain arguments from the theory that superficially appeared to support change in sex roles. For example, Betty Friedan argued that one of the negative consequences of excluding women from employment is that the full-time housewife is too powerful a mother in the lives of her sons and that her overprotectiveness is responsible for "the homosexuality that is spreading like a murky smog over the American scene."[62] Early feminist psychoanalysis also wholly incorporated male identity arguments about men's fear and hatred of women as the result of the male child's identification with the mother.[63]

60. S. Bem, "Psychology Looks at Sex Roles: Where Have All the Androgynous People Gone?" (paper presented at UCLA Symposium on Sex Differences, 1972): S. Bem, "The Measurement of Psychological Androgyny," *Journal of Clinical and Consulting Psychology* 42(1974):155–162; S. Bem, "Probing the Promise of Androgyny," in *Beyond Sex Role Stereotypes: Toward a Psychology of Androgyny*, ed. A. Kaplan and J. Bean (Boston: Little, Brown, 1976); J. T. Spence, R. Helmreich, and J. Stapp, "The Personal Attributes Questionnaire: A Measure of Sex Role Stereotypes and Masculinity–Femininity," *JSAS Catalog of Selected Documents in Psychology* 4(1974):43; J. Spence and R. Helmreich, *Masculinity and Femininity: Their Psychology Dimensions, Correlates, and Antecedents* (Austin: University of Texas, 1978).

61. Biller and Borstelmann, "Masculine Development"; H. Biller, "A Multiaspect Investigation of Masculine Development in Kindergarten Age Boys," *Genetic Psychology Monographs* 78(1968):89–138; and J. Gonen and L. Lansky, "Masculinity, Femininity and Masculinity–Femininity: A Phenomenological Study of the MF Scale of the MMPI," *Psychological Reports* 12(1968):183–194.

62. B. Friedan, *The Feminine Mystique* (New York: Norton, 1963), p. 265.

63. N. Chodorow, "Being and Doing: A Cross-Cultural Examination of the Socialization of Males and Females," in *Women in Sexist Society*, ed. V. Gornick and B. K. Moran (New York: Basic Books, 1971); and N. Chodorow, "Family Structure and Feminine Personality," in *Women, Culture, and Society*, ed. M. Z. Rosaldo and L. Lamphere (Stanford: Stanford University Press, 1974).

Another example is Farrell's recommendation of greater paternal participation in childrearing because it will reduce male homosexuality.[64] More recent feminist works use such arguments increasingly less frequently.[65]

Because of these developments in both research and social attitudes, the theory of male sex-role identity is no longer a dominant paradigm in psychology. Rather, it is now an event in psychology's history. Consideration of this history will help contribute to new paradigms in the study of sex roles that are more relevant to the need of contemporary society.

64. W. Farrell, *The Liberated Man* (New York: Random House, 1974).
65. E.g., N. Chodorow, *The Reproduction of Mothering: Psychoanalysis and the Sociology of Gender* (Berkeley: University of California Press, 1978).

2

The Case for Men's Studies

Harry Brod

> *After all, men have been the subject of nearly all research to date, which has constituted "men's studies," so why should feminists add to this?*
> Sue Wise and Liz Stanley, "Sexual Politics"

In this chapter I attempt to establish the validity of the emerging field of men's studies, primarily by articulating its distinctive contributions to the ongoing feminist reconstruction of knowledge. I contend that men's studies perspectives are essential to, not merely compatible with, the academic and political projects initiated by women's studies two decades ago. In the course of this discussion, I propose a general theory of men's studies as an academic field, analyze some illustrative examples of men's studies research, and contrast various political perspectives on men's studies.

MEN'S STUDIES DEFINED

To assess men's studies claims to inclusion in the academy, its specific contributions must first be articulated. Given the women's studies critique of traditional scholarship, it may seem, at least initially, that men's studies represents an attempt to undermine rather than contribute to feminist scholarship, since it appears to threaten the fundamental premise of women's studies. Briefly, women's studies emerges from the proposition that traditional scholarship embodies a bias that is male oriented or androcentric. Women's experiences and perspectives have been systematically not incorporated into, or written out of, what has been accepted as knowledge. Thus traditional scholarship, while claiming to be objective and neutral, has been a *de facto* program of "men's studies."[1] The goal of women's studies, then, is to reconstitute knowledge to rectify that deficiency, by supplementing the traditional canon with additional information about women and, in many cases, by bringing about a fundamental revision of the form and content of traditional academic disciplines to produce a gynocentric rather than androcentric vision. "Men's studies" appears as the problem, not the solution.

The new men's studies, however, does not recapitulate traditionally male-biased scholarship. Like women's studies, men's studies aims at the emasculation of patriarchal ideology's masquerade as knowledge. Men's studies argues that while women's studies corrects the exclusion of women from the traditional canon caused by androcentric scholarship's elevation of *man* as male to *man* as generic human, the implications of this fallacy for our understanding of men have gone largely unrecognized. While *seemingly* about men, traditional scholarship's treatment of generic man as the human norm in fact systematically excludes from consideration what is unique to men *qua* men. The overgeneralization from male to generic human experience not only distorts our understanding of what, if anything, is truly generic to humanity but also precludes the study of masculinity as a *specific male* experience, rather than a universal paradigm for *human* experience. The most general definition of men's studies is that it is the study of masculinities and male experiences as specific and varying social–historical–cultural formations. Such studies situate masculinities as objects of study on a par with femininities, instead of elevating them to universal norms.

For the feminist project that undergirds both to be completed, men's studies then emerges as a necessary complement to women's studies. For not only do old soldiers not die, they do not even fade away. No feminist theory can move women from the margin to the center, if one accepts this central metaphor of Bell Hooks's recent book on feminist theory, by ignoring men.[2] If men are to be removed from center stage and a feminist vision fulfilled, that feminist vision must be explicitly focused on men to move them off center. Men's studies views men precisely in this manner. While women have been obscured from our vision by being too much in

1. See Dale Spender, ed., *Men's Studies Modified: The Impact of Feminism on the Academic Discipline* (Elmsford, N.Y.: Pergamon, 1981); Janice G. Raymond, "Women's Studies: A Knowledge of One's Own," in *Gendered Subjects: The Dynamics of Feminist Teaching*, ed. Margo Culley and Catherine Portuges (London: Routledge & Kegan Paul, 1985), pp. 49–50; Judith Shapiro, "Anthropology and the Study of Gender," in *A Feminist Perspective in the Academy: The Difference It Makes*, ed. Elizabeth Langland and Walter Gove (Chicago: University of Chicago Press, 1981), p. 111.

2. Bell Hooks, *Feminist Theory: From Margin to Center* (Boston: South End Press, 1984).

the background, men have been obscured by being too much in the fore-ground.[3] Without a particular focus on men, the danger remains that even new knowledge about women will remain knowledge of the "other," not quite on a par with knowledge of men. The "woman question" must be supplemented by the "man question" for either to be addressed fully.

Men's studies raises new questions and demonstrates the inadequacy of established frameworks in answering old ones. I here allude only to several illustrative questions guiding research in various key areas.

Work and Family

Why are women parents in the paid labor force seen as working mothers, while statistics on levels of fatherhood in the workforce are unavailable, not even collected by the Census Bureau?[4] Is there an unacknowledged darker side to fathers' feelings toward their sons — what could be called a *Laius complex*— in which men fear their sons' impending ascension to power?[5] Has new research on fathering simply changed pronouns from earlier research on mothering, uncritically using concepts that speak more to female than male life cycles, thereby failing fully to capture male di-mensions of parenting?[6] To focus this problem more sharply, take cogni-zance of how dual labor market analysis has shown that the working mother concept means not only that some women have children but that the work women as a group do, even in the paid labor force, is a "mother-ing" (i.e., service) kind of work.[7] The noun *mother* remains as women's putative essence, in some cases modified by the adjective *working* and in other cases not. To coin a phrase, the analogous concept for men would be *fathering workers*, not *working fathers*. With parenting conceived on the female model, where the private is seen as antecedent to and constitutive of the public, we have not sufficiently investigated how men's supposedly essential public roles have an impact on their private fathering functions. For example, do men see parenting as more of a "job," with discrete tasks,

3. The metaphor is from David Morgan, "Men, Masculinity and the Process of Sociologi-cal Enquiry," in *Doing Feminist Research*, ed. Helen Roberts (London: Routledge & Kegan Paul, 1981), p. 94.

4. See Lorna McKee and Margaret O'Brien, eds., *The Father Figure* (London: Tavistock, 1982).

5. See Samuel Osherson, *Finding Our Fathers: The Unfinished Business of Manhood* (New York: Free Press, 1986), chap. 1.

6. This argument is made in Martin P. M. Richards, "How Should We Approach the Study of Fathers?" in McKee and O'Brien, eds., *Father Figure*.

7. See Ruth Milkman, "Organizing the Sexual Division of Labor: Historical Perspectives on 'Women's Work' and the American Labor Movement," *Socialist Review* 49, no. 1 (January–February 1980):95–150.

than women do? Further, on the normative female model, male differences in parenting styles inevitably appear as deficiencies. They may well be, but this would need to be established, not assumed. Nor have we investigated how fathering relates to men's life cycles and career development patterns, as we have investigated mothering in women's lives.[8]

Violence

What is the connection between masculinity and militarism? Consider, for example, the change in rhetoric of the peace movement in the relatively short time from the early days of Vietnam draft resistance when the profile of the hero changed from the soldier to the resister, but women's function as support and trophy remained unquestioned ("Girls say yes to guys who say no," as the slogan then had it), to the current climate in which the women's peace movement has made a critical analysis of masculinity part of mainstream rhetoric, to the extent that Helen Caldicott published an antinuclear book entitled *Missile Envy*, with all its Freudian connotations.[9] Further, what concepts of men as citizen – warriors have shaped our traditions of political theory and practice in which questions of war and peace, as well as questions of the general welfare, are framed?[10]

Health

How much more would we know about health science if gender bias had not prevented us from looking for DES sons, for example, and the miscar-

8. Good steps in this direction are Byran E. Robinson and Robert L. Barret, *The Developing Father* (New York: Guilford, 1986); Joseph H. Pleck, "The Work – Family Role System," in *Work and Family: Changing Roles of Men and Women*, ed. Patricia Voydanoff (Palo Alto, Calif.: Mayfield, 1984); Robert A. Lewis and Robert E. Salt, eds., *Men in Families* (Beverly Hills, Calif.: Sage, 1986); Robert A. Lewis and Marvin B. Sussman, eds., *Men's Changing Roles in the Family* (New York: Haworth, 1986).

9. Helen Caldicott, *Missile Envy* (New York: Bantam, 1985). In Caldicott's own words: "That's why I call my book *Missile Envy*, after Freud. That's the dynamic: mine's bigger than yours, or I want one that's as big as yours." "Nuclear Madness: Excerpts from Helen Caldicott's Farewell Speech," *National Women's Studies Association Perspectives* 4, no. 4 (Fall 1986):3. See also Brian Easlea, *Fathering the Unthinkable: Masculinity, Scientists, and the Nuclear Arms Race* (London: Pluto, 1983).

10. See Judith Stiehm, ed. *Women and Men's Wars* (Elmsford, N.Y.: Pergamon, 1983) and *Women's Views of the Political World of Men* (Transnational, 1984). For studies which revise standard interpretations of major political theorists by establishing the centrality of their views on masculinity, see *Fortune Is a Woman: Gender and Politics in the Thought of Niccolo Machiavelli*, Hanna Fenichel Pitkin (University of California Press, 1984) and *The Orwell Mystique: A Study in Male Ideology*, Daphne Patai (University of Massachusetts, 1984).

riages and birth defects among offspring of males working with hazardous genotoxic substances as quickly as we moved to protect the supposedly frailer vessels of female bodies?[11] How are codes of masculinity and Type A cardiovascular disease personalities related?[12]

Sexuality

What are the determinants of heterosexuality and homosexuality, as activities and identities?[13] Is pornography constitutive, expressive, or distortive of male sexuality?[14] Is "womb envy" an adequate explanatory concept for much of male behavior?[15]

Culture

What do changing styles in genres such as adventure and detective stories tell us about masculinities?[16] How have concepts of the hero been shaped by the rhythms of male life cycles, with their particular patterns of separation and return and distinctive individuating trajectories, and by male

11. Janice M. Swanson and Katharine A. Forrest, eds., *Men's Reproductive Health* (New York: Springer, 1984); Michael Castlemen, "Why Johnny Can't Have Children," in Francis Baumli, ed., *Men Freeing Men* (Jersey City, N.Y.: New Atlantis Press, 1985); and Phil Korman, "Hazards in the Workplace," *Changing Men: Issues in Gender, Sex and Politics* 16, Summer 1986.

12. See Meyer Friedman and Ray H. Rosenman, *Type A Behavior and Your Heart* (New York: Knopf, 1974). For a critical analysis of how this question was raised, see "Dreams of the Heart: Cardiology Rewrites the Masculine Script," chap. 6 in Barbara Ehrenreich, *The Hearts of Men: American Dreams and the Flight from Commitment* (New York: Anchor-Doubleday, 1983).

13. See, for example, Andy Metcalf and Martin Humphries eds., *The Sexuality of Men* (London: Pluto, 1985), Alan P. Bell and Martin S. Weinberg, *Homosexualities: A Study of Diversity among Men and Women* (New York: Simon and Schuster, 1978); or John D'Emilio, *Sexual Politics: The Making of a Homosexual Minority in the United States, 1940–1970* (Chicago: University of Chicago Press, 1983).

14. See the chapter on "Male and Female Sexuality in Capitalism" in Alan Soble's *Pornography: Marxism, Feminism, and the Future of Sexuality* (New Haven: Yale University Press, 1986); and Harry Brod, "Eros Thanatized: Pornography and Male Sexuality," *Humanities in Society* 7, nos. 1–2(Winter–Spring 1984).

15. Eva Feder Kittay, "Womb Envy: An Explanatory Concept," in *Mothering: Essays in Feminist Theory*, ed. Joyce Trebilcot (Totowa, N.J.: Rowman & Allanheld, 1984).

16. See the chapter on "Gender and Genre: Men's Stories" in *Rewriting English: Cultural Politics of Gender and Class*, ed. Janet Batsleer, Tony Davies, Rebecca O'Rourke, and Chris Weedon (London: Methuen, 1985). See also Ernest Mandel, *Delightful Murder: A Social History of the Crime Story* (Minneapolis: University of Minnesota Press, 1984).

predilections for clearly demarcated, agonistic situations?[17] The literature solely on gender and Shakespearean protagonists has practically become a subgenre. Several books focus on masculinity.[18] As Kahn writes of Shakespeare's plays, "Much of their enduring value also lies in how they present specifically masculine experience."[19]

These and many other questions form some of the core concerns of men's studies. In the following section, I discuss two such problematics at greater length. First, however, it may be helpful to discuss the propitiousness of such inquiries.

Current interest in the new men's studies has identifiable academic, social, and political roots. Academically, women's studies has for some time been broadening its goal from supplementing or compensating for the traditional curriculum to fundamentally revising that curriculum. This shift has engendered deeply probing questions, not simply about the status of women in sexist society, but about the nature of the gender division itself. Such questions inevitably focus attention on masculinity as well as femininity. Men's studies extends and highlights such trends in feminist scholarship.

Socially, numerous factors contribute to interest in male role changes. Forces are at work specific to male spheres of activity, in addition to the more obvious demands for change occasioned by the women's movement. The breadwinner role, arguably the traditional core of male identity, is threatened not only by the increased entry of women into the paid workforce but also by changes in the nature of work, such as increasing empha-

17. Men's studies has yet fully to integrate such earlier works as Joseph Campbell's *The Hero with a Thousand Faces* (New York: Meridian–World, 1956) or the title essay in Otto Rank's *The Myth of the Birth of the Hero and Other Writings*, ed. Philip Freund (New York: Vintage–Random, 1964). Published before *The Second Sex*, Simone de Beauvoir's *The Ethics of Ambiguity*, trans. Bernard Frechtman (Secaucus, N.J.: Citadel, 1970), prefigures contemporary discussions such as Carol Gilligan's of women's greater tolerance for ambiguity, for *both–and* rather than *either–or* categories. See also Eugene R. August, "'Modern Men,' or Men's Studies in the 80's," *College English* 44, no. 6 (October 1982); and William J. Goode, *The Celebration of Heroes: Prestige as a Control System* (Berkeley: University of California Press, 1978).

18. Coppélia Kahn, *Man's Estate: Masculine Identity in Shakespeare* (Berkeley: University of California Press, 1981); Marilyn French, *Shakespeare's Division of Experience* (New York: Summit, 1981); Marianne L. Novy, *Love's Argument: Gender Relations in Shakespeare* (Chapel Hill: University of North Carolina Press, 1984); Diane E. Dreher, *Domination and Defiance: Fathers and Daughters in Shakespeare* (Lexington: University Press of Kentucky, 1986); Peter Erickson, *Patriarchal Structures in Shakespeare's Drama* (Berkeley: University of California Press, 1985).

19. Kahn, *Man's Estate*, p. 20; On masculinity in modern literature, see Peter Schwenger, *Phallic Critiques: Masculinity and Twentieth-Century Literature* (London: Routledge & Kegan Paul, 1984) and Bruce Woodcock, *Male Mythologies: John Fowles and Masculinity* (Sussex: Harvester, 1984).

sis on mental rather than manual labor. Such changes are especially notable in advanced industrial nations undergoing a shift from manufacturing
to service economies, paradigmatically the United States. This shift is
accompanied by a change from a work ethic, emphasizing renunciation or
delayed gratification of one's desires in the interests of efficient production, to a consumer ethic, emphasizing the cultivation and satisfaction of
desires through consumption. Greater consciousness of and interest in
more personal and psychological aspects of male roles arises in response to
the new status of men as consumers.[20] Moreover, the traditional heroism
of the male warrior is rendered obsolete by the advent of the electronic
battlefield and nuclear weaponry. Proving one's identity by sexual conquest has also been rendered problematic by the women's and gay liberation movements, and by other changes in sexual ethics. The benchmarks
of masculinity are noticeably in flux, giving rise to interest in examining
male identities.

Politically, men's studies is rooted in the profeminist men's movement,
analogously to women's studies rootedness in feminism. (It should nonetheless be noted that not all men's studies practitioners are male, just as not
all women's studies practitioners are female.) There is, in the United States
as elsewhere, a small but growing men's movement. The Men's Studies
Association is the largest organizational component of the movement's
major national organization, the National Organization for Changing
Men. The association has been instrumental in organizing men's studies
activities since its inception in 1983.[21] This connection should not be
disavowed in the new field's quest for academic respectability. Women's
studies gains much of its vitality from its connection to the feminist movement, whereby its feminist commitments have not been minimized or
negated in pursuit of an ephemeral goal of apolitical objectivity. Similarly,
men's studies should be unabashedly explicit about its roots in the search
for progressive, profeminist change in male roles. If certain traditionalists
wish to castigate men's studies as "merely" a form of political activism and
not a scholarly pursuit, the response of men's studies should be to wear its
activism as a badge of honor rather than shame. Such a charge can be made
only by practitioners ignorant of the history of their own disciplines, for all
knowledge, even that stemming from disciplines now firmly ensconced in
the academic establishment, originates in the search for human better-
ment. To provide an example: When it was founded more than a hundred

20. An example of the advertising industry's response to changes in men is *Men's Changing Role in the Family of the 80's: An American Consensus Report* (New York: Benton & Bowles
Research Services, 1980).
21. The full address is: National Organization for Changing Men, P.O. Box 451, Wat-
seka, IL 60970.

years ago, the Modern Language Association, now perhaps the quintessential professional organization, was self-consciously the product of a
social movement aimed at democratizing higher education and making it
relevant to then-current needs. Then, too, there were those who argued
that teaching modern languages instead of the classics would destroy the
integrity of the university, since such teaching was clearly a passing fad.

I have more to say of the politics of men's studies later in the chapter.
Because I believe knowledge cannot ultimately be severed from its social
roots and repercussions, in the discussion of men's studies research perspectives that follows I intertwine analysis of scholarly paradigm shifts with
analysis of their political ramifications.

MASCULINITY DEMYSTIFIED

New women's history, written since the 1960s, has decisively changed the
understanding and writing of history, not by elevating a few select women
to the ranks of the "great men" of male historiography, but by joining
ranks with the social history emergent since the early twentieth century to
change the construction of historical narratives. The new women's social
history focuses on the lives led by the majority of women in all strata of
society, based on a wide range of sources from diaries to demographics.
Similarly, the new men's history, as practiced by men's studies, is not a
succession of biographies of great men; neither is it a tale of campaigns,
military and political, won and lost. Instead, new men's history deals with
the daily lives of the majority of men in the past. Just as one of the leading
questions raised by women's history has been the extent to which women
acted *as women*, on the basis of some more or less articulated normative
femininity, so too men's history questions how specific concepts and social
forms of masculinity interacted in men's lives and either formed the basis
of or emerged as reflections on their actions. While the dominant trend in
the new men's history is in the tradition of social history, some psychohis-
torical studies, augmented by a more critical analysis of masculinity than
that found in mainstream psychoanalytic literature, also have been incorporated into men's studies.

Men's history lays decisive emphasis on dispelling the commonly held
belief that the contemporary period is uniquely tumultuous and troubling
for beleaguered male egos. It reveals that constructs of masculinity have
always resulted from conflicting pressures. To cite the contemporary example: The nostalgic male eye that looks longingly back to the 1950s,
ostensibly the last time when men were men and everyone knew what that

meant, forgets that this was also a period of pervasive fear among the white middle class that men were being emasculated by being turned into robotized organization men in indistinguishable gray flannel suits. One of the apotheotic films of the decade, *Rebel without a Cause*, contains scenes in which the James Dean character's juvenile delinquency is clearly attributed to his father's wearing an apron. The 1950s were also the era of the beatniks, and the decade was ushered in by the 1949 premiere of Arthur Miller's *Death of a Salesman*, to my mind still the most eloquently profound single statement of mainstream contemporary American male dilemmas. These are but a few among many signs that all was not well in the kingdom.

To go back farther, the 1890s in the United States was a decade widely perceived as encompassing an acute "crisis of masculinity." Articles on the subject abounded in the popular press, and instructional manuals to solve male problems proliferated. Many factors contributed to the male malaise, among them the wane of Victorianism, the emergence of the "new woman," the continuing impacts of industrialization and urbanization, and the closing of the frontier. It is impossible to understand fully the culture and politics of this and the subsequent period without understanding much of it, including the amalgam of forces that brought Teddy Roosevelt and the Progressive movement to national leadership, as attempts to resolve the crisis.[22]

There is currently a neglected analogue to this earlier male shift in political consciousness, obscured by the skewed vision that men's studies corrects. Volumes have been written to explain the "gender gap," a divergence between men's and women's voting patterns that came to national significance in the 1980 presidential elections. Analysts have tried to explain the shift in women's political consciousness that produced the gap. As usual, males as such are not addressed in this discourse. Male voting patterns instead form the assumed norm against which female deviations must be explained. One anomaly such explanations of the gender gap must explain, often with great difficulty, is that the gap emerges most clearly, not on so-called women's issues — Equal Rights Amendment (ERA), abortion, day care — but on mainstays of male politics, issues of war and peace and military versus welfare expenditures. Men's studies solves this conundrum. The key to the gender gap lies in the study of men, not women. Closer analysis of voting patterns reveals that men have shifted to the right, not that women have shifted to the left. As Elshtain appropriately writes:

---

22. See Joe L. Dubbert, *A Man's Place: Masculinity in Transition* (Englewood Cliffs, N.J.: Prentice-Hall, 1979); and Peter Gabriel Filene, *Him / Her / Self: Sex Roles in Modern America*, rev. ed. (Baltimore: Johns Hopkins University Press, 1986).

Women's votes in 1980 largely followed party lines and showed little change from 1976. . . . But *men* showed a significant shift *to* Reagan, and it was this change in male voting patterns that highlighted a gender gap. . . . One could make the argument that it was the men whose 1980 voting behavior really should be explained.[23]

Contemporary social and political life cannot be understood without men's studies perspectives. Ehrenreich's *The Hearts of Men: American Dreams and the Flight from Commitment* similarly turns the tables by arguing that many life-style changes commonly attributed to feminism should be attributed to changes in male consciousness.[24]

Recapturing the historical ambiguities of masculinities enables men to respond to current and future male role changes. Most men today are nostalgic for a past they conceptualize as having contained a secure and stable male identity. This nostalgia tends to be an immobilizing and conservative force, as it leads men not only to be less responsive to contemporary demands but also to feel more justifiably intransigent, since they can claim to be championing a continuous uniform tradition against unique assaults on it. This attitude is nowhere more succinctly expressed than in one ultra-right-wing writer's reference to the current period as the "Gelded Age."[25] Pointing out the historical inaccuracies of their mythologization of the past can liberate men's attention to face more directly present realities. Even this mythologizing is not unique, after all, to the contemporary period. Our inherited mythology of American western heroes was a romanticization of an era vanished in the West even as it was being glorified in the eastern press. For example, the most famous single gunfight in western history, the shootout at the OK Corral between the Earps and the Clantons, can in many ways be more accurately conceptualized in contemporary terms as rival gang warfare than as a battle of law and order against criminality.

Unfortunately, some attempts to further progressive change only perpetuate a monolithic, static view of the past. All too many writers simply contrast "modern" versus "traditional" male roles. This approach denies the diversity of the past and the complexities of historical change, making it seem as if the current wave of questioning the nature of masculinity arose *ex nihilo*. There is, however, a history of male gender role nonconformity as well as a history of explicitly profeminist, antisexist men. Reclaiming knowledge of one's antecedents is essential to carrying on such work.

---

23. Jean Bethke Elshtain, "The Politics of Gender: Why Women Sound a Different Note," *Progressive* 48, no. 2 (February 1984):22. Cf. Ethel Klein, *Gender Politics* (Cambridge: Harvard University Press, 1984).

24. Ehrenreich, *Hearts of Men*.

25. Allan C. Carlson, "The Gelded Age," *Chronicles* 10, no. 6 (June 1986).

While women's studies has documented how women have been written out of male history, profeminist men have as yet been insufficiently written into the new women's history. As Strauss writes: "Where are the men in women's history? Are women historians perpetuating the same kinds of distortions perpetrated by those historians who wrote histories devoid of women?"[26]

The history of antisexist men is an essential part of the history of feminism. In the nineteenth century, for example, many men supported feminist demands; many of them were also active as abolitionists — William Lloyd Garrison, Frederick Douglass, Thomas Wentworth Higginson, Parker Pillsbury, and Samuel Joseph May. Some supportive husbands of suffrage leaders, such as Henry Blackwell, husband of Lucy Stone, and James Mott, husband of Lucretia Mott, were activists for women's rights in their own right as well.[27] The history of profeminist men includes not only support of women but also men's relationships reconstructed to feminist or humanitarian standards, rather than patriarchal "male bonding." These positive elements of male homosociality, the realm of male companionship, also await their chroniclers.

There are many other instances of cross-sex feminist alliances. For example, in a 1971 Modern Language Association list of courses in the history of women in American colleges, of 17 of 20 listed by full name (3 have only title or initial plus last name), assuming sex-typical names, 6 are men.[28] Given women's studies early stage of development at the time — the field is identified as Female Studies — I do not believe the participation of these men can be conceptualized as men coopting women's work. I believe it is an example of women and men educating themselves and moving forward together. The approximately one-third proportion of men happens also to be the percentage of male signatories to the landmark 1848 Seneca Falls Declaration of Sentiments and Resolutions. All these men are an important part of men's and women's histories, and their work must be reclaimed.

Men's, like women's, history is ultimately not simply a matter of accumulating information. At its deepest level, it involves a reconceptualization of previous data. In historical studies, much of the effort expended on

26. Sylvia Strauss, *"Traitors to the Cause": The Men's Campaigns for Women's Rights* (Westport, Conn.: Greenwood Press, 1982), p. xv.

27. See the regular feature on men's history, "Before Us," by Sally Roesch Wagner, in *Changing Men: Issues in Gender, Sex and Politics;* and the section on "Male Feminism and Social Science" in William Leach, *True Love and Perfect Union: The Feminist Reform of Sex and Society* (New York: Basic Books, 1980), pp 300–316.

28. Dolores Barracano Schmidt, in collaboration with Earl Robert Schmidt, "The Invisible Women: The Historian as Professional Magician," in *Women Out of History: An Herstory Anthology,* ed. Ann Forfreedom (Venice, Calif.: Ann Forfreedom, 1972), p. 101.

such reconceptualizations focuses on the question of reperiodization. Extant college-level textbooks in men's studies — Doyle's *The Male Experience* and Franklin's *The Changing Definition of Masculinity*— accept the periodization for the history of the United States established by the Plecks in their anthology *The American Man:* Agrarian Patriarchy (1630–1820), the Commercial Age (1820–1860), the Strenuous Life (1861–1919), Companionate Providing (1920–1965), and the period following 1965, marked by the women's, gay, and men's liberation movements.[29]

In the longer term, there is greater disagreement. Doyle, for example, presents the contemporary male as a composite of centuries of Western male role ideals: epic (800–100 B.C.), spiritual (A.D. 400–1000), chivalric (twelfth century), Renaissance (sixteenth century), and bourgeois (eighteenth century).[30] In contrast, Hoch argues on the basis of Marxist theory:

> For the past three thousand years the manly ideal of the leading social classes has oscillated sharply between these two basic poles: on the one side a sort of hard-working, hard-fighting "puritan" hero who adheres to a production ethic of duty before pleasure; and, on the other, a more aristocratic "playboy" who lives according to an ethic of leisure and sensual indulgence. . . . Leisure ethic masculinity involves the extravagances of dress, lifestyle, and sexual affairs that we associate with the Roman patricians of the Empire period, the courtiers of the Renaissance and Tudor England, the Cavalier gallants of the eighteenth century Enlightenment, and the wealthy playboys of the present consumer society. When the economic surplus and class polarisation necessary to support such a leisure class is not present, the predominant standard of masculinity necessarily revolves around some sort of production ethic. This seems to have been the case with the farmer–warriors of early Rome, the knights of the Dark and Middle Ages (at least to the flowering of court life from the end of the twelfth century), the Puritans of the Calvinist Reformation and the Cromwellian period, and the nineteenth century Victorians and American frontiersmen.[31]

In another common variant, historians such as Peter Stearns and Donald Bell see changes in work and industrialization as signposts of men's history.[32] In much of this work, the level of somewhat sweeping generalizations attests to men's studies still being in its infancy (as many of these

29. James A. Doyle, *The Male Experience* (Dubuque, Iowa: Wm. C Brown, 1983); Clyde W. Franklin II, *The Changing Definition of Masculinity* (New York: Plenum, 1984); and Elizabeth H. Pleck and Joseph H. Pleck, *The American Man* (Englewood Cliffs, N.J.: Prentice-Hall, 1980).

30. Doyle, *Male Experience*, pp. 23–35.

31. Paul Hoch, *White Hero, Black Beast: Racism, Sexism, and the Mask of Masculinity* (London: Pluto, 1979), 118–120.

32. Peter N. Stearns, *Be a Man: Males in Modern Society* (New York: Holmes & Meier, 1979); and Donald H. Bell, "Up from Patriarchy: The Male Role in Historical Perspective," in *Men in Difficult Times: Masculinity Today and Tomorrow*, ed. Robert Lewis (Englewood Cliffs, N.J.: Prentice-Hall, 1981).

authors would be the first to admit), as does the widespread tendency to speak in the singular of *the* male sex role rather than different modes of masculinity that vary by race, class, ethnicity, sexual orientation, nationality, and so on. Nonetheless, even in its early stages this new men's history is a far cry indeed from the men's history castigated by women's studies. It clearly can contribute greatly to feminist historical understanding.

I would like to elucidate another area in which men's studies perspectives are of singular note, where new perspectives on masculinity are having dramatic practical results. The most dynamic aspect of the men's movement is its antiviolence component. Across the United States, dozens of men's groups are working with violent men to change their behavior. A recent meeting of the California Men's Alternatives to Violence Task Group brought together representatives of 17 such groups in California alone. They work with men who batter, rape, and commit abuses of all sorts. Activities range from long- and short-term counseling programs and crisis-intervention hotlines to political demonstrations, legislative lobbying, and public education projects. The two leading groups in this movement are in St. Louis — RAVEN (Rape and Violence End Now) — and in Boston — EMERGE: A Men's Counseling Service on Domestic Violence. Both claim to have developed therapeutic techniques with higher-than-standard success rates. Their therapies are based on men's studies perspectives.[33]

In the standard frame of reference, violent men are deviants or nonconformists, having failed to internalize society's condemnation of violence. The goal of therapy is belatedly to socialize these men into conformity with social norms. Men's studies, in contrast, argues that to look at the norms of a genderless "society" is insufficient. One must look specifically at *male* socialization. What then emerges is a picture of considerable socialization *toward* violence. Whether learned in gangs, sports, the military, at the hands (often literally) of older males, or in simple acceptance that "boys will be boys" when they fight, attitudes are conveyed to young males ranging from tolerance to approval of violence as an appropriate vehicle for conflict resolution, perhaps even the most manly means of conflict negation. From this perspective, violent men are not deviants or *non*conformists; they are *over*conformists, men who have responded all too fully to a particular aspect of male socialization.[34] Consequently, the therapeutic task is *not* to inculcate more deeply society's mores into these men but to

33. Edward W. Gondolf, *Men Who Batter: An Integrated Approach for Stopping Wife Abuse* (Holmes Beach, Fla.: Learning Publications, 1985).

34. Cf. Diana E. H. Russell's concept of the "virility mystique" in the chapter on "Rape and the Masculine Mystique" in her *The Politics of Rape: The Victim's Perspective* (Briarcliff Manor, N.Y.: Stein and Day, 1975).

enable them to distance themselves from their socialization and individuate. In what may seem a paradoxical result, the key to helping men
become less aggressive is to help them be more assertive as individuals.
The question for men's studies in relation to male violence, then, is not the
standard "What is wrong with these men and how can we bring them up to
par?" but the more significant "How can we strengthen the mechanisms
of resistance by which nonviolent men have avoided acting on society's
prescriptions for male violence, and how can we eliminate such
prescriptions?"

Not only goals of treatment, but particular counseling strategies as well
are derived from the specifics of male socialization. For example,
EMERGE bases its group-therapy mode on aspects of male socialization.
They argue that since so much of male role learning takes place in groups,
its unlearning is also facilitated by group situations. Positively, group interaction allows for the feeling of commonality with men who share similar
behavior patterns to emerge sufficiently for men to support one another in
undertaking painful self-evaluations, a process anathema to mainstream
masculinity. Negatively, groups avoid dyadic counseling situations, threatening to many men as too feminine a setting because of male socialization
regarding intimacy. EMERGE reports that when domestic violence is
treated in the common couples-counseling mode, men often become defensive because they feel that even the male therapist is siding with the
woman, predominantly because of the intimate setting and mode of expression rather than the content of anything the therapist may have said.
They also argue that while it has the laudable intention of enabling the
man to cope better with the problem by not burdening him with excessive
guilt, the common couples-counseling strategy of treating domestic violence as a problem between the couple, often involving communication
problems, is all too easily used by the male to blame the victim and avoid
taking personal responsibility for his actions, which is the prerequisite for
change. Here, too, treating violence as a specifically male rather than a
diffused social problem seems most effective.[35]

Much more can be said about men's studies' examination of male violence. Many theses are salient, such as the alienation of men from their
emotions and bodies that underlies the myth of violent men being overtaken by their passions, drugs, or alcohol, performance pressures of all
sorts, including economic and sexual, and militarism. It is highly significant, for example, that some of the impetus to establish counseling pro-

35. *Organizing and Implementing Services for Men Who Batter* (EMERGE, 1980; 25 Huntington Avenue, Boston, MA 02116); and David Adams and Isidore Penn, "Men in Groups:
The Socialization and Resocialization of Men Who Batter" (paper presented at the annual
meeting of the American Orthopsychiatric Association, April 1981).

grams for Vietnam veterans came when women staffing battered women's shelters reported that disproportionate numbers of the women they were seeing were wives or lovers of these men—a classic case of bringing the war back home.

Suffice it to say that in many ways the treatment of male violence sketched above is a specific application of a wider, highly influential men's studies paradigm developed by Pleck in *The Myth of Masculinity*.[36] In this seminal work Pleck, the leading scholar in men's studies as an academic field, articulates in 11 propositions the male sex-role identity paradigm (MSRI) he demonstrates has dominated research on masculinity and argues that it is fundamentally flawed and should be replaced by what he calls the sex role strain paradigm (SRS). A summary of the work is beyond the scope of this essay (see Chapter 1), but I can briefly expound on some implications. While the MSRI model holds that a strong self-concept as masculine is essential, the SRS model holds that it may be harmful to one's mental and physical health. On the latter model, stress in men's lives is caused, not by the individual's failure to socialize properly as a male (as on the former), but by the contradictory demands of the male sex role itself.

Clear articulation of the two paradigms reveals that many who believe they are allied in supporting male role changes are actually in fundamental opposition. Consider the now widely accepted proposition that men should be more actively involved in childrearing and early childhood education. The most common supporting argument cites the difficulty young males have in establishing their male identity growing up without male role models, since so much of the childrearing in our society is done by women. This relies on the MSRI paradigm's contention that a strong sense of oneself as male is desirable. It supports men's involvement with male children in order to make gender identification more readily obtainable and secure for young males. Others, however, support greater male involvement with children of either sex because nurturing behavior is not part of traditional male roles. Having children of both sexes, as well as adults, experience men functioning in this mode will therefore help break down traditionally sex-stereotyped behavior. On this line of reasoning, stemming from the SRS paradigm, the goal of greater male involvement with children is to break down the fixed male identity supposedly being bolstered by this same activity on the MSRI line of argument. The ostensibly mutually supportive arguments in favor of this specific male role change are in fact incompatible.

I have hitherto invoked a unified conception of men's studies. There are, however, important differences in perspectives in men's studies,

36. Jospeh H. Pleck, *The Myth of Masculinity* (Cambridge: MIT Press, 1981). Key theses are summarized in Doyle, *Male Experience*, pp. 131–141.

which have significant consequences for the directions the field will take
and its reception in the academy and the society at large. I turn now to
address these differences.

ARGUMENTS FOR MEN'S STUDIES: DAMOCLES' SWORD
VERSUS ACHILLES' HEEL

Proponents of men's studies use various arguments, distinguishable by
whether they conceive men or women as their principal audience or constituency, to defend its utility. I designate these *male-identified* versus *female-identified* arguments for men's studies. The sword of Damocles serves
as a useful symbol of the male-identified approach to men's studies. The
sword of Damocles is an ancient symbol of the perils of power. In its most
encapsulated form, the story runs as follows:

> Damocles, a sycophant of Dionysius the Elder, of Syracuse, was invited by the tyrant to
> try the felicity he so much envied. Accepting, he was set down to a sumptuous banquet,
> but overhead was a sword suspended by a hair. Damocles was afraid to stir, and the
> banquet was a tantalizing torment to him.[37]

The idea that consciousness of the double-edged nature of power makes
one willing, if not eager, to relinquish that power is the guiding theme of
the male-identified understanding of the positive political ramifications of
men's studies. It relies on a particular variant of a theory of false consciousness. Usually, claims to have uncovered cases of false consciousness are
made on behalf of oppressed groups whose interests are being systematically thwarted by a society they erroneously believe is working in their
interests. In the case of men, however, the claim cannot be that men's
interests are not being materially advanced by the society, since such a
claim would deny the feminist foundations of both women's and men's
studies. Instead, the claim must be that the sorts of interests being advanced are interests men would in some meaningful sense be better off
without. It is the *nature* of men's interests, not the calculus as to their
satisfaction, that is radically questioned by men's studies. The argument
has two steps. First, it is claimed that the material rewards conferred on
men as a group by patriarchy — rewards of a legal, economic, social, and
political nature — come at too high a personal cost. Male sex roles are
damaging to men, as evidenced in part by disproportionately high male

37. William Rose Benet, ed. *The Reader's Encyclopedia* (New York: Crowell, 1963),
p. 270.

rates of ulcers, suicides, hypertension, heart attacks, and even earlier deaths (seven to eight years on the average in the industralized nations), as well as more subjectively experienced dissatisfactions. Second, it is argued that men's studies' elucidation of these factors will play a crucial role in mobilizing significant numbers of men to join with women in common cause against patriarchal privilege. This line of argument plays a major role in accounting for the largely psychological orientation of much of men's studies, since the disadvantages of male roles enumerated here are predominantly psychological in nature. (Other factors also contribute to the high proportion of psychologists in men's studies, such as the prior existence of the psychology of sex roles field, which served as prolegomenon to much men's studies research, the salience of gender issues in therapeutic contexts, and a certain appeal a "soft" field such as counseling might have to men interested in alternative sex roles.)

This line of reasoning, in its most common form, is a corollary of liberal forms of feminism. It accepts the liberal conception of feminism as interest-group politics in behalf of women. Transferring this conception to men's studies, it sees men as its obvious constituency. It displays the liberal predilection to seek common ground among all members of society. In contrast, female-identified arguments for women's studies show greater affinities to more radical forms of feminism in their emphasis on divergent interests between conflicting groups. (I mean here not only what is specifically referred to as *radical feminism* but also other left-of-liberal forms of feminism.) While these forms of feminism could, in principle, accept the former of the claims made above, concerning male roles being damaging to men, they would tend to doubt the latter claim that men might be thereby motivated to act against patriarchal privileges.

While acknowledging the considerable historical basis for such skepticism, I believe that at least some men may indeed join feminist ranks, although precisely which men might be so motivated and under what circumstances remains one of the critical unanswered questions for men's studies.[38] In discussing the claims radical feminisms might make on men's allegiances, I have argued elsewhere that while liberal feminism is at least tenable for women, even if regarded by some (myself included) as insufficient, liberal feminism for men is untenable as a basis for a men's political stance because liberalism's idea of feminism as interest-group politics means that on the liberal agenda men must, on the whole, correspondingly lose as women gain, specific areas of male gain notwithstanding (e.g., paternity leave, widower's benefits). In contrast, the more radical forms of

38. See Arnold Kahn, "The Power War: Male Response to Power Loss under Equality," *Psychology of Women Quarterly* 8, no. 3(Spring 1984):234–247.

feminism stand for revolution against, rather than a redistribution of, power. They aim to dismantle the power structures that damage male psyches, structures that liberal feminism leaves on the whole intact, generally seeking only greater access to them for women. Consequently, they hold out the greater possibility of men gaining from radical social reconstruction to alleviate or eliminate male and female role restrictions and debilities.[39] In *The Women's Movement* Deckard captures the core of the difference between liberal and more radical forms of feminism by contrasting the slogans "Let us in" and "Set us free."[40] Since they are already "in," men can ultimately benefit only from a politics aimed at setting all free. The greater emphasis on "the personal as political" of more radical feminisms also renders them more suited to male feminist politics than liberal feminism, which more readily accepts the public–private distinction at the core of liberal political theory, since such politics must emphasize issues of personal life more than issues of public access because men already have access to public power. If men's studies is to advance significantly the search for gender justice, arguments addressed only to men's interests or to their altruism, though essential and valid as far as they go, are ultimately insufficient. Arguments must also be advanced that more directly and broadly address more sweeping goals of feminist transformation.

I now turn to consider the seemingly paradoxical proposition that men's studies is in women's interests. Consider the following:

> Why not turn our sights toward those who hold control, with a view to giving a clearer understanding of their activities to those whose lives they affect? This is often a difficult task, for the well-endowed are less vulnerable to scholarly scrutiny than those who have no choice but to let themselves be studied; we should accept this as a challenge.[41]

The quotation, used in support of men's studies, is entirely out of context. It appears in an article analyzing scholarship on world hunger, in the context of an argument that scholars seeking to explain trends in underdeveloped countries should not focus their attention solely on the Third World but should study the First World, where the Third World's problems originate. Yet it expresses the core element of the female-identified rationale for men's studies. The guiding theme is expressed in such

39. "Feminism for Men: Beyond Liberalism," *Brother: The Newsletter of the National Organization for Changing Men* 3, no. 3(June 1985):2–5.

40. Barbara Sinclair Deckard, *The Women's Movement: Political, Socioeconomic, and Psychological Issues* (New York: Harper & Row, 1975).

41. Susan George, "Scholarship, Power, and Hunger," in *First Harvest: The Institute for Policy Studies 1963–83*, ed. John S. Friedman (New York: Grove Press, 1983), p. 67.

aphorisms as "Knowledge is power" or "Know thine enemy." A female-identified perspective on men's studies is oriented toward female empowerment, not male enlightenment. Men's studies is here conceived of, not as outreach to men, as male-identified arguments would have it, but as feminist encroachment on previously male terrain. The lack of analysis of male roles as such is, along this line of reasoning, attributed not so much to ignorance as to obfuscation, to the vested interest of the privileged in obscuring the source of their privileges. Leaving men's lives unexamined leaves male privilege unexamined, and hence more powerful precisely because more secretive. A female-identified view of men's studies has been expressed by two women as follows: "Until we know *how* it is that men do sexual politics we can't stop them; and we know for sure that they won't stop themselves, for they've far too much invested in the successful continuance of patriarchy."[42]

Achilles' heel is a useful symbol of this approach to men's studies. In contrast to the sword of Damocles, whose primary purpose is to enlighten Damocles himself, Achilles' heel not only reminds the seemingly invincible warrior of his own vulnerability but is also where an opponent may successfully attack.[43] Men's studies de-powers the masculine mystique by shedding light on its true nature, revealing it to be vulnerable and mutable, perhaps not a paper tiger but not a roaring one either. As one feminist scholar put it: "Men's studies from a feminist perspective also 'turns the tables on men.' I assume women are normal, and men are curiosities."[44]

The two approaches are not necessarily incompatible. The difference between them may in some cases be primarily a matter of emphasis. Although I argued above that the male-identified approach is ultimately insufficient, nonetheless much valuable work proceeds from its premises. The dispute between them turns in large part on disagreement as to the greater likelihood of men's studies leading significant groups of women or men toward profeminist consciousness and action, with adherents of female-identified perspectives being more pessimistic about men's potentialities and adherents of male-identified perspectives laying greater stress on common interests across gender lines.

42. Sue Wise and Liz Stanley, "Sexual Politics—An Editorial Introduction," *Women's Studies International Forum* 7, no. 1(1984): 2.

43. To judge by its literature, antisexist men's politics in Britain is significantly to the left of the U.S. men's movement. While the major U.S. movement's magazine was originally titled *M. Gentle Men for Gender Justice* (now *Changing Men: Issues in Gender, Sex and Politics,* the name change precipitated by a legal settlement between it and a slick men's fashion magazine called *M—The civilized man*), its British counterpart is *Achilles Heel.* I take this as validating my choice of imagery.

44. Judith Hicks Stiehm, quoted in Karen J. Winkler, "USC Program Extends Feminist Scholarship to Include 'Men's Studies,'" *Chronicle of Higher Education,* June 20, 1984, p.8.

The difference also emerges in how certain themes are treated. Here, female-identified perspectives emerge as more comprehensive in their cognizance of issues of power. For example, male-identified perspectives might concentrate on documenting how male role constraints on emotional display inhibit and repress men, while female-identified perspectives would add to this an analysis of how these restraints also confer power on men, in large part by effectively withholding information about oneself, and showing the interrelationships of both sides of the question.[45] Similarly, men's studies analyses of male sexuality must be more than simply self-help manuals aiming at greater male sexual satisfaction. They must also show the relationships between constraints on male sensuality and various forms of domination. Adhering to the feminist thesis that a fundamental structural feature of Western culture is captured in the analogy "Woman : Nature = Man : Culture," women's studies has seen much of its mission as "enculturating" women.[46] As Davis has argued, with this as one's point of departure one can say that men's studies must work at "embodying" men.[47] The goal of men's studies treatment of male sexuality, then, should not simply be to add greater sexual satisfaction to the range of male privileges but to rectify the Western mind–body dualism and objectification of the body that have often been particularly detrimental to women.

I conclude by considering two problematic issues for the development of men's studies: potential conflicts with women's studies over allocation of resources, and relationships between men's, gender, and gay studies.

Feminist women have often expressed agreement that men's studies of the sort I have sketched would, in principle or in some ideal world, be a fine thing, but they hesitate to support or even feel compelled to argue against it in the real world of practical politics. Proposals to advance men's studies raise fears for these women that when many women's studies programs

45. See Harry Brod, "Fraternity, Equality, Liberty," *Changing Men* 16(Summer 1986). Reprint in Franklin Abbott, ed. *New Men, New Minds: Breaking Male Tradition* (Freedom, Calif.: Crossing Press, 1987).

46. See Carol MacCormack and Marilyn Strathern, eds., *Nature, Culture and Gender* (Cambridge: Cambridge University Press, 1980); and Sherry B. Ortner, "Is Female to Male as Nature Is to Culture?" in *Women and Values: Readings in Recent Feminist Philosophy*, ed. Marilyn Pearsall (Belmont, Calif.: Wadsworth, 1985).

47. Ted Davis, "Men's Studies: Defining Its Contents and Boundaries" (paper presented at the Tenth National Conference on Men and Masculinity, St. Louis, Missouri, June 1985). On men's perceptions of their body images, see Marc E. Mishkind, Judith Rodin, Lisa R. Silberstein, and Ruth H. Striegel-Moore, "The Embodiment of Masculinity: Cultural, Psychological, and Behavioral Dimensions," *American Behavioral Scientist* 29, no. 5(May/June 1986):545–562; and Philip Corrigan, "'My' Body, My 'Self'? Trying to See My Masculine Eyes," *Resources for Feminist Research / Documentation sur la Recherche Féministe* 12, no. 4(December/January 1983–1984):29–32.

must retrench in the face of efforts to marginalize or eliminate them, opponents of women's studies will seize on men's studies as a way of siphoning off all-too-scarce resources. Given society's patriarchal values, they fear men's studies will triumph over women's studies in competition for funds, faculty positions, media attention, and so forth. These fears are well grounded and must be addressed by men's studies proponents. A precedent for the resolution of such conflicts fortunately exists in relationships between the men's and women's antiviolence movements discussed earlier in this chapter. Similar conflicts arise in that context. Laudable programs for counseling violent men compete for funding at all levels with a variety of women's services: shelters, hotlines, counseling programs, legal aid, and so on. Indeed, the problem is even more acute here than in the academic context. Since many women's services of this nature treat women, by and large, after the violence has occurred, and many men's programs are preventive in nature, one could argue, on the grounds that an ounce of prevention is worth a pound of cure, that money would be better spent on men than women. The irony of giving money to the perpetrators rather than victims of the crime is fortunately usually sufficient to prevent such arguments from carrying the day.

Of crucial importance are the steps men's antiviolence organizations have taken to prevent such conflicts from arising, or to resolve them when they do. Such steps include having representatives of women's antiviolence groups on the governing boards of men's groups, agreement to presubmit funding proposals to local feminist groups, and agreement on principle not to engage in competitive fund raising. I envisage analogous institutional arrangements between men's and women's studies. Having on occasion been accused of selling men out by taking such a stance, I would add that I advocate such measures, *not* as a compromise of men's interests in the face of anticipated feminist political pressures, but in men's interests as well. As a feminist, I believe men's and women's sex role problems can be resolved only by the empowerment of women that women's studies represents. Such empowerment requires women's leadership on appropriate questions.[48]

The designation of the field now called women's studies has been a matter of controversy from the outset. Early writings refer to female, women, or feminist studies, among others. Were we naming the field *ab initio,* I would consider *feminist studies* the most accurate label for the enterprise in which both women's and men's studies are engaged. Given the current prevalence of the nomenclature of women's studies, however,

48. This and other issues raised below are discussed at greater length in Harry Brod, "The New Men's Studies: From Feminist Theory to Gender Scholarship," *Hypatia: A Journal of Feminist Philosophy* 2, no. 1(Winter 1987).

the question must be raised whether men's studies should seek integration with women's studies under the new terminology of *gender studies* or pursue a more autonomous course? Gender studies may seem desirable because it is more inclusive and because, as mentioned earlier, women's studies' treatment of questions of gender provides some of the impetus for men's studies. Nevertheless, gender studies betokens a spurious parity between women's and men's studies.[49] It can all too easily encourage the belief that men's studies is about equal time for men under some misconceived fairness doctrine, a belief that bespeaks an antifeminist understanding of men's studies. Such a perspective would see it as some sort of corrective for alleged deficiencies in women's studies, correcting the balance in some way by preventing extremism, competing against rather than extending feminist scholarship. Such views ignore or misunderstand the feminist basis of men's studies. Men's studies calls for qualitatively different, not quantitatively more, attention to men. We should be clear that men's studies is a complement, not a cooptation, of women's studies.

For these reasons it seems best to eschew the conceptualization at the field as gender studies and retain the terminology of women's and men's studies, for the foreseeable future at any rate. This is not an argument that men's and women's studies should not be institutionally merged into a single program at certain institutions. There may well be good reasons for doing so, not the least of which is the need for men's studies to develop in close consultation with women's studies. It is simply an argument that if they are so merged, they should nonetheless retain distinct identities rather than be subsumed under a new rubric. If need be, a locution such as *gender scholarship* could be used as an overarching term to designate work being done in women's and men's studies jointly considered, since this is less likely to be taken as a replacement for women's studies, a status some have urged for gender studies.[50] Or, it may well be that one side effect of men's studies will be a revival of the popularity of the term *feminist studies*.

Even if the validity of the concept is accepted, a line of argument objecting to the establishment of men's studies remains. Since, as noted, much of the inspiration for men's studies comes from women's studies' analysis of masculinity, should we not simply recognize that women's studies already

49. See Gloria Feman Orenstein, "Is Equality Still Inequality," *Journal of the National Association for Women Deans, Administrators, and Counselors* 49, no. 4(Summer 1986):22–28; Marilyn J. Boxer, "For and About Women: The Theory and Practice of Women's Studies in the United States," *Signs* 7, no. 3 (Spring 1982): 661–95; Judith Shapiro, "'Women's Studies': A Note on the Perils of Markedness," *Signs* 7, no. 3 (Spring 1982): 717–721.

50. This was the strategy of the University of Southern California Program for the Study of Women and Men in Society conference, "The New Gender Scholarship: Women's and Men's Studies," February 13–15, 1987.

studies men? Hence, there is no need for men's studies. This is reminiscent of defensive reactions against women's studies in its early days. The first line of defense is to deny the validity of specifically studying women or men. But once the legitimacy of the subject is established, the fallback position is to claim that to the extent such work has validity, it already is or can be carried out under existing rubrics. Hence there is no need for new programs. But scattered insights or findings, however profound or important, are no substitute for consolidated analysis. It is this sustained, systematically focused study of masculinities that only men's studies can provide.

Both methodologically and substantively, men's studies has a crucial relationship to gay studies. In a trend analogous to that in women's studies discussed earlier, gay studies has moved from simply supplying supplemental information about gay men to questioning the nature of the categorizations heterosexual and homosexual. It is therefore becoming increasingly difficult to draw a clear line between gay and men's studies. For example, while the *berdache* Native American Indian tradition has traditionally been seen as a homosexual role, new research reveals it more akin to a third sex, which challenges our polar notions of gender.[51] Studies such as these and others in areas of common interest, such as the effects of homophobia on the general population, blur the boundaries between men's and gay studies. Furthermore, gay studies serves as a model to correct the unfortunate tendency in men's studies to assume too much commonality among men. Both by virtue of its content and its methodological commitment to specificity, gay studies helps to rectify this deficiency.

A final word. It may be objected that the arguments I have put forward prove too much. An attempt to refute my position via a *reductio ad absurdum* would present analogous arguments for the establishment of white studies, straight studies, ruling-class studies, Gentile studies, and so on. Does a commitment to men's studies indeed imply a commitment to all of the above? I think not. What, then, differentiates men's studies? The answer lies in the fundamental feminist contention that gender is a fundamental component of one's identity and not simply an external mark of oppression. Men's studies adapts from women's studies the contention that consideration of one's identity as male per se is indispensable. This is not to claim that masculinity is invariant but that there is a sufficiently unitary object of study denoted by the concept of masculinity to justify its investigation under one rubric. Such is not the case for whites, ruling classes,

51. Walter L. Williams, *The Spirit and the Flesh: Sexual Diversity in American Indian Culture* (Boston: Beacon, 1986). For an argument that gay studies should find a home in men's studies, see Williams's "Gay Studies and Men's Studies," *Journal of the National Association of Women Deans, Administrators, and Counselors* 49, no. 4(Summer 1986):38–41.

straights, or Gentiles. At least, to the best of my knowledge, such cases have not yet been adequately made. Should a case be successfully made that whiteness, for example, or *albosity*, as I have heard it referred to, was such a fundamental concept and not simply an overarching, externally imposed grouping of intrinsically radically disparate national and ethnic identities, I would have to reverse my stance and accept the validity of white studies. Certain aspects of men's studies may indeed share principles in common with studies of other ruling groups, as Goode suggests in his sketch of a "sociology of superordinates."[52] But the concept of gender has been shown to be of unique utility in understanding both sides of the divisions it creates. For now, at least, men's studies is the sole purveyor of its unique craft.

AUTHOR'S NOTE: An abridged and revised version of this essay appears as "New Perspectives on Masculinity: A Case for Men's Studies," in *Changing Men: New Directions in Research on Men and Masculinity*, ed. Michael Kimmel (Beverly Hills, Calif.: Sage, 1987). It has benefited from comments on earlier drafts by many individuals I would like to thank: Lois Banner, Helen Heise, Alison Jaggar, Mark Kann, Michael Kimmel, Maria Papacostaki, Joseph Pleck, Michael Shiffman, Sally Roesch Wagner, anonymous reviewers, and members of the audience at the Gender and the Curriculum Project at the College of Saint Benedict and Saint John's University (which published an earlier version as a pamphlet, *Making a Case for Men's Studies*), Symposium on Women's Studies and Men's Studies and the Liberal Arts at Oxford College of Emory University, Society for Women in Philosophy Pacific Division, and Women's Studies programs at the University of California at Santa Cruz and Los Angeles.

52. William J. Goode, "Why Men Resist," in *Rethinking the Family: Some Feminist Questions,* ed. Barrie Thorne with Marilyn Yalom (White Plains, N.Y.: Longman, 1982).

3

Toward a New Sociology
of Masculinity

Tim Carrigan, Bob Connell, and John Lee

The upheaval in sexual politics of the past 20 years has mainly been discussed as a change in the social position of women. Yet change in one term of a relationship signals change in the other. From very early in the history of women's liberation it was clear that its politics had radical implications for men. A small "men's liberation" movement developed in the 1970s among heterosexual men. Gay men became politicized as the new feminism was developing, and gay liberation politics have continued to call into question the conventional understanding of what it is to be a man. Academic sex-role research, though mainly about women in the family, was easily extended to the "male role." From several different directions in the 1970s, critiques and analyses of masculinity appeared. Quite strong claims about the emergence of a new area of study, and a new departure in sexual politics, were made. The purpose of this article is to bring together these attempts, evaluate them, and propose an alternative.

We think it important to start with the "prehistory" of this debate — early attempts at a sociology of gender, the emergence of the "sex-role" framework, and research on masculinity *before* the advent of women's liberation. In this dusty literature are the main sources of the framework that has governed most recent writing on masculinity. It includes an agenda about modernization, a characteristic blindness about power, and a theoretical incoherence built into the "sex-role" paradigm. There are also, in some nearly forgotten writing, pointers to a much more powerful and interesting analysis.

Approaching the recent literature, we were concerned with three

This chapter was originally published in *Theory and Society*, 5 (14) September 1985, Elsevier, Amsterdam, by permission of Martinus Nijhoff Publishers, Dordrecht, The Netherlands. It is a shortened version of the original article.

things: its empirical discoveries, its political assumptions and implications, and its theoretical framework. Its empirical content turns out to be slight. Though most social science is indeed about men, good-quality research that brings *masculinity* into focus is rare. Ironically, most recent studies are not up to the standard set by several researchers in the 1950s. There is, however, a notable exception, a new body of work on the history of homosexual masculinity, which has general implications for our understanding of the historical construction of gender categories.

The political meaning of writing about masculinity turns mainly on its treatment of power. Our touchstone is the essential feminist insight that the overall relationship between men and women is one involving domination or oppression. This is a fact about the social world that must have profound consequences for the character of men. It is a fact that is steadily evaded, and sometimes flatly denied, in much of the literature about masculinity written by men—an evasion wittily documented by Ehrenreich in *The Hearts of Men*.[1]

There are, however, some accounts of masculinity that have faced the issue of social power, and it is here that we find the bases of an adequate theory of masculinity. But they too face a characteristic danger in trying to hold to feminist insights about men, for a powerful current in feminism, focusing on sexual exploitation and violence, sees masculinity as more or less unrelieved villainy and all men as agents of the patriarchy in more or less the same degree. Accepting such a view leads to a highly schematic view of gender relations, and leads men in particular into a paralyzing politics of guilt. This has gripped the "left wing" of men's sexual politics since the mid 1970s.

It is necessary to face the facts of sexual power without evasion but also without simplification. A central argument of this is that the theoretical bases for doing so are now available, and a strong radical analysis of masculinity has become possible. Three steps open this possibility up. First, the question of sexual power has to be taken more seriously and pursued *inside* the sex categories. In particular the relations between heterosexual and homosexual men have to be studied to understand the constitution of masculinity as a political order, and the question of what forms of masculinity are socially dominant or hegemonic has to be explored. The writings of gay liberation theorists already provide important insights about this problem. Second, the analysis of masculinity needs to be related as well to other currents in feminism. Particularly important are those that have focused on the sexual division of labor, the sexual politics of workplaces, and the interplay of gender relations with class dynamics. Third, the analy-

1. B. Ehrenreich, *The Hearts of Men: American Dreams and the Flight from Commitment* (London: Pluto, 1983).

sis needs to use those developments in social theory in the last decade or so that offer ways past the dichotomies of structure versus individual, society versus the person, that have plagued the analysis of gender as much as the analysis of class. These developments imply a focus on the historical production of social categories, on power as the ability to control the production of people (in both the biological and psychological senses), and on large-scale structures as both the objects and effects of collective practice. In the final section of this article we sketch a sociology of masculinity that draws on these sources.

We hope for a realistic sociology of masculinity, built on actual social practices rather than discussion of rhetoric and attitudes. And we hope for a realistic politics of masculinity, neither fatuously optimistic nor defeatist. We see such an enterprise as part of a radical approach to the theory of gender relations in general, made possible by convergences among feminism, gay liberation, contemporary socialism, psychoanalysis, and the history and sociology of practice. The theme of masculinity makes sense only in terms of that larger project. At the same time it is, we think, an important part of it.

ORIGINS

The Early Sociology of Gender and the "Sex-Role" Framework

"The problem of women" was a question taken up by science generally in the second half of the nineteenth century, at first in a mainly biological framework. This was not simply part of the widening scope of scientific inquiry. It was clearly also a response to the enormous changes that had overtaken women's lives with the growth of industrial capitalism. And, toward the end of the century, it was a response to the direct challenge of the women's emancipation movement.

The relationship of the emerging social sciences to this nineteenth- and early twentieth-century discourse on women was profound. In a useful sociology of knowledge investigation of the growth of the discourse, Viola Klein observed that "there is a peculiar affinity between the fate of women and the origins of social science, and it is no mere co-incidence that the emancipation of women should be started at the same time as the birth of sociology."[2] The political stakes were particulary evident in psychological research. The area usually referred to today as "sex-difference research"

2. V. Klein, *The Feminine Character: History of an Ideology* (London: Routledge & Kegan Paul, 1971) p. 17.

has been a major component in the development of social science work on gender. In the view of one prominent observer of the field, this work was originally "motivated by the desire to demonstrate that females are inherently inferior to males. . . . But from 1900 on, the findings of the psychologists gave strong support to the arguments of the feminists."[3]

Rosalind Rosenberg has documented the pioneering, and subsequently forgotten, research by American women into sex differences in the first two decades of this century. She established the importance of the work of Helen Thompson, Leta Hollingworth, Jessie Taft, Elsie Clews Parsons, and others across a range of disciplines into questions of intelligence, the socialization of women, and American sexual mores. There were serious obstacles in the way of the academic careers of these women, but Rosenberg revealed the influence they had on such later social theorists as W. I. Thomas, Robert Lowie, John Dewey, and Margaret Mead.[4]

Establishing the social basis of sex differences was one thing (though biological claims and assumptions recur in this work right up to the present). Developing a sociological account of femininity was quite another. The "marginal man" perspective, for example, was used by Park and other sociologists at the University of Chicago from the late 1920s to refer to the ways in which groups such as Jewish and black people experienced the conflict of living in two cultures. As Rosenberg observed, this was quite comparable to how Taft had conceived the position of women a decade before. Yet it was not until the 1950s that the "marginal man" or "minority" perspective was applied to women, by Helen Hacker.[5] By then, however, the development of an adequate sociology of femininity was inhibited by the ascendancy of functionalism; for this meant that the radical implications of the early research into femininity were pretty well lost.

By midcentury, functionalist sex-role theory dominated the Western sociological discourse on women. The key figure in this development was Talcott Parsons, who in the early 1950s wrote the classic formulation of American sex role theory, giving it an intellectual breadth and rigor it had never had. The notion of *role* as a basic structural concept of the social sciences had crystallized in the 1930s, and it was immediately applied to questions of gender. Two of Parsons's own papers of the early 1940s talked "freely of sex roles." In the course of his argument he offered an interesting account of several options that had recently emerged within the female role. There was, however, little sense of a power relation be-

3. L. Tyler, *The Psychology of Human Differences* (New York: Appleton Century Crofts, 1965), p. 240.

4. R. Rosenberg, *Beyond Separate Spheres: Intellectual Roots of Modern Feminism* (New Haven and London: Yale University Press, 1982).

5. H. M. Hacker, "Women as a Minority Group," *Social Forces* 30(October 1951):60–69.

tween men and women; and the argument embedded the issue of sex and gender firmly in the context of the family.[6]

For the rest of the 1940s, Parsons was mainly occupied with the system building for which he is now famous. When he returned to the theme of sex, it was with questions of structure behind him, and questions of how people were fitted into structures — what he called "socialization" — uppermost in his mind. The main tool he used on this problem was psychoanalysis, and his work thus is the first important encounter of Freudian thought on sexuality with the American sociology of gender — even if it was the rather bland version of psychoanalysis being naturalized in the United States at the time.

In the two chapters of the collaborative volume *Family, Socialization, and Interaction Process* (1953) that represent the culmination of this development, Parsons achieved a notable synthesis. He brought together a structural account of kinship, the socialization problem in sociology, psychoanalytic accounts of personality formation, the internal interaction patterns of the household, and the sexual division of labor into a coherent argument. The theme of the differentiation and learning of sex roles provided the solvent that blended all these ingredients. It follows that in most of Parsons's argument "sex roles" themselves were a taken-for-granted fact. What was at issue was the processes and structures that called them into play.

At a key point, however, Parsons did make sex-role differentiation the problem, asking how it was to be explained. He rejected the biological-difference argument as utterly incapable of explaining the social pattern of sex roles. Rather, he derived it from a general sociological principle, the imperative of structural differentiation. Its particular form here was explained by the famous distinction between "instrumental" and "expressive" leadership. Parsons treated sex roles as the instrumental – expressive differentiation that operated within the conjugal family. And he treated the conjugal family both as a small group and as the specific agency of the larger society entrusted with the function of socializing the young. Thus he deduced the gender patterning of roles, and their reproduction across generations, from the structural requirements of any social order whatever.

To this tour de force of reasoning Parsons added a sophisticated account of role acquisition, in the sense of how the role gets *internalized*. This is where psychoanalysis, with its account of the production of masculinity and femininity through different patternings of the Oedipal crisis, came

---

6. T. Parsons, "Age and Sex in the Social Structure of the United States," in *Essays in Sociological Theory* (New York: Free Press, 1964), pp. 89–103; and, in the same volume, "The Kinship System of the Contemporary United States," pp. 177–196.

into play. In effect, sex role becomes part of the very constitution of the person, through the emotional dynamics of development in the nuclear family.

Thus Parsons analyzed the acquisition of sex roles as a matter of the production, from one generation to the next, of what we might call *gender personalities*. For example:

> Relative to the total culture as a whole, the masculine personality tends more to the predominance of instrumental interests, needs and functions, presumably in whatever social system both sexes are involved, while the feminine personality tends more to the primacy of expressive interests, needs and functions. We would expect, by and large, that other things being equal, men would assume technical, executive and "judicial" roles, women more supportive, integrative and "tension-managing" roles.[7]

This notion provided Parsons then, as it provides role theorists still, with a powerful solution to the problem of how to link person and society. But its ability to do so was based on a drastic simplification. As phrases like "the masculine personality" show, the whole argument is based on a normative standard case. Parsons was not in the least concerned about how many men (or women) are actually like that. Even the options within a sex role that he had cheerfully recognized in the earlier papers had vanished. All that was left in 'he theory was the normative case on the one hand, and on the other, deviance. Homosexuality, he wrote only a couple of pages after the passage just quoted, is universally prohibited so as to reinforce the differentiation of sex roles.

Apart from being historically false (homosexuality was and is institutionalized in some societies), such a theory fails to register tension and power processes *within* gender relations. Parsons recognizes many forms of "role strain," but basically as a result of problems in the articulation of the different subsystems of society. For instance, in his account the relation between the family and the economy is the source of much of the change in sex roles. The underlying structural notion in his analysis of gender is always differentiation, not relation. Hence his automatic assumption is that the connection between the two sex roles is one of complementarity, not power.

This version of the role framework fitted comfortably with the intense social conservatism of the American intelligentsia in the 1950s, and with the lack of any direct political challenge from women. For functionalist sociology, "the problem of women" was no longer how to explain their social subordination. It was how to understand the dysfunctions and strains involved in women's roles, primarily in relation to the middle-class

7. T. Parsons and R. F. Bales, *Family, Socialization and Interaction Process* (London: Routledge & Kegan Paul, 1953), p. 101.

family. Given the normative emphasis on the family, the sociological focus was strongly on "social problems": the conflicts faced by working wives, "maternal deprivation," divorce rates and juvenile delinquency, and intergenerational family conflict. The sense of conflict is strong in the work of Mirra Komarovsky, who, after Parsons, made the most impressive application of the functionalist framework to sex roles in the 1940s. She developed a general argument about modernization producing a clash between a feminine "homemaker" ideal and a "career girl" ideal. The implications remained vague, but there was much more sense of complexity within sex roles than in Parsons's grand theorizing.[8]

Through the 1950s and 1960s the focus of sex-role research remained on women in the family. And the field of sex-role research remained a distinctly minor one within the overall concerns of sociology. This changed dramatically with the impact of second-wave feminism. There was a spectacular growth in the volume of work produced under the general rubric of "sex-role research," and this field also claimed a much greater proportion of sociological research interest (see Figs. 1 and 2). It was not only a matter of establishment social science registering the issues raised by the new feminism. Academic feminists themselves began a process of rejuvenating the discourse. On the one hand there was a huge increase in the volume of research on women, feeding into the growth of women's studies courses. On the other, attention was directed to the way an analysis of the subordination of women had been "contained" by the social–scientific discourse itself. For although sex-role theory was nominally about both sexes, the conventional pattern had been an almost exclusive concentration on women's roles, ignoring their relation to men's roles and to larger societal structures. Thus one immediate reform called for was a greater attention to men's roles. Research and writing on men's roles did in fact rise markedly from the late 1960s, producing about half the volume of the work on women's.

The institutional power that role theory enjoyed in sociology, especially in the United States—where as recently as the mid 1970s Komarovsky could describe it simply as "the generally accepted arsenal of sociological conceptual tools"[9]—ensured that feminist questions would be posed in that framework, at least at the start. Could this framework encompass feminist propositions? Especially could it incorporate the notion of *oppression,* or as it was more often called in this literature, the power differential between men and women?

8. M. Komarovsky, "Cultural Contradictions and Sex Roles," *American Journal of Sociology* 52(November 1946):184–189; and Komarovsky, "Functional Analysis of Sex Roles," *American Sociological Review* 15(August 1950):508–516.

9. M. Komarovsky, *Dilemmas of Masculinity* (New York: Norton, 1976), p. 7.

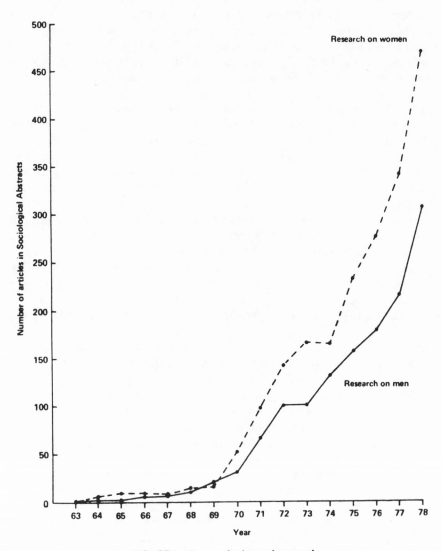

FIGURE 1. The growth of sex-role research

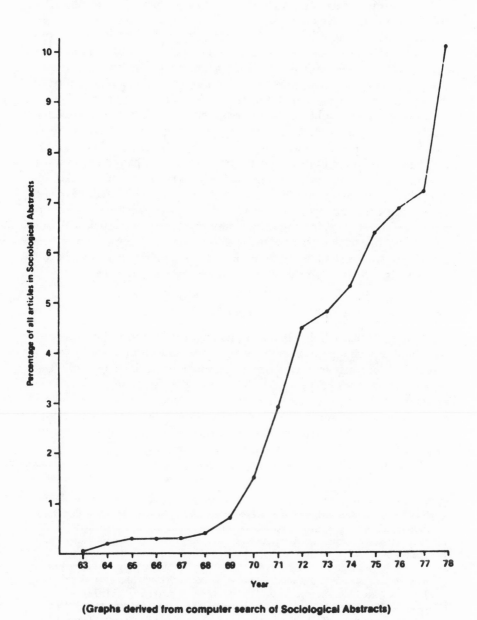

(Graphs derived from computer search of Sociological Abstracts)

FIGURE 2. How sex-role research claimed a growing share of research interests.

Some feminist sociologists argued that this was perfectly possible; that role theory had been misapplied, misunderstood, or had not been extended to its full potential.[10] Yet by the late 1970s, other feminist sociologists were arguing that the sex-role framework should be abandoned. Not only had the notion of "role" been shown to be incoherent. The framework continued to mask questions of power and material inequality; or worse, implied that women and men were "separate but equal."[11]

These criticisms underlined a more general problem: the discourse lacked a stable theoretical object. "Sex-role" research could, and did, wobble from psychological argument with biological assumptions, through accounts of interpersonal transactions, to explanations of a macrosociological character, without ever having to resolve its boundaries. The elusive character of a discourse where issues as important as that of oppression could appear, disappear, and reappear in different pieces of writing without anything logically compelling authors to stick with and solve them no doubt lies behind much of the frustration expressed in these criticisms. As we shall see, this underlying incoherence was to have a devastating influence on the sociological literature about men.

The "Male Role" Literature before Women's Liberation

A sociology of masculinity, of a kind, had appeared before the "sex-role" paradigm. Specific groups of boys and men had become the object of research when their behavior was perceived as a "social problem." Two notable instances are juvenile delinquency and educational underachievement—topics whose significance in the history of sociology can hardly be exaggerated. Studies such as Thrasher's *The Gang* (1927) and Whyte's *Street Corner Society* (1943) talked extensively about masculinity without directly proclaiming sex roles as their object.[12]

Through the 1950s and 1960s the most popular explanation of such

10. See, for example, M. Komarovsky, "Presidential Address: Some Problems in Role Analysis," *American Sociological Review* 38(December 1973):649–662; M. Millman, "Observations on Sex Role Research," *Journal of Marriage and the Family* 33(November 1971):772–776; and E. Peal, "'Normal' Sex Roles: An Historical Analysis," *Family Process* 14(September 1975):389–409.

11. See, for example, A. R. Edwards, "Sex Roles: A Problem for Sociology and for Women," *Australian and New Zealand Journal of Sociology* 19(1983):385–412; S. Franzway and J. Lowe, "Sex Role Theory, Political Cul-de-sac?" *Refractory Girl* 16(1978):14–16; M. Gould and R. Kern-Daniels, "Toward a Sociological Theory of Gender and Sex," *American Sociologist* 12(November 1977):182–189; and H. Z. Lopata and B. Thorne, "On the Term 'Sex Roles,'" *Signs* 3(Spring 1978):718–721.

12. F. M. Thrasher, *The Gang* (Chicago: University of Chicago Press, 1927); W. F. Whyte, *Street Corner Society* (Chicago: University of Chicago Press, 1943).

social problems was "father absence," especially from poor or black families. The idea of "father absence" had a broader significance, since the historical tendency of capitalism has been to separate home from workplace. Most fathers earning wages or salaries are therefore absent from their families much of the time. This imbalance was the focus of one of the first sociological discussions of the *conflicts* involved in the construction of masculinity.

Ruth Hartley, in a paper published in 1959, related the absence of fathers and the overwhelming presence of mothers to a widespread anxiety among American boys, which was centered in the whole area of sex-connected role behaviors, "an anxiety which frequently expresses itself in overstraining to be masculine, in virtual panic at being caught doing anything traditionally defined as feminine and in hostility toward anything even hinting at "femininity," including females themselves." [13]

Hartley's interviews produced a picture of boys who had distant relationships with their fathers, who had been taught to eschew everything feminine from a very early age while having to live in an environment dominated by women, and who consequently constructed an oversimplified and overemphasized understanding of masculinity within their peer groups. For Hartley, the basic problem was not "father absence" as such, so much as a pattern of masculine socialization rigidly upheld by adults in a society where feminine roles were changing rapidly and the emancipation of women was well advanced.

Other sociologists, including David Riesman, proposed that in the modern male role, expressive functions had been added to the traditional instrumental ones.[14] The idea was clearly formulated by Helen Hacker in a notable paper called "The New Burdens of Masculinity," published in 1957: "As a man, men are now expected to demonstrate the manipulative skill in interpersonal relations formerly reserved for women under the headings of intuition, charm, tact, coquetry, womanly wiles, et cetera. They are asked to bring patience, understanding, gentleness to their human dealings. Yet with regard to women they must still be sturdy oaks."[15]

This argument has become virtually a cliché in more recent writing. Hacker's paper is striking in its emphasis on conflict within masculinity. She pointed out that though the husband was necessarily often absent from his family, he was "increasingly reproached for his delinquencies as

---

13. R. E. Hartley, "Sex Role Pressures in the Socialization of the Male Child," *Psychological Reports* 5(1959):458.

14. D. Riesman, *The Lonely Crowd* (Garden City, N.Y. Doubleday Anchor, 1953).

15. H. M. Hacker, "The New Burdens of Masculinity," *Marriage and Family Living* 19(August 1957):229.

father." To compound the problem, men were also under pressure to evoke a full sexual response on the part of women. The result was the growing social visibility of impotence.

Male homosexuality was also becoming increasingly visible, and this was further evidence that "all is not well with men." It is notable that Hacker did not conceive of homosexuality in terms of the current medical model but in relation to the strong differentiation between masculine and feminine social roles. "The 'flight from masculinity' evident in male homosexuality may be in part a reflection of role conflicts. If it is true that heterosexual functioning is an important component of the masculine role in its social as well as sexual aspects, then homosexuality may be viewed as one index of the burdens of masculinity." [16]

Though Hacker probably viewed (more equal) heterosexual relations as the natural order of things, her remark in fact prefigured the perspective reached within the gay liberation movement 12 years later. Almost all subsequent sociological writing, however, has ignored Hacker's brief comments, as well as the gay movement's arguments, and has continued to take the heterosexual definition of masculinity for granted.

The consideration of male homosexuality suggested the need to establish empirically "a typology of men, perhaps according to family constellation or social class position, in terms of their interpretation of the demands of masculinity and their felt capacity to fulfill them." [17] In short, masculinity varies as it is constructed in different situations.

Hacker never lost sight of the fact that masculinity exists as a power relation. Her appreciation of the effects of power led her to describe the possible range of masculine types as more restricted than that of feminine types. It also led to the suggestion (reminiscent of Chodorow's later work) that "masculinity is more important to men than femininity is to women." [18]

There is something motherly in Hacker's approach to men. Her feminism, if advanced at the time, certainly seems tame 25 years later. But the striking fact is that most research on masculinity in the meantime has not improved on her analysis. Indeed, much of it has been a good deal more primitive. For instance, *The Male in Crisis* (1970), by the Austrian author Karl Bednarik, suggests that alienation at work, bureaucracy in politics and war, and the commercialization of sexuality all undermine masculinity. Bednarik made some acute observations on the way the commercialization of sexuality connects it with aggressiveness. And his stress on the

16. Ibid., p. 231.
17. Ibid., p. 232.
18. Ibid., p. 231.

contradication between the hegemonic male image and the real conditions of men's lives is notable. But he never questioned that the traditional image *is* the primordial, true nature of man.[19] Nor did the American Patricia Sexton in her widely quoted book *The Feminized Male* (1969). "What does it mean to be masculine? It means, obviously, holding male values and following male behavior norms. . . . Male norms stress values such as courage, inner direction, certain forms of aggression, autonomy, mastery, technological skill, group solidarity, adventure, and a considerable amount of toughness in mind and body."[20]

In her account, however, the main force pushing American boys away from true masculinity was women. Schoolteachers and mothers, through their control of childrearing and rewarding of conformity and academic success, were making them into sissies. It is not surprising to find that Sexton romanticized working-class boys and their "boy culture," and was hostile to the "visibly feminized" soft men of the New Left and counterculture ("a new lumpen leisure-class of assorted hippies, homosexuals, artistic poseurs, and 'malevolent blacks'").[21]

But there was something more here: an appreciation of power that had a distinctly feminist flavor. The reason women were engaged in feminizing boys, Sexton argued, was that women have been excluded from all *other* positions of authority. She documented not only the hazards of being male, citing statistics on the higher death and illness rates among men that were soon to become another cliché of the literature. She also recited at length the facts of men's power. Basically the reform she wanted was a change in the sexual division of labor, and in this regard her argument was in line with the feminism of 10 years later. But she had no sense that the "male values" and "male norms" she admired are as much effects of the structure of power as the women's behavior she condemned.

Lionel Tiger's *Men in Groups*, published in the same year in Britain, was also a paradigmatic treatment of masculinity. It extensively documented men's control of war, politics, production, and sports, and argued that all this reflected a genetic pattern built into human beings at the time when the human ancestral stock took up cooperative hunting. Greater political participation by women, of the kind argued for by Sexton, would be going against the biological grain.

The notion that there is a simple continuity between biology and the social has been very powerful as ideology. So has another important feature of Tiger's argument, the way *relations* are interpreted as *differences*.

19. K. Bednarik, *The Male in Crisis* (New York: Knopf, 1970).
20. P. Sexton, *The Feminized Male* (New York: Random House, 1969), p. 15.
21. Ibid., p. 204.

The greater social power of men and the sexual division of labor are interpreted as "sexual dimorphism" in behavior. With this, the whole question of social structure is spirited away. Tiger's scientific-sounding argument turns out to be pseudo-evolutionary speculation, overlaying a more sinister political message. Its drift becomes obvious in the book's closing fantasy about masculinity and its concern with "hard and heavy phenomena," with warmongering being part of "the masculine aesthetic," and arguments about what social arrangements are and are not "biologically healthy."[22]

It will be obvious from these cases that there was a reasonably complex and sometimes sophisticated discussion about masculinity going on before the main impact of feminism. It is also clear that this discussion was intellectually disorganized, even erratic.

What coherence it had was provided by role concepts; and in one case this framework did give rise to a notable piece of research. Komarovsky's *Blue Collar Marriage* is one of the best pieces of empirical research on any topic produced by American sociology in its heyday.[23] Based on long interviews conducted in the late 1950s, the study yielded a vivid account of the interactions that actually constitute the politics of everyday life. From a bitter sketch of the sexual frustration of one heavily subordinated wife, to reflections on husbands' violence, to an illuminating (if overmoralistic) account of the emotional importance of mothers-in-law, Komarovsky traced the construction of relationships under pressure. She delivered some shrewd knocks to the bland assumptions made by conventional theorists, Parsons among them, about how "the American family" worked.

Out of this came a picture of masculinity that was both more subtle and harsher than anything else written in its period. Though she did not use this terminology, she painted a picture of masculinity as something constructed in a very complex and often tense process of negotiation, mostly with women, that stretched right through adult life. The outcomes are never guaranteed; and there is a lot of variation in the pattern Komarovsky found. Nevertheless, there was a general sense of unease. The working men she found in her American steel town were on the whole an unhappy lot, with little real communication with their wives and constricted views of the world outside. There was a lot of prejudice and aimless anger around. Ten years later, these themes were to be made a centerpiece of the "men's movement" account of masculinity in general. Unlike most role research, Komarovsky did have a lot to say about power. She was sensitive to the role

22. L. Tiger, *Men in Groups* (London: Nelson, 1969), p. 209.
23. M. Komarovsky, *Blue Collar Marriage* (New York: Vintage, 1964).

of family violence, and to the economic resources of husband and wife. Like the slightly earlier Australian research by Fallding, much less known though similar in style, and Bott's *Family and Social Network*,[24] she was able to show a difference between more patriarchal and more egalitarian patterns of marriage. Nevertheless, this variation was limited. Komarovsky acutely observed that in the case where the husband's power had been so far eroded that the wife was dominant in the marriage, it still was not acceptable for the wife to deny her husband's supremacy in public, among friends, neighbors, or relations. But here the analysis stopped. To push further required the concepts that were still to be provided by second-wave feminism. (In the original version of this paper, a review and critique of the 1970s literature on masculinity and "men's liberation" appeared here. This may be found in *Theory & Society*, 5 (14) September 1985, pp. 564–578.)

TOWARD REDEFINITION

Sex Roles Revisited

The very idea of a "role" implies a recognizable and accepted standard, and sex-role theorists posit just such a norm to explain sexual differentiation. Society is organized around a pervasive differentiation between men's and women's roles, and these roles are internalized by all individuals. There is an obvious common-sense appeal to this approach. But the first objection to be made is that it does not actually describe the concrete reality of people's lives. Not all men are "responsible" fathers, nor "successful" in their occupations, and so on. Most men's lives reveal some departure from what the "male sex role" is supposed to prescribe.

The problem here is that the sex-role literature does not consistently distinguish between the expectations made of people and what they in fact do. The framework often sees variations from the presumed norms of male behavior in terms of "deviance," as a "failure" in socialization. This is particularly evident in the functionalist version of sex-role theory, where "deviance" becomes an unexplained, residual, and essentially nonsocial category.

When variation and conflict in the male role are recognized to be more typical, there are two possible explanations for sex-role theorists. Some see this conflict as a result of the blurring of men's and women's roles so that men find they are expected to add expressive elements to their traditional instrumental roles. It is not obvious why men, perhaps allowing for some

24. H. Fallding, "Inside the Australian Family," in *Marriage and the Family in Australia*, ed. A. P. Elkin (Sydney: Angus and Robertson, 1957); E. Bott, *Family and Social Network* (London: Tavistock, 1957).

initial confusion, could not internalize this new male role just as they did the original one. The answer for authors such as Bednarik and Sexton was that these changes in men's lives are going against the grain.[25] Hegemonic masculinity *is* the true nature of men, and social harmony arises from promoting this idea, not impeding it. "Masculinity" in these terms is a nonsocial essence — usually presumed to arise from the biological makeup or genetic programing of men.

In the alternative explanation of role conflict, the focus is more narrowly on the individual. There is variation in masculinity, arising from individual experiences, that produces a range of personalities — ranging in one conception along a dimension from "hard" to "soft," in another from higher to lower levels of androgyny. Conflict arises when society demands that men try to live up to an impossible standard at the hard or gynephobic ends of the scales; this is "dysfunctional." The "male role" is unduly restrictive because hegemonic masculinity does *not* reflect the true nature of men. The assumption is of an essential self whose needs would be better met by a more relaxed existence nearer the soft or androgynous poles. In this argument, masculinity is fundamentally the social pressure that, internalized, prevents personal growth.

The role framework, then, depending on which way one pushes it, can lead to entirely opposite conclusions about the nature of masculinity. One is reminded of the wax nose mentioned by Marc Bloch, which can be bent either to the right or to the left.[26] Role theory in general and sex-role theory in particular lack a stable theoretical object; there is no way that these different lines of argument about masculinity can be forced to meet. As argued in detail elsewhere, this is a consequence of the logical structure of the role framework itself; it is internally incoherent.[27]

As social theory, the sex role framework is fundamentally static. This is not to say that it cannot recognize social change. Quite the contrary. Change has been a leading theme in the discussion of men's sex roles by authors such as Pleck and Brannon.[28] The problem is that they cannot grasp it as history, as the interplay of praxis and structure. Change is always something that *happens to* sex roles, that impinges on them — whether

25. Bednarik, *Male in Crisis;* Sexton, *Feminized Male.*

26. M. Bloch, *The Historian's Craft* (Manchester: University Press, 1984).

27. R. W. Connell, "The Concept of 'Role' and What To Do With It," *Australian and New Zealand Journal of Sociology* 15(1979):7–17; reprinted in Connell, *Which Way Is Up?* (Sydney: Allen and Unwin, 1983), chap. 10.

28. J. H. Pleck, "The Male Sex Role: Definitions, Problems and Sources of Change," *Journal of Social Issues* 32(1976):155–164; J. H. Pleck, *The Myth of Masculinity* (Cambridge: MIT Press, 1981); and D. S. David and R. Brannon, *The Forty-Nine Percent Majority* (Reading, Mass.: Addison-Wesley, 1976).

from the direction of the society at large (as in discussions of how technological and economic change demands a shift to a "modern" male sex role) or from the direction of the asocial "real self" inside the person, demanding more room to breathe. Sex-role theory cannot grasp change as a dialectic arising within gender relations themselves.

This is quite simply inherent in the procedure by which any account of "sex roles" is constructed: generalizing about sexual norms, and then applying this frozen description to men's and women's lives. This is true even of the best role research. Komarovsky in *Blue Collar Marriage* gives a wonderful account of the tangled process of constructing a marriage, the sexual dilemmas, the struggles with in-laws over money and independence, and so on; and then theorizes this as "learning conjugal roles," as if the scripts were just sitting there waiting to be read. Because the framework hypostatizes sex roles, it ultimately takes them for granted; and so remains trapped within the ideological context of what it is attempting to analyze.

The result of using the role framework is an abstract view of the *differences* between the sexes and their situations, not a concrete one of the *relations* between them. As Franzway and Lowe observe in their critique of the use of sex-role theory in feminism, the role literature focuses on attitudes and misses the realities that the attitudes are about.[29] The political effect is to highlight the attitudes and pressures that create an artificially rigid *distinction* between men and women and to play down the *power* that men exercise over women. (As some critics have observed, we do not speak of "race roles" or "class roles" because the exercise of power in these areas of social relations is more immediately evident to sociologists.) Where sex-role analysis does recognize power, it is typically in a very restricted context. Once again, Komarovsky, because her field research is very good, provides a clear example. She recognizes power as a balance within marriage; her analysis of this is subtle and sophisticated. And she reports that in the cases where the wife had achieved dominance within the marriage, it was still not acceptable for this to be shown in public. But she cannot theorize this, though it is a very important point. The notion of the overall social subordination of women, institutionalized in the marital division of labor, but consistent with a fluctuating and occasionally reversed power situation in particular relationships, is not a conception that can be formulated in the language of role theory.

The consequence of the evasion and blurring of issues of power is, we feel, a persistent and serious misjudgment of the position of heterosexual men in the sexual politics of the advanced capitalist countries. The inter-

29. Franzway and Lowe, "Sex Role Theory."

pretation of oppression as overrigid role requirements has been important in bolstering the idea, widely argued in the "men's movement" literature of the 1970s, that men in general stand to *gain* from women's liberation. This notion is naive at best, and at worst dishonest. The liberation of women must mean a *loss* of power for most men; and given the structuring of personality by power, also a great deal of personal pain. The sex-role literature fairly systematically evades the facts of men's *resistance* to change in the distribution of power, in the sexual division of labor, and in masculinity itself, a point about which we shall have more to say in a moment.

The role framework, then, is neither a conceptually stable nor a practically and empirically adequate basis for the analysis of masculinity. Let us be blunt about it. The "male sex role" does not exist. It is impossible to isolate a "role" that constructs masculinity (or another that constructs femininity). Because there is no area of social life that is not the arena of sexual differentiation and gender relations, the notion of a sex role necessarily simplifies and abstracts to an impossible degree.

What should be put in its place? Partly that question is unanswerable; the only thing that can occupy the conceptual and political place of sex-role theory is sex-role theory itself. It has a particular intellectual pedigree. It is connected with a definite politics (liberal feminism and its "men's movement" offshoot), to which it supplies answers that seem to satisfy. And it is, of course, now institutionalized in academia and plays a very material part in many academic careers. Nothing else will do just that.

But we may still ask for alternatives in another sense. We have argued that the questions that were posed in the language of role theory are real and important questions. If so, they should arise in other approaches to gender relations and sexual politics, though they may take a different shape there.

Resistance and Psychoanalysis

How are we to understand the deep-seated resistance to change in masculinity that has become steadily more evident since the mid 1970s? As we have noted, the sex-role literature mainly analyzes the acquisition of masculinity by means of a simple social-learning, conformity-to-norms model. This gives no grip on the general question of resistance, let alone such specifics as the violence experienced by gay men and many women at the hands of heterosexual men. (Both of these are notable absences in one of the rare discussions of men's resistance, by Goode, which remains staunchly optimistic that men will finally accept the equality of women despite being unable to find very much evidence of such a tendency at present.)[30] But since Parsons's work 30 years ago, role literature has had available a more complex and powerful tool for work on this issue, psychoanalysis.

It is instructive to see what has become of this. Parsons himself made a very selective reading of Freud, taking the theory of the Oedipus complex as the psychological side of role differentiation in the family, and leaving out much of the emotional complexity Freud had documented within masculinity.[31] Later sex-role theorists have taken even less. On the whole, they have simply ignored psychoanalytic work on gender. The influence of the "growth movement" on the masculinity literature of the 1970s is part of this story: There is no room for the unconscious, let alone intractable unconscious conflict, within its woolly minded voluntarism. Another part is the blinkering effect of the research conventions in role research: If you can't measure it, then it can't exist. Some sex-role theorists, such as Pleck, are, however, quite explicit about the expulsion of depth psychology from the domain of their argument.[32]

There has been rather more receptiveness to psychoanalysis in accounts of masculinity given by writers on the political left, though not very much clarity. Tolson has a rather confused reference to the Oedipal relationship between father and son. Hoch presents a sub-Reichian argument about the links between capitalism, sexual repression, and the production of masculinity that is so scrambled it is difficult to take seriously. Psychoanalytic ideas appear and disappear more or less randomly in the French men's movement treatise *Holy Virility* by Reynaud.[33]

Zaretsky provides a more substantial account in a paper called "Male Supremacy and the Unconscious." To our knowledge, he is the only author to consider what Mitchell's interpretation of Freud might mean for the psychology of masculinity. While his treatment of "male supremacy" is fairly cursory, Zaretsky usefully marshals Freud's explicit arguments about the unconscious workings of masculinity. The three main ones concern men's disparagement of women as castrates, the structured tension in masculinity between love and desire, and the high level of resistance among men to expressing passive attitudes toward other men. Quite how this picture fits into a broader conception of masculinity as a continuous process with variable expressions Zaretsky does not ask; but he does pro-

30. W. J. Goode, "Why Men Resist," in *Rethinking the Family: Some Feminist Questions*, ed. B. Thorne and M. Yalom (New York: Longman, 1982).

31. Parsons and Bales, *Family, Socialization and Interaction Process*.

32. J. H. Pleck, "Masculinity–Femininity: Current and Alternative Paradigms," *Sex Roles* 1(June 1975):161–178; and Pleck, *Myth of Masculinity*, p. 112

33. A. Tolson, *The Limits of Masculinity* (London: Tavistock, 1977); P. Hoch, *White Hero, Black Beast* (London: Pluto, 1979); and E. Reynaud, *Holy Virility* (London: Pluto, 1983).

vide a clear case for the relevance of psychoanalysis for making psychological sense of masculinity.[34]

The more imaginative use of Freudian concepts has been by feminist women, among whom psychoanalysis came into widespread use in the 1970s as a tool for the analysis of femininity. Chesler suggests one line of thought on masculinity, though only in very general terms: a connection between fear of the father, male-to-male violence, and the subordination of women as a way of absorbing that violence.[35] Stockard and Johnson argue for a different emphasis. In a brief survey of psychoanalytic work they distinguish a "gynocentric" approach, which takes the construction of masculinity to be problematic, from a "phallocentric" approach (illustrated by Mitchell and Rubin), which stresses instead the problematic nature of femininity. Stockard and Johnson emphasize a connection between the exclusive care of children by women and men's subsequent difficulty in establishing a masculine identity after their initial "feminine" identification — an argument in some ways reminiscent of Sexton's. But they argue that there is a general reaction from this. Men's urge to domination is thus a result of their assertion of a tenuous identity in the face of a continuing fear of the power of the mother, and their envy of women's reproductive capacity.[36]

The most detailed feminist argument moves away from the high but cloudy territory of men's lust for power to the concrete reality of diaper changing. Chodorow's *The Reproduction of Mothering* is an ambitious synthesis of psychoanalysis and sociology that attempts to explain why men do not mother, as well as why women do. The argument involves her in developing a general theory of the production of masculinity, drawing mainly on the "object relations" school of psychoanalysis. Given primary parenting by women, the rupture of the little boy's primary identification with his mother (in contrast to the continuity of the girl's) is central to the emotional dynamics of adult masculinity. It produces a personality with reduced capacity for relationships, stronger ego boundaries, and less motive to find completeness in constructing new relationships with the young. The family sexual division of labor in child care thus reproduces itself from one generation to another by the formation of gender personalities.[37]

34. E. Zaretsky, "Male Supremacy and the Unconscious," *Socialist Revolution* 4(1975): p. 7–55.

35. P. Chesler, *About Men* (London: Woman's Press, 1978).

36. J. Stockard and M. Johnston, *Sex Roles* (Englewood Cliffs, N.J.: Prentice-Hall, 1980), chap. 9; J. Mitchell, *Psychoanalysis and Feminism* (Harmondsworth, England: Penguin, 1974); G. Rubin, "The Traffic in Women: Notes on the 'Political Economy' of Sex," in *Toward an Anthropology of Women*, ed. R. Reiter (New York: Monthly Review Press, 1975), pp. 157–210.

37. N. Chodorow, *The Reproduction of Mothering* (Berkeley: University of California Press, 1978).

On this point, as on others, the similarity to Parsons's argument is quite striking. The difference is mainly in the evaluations. Chodorow infers from the analysis that a changed sexual division of labor in child care is crucial to any strategy for major change in masculinity or femininity. Much the same criticisms can be made of her argument as of Parsons's, the concentration on a normative standard case in particular. It is therefore appropriate to turn to what is emphatically not a normative standard case, and look at the analysis of masculinity offered by homosexual men.

Gay Liberation and the Understanding of Masculinity

The masculinity literature before women's liberation was frankly hostile to homosexuality, or at best very wary of the issue. What is post – women's liberation is also post – gay liberation. Gay activists were the first contemporary group of men to address the problem of hegemonic masculinity outside of a clinical context. They were the first group of men to apply the political techniques of women's liberation, and to align with feminists on issues of sexual politics — in fact to argue for the importance of sexual politics. . . .

None of the 1970s books about men made a serious attempt to come to grips with gay liberation arguments or to reckon with the fact that mainstream masculinity is heterosexual masculinity. Nor did the "men's movement" publicists ever write about the fact that beside them was another group of men active in sexual politics; or discuss their methods, concerns or problems. The reason is obvious enough. Homosexuality is a theoretical embarrassment to sociobiologists and social-learning theorists alike, and a practical embarrassment to the "men's movement." How they got away with it is another matter. It required them to avert their gaze, not only from gay liberation, but also from contemporary developments in women's liberation (Jill Johnston's *Lesbian Nation* came out in 1973, for instance) and from basic concepts in the analysis of sexuality (notably the theory of bisexuality).[38]

The gay movement has been centrally concerned with masculinity as part of its critique of the political structure of sexuality. In this, it should be noted, the contemporary movement represents a distinct break with previous forms of homosexual activism. It has gone well beyond earlier campaigns for the social rights of homosexual people and the accompanying efforts to foster tolerance in the heterosexual population toward a "sexual minority." Instead, gay liberationists attacked the social practices and psychological assumptions surrounding gender relations, for a prominent theme in their arguments is an attempt to explain the sources of homosex-

---

38. J. Johnston, *Lesbian Nation* (New York: Simon and Schuster, 1973).

ual oppression in these terms. The British gay liberation newspaper *Come Together* declared in 1970: "We recognize that the oppression that gay people suffer is an integral part of the social structure of our society. Women and gay people are both victims of the cultural and ideological phenomenon known as sexism. This is manifested in our culture as male supremacy and heterosexual chauvinism."[39]Activists argued that homosexual people were severely penalized by a social system that enforced the subservience of women to men and that propagated an ideology of the "natural" differences between the sexes. The denial and fear of homosexuality were an integral part of this ideology because homosexuals were seen to contradict the accepted characteristics of men and women, and the complementarity of the sexes that is institutionalized within the family and many other areas of social life.[40]

Not surprisingly, then, the gay movement has been particularly critical of psychiatric definitions of homosexuality as a pathology, and of the concern with "curing" homosexuals, a phenomenon of twentieth-century medicine marked by both theoretical incoherence and practical failure. Activists readily observed the ways in which notions such as "gender inversion" were a transparent rationalization of the prevailing relationships between men and women. For the whole medical model of homosexuality rested on a belief in the biological (or occasionally socially functional) determination of heterosexual masculinity and femininity. The gay liberation tactic in this and many other areas was one of a defiant reversal of the dominant sexual ideology. In affirming a homosexual identity, many gay liberationists embraced the charge of effeminacy and declared that the real problem lay in the rigid social definitions of masculinity. It was society, not themselves, that needed to be cured.[41]

For some, this led to experiments with what was known as "radical drag." An American activist declared, "There is more to be learned from wearing a dress for a day than there is from wearing a suit for life."[42] The point was not to imitate a glamorous image of stereotypical femininity (*à la* Danny La Rue or Les Girls) but to combine feminine images with masculine ones, such as a dress with a beard. The aim was described as gender confusion, and it was advocated as a means both for personal liberation from the prescriptions of hegemonic masculinity and for subverting the accepted gender categories by demonstrating their social basis, as indicated by its technical name, a "gender fuck." Radical drag was hardly an

39. A. Walter, ed., *Come Together* (London: Gay Men's Press, 1980), 49.

40. M. Mieli, *Homosexuality and Liberation* (London: Gay Men's Press, 1980); D. Fernbach, *The Spiral Path* (London: Gay Men's Press, 1981).

41. R. Bayer, *Homosexuality and American Psychiatry* (New York: Basic Books, 1981).

42. Mieli, *Homosexuality and Liberation*, 193.

effective strategy for social change, but it contained far more political insight than did the notion of androgyny that was beginning to be popularized by sex-role theorists at about the same time.

To understand gay liberation's political responses, we should observe how the gender dichotomy acts to define homosexual men not only as "outside" of patriarchal sexual relations but "within" them as well. In the first case, as we have just noted, homosexual men are penalized for failing to meet the criteria of masculinity and are told that they are weak, effeminate, maladjusted, and so on. But they have often been defined "within" patriarchal sexual relations by being divided into "active" and "passive" types. Gay activists argued very strenuously that when homosexual men consequently organized a relationship in terms of husband and wife "roles," they were expressing self-hatred in a futile attempt to win heterosexual tolerance. More centrally, activists attacked sexual "role playing" or concepts of oneself as "butch" or "femme." The objection was not simply that this was sexist and bizarrely conformist; there was an agonizing personal trap for homosexual men in such a conception.

If a man identified as "femme," could he ever be satisfied to love a "butch" partner who returned his love? Would not a "real" man love only women (the homosexual "tragedy" explored by Proust and to an extent also Genet)? The gay liberation response was to urge homosexual men to love each other and to direct considerable criticism and satire at the masculine posturing of straight men. In these terms, the assertion of a strong gay identity that incorporates a confidence that homosexual men are perfectly capable of giving each other sexual pleasure is an attack on the power of heterosexual men.

The gay movement, then, did not speak only to homosexual people. A common sentiment, especially in the early days of the movement, was that "every straight man is a target for gay liberation." Activists often drew on Freud's conviction of universal bisexuality and claimed that heterosexual men suffered from their repressed homosexual desire; to reject it they had constantly to prove their manliness, which resulted in their oppression of women.

There are serious theoretical problems in these early gay liberation arguments, but their significance remains. Consider this contrast. Quentin Crisp has described his conviction during the interwar years that to have sexual relations with a man he desired would destroy the relationship; that man would have revealed a fatal flaw in his masculinity.[43] Forty years later, gay liberationists had sexual relations, on occasions, with heterosexual men in which the latter hoped to liberate their repressed homosexuality,

43. Q. Crisp, *The Naked Civil Servant* (London: Jonathon Cape, 1968).

and to prove they were politically on-side. This is a minor, though striking, aspect of a larger process in which gay liberationists have contested the power in gender relations; a process in which resistance among homosexual men has been generated and in which identities have changed.

The most general significance of the gay liberation arguments (and no doubt a central reason for the "men's movement" ignoring them) was that they challenged the assumptions by which heterosexuality is taken for granted as the natural order of things. It is, for example, a fundamental element of modern hegemonic masculinity that one sex (women) exists as potential sexual object, while the other sex (men) is negated as a sexual object. It is women, therefore, who provide heterosexual men with sexual validation, whereas men exist as rivals in both sexual and other spheres of life. The gay liberation perspective emphasized that the institutionalization of heterosexuality, as in the family, was achieved only by considerable effort, and at considerable cost not only to homosexual people but also to women and children. It is, then, precisely within heterosexuality as it is currently organized that a central dimension of the power that men exercise over women is to be found.

The gay movement's theoretical work, by comparison with the "sex-role" literature and "men's movement" writings, had a much clearer understanding of the reality of men's power over women, and it had direct implications for any consideration of the hierarchy of power among men. Pleck was one of the few writers outside gay liberation to observe that the homosexual–heterosexual dichotomy acts as a central symbol in *all* rankings of masculinity. Any kind of powerlessness, or refusal to compete, among men readily becomes involved with the imagery of homosexuality.[44]

What emerges from this line of argument is the very important concept of *hegemonic masculinity,* not as "the male role," but as a particular variety of masculinity to which others—among them young and effeminate as well as homosexual men—are subordinated. It is particular groups of men, not men in general, who are oppressed within patriarchal sexual relations, and whose situations are related in different ways to the overall logic of the subordination of women to men. A consideration of homosexuality thus provides the beginnings of a dynamic conception of masculinity as a structure of social relations.

Gay liberation arguments further strengthen a dynamic approach to masculinity by providing some important insights into the historical char-

44. J. H. Pleck, "Men's Power with Women, Other Men and Society: A Men's Movement Analysis," in E. H. Pleck and J. H. Pleck, eds., *The American Man* (Englewood Cliffs, N.J.: Prentice-Hall, 1980).

acter of gender relations. Homosexuality is a historically specific phenomenon, and the fact that it is socially organized becomes clear once we distinguish between homosexual *behavior* and a homosexual *identity*. While some kind of homosexual behavior may be universal, this does not automatically entail the existence of self-identified or publicly labeled homosexuals. In fact, the latter are unusual enough to require a historical explanation. Jeffrey Weeks and others have argued that in Western Europe, male homosexuality did not gain its characteristically modern meaning and social organization until the late nineteenth century.[45] That period witnessed the advent of new medical categorizations, homosexuality being defined as a pathology by the German psychiatrist Westphal in 1870. There were also new legal prescriptions, so that all male homosexual behavior was subject to legal sanctions in Britain by the end of the century (one of the first victims of these laws being Oscar Wilde). Such medical and legal discourses underlined a new conception of the homosexual as a specific type of person in contrast to the older one of homosexuality as merely as potential in the lustful nature of all men — or indeed a potential for disorder in the cosmos.[46] Correspondingly, men with same-sex preferences had more reason than previously to think of themselves as separate and distinct; and the homosexual subculture of the time in cities such as London gained its recognizably modern form.

These developments have yet to be fully explained. But they do highlight an important change in gender relations. It it clear that the early medical categorizations of homosexuality typically relied on the idea of gender inversion; and what is known of the early homosexual subcultures (say in the "Molly houses" of London from the late seventeenth century[47]) suggests that they were characterized by a high degree of effeminacy and what is now known as "transvestism." Thus the emergence of both the medical discourses on homosexuality and the corresponding self-conception of homosexuals in the nineteenth century need to be related to particular societal conceptions of masculinity, and the process of its social reorganization. Just as "the housewife," "the prostitute," and "the child" are historically specific "types" that should be understood in the context of gender relations of the time, so too "the homosexual" represents the modern definition of a new "type" of adult male. It was a man who was

45. J. Weeks, *Coming Out* (London: Quartet, 1977); J. Weeks, *Sex, Politics and Society* (London: Longman, 1981); and K. Plummer, ed., *The Making of the Modern Homosexual* (London: Hutchinson, 1981).

46. A. Bray, *Homosexuality in Renaissance England* (London: Gay Men's Press, 1982).

47. M. McIntosh, "The Homosexual Role," *Social Problems* 16(Fall, 1968):182–192; and Bray, *Homosexuality in Renaissance England*, chap. 4.

classified as an invert, and who, frequently at least, understood himself to possess a "woman's soul in a man's body."

The subsequent career of the category of homosexuality, and of the identities of homosexual men, similarly point to broader changes in masculinity. For the idea of inversion has now been theoretically discredited, and male homosexuals typically identify themselves as men (however problematic they may find the general social elaboration of masculinity). The changes that have taken place in the definition of the gender of homosexual men, in their own identities, and in the level of this oppression need to be understood in the light of changes in the general power relationship between men and women. The "social space" that homosexuals at present occupy, and that the gay movement has struggled to expand, reflects a contestation of the subordination of women to men. For it is now possible to depart publicly from the prescriptions of hegemonic masculinity without being defined, and accepting oneself, as "really" a woman. Homosexual relationships are now much less marked, to borrow Rubin's terms, by the rules of the gender division and obligatory heterosexuality.[48] The distinctions between the "invert"/"pervert," the "active"/"passive," and the "masculine"/"feminine" homosexual man, all of which acted to give a *heterosexual* meaning to an anomalous relationship, have lost their former saliency. As long as a very rigid distinction is maintained between the social categories of "man" and "woman," there is relatively little space in which homosexual men can exist; the very idea of a *homosexual man* may be inconceivable if "man" is a strictly heterosexual category. Thus it can scarcely be an accident that the first wave of feminism in nineteenth-century Europe was accompanied by some substantial efforts to achieve the emancipation of homosexuals; just as over the past 15 years there has been an indispensable link between the gay and women's movements.

The emerging history of male homosexuality, then, offers the most valuable starting point we have for constructing a historical perspective on masculinity at large. The technical superiority of the work of gay historians over the histories of masculinity and the "male role," to be found in works like Hoch, Dubbert, Stearns, and Pleck and Pleck, is so marked as to be embarrassing. Conceptually, gay history moves decisively away from the conception underlying those works, that the history of masculinity is the story of the modulation, through time, of the expressions of a more or less fixed entity.[49]

The history of homosexuality obliges us to think of masculinity not as a

48. Rubin, "The Traffic in Women."

49. P. Hoch, *White Hero, Black Beast* (London: Pluto Press, 1979); T. L. Dubbert, *A Man's Place* (Englewood Cliffs, N.J.: Prentice-Hall, 1979); P.N. Stearns, *Be a Man* (New York: Holmes & Meier, 1979); Pleck and Pleck, *American Man.*

single object with its own history but as being constantly constructed within the history of an evolving social structure, a structure of sexual power relations. It obliges us to see this construction as a social struggle going on in a complex ideological and political field in which there is a continuing process of mobilization, marginalization, contestation, resistance, and subordination. It forces us to recognize the importance of violence, not as an expression of subjective values or of a type of masculinity, but as a constitutive practice that helps to make all kinds of masculinity— and to recognize that much of this violence comes from the state, so the historical construction of masculinity and femininity is also struggle for the control and direction of state power. Finally it is an important corrective to the tendency, in left-wing thought especially, to subordinate the history of gender to the history of capitalism. The making of modern homosexuality is plainly connected to the development of industrial capitalism, but equally clearly has its own dynamic.

OUTLINE OF A SOCIAL ANALYSIS OF MASCULINITY

Men in the Framework of Gender Relations

The starting point for any understanding of masculinity that is not simply biologistic or subjective must be men's involvement in the social relations that constitute the gender order. In a classic article Rubin has defined the domain of the argument as "the sex/gender system," a patterning of social relations connected with reproduction and gender division that is found in all societies, though in varying shapes.[50] This system is historical, in the fullest sense; its elements and relationships are constructed in history and are all subject to historical change.[51] It is also internally differentiated, as Mitchell argued more than a decade ago.[52] Two aspects of its organization have been the foci of research in the past decade: the division of labor and the structure of power. (The latter is what Millett originally called "sexual politics"[53] and is the more precise referent of the concept "patriarchy.") To these we must add the structure of cathexis, the social organization of sexuality and attraction—which as the history of homosexuality demonstrates is fully as social as the structures of work and power.

The central fact about this structure in the contemporary capitalist

50. Rubin, "Traffic in Women."
51. R. W. Connell, "Theorising Gender," *Sociology* 19(May 1985):260–272.
52. J. Mitchell, *Woman's Estate* (Harmondsworth, England: Penguin, 1971).
53. K. Millett, *Sexual Politics* (New York: Doubleday, 1970).

world (like most other social orders, though not all) is the subordination of women. This fact is massively documented and has enormous ramifications — physical, mental, interpersonal, cultural — whose effects on the lives of women have been the major concerns of feminism. One of the central facts about masculinity, then, is that men in general are advantaged through the subordination of women.

To say "men in general" is already to point to an important complication in power relations. The global subordination of women is consistent with many particular situations in which women hold power over men, or are at least equal. Close-up research on families shows a good many households where wives hold authority in practice.[54] The fact of mothers' authority over young sons has been noted in most discussions of the psychodynamics of masculinity. The intersections of gender relations with class and race relations yield many other situations where rich white heterosexual women, for instance, are employers of working-class men, patrons of homosexual men, or politically dominant over black men.

To cite such examples and claim that women are therefore not subordinated in general would be crass. The point is, rather, that contradictions between local situations and the global relationships are endemic. They are likely to be a fruitful source of turmoil and change in the structure as a whole.

The overall relation between men and women, further, is not a confrontation between homogeneous, undifferentiated blocs. Our argument has perhaps established this sufficiently by now; even some role theorists, notably Hacker,[55] recognized a range of masculinities. We would suggest, in fact, that the fissuring of the categories of "men" and "women" is one of the central facts about patriarchal power and the way it works. In the case of men, the crucial division is between hegemonic masculinity and various subordinated masculinities.

Even this, however, is too simple a phrasing, as it suggests a masculinity differentiated only by power relations. If the general remarks about the gender system made above are correct, it follows that masculinities are constructed not just by power relations but by their interplay with a division of labor and with patterns of emotional attachment. For example, as Bray has clearly shown, the character of men's homosexuality, and of its regulation by the state, is very different in the mercantile city from what it was in the precapitalist countryside.[56]

The differentiation of masculinities is psychological — it bears on the

54. G. Dowsett, "Gender Relations in Secondary Schooling," *Sociology of Education* 58(January 1985):34–48.
55. Hacker, "New Burdens of Masculinity."
56. Bray, *Homosexuality in Renaissance England.*

kind of people that men are and become — but it is not only psychological. In an equally important sense it is institutional, an aspect of collective practice. In a notable recent study of British printing workers, Cynthia Cockburn has shown how a definition of compositors' work as hypermasculine has been sustained despite enormous changes in technology.[57] The key was a highly organized practice that drove women out of the trade, marginalized related labor processes in which they remained, and sustained a strongly marked masculine "culture" in the workplace. What was going on here, as many details of her study show, was the collective definition of a hegemonic masculinity that not only manned the barricades against women but at the same time marginalized or subordinated other men in the industry (e.g., young men, unskilled workers, and those unable or unwilling to join the rituals). Though the details vary, there is every reason to think such processes are very general. Accordingly we see social definitions of masculinity as being embedded in the dynamics of institutions — the working of the state, of corporations, of unions, of families — quite as much as in the personality of individuals.

Forms of Masculinity and Their Interrelationships

In some historical circumstances, a subordinated masculinity can be produced collectively as a well-defined social group and a stable social identity, with some well-recognized traits at the personal level. A now familiar case in point is the "making of the modern homosexual" (to use Plummer's phrase[58]) in the late nineteenth and early twentieth centuries. One aspect of the collective process here was a change in forms of policing that criminalized homosexuality as such, creating a criminal sexual "type." And one aspect of the psychological process was the creation of "camp" personal style, both internalizing and sardonically transforming the new medical and clinical definition of the homosexual as a type of person.

In other circumstances, a subordinated masculinity may be a transient identity. The printing apprentices in Cockburn's study provide one example of this. Another is provided by the New Guinea culture studies by Herdt, where younger men gain their masculinity through ritualized homosexuality under the guardianship of older men.[59] In other cases again, the collective and individual processes do not correspond. There may be stable enough personalities and configurations of motive produced, which for various reasons do not receive a clear social definition. A historic case

57. C. Cockburn, *Brothers: Male Dominance and Technological Change* (London: Pluto, 1983).
58. Plummer, *Making of the Modern Homosexual*.
59. G. H. Herdt, *Guardians of the Flutes* (New York: McGraw-Hill, 1981).

of this is the vague social identity of English homosexuality before the advent of "Molly" at the end of the seventeenth century. Closer to home, another example would seem to be the various forms of effeminate hetero-sexual masculinity being produced today. There are attempts to give such masculinities an identity: for instance, by commercial exploitation of hip-pie styles of dress; and by conservative transvestite organizations such as the Beaumont Society (United Kingdom) or the Seahorse Club (Australia). But for the most part there is no very clear social definition of heterosexual effeminacy. It is popularly assimilated to a gay identity when it is noticed at all—an equation its publicists furiously but unavailingly protest.

The ability to impose a particular definition on other kinds of masculin-ity is part of what we mean by "hegemony." Hegemonic masculinity is far more complex than the accounts of essences in the masculinity books would suggest. It is not a "syndrome" of the kind produced when sexolo-gists like Money reify human behavior into a "condition,"[60] or when clinicians reify homosexuality into a pathology. It is, rather, a question of how particular groups of men inhabit positions of power and wealth, and how they legitimate and reproduce the social relationships that generate their dominance.

An immediate consequence of this is that the culturally exalted form of masculinity, the hegemonic model so to speak, may only correspond to the actual characters of a small number of men. On this point at least the "men's liberation" literature had a sound insight. There is a distance, and a tension, between collective ideal and actual lives. Most men do not really act like the screen image of John Wayne or Humphrey Bogart; and when they try to, it is likely to be thought comic (as in the Woody Allen movie *Play It Again, Sam*) or horrific (as in shootouts and "sieges"). Yet very large numbers of men are complicit in sustaining the hegemonic model. There are various reasons: gratification through fantasy, compensation through displaced aggression (e.g., poofter-bashing by police and working-class youths), and so on. But the overwhelmingly important reason is that most men benefit from the subordination of women, and hegemonic masculin-ity is centrally connected with the institutionalization of men's dominance over women. It would hardly be an exaggeration to say that hegemonic masculinity is hegemonic so far as it embodies a successful strategy in relation to women.

This strategy is necessarily modified in different class situations, a point that can be documented in the research already mentioned on relation-ships inside families. A contemporary ruling-class family is organized

60. J. Money, "Sexual Dimorphism and Homosexual Gender Identity," *Psychological Bulletin* 74(1970):425–440.

around the corporate or professional career of the husband. In a typical case the well-groomed wife is subordinated not by being under the husband's thumb — he isn't in the house most of the time — but by her task of making sure his home life runs on wheels to support his self-confidence, his career advancement, and their collective income. In working-class homes, to start with, there is no "career"; the self-esteem of men is eroded rather than inflated in the workplace. For a husband to be dominant in the home is likely to require an assertion of authority without a technical basis; hence a reliance on traditional ideology (religion or ethnic culture) or on force. The working man who gets drunk and belts his wife when she doesn't hold her tongue, and belts his son to make a man of him, is by no means a figure of fiction.[61]

To think of this as "working-class authoritarianism" and see the ruling-class family as more liberal would be to mistake the nature of power. Both are forms of patriarchy; and the husbands in both cases are enacting a hegemonic masculinity. But the situations in which they do so are very different, their responses are not exactly the same, and their impact on wives and children is likely to vary a good deal.

The most important feature of his masculinity, alongside its connection with dominance, is that it is heterosexual. Though most literature on the family and masculinity takes this entirely for granted, it should not be. Psychoanalytic evidence goes far to show that conventional adult heterosexuality is constructed, in the individual life, as one among a number of possible paths through the emotional forest of childhood and adolescence. It is now clear that this is also true at the collective level, that the pattern of exclusive adult heterosexuality is a historically constructed one. Its dominance is by no means universal. For this to become the hegemonic form of masculine sexuality required a historic redefinition of sexuality itself, in which undifferentiated "lust" was turned into specific types of "perversion" — the process documented, from the underside, by the historians of homosexuality already mentioned. A passion for beautiful boys was compatible with hegemonic masculinity in Renaissance Europe, emphatically not so at the end of the nineteenth century. In this historical shift, men's sexual desire was to be focused more closely on women — a fact with complex consequences for them — while groups of men who were visibly not following the hegemonic pattern were more specifically labeled and attacked. So powerful was this shift that even men of the ruling classes found wealth and reputation no protection. It is interesting to contrast the experiences of the Chevalier d'Eon, who managed an active

61. See, for example, Kessler *et al.*, "Gender Relations in Secondary Schooling"; and V. Johnson, *The Last Resort* (Ringwood: Penguin, 1981).

career in diplomacy while dressed as a woman (in a later era he would have been labeled a transvestite), with that of Oscar Wilde a hundred years later.

"Hegemony," then, always refers to a historical situation, a set of circumstances in which power is won and held. The construction of hegemony is not a matter of pushing and pulling between ready-formed groupings but is partly a matter of the *formation* of those groupings. To understand the different kinds of masculinity demands, above all, an examination of the practices in which hegemony is constituted and contested—in short, the political techniques of the patriarchal social order.

This is a large enterprise, and we can note only a few points about it here. First, hegemony means persuasion, and one of its important sites is likely to be the commercial mass media. An examination of advertising, for instance, shows a number of ways in which images of masculinity are constructed and put to work: amplifying the sense of virility, creating anxiety and giving reassurance about being a father, playing games with stereotypes (men washing dishes), and so on.[62] Studying versions of masculinity in Australian mass media, Glen Lewis points to an important qualification to the usual conception of media influence.[63] Commercial television in fact gives a lot of airplay to "soft" men, in particular slots such as hosts of daytime quiz shows. What comes across is by no means unrelieved *machismo;* the inference is that television companies think their audiences would not like that.

Second, hegemony closely involves the division of labor, the social definition of tasks as either "men's work" or "women's work," and the definition of some kinds of work as more masculine than others. Here is an important source of tension between the gender order and the class order, as heavy manual labor is generally felt to be more masculine than white-collar and professional work (though perhaps not management).[64] Third, the negotiation and enforcement of hegemony involves the state. The criminalization of male homosexuality as such was a key move in the construction of the modern form of hegemonic masculinity. Attempts to reassert it after the struggles of the last 20 years, for instance by fundamentalist right-wing groups in the United States, are very much addressed to the state—attempting to get homosexual people dismissed as public school teachers, for instance, or erode court protection for civil liberties. Much more subtly, the existence of a skein of welfare rules, tax conces-

62. R. Atwan, D. McQuade, and J. W. Wright, *Edsels, Luckies and Frigidaires* (New York: Delta, 1979).

63. G. Lewis, *Real Men Like Violence* (Sydney: Kangaroo Press, 1983).

64. Tolson, *Limits of Masculinity.*

sions, and so on that advantage people living in conventional conjugal households and disadvantage others[65] creates economic incentives to conform to the hegemonic pattern. To argue that masculinity and femininity are produced historically is entirely at odds with the views that sees them as settled by biology, and thus as presocial categories. It is also at odds with the now common view of gender, which sees it as a social elaboration, amplification, or perhaps exaggeration of the biological fact of sex — where biology says "what" and society says "how." Certainly, the biological facts of maleness and femaleness are central to the matter; human reproduction is a major part of what defines the "sex/gender system." But all kinds of questions can be raised about the nature of the *relation* between biology and the social. The facts of anatomical and physiological variation should caution us against assuming that biology presents society with clear-cut categories of people. More generally, it should not be assumed that the relation is one of *continuity*.

We would suggest that the evidence about masculinity, and gender relations at large, makes more sense if we recognize that the social practice of gender arises — to borrow some terminology from Sartre — in *contradiction* to the biological statute.[66] It is precisely the property of human sociality that it transcends biological determination. To transcend is not to ignore: The bodily dimension remains a presence within the social practice. Not as a "base," but as an *object of practice*. Masculinity invests the body. Reproduction is a question of strategies. Social relations continuously take account of the body and biological process and interact with them. "Interact" should be given its full weight. For our knowledge of the biological dimension of sexual difference is itself predicated on the social categories, as the startling research of Kessler and McKenna makes clear.[67]

In the field of this interaction, sexuality and desire are constituted, being both bodily pain and pleasure, and social injunction and prohibition. Where Freud saw the history of this interaction only as a strengthening prohibition by an undifferentiated "society," and Marcuse as the by-product of class exploitation,[68] we must now see the construction of the unconscious as the field of play of a number of historically developing power

65. C. V. Baldock and B. Cass, eds., *Women, Social Welfare and the State* (Sydney: Allen and Unwin, 1983).

66. R. W. Connell "Class, Patriarchy and Sartre's Theory of Practice," *Theory and Society* 11(1982):305–320.

67. S. J. Kessler and W. McKenna, *Gender: An Ethnomethodological Approach* (New York: Wiley, 1978).

68. S. Freud, "Civilization and its Discontents," *Standard Edition of the Complete Psychological Works,* vol. 21(London: Hogarth, 1930); and H. Marcuse, *Eros and Civilization* (London: Sphere Books, 1955).

relations and gender practices. Their interactions constitute masculinities and femininities as particular patterns of cathexis.

Freud's work with his male patients produced the first systematic evidence of one key feature of this patterning. The repressions and attachments are not necessarily homogeneous. The psychoanalytic exploration of masculinity means diving through layers of emotion that may be flagrantly contradictory. For instance in the "Wolf Man" case history,[69] the classic of the genre, Freud found a promiscuous heterosexuality, a homosexual and passive attachment to the father, and an identification with women, all psychologically present though subject to different levels of repression. Without case-study evidence, many recent authors have speculated about the degree of repression that goes into the construction of dominant forms of masculinity: the sublimated homosexuality in the cult of sports, repressed identification with the mother, and so on. Homosexual masculinity as a pattern of cathexis is no less complex, as we see for instance in Genet. If texts like *Our Lady of the Flowers* are, as Sartre claims, masturbatory fantasies,[70] they are an extraordinary guide to a range and pattern of cathexes—from the hard young criminal to Divine herself—that show, among other things, Genet's homosexuality is far from a mere "inversion" of heterosexual object choice.

In this perspective the unconscious emerges as a field of politics. Not just in the sense that a conscious political practice can address it, or that practices that do address it must have a politics, as argued (against Freud) by the Red Collective in Britain.[71] More generally, the organization of desire is the domain of relations of power. When writers of the books about men ejaculate about "the wisdom of the penis" (H. Goldberg, who thinks the masculine ideal is a rock-hard erection), or when they dilate on its existential significance ("a firm erection on a delicate fellow was the adventurous juncture of ego and courage"—Mailer), they have grasped an important point, though they have not quite got to the root of it. What is at issue here is power over women. This is seen by authors such as Lippert, in an excellent paper exploring the connections of the male-supremacist sexuality of American automobile workers with the conditions of factory work. Bednarik's suggestion about the origins of popular sadism in the commercialization of sex and the degradation of working life is a more complex case of how the lines of force might work.[72]

69. S. Freud, "From the History of an Infantile Neurosis," *Standard Edition of the Complete Psychological Works*, vol. 17(London: Hogarth, 1918).

70. J. P. Sartre, *Saint Genet* (London: W. H. Allen, 1964).

71. Red Collective, *The Politics of Sexuality in Capitalism* (London: Red Collective/PDC, 1978).

72. Goldberg, *Hazards of Being Male;* N. Mailer, *The Prisoner of Sex* (London: Weidenfeld and Nicolson, 1971); J. Lippert, "Sexuality as Consumption," in Snodgrass, *For Men Against Sexism*, pp. 207–213; Bednarik, *Male in Crisis*.

The psychodynamics of masculinity, then, are not to be seen as a separate issue from the social relations that invest and construct masculinity. An effective analysis will work at both levels; and an effective political practice must attempt to do so too.

Transformations

An "effective political practice" implies something that can be worked on and transformed. The question of transformation, its possibilities, sources, and strategies, should be central to the analysis of masculinity.

It has had a very ambiguous status in the literature so far. The "male role" literature has spoken a lot about changes in the role, but has had no very clear account of how they come about. Indeed, this literature generally implies, without arguing the point very explicitly, that once a man has been socialized to his role, that is more or less the end of it. On the other side, the gay movement, in its contest with psychiatrists who wished to "cure" homosexuality, has had its own reasons for claiming that homosexual masculinity, once formed, is settled.

The strength of sexual desire as a motive is one reason why a pattern of cathexis may remain stable for most of a lifetime. Such stability can be found even in the most implausible patterns of cathexis, as the literature of sexual fetishism has abundantly shown, ever since Krafft-Ebing introduced his Middle European hair, handkerchief, corset, and shoe enthusiasts back in the 1880s.[73] Yet the strength of desire can also be a mighty engine of change, when caught up in contradiction. And as the last two sections have suggested, contradiction is in fact endemic in the processes that construct masculinity.

The psychodynamics of change in masculinity is a question that so far has attracted little attention. There is one exception: the highly publicized, indeed sensationalized, case of male-to-female "transsexuals." Even this case has not brought the question quite into focus because the transsexuals are mostly saying they are really women and their bodies should be adjusted to match, while their opponents say their bodies show they are really men and their psyches should be adjusted to match. Both look on masculinity and femininity as pure essences, though of different kinds. Roberta Perkins's fascinating study shows the true situation is much more complex and fraught.[74] The conviction of being really a woman may grow, rather than be present from the start. It may not be complete; ambiguity and uncertainty are common. Those who push on must negotiate their way out of the social position of being a man and into that of being a woman, a

---

73. R. von Krafft-Ebing, *Psychopathia Sexualis* 1886; New York: Paperback Library, 1965).
74. R. Perkins, *The Drag Queen Scene* (Sydney: Allen and Unwin, 1983).

process liable to corrode family relationships, lose jobs, and attract police attention. (The social supports of conventional masculine identities are very much in evidence.) Sexual ambiguity is exciting to many people, and one way of surviving — if one's physique allows it — is to become a trans-sexual prostitute or showgirl. But this tends to create a new gender category — one becomes known as "a transsexual" — rather than make a smooth transition into femininity. There is, in short, a complex interplay between motive and social circumstance; masculinity cannot be abandoned all at once, nor without pain.

Although very few are involved in a process as dramatic and traumatic as that, a good many men feel themselves to be involved in some kind of change having to do with gender, with sexual identity, with what it is to be a man. The "androgyny" literature of the late 1970s spoke to this in one way, the literature about the importance of fathering in another.[75] We have already seen some reasons to doubt that the changes discussed were as decisive as the "men's movement" proclaimed. But it seems clear enough that there have been recent changes in the constitution of masculinity in advanced capitalist countries, of at least two kinds: a deepening of tensions around relationships with women, and the crisis of a form of heterosexual masculinity that is increasingly felt to be obsolete.

The psychodynamics of these processes remain obscure; we still lack the close-up research that would illuminate them. What is happening on the larger scale is somewhat clearer. Masculinities are constituted, we argued above, within a structure of gender relations that has a historical dynamic as a whole. This is not to say it is a neatly defined and closely integrated system — the false assumption made by Parsons, Chodorow, and a good many others.[76] This would take for granted what is currently being fought for. The dominion of men over women, and the supremacy of particular groups of men over others, is sought by constantly reconstituting gender relations as a system within which that dominance is generated. Hegemonic masculinity might be seen as what would function automatically if the strategy were entirely successful. But it never does function automatically. The project is contradictory, the conditions for its realization are constantly changing, and, most important, there is resistance from the groups being subordinated. The violence in gender relations is not part of the essence of masculinity (as Fasteau, Nichols, and Reynaud, as well as

75. J. L. Bem, "The Measurement of Psychological Androgyny," *Journal of Consulting and Clinical Psychology* 42(1974):155–162; and B. Russell, *The Changing Role of Fathers* (St.Lucia: University of Queensland Press, 1983).

76. Parsons and Bales, *Family, Socialization and Interaction Process;* and Chodorow, *Reproduction of Mothering.*

many radical feminists, present it)[77] as much as a measure of the bitterness of this struggle.

The emergence of women's liberation at the end of the 1960s was, as feminists are now inclinced to see it, the heightening of a resistance that is much older and has taken many other forms in the past. It did nevertheless represent two new and important things. First, the transformation of resistance into a liberation project addressed to the whole gender order. Second, a breakdown of masculine authority; if not in the society as a whole, at least in a substantial group, the younger professional intelligentsia of Western cities. Though it has not widened its base as fast as activists expected, the new feminism has also not gone under to the reaction that gained momentum in the late 1970s. Like gay liberation, it is here to stay; and at least in limited milieus the two movements have achieved some changes in power relations that are unlikely to be reversed.

This dynamic of sexual politics has met up with a change in class relations that also has implications for masculinity. In a very interesting paper, Winter and Robert suggest that some of the familiar economic and cultural changes in contemporary capitalism—the growth of large, bureaucratized corporations, the integration of business and government, the shift to technocratic modes of decision making and control—have implications for the character of "male dominance."[78] We think they overgeneralize, but at least they have pointed to an important conflict within and about hegemonic masculinity. Forms of masculinity well adapted to face-to-face class conflict and the management of personal capital are not so well suited to the politics of organizations, to professionalism, to the management of strategic compromises and consensus.

One dimension of the recent politics of capitalism, then, is a struggle about the modernization of hegemonic masculinity. This has by no means gone all one way. The recent ascendancy of the hard-liners in the American ruling class has involved the systematic reassertion of old-fashioned models of masculinity (not to mention femininity—*vide* Nancy Reagan).

The politics of "men's liberation" and the search for androgyny have to be understood in this field of forces. They are, explicitly, a response to the new feminism—accepting feminism in a watered-down version, hoping that men could gain something from its advent. This required an evasion of the issue of power, and the limits were clearly marked by the refusal of

77. M. Fasteau, *The Male Machine* (New York: McGraw-Hill, 1974); J. Nichols, *Men's Liberation* (New York: Penguin, 1975); Reynaud, *Holy Virility;* and A. Dworkin, *Pornography: Men Possessing Women* (London: The Women's Press, 1981).

78. M. F. Winter and E. R. Robert, "Male Dominance, Late Capitalism, and the Growth of Instrumental Reason," *Berkeley Journal of Sociology* 24/25(1980):249–280.

any engagement with gay liberation. Yet there was an urgency about what the "men's movement" publicists were saying in the early 1970s, which drew its force partly from the drive for the modernization of hegemonic masculinity already going on in other forms.[79] The goal (to simplify a little) was to produce forms of masculinity able to adapt to new conditions but sufficiently similar to the old ones to maintain the family, heterosexuality, capitalist work relations, and American national power (most of which are taken for granted in the books about men). The shift in the later 1970s that produced "Free Men" campaigning for fathers' rights, and the ponderings of conservative ideologues like Stearns on how to revive intelligent paternalism, is clearly connected with the antimodernist movement in the American ruling class. This offered strategies for repairing men's authority in the face of the damage done by feminism, much as the Reagan foreign policy proposed to restore American hegemony internationally, and monetarism proposed a drastic disciplining of the working class. The political appeal of the whole package — mainly to men, given the "gender gap" — is notable.

The triumph of these ideas is not inevitable. They are strategies, responding to dilemmas of practice, and they have their problems too. Other responses, other strategies, are also possible; among them much more radical ones. The ferment started by the New Left, which produced the counterculture, the new feminism, gay liberation, and many attempts at communal households and collective child care, has also produced a good deal of quiet experimentation with masculinity and attempts to work out in practice unoppressive forms of heterosexuality. This is confined at present to a limited milieu and has not had anything like the shape or public impact of the politics of liberation among gay men.

The moment of opportunity, as it appeared in the early 1970s, is past. There is no easy path to a major reconstruction of masculinity. Yet the initiative in sexual politics is not entirely in the hands of reaction, and the underlying tensions that produced the initiatives of 10 years ago have not vanished. There are potentials for a more liberating politics, here and now — not in the form of grand schemes of change, but at least in the form of coalitions among feminists, gay men, and progressive heterosexual men that have real chances of making gains on specific issues.

79. Ehrenreich, *Hearts of Men.*

History and Danger

Opposition to the reification of gender lies at the core of men's and women's studies. Understanding the historical vicissitudes of masculinities is essential to this project. In this section Peter Filene discusses the progress men's history has made and can make in understanding both continuity and change in men's lives, Michael Kimmel discovers recurrent patterns of change, and Clyde Franklin reminds us that change is not necessarily progress.

"The Secrets of Men's History" follows the lead of women's historians during the past 15 years in recognizing how most behaviors and attitudes are influenced by gender. Examination of Lincoln Steffens's famous *Autobiography*, for example, reveals how, in typically male fashion, he hid his private behind his public self. Steffens is shown to be one of many famous American men — Eugene V. Debs, Alfred Steiglitz, Woodrow Wilson, and others — who had significant secrets that historians (and often the men themselves) ignored. Marital infidelity may not seem a particularly surprising secret, but fidelity, dependency on wives, and powerful longings for children may be more surprising. All these secrets greatly affected the men's development, including their careers, but have escaped historians' attention because the men's private lives have been deemed "insignificant." Looking ahead, Filene argues that men's history must go beyond individual biographies to aggregate analysis, demonstrating the male dimensions of gender's effects on economic and political institutions, as well as personal aspects of class and power.

Although still at a rudimentary stage, an analysis of 25 recent
scholarly historical studies indicates that path-breaking work is
under way.

"The Contemporary 'Crisis' of Masculinity in Historical
Perspective" finds significant structural similarities in three
periods of widespread gender confusion: Restoration England,
turn-of-the-century United States, and the contemporary United
States. Its gender relation model indicates that changes in
masculinity are reactive to those in femininity, responding to
intergroup renegotiations of status and obligations precipitated
by economic and social upheavals. The pamphlet wars of
Restoration England and modern men's varied responses to
women's demands are examples of the resulting sexualization of
political discourse in such periods.

"Surviving the Institutional Decimation of Black Males:
Causes, Consequences, and Intervention" analyzes the systematic
removal of black men from the civilian population through
penal, military, educational, healthcare, and other institutions.
Contradictions between the norms of different groups that
influence black men — their immediate peer group, the black
community, and white society — create damaging conflicts of
allegiances for black men. Such conflicts have recently intensified,
as an earlier, prosurvival ethos of role interchange in the black
community has given way to greater gender rigidity. Healthier
male socialization patterns must be established in formal black
community settings and the informal sites where men gather,
such as barbershops, bars, and street corners.

4
The Secrets of Men's History

Peter Filene

When Gerda Lerner began her dissertation in 1963 on two nineteenth-century sisters named Grimké, she had to justify choosing this "exotic specialty."[1] Twenty years later, women's historians need no justifications. Quite the contrary; they have established a thriving field all their own. At the annual Berkshire Conference, hundreds of speakers unapologetically discuss nothing but female history. In such journals as *Signs, Feminist Studies,* and *Women's Review of Books,* they publish erudite articles. In a hundred universities and colleges, students can earn degrees in women's studies, while countless history departments have hired one or more scholars specializing in women of some era or nation.[2] Gender history has arrived — half of it, at least.

"But what do you mean when you say you're studying 'men's history'?" the woman asked me in a puzzled tone. Standing behind the podium at a scholarly conference in 1982, I had a wry flash of *déja vu.* In her question I heard echoes of the challenge to scholars of women 20 years ago. Addressed to the male gender, however, it took a very different form. "After all," my interrogator continued, "hasn't all history been about men?" This was — and is — the fundamental question. Whereas women's historians rescued their subjects from almost total obscurity, what was there for a historian of men to discover? Male activities and ideas dominated the landscape of the recorded past as far as the eye could see, from the biblical plains to New York skyscrapers. The usual "history of man" was precisely that. So what in the world remained to be said on his behalf?

1. Gerda Lerner, *The Majority Finds Its Past: Placing Women in History* (New York: Oxford University Press, 1979), p. xx.
2. "Out of the Academic Ghetto," *Newsweek* 102(October 31, 1983):86.

The answer has to do with *how* more than *what*. Men's history—masculine history, if you will—begins when we redefine our usual notion of historical significance and when we shift our usual frame of reference. Once we have made these two conceptual adjustments, we uncover some secrets hidden in the familiar landscape of the past. More often—and ultimately more important—as we shift our angle of vision, we recognize new meanings in the evidence that lay in front of our eyes all along.

Our male ancestors debated in legislatures, preached hellfire sermons in churches, harvested wheat under burning sun, and forged steel in factories. They also drank in saloons, watched or played baseball, earned Boy Scout badges, and belonged to fraternities and Rotary Clubs; but historians have paid little attention to these recreational activities in the semipublic realm. And, of course, men also were boys, lovers, husbands, and fathers; but historians have given even less attention to these private roles. Private and semipublic life becomes important—becomes *history*—only if it causes the public front to collapse. When Edward VIII gave up the throne "for the woman I love," the usual monarchical framework widened for a moment. Men's drinking habits became noteworthy during the Prohibition controversy. Because Franklin Roosevelt overcame polio and Randolph Churchill succumbed to syphilis, historians briefly shifted their gaze from politics to bodies. Except for traumatic episodes like these, we are supposed to believe that men spend all their energy and emotion—at least all that is worth writing about—in public. Men, apparently, find their primary sense of self apart from boyhood, family, recreation, and love.

Until recently, few historians questioned this lopsided rendition. Most of them left to playwrights and novelists the job of portraying prodigy composers placating their fathers or newspaper magnates daydreaming of boyhood sleds. This was, after all, fiction. In the realm of nonfiction, biographers made gestures toward integrating their subjects' private and public lives, but even they often vaulted boyhoods in a chapter and thrust marriages, children, and male friendships into paragraphs here and there. Only so-called psychohistorians insisted on the importance of childhood and of interior, not-always-rational influences. But conventional scholars scorned psychohistory, complaining that it reduced people to little more than an Oedipal complex or sibling rivalry. Regular history held its attention to grown-up men in the public world.

This frame of reference derived from a particular presumption about what is historically *significant*. Power was significant, and the extraordinary was significant. Presidents, not automobile salesmen. Elections and depressions; not meals, marriage, and sports (what used to be called "pots and pans history"). Given this presumption, it is hardly surprising that women were denied their past. The typical woman, after all, was "just a housewife" trudging through the daily domestic rounds or — from a longer perspective — traveling the cycle of marriage, motherhood, and death. Either way, mundane or universal, she fell short of significance. But women were not the only ones left out. Most men also failed to put their names in the history books. At best they showed up as voting statistics, revolutionary mobs, or labor forces. Traditional history remained a matter of extraordinary public men.

That was where matters stood a quarter-century ago. Then came the decade of the 1960s, which, along with its many other tumults, brought an upheaval within the historical profession. New Left historians — soon part of a larger school known as social historians — set to work turning the traditional premises upside down. Focusing on the grass roots instead of the seats of power, listening to the inarticulate instead of the elite, documenting the nonwhite, nonmale, and nonwealthy, these new historians have asked us to reconsider what or who is significant. Andrew Carnegie, a few union leaders, or thousands of nameless steel workers? Andrew Jackson or the Jacksonians? The cotton kingdom or family life among the slaves? New questions, new answers.

Amid this redefinition of the past, women — the minority group that is a majority — inevitably played a leading role. Toward the end of the 1960s, historians of women launched an assault on the "andocentric frame of reference." Traditional history, they announced, was the history of men. "The very term 'Women's History,'" Gerda Lerner declared, "calls attention to the fact that something is missing from historical scholarship and it aims to document and reinterpret that which is missing."[3]

This retrieval effort has come up with astonishing results. We now know about alewives, midwives, and prostitutes; subcultures of female friendship, female homosexuality, and female slaves; quilting and housework; Abigail Adams, Zelda Fitzgerald, and dozens of other famous men's wives who merit spotlights of their own. By now, every publisher boasts that its introductory textbook gives "ample" coverage to all minorities, from blacks to women to Native Americans. A few have even published surveys exclusively of women — "herstory," as one was titled, in case anybody missed the point. Who can have failed to notice that the past has been widened? History his and hers.

Well, not exactly. Look in the indexes of American history textbooks under *W* and you find woman's suffrage, women's employment, or simply women. But look under *M* and you find nothing between Manifest Destiny and Mexican War. Historians have heeded Gerda Lerner's call to fill in the "something missing" from the female past, but have not yet recognized

3. Lerner, *Majority*, p xiv.

that gender refers to two sexes. Something is also missing in men's own history. The time has come to fill in the blanks.

EXTRAORDINARY MEN WITH ORDINARY SECRETS

To begin with, we can tell men's secrets aloud. Significant secrets, I should add. Merely to chip away at plaster heroes and uncover scandals, as "debunking" biographers delight in doing, is not the point. George Washington did not chop down the cherry tree, Grover Cleveland may have fathered a bastard, John F. Kennedy probably carried on an affair with the girlfriend of Mafia mobsters. But that is gossip, not history. Digging up skeletons in heroes' closets is basically no different from digging up Oedipal complexes—a reduction rather than expansion of our understanding a man. The point is not the secret but the interplay between the secret and the rest of his behavior and attitudes. When we learn that an apparently upright man was limping through life, desperately balancing infidelity against honor, then we are learning significant masculine truth.

Eugene Debs, for example, has been a patron saint of reformers because he worked selflessly for the lower class. The fact also is that, after 30 years of loveless, childless marriage, Debs fell in love with a married woman named Mabel Curry. "You seem always to have been in my heart and my life and I can not think of a time when you were not with me." But it was hardly that simple. His Victorian code of ethics would not let him divorce Mrs. Debs, while his emotional inhibitions kept him from fully embracing Mrs. Curry. During the last two decades of his life, he and Mabel had a passionate, furtive affair, mostly through love letters. In the second of those decades, he slid into despair, partly because the federal courts had sentenced him to prison for wartime sedition, partly because Debs had sentenced himself to a prison of unrequited love.[4]

Does his secret make a difference? Not in an obvious way. We do not have to rewrite the Pullman strike, socialism, and the 1920 election. But the affair is a window on Debs's concept of manhood, which in turn, according to Nick Salvatore's fine biography, influenced his social–economic philosophy. For one thing, Debs presumed that women would and should stay at home while their husbands, fathers, and brothers governed the world. More generally, because he believed that "no man can

---

4. Debs to Curry, n.d. [1917–1919], quoted by Nick, Salvatore, *Eugene V. Debs: Citizen and Socialist* (Urbana: University of Illinois Press, 1982), p. 277. See also pp. 278, 339–340, and chap. 10.

rightly claim to be a man unless he is free and self-reliant" — a man and not "a hand" — Debs never adopted a deterministic, class-conflict version of socialism.[5] Thus his private preoccupation with his own manhood mingled with his public quest for a brotherhood of workers. In other words, the personal story was not "merely personal"; it shaped the career as much as the career shaped the personal life.

Alfred Stieglitz seems the antithesis of Debs in every way but gender and date of birth. He grew up in New York City, not Terre Haute; in a Jewish rather than a Christian family; in the upper middle, not the lower middle, class. Whereas Debs left home at age 15 to work on the railroad and "prove that I can act manly," Stieglitz went to the Berlin Polytechnikum to study mechanical engineering.[6] Soon he discovered he had no fondness for engineering and a passion for making photographs. On his return to New York, he joined a photoengraving firm, but business was no more his calling than engineering had been. He was to be a man of art, not commerce, and his marriage to wealthy Emmeline Obermeyer permitted him that luxury. Living on her money, he dedicated himself to a nonprofit-making career as impresario of American artistic photography.

Apparently Stieglitz and Debs would have found almost nothing to say to each other, yet the aesthete and the labor leader had two fundamental things in common: unhappy marriages and the Victorian code of manliness. For 25 years, Stieglitz disliked his wife and stayed coldly, often contemptuously faithful to her. In 1918, at the age of 54, he fell in love with the painter Georgia O'Keeffe and stopped the charade. Emmeline issued an ultimatum: Either she goes or you go. Alfred packed within 48 hours and left. Almost at once, the passionate relationship with O'Keeffe rejuvenated his photographic vision. Taking intense close-ups of her nude body, he radically altered photographic portraiture. Later, when he pointed his camera toward the clouds and produced the series of abstract "Equivalents," he brought photography into modernist art. His history is not reducible to love, but neither is it entirely explained without it.[7]

Infidelity has been a secret, of course. But in a sense there has also been a secret about fidelity. When Theodore Roosevelt's first wife died, he forbade her name to be mentioned in his presence. "For joy or sorrow, my life

5. Quotation from Debs, speech to AFL, August 12, 1908, quoted in ibid., p. 228. See also pp. 171, 228–231.

6. Debs to Louise Debs, October 8, 1874, quoted in ibid., p. 19.

7. Sue Davidson Lowe, *Stieglitz: A Memoir / Biography* (New York: Farrar, Straus, & Giroux, 1983), esp. chap. 7 and pp. 100–101, 216–217, 222, 260. For his artistic significance, see Jonathan Green, *American Photography: A Critical History, 1945 to the Present* (New York: Abrams, 1984), pp. 14–17; and Beaumont Newhall, *The History of Photography, From 1839 to the Present Day*, rev. ed. (New York: Museum of Modern Art, 1964), pp. 102–106, 111–114.

has now been lived out," he wrote in his diary. But the secret was not her name, nor was it his heartrending grief. The secret that lay beneath them, and that they signaled, was how profoundly he depended on his wife. If the secret of men's marriages has all too often been adultery, the no-less-frequent secret has been dependency. In the 2 years after Alice died, Roosevelt plunged deeper into Republican party politics and then, in the Dakota Badlands, pitched himself against bears and blizzards. Clearly his energy for doing was far from "lived out," but so was his need for loving. Widowed less than 2 years, Roosevelt became engaged to a childhood friend, Edith Carow. Their 33-year marriage and four children gave him all the joy and sorrow—mostly joy—that he had momentarily believed to have been buried with Alice. Of course, one cannot claim that, without domestic happiness, he would not have gone on to his spectacular political achievements. But domesticity played a part. In Roosevelt's opinion, it played a large part. "No man can be a good citizen," he proclaimed, "who is not a good husband and a good father."[8]

Woodrow Wilson disagreed with Roosevelt on trusts, military preparedness, and other policies, but on the importance of a wife's love, the Roughrider and the preacher president were unanimous. "My own darling," young Wilson wrote to his fiancée, Ellen Axson:

> I suppose there never was a man more dependent than I on love and sympathy, more devoted to home and home life; and, my darling, my heart is overflowing with gratitude and gladness because of the assurance that it now has a new love to lean upon—a love which will some day be the centre of a new home and the joy of new home life. I shall not begin to live a complete life, my love, until you are my wife.[9]

As he moved steadily from college campus to statehouse to White House, Woodrow's ardor for Ellen never flagged because his need for her never diminished. And when she died, midway through his first presidential term, he pushed aside his aides' warnings and remarried within 18 months. Let the public criticize him for unseemly haste. Without a wife, Woodrow was not "complete." After his incapacitating stroke several years later, the second Mrs. Wilson would become virtually the acting president of the United States.

8. Edmund Morris, *The Rise of Theodore Roosevelt* (New York: Coward, McCann and Geoghan, 1979), chaps. 10–12 and pp. 313–314. Diary is quoted on p. 244. On fatherhood, see address to Liberal Club, Buffalo, New York, January 26, 1893, quoted in Dewey W. Grantham, ed, *Theodore Roosevelt* (Englewood Cliffs, N.J.: Prentice-Hall, 1971), p. 41.

9. Wilson to Axson, October 2, 1893, in Eleanor Wilson McAdoo, ed., *The Priceless Gift: The Love Letters of Woodrow Wilson and Ellen Axson Wilson* (New York: McGraw-Hill, 1962), p. 19.

And when a man had a wife whom he did not love, and a wife he loved whom he could not marry, he invented substitutes. Toward the end of his life, Debs increasingly leaned on his younger brother. "Theo has been a big sister to the little brother in me," he confided to a friend. On another occasion, Theo had "the heart of a mother."[10] Even a cultural rebel like Hutchins Hapgood, who preached sexual freedom and practiced extramarital affairs, found that he could not "achieve emotional independence" of his wife.[11]

Whether marital or extramarital, this emphatic reliance on a woman was a secret, but, in retrospect, it is not a mystery. It was the other side of manly independence, the emotional counterweight to the lonely demands of success. Out there in the world, the "true man" sought to be self-reliant, hardworking and brave, proving his worth through what Roosevelt called the "strenuous life." Against such odds, it is no wonder that a man — not only the one who was losing but equally the one who was winning — needed a home as haven and a wife as comforter of his fears, tears, and other soft feelings. He depended on his other half to make him whole.[12]

Men need women. They also want children. Such a statement is hardly newsworthy when applied to a woman like Abigail Adams, who single-handedly tended five children while her husband was off at Philadelphia and Paris being a Founding Father. Nor is it very surprising when applied metaphorically to an unmarried woman like Jane Addams, who mothered the slum dwellers around Hull House and the child laborers throughout the nation. For biological and cultural reasons, children have played a prominent, usually decisive role in women's lives. For the same reasons, we have discounted the meaning of fatherhood. Just as pre-Lamaze hospitals banished expectant husbands to waiting rooms while their wives gave birth, historians have treated parenthood as motherhood.

But many fathers have said otherwise. "My dear Nabby, Johnny, Charly and Tommy," John Adams wrote from Philadelphia, "I long to see you, and to share with your Mamma the Pleasures of your Conversation." Another Massachusetts man, Timothy Pickering, showered his wife with paternal questions about their infant son: "How could you forbear telling me often how fast he grew? Whether he was quiet? and what signs of understanding he discovered?" When William Palfrey was away from

10. Debs to David Karsner, September 11, 1922, and to Mabel Curry, n.d., quoted in Salvatore, *Debs*, pp. 217–218.

11. Quoted in Gerald L. Marriner, "A Victorian in the Modern World: The 'Liberated' Male's Adjustment to the New Woman and the New Morality," *South Atlantic Quarterly* 76(Spring 1977):199.

12. Peter G. Filene, *Him / Her / Self: Sex Roles in Modern America* 2nd ed. (Baltimore: Johns Hopkins University Press, 1986), chap. 3.

home on business and received news of the death of his 7-year-old daughter Polly, he sat down "cooly and calmly" to write a letter consoling his wife. But all at once he gave way: "O my poor dear little Polly—never to see her again! Never to see her dance Nancy Dawson again—I can't bear the thoughts—This letter you will see is wet with my Tears—I go about crying like a fool whenever I think of her."[13]

These were eighteenth-century fathers. During the course of nineteenth-century industrial development, the split between work and home —his sphere and hers—increasingly defined childrearing as a mother's responsibility. There were mothers' discussion clubs rather than parents' discussion clubs; Mothers' Magazine and motherhood advice manuals; and, by 1914, Mother's Day—but Father's Day arrived merely as a commercial afterthought. Along with this partition of gender roles, children may have become less important to men. Possibly, but the question deserves to be followed into men's letters and diaries before we presume the answer. After all, who knows how many other fathers were like Henry James, Sr., who returned from a lecture trip after 36 hours instead of 2 weeks, hurrying home when he could not bear to be away from his wife and children?[14]

Because fathers were banished to the waiting rooms of history, we do not know how much they valued children. In fact, given the bias of American culture, they themselves may not have known. In the course of the 900 pages of Lincoln Steffens's famous Autobiography (1931), we encounter the author in many roles and many places. We meet the California boy who galloped between deviltry and penitence; the young journalist who muckraked city bosses in the United States and then the Allied leaders in postwar Versailles; and finally the aging liberal who "went over into the future" of the Bolshevik revolution and came back as an undogmatic radical. In this exuberant story a reader cannot detect—because Steffens himself did not fully admit—that a deep emotional frustration churned beneath the surface of his life. "My wife died, and then her mother. A short sentence that, but it covers a long story"—that is all he told his public audience. In private letters, by contrast, he confessed that his mar-

13. John Adams to Abigail Adams, July 7, 1775, in L. H. Butterfield, Marc Friedlander, and Mary-Jo Kline, eds., The Book of Abigail and John: Selected Letters of the Adams Family, 1762–1784 (Cambridge: Harvard University Press, 1975), p. 95; Timothy Pickering to Rebecca Pickering, August 30, 1777, and William Palfrey to Susannah Palfrey, September 19, 1772, quoted by Mary Beth Norton, Liberty's Daughters: The Revolutionary Experience of American Women, 1750–1800 (Boston: Little, Brown, 1980), pp. 92, 90.

14. E. Anthony Rotundo, "Manhood in America: The Northern Middle Class, 1770–1920" (Ph.D. dissertation, Brandeis University, 1982), chap. 5, esp. pp. 197–210, 220–222, and chap. 8, esp. pp. 338–347. Leon Edel, Henry James: The Untried Years, 1843–1876 (New York: Lippincott, 1953), p. 44.

riage had been "barren" for years. "I need a home," the lonely widower wrote plaintively to his sister. "I must have a wife."[15]

But shortly after remarrying at the age of 57, he discovered that his need went beyond a wife. "One of the deepest secret desires of my life is about to be fulfilled," Steffens exclaimed to his sister: He was going to become a father. Need turned into desire, marriage turned into father-hood, and then the father found himself falling passionately in love with his son: "The hold Little Pete has on me is the most violent force that has ever gripped me." In his *Autobiography* 7 years later, however, Pete Steffens made merely a one-paragraph appearance at the end of a chapter on Mussolini—a trivial incident rather than a grand fulfillment. For some reason, the father–autobiographer kept his deepest desire a secret in all but name.[16]

We are hardly astonished by this discrepancy between the private and the public versions. As Justin Kaplan remarks in his perceptive biography of Steffens, "A man's life is one thing and his autobiography something else altogether. . . . " When a man writes down his life, he is not simply assembling the facts; he is composing himself. He tries to re-create who he was, but in so doing, he ratifies who he has become or who he would like to have been. Disclosure becomes disguise. The history of self always veers along the brink of fiction.[17]

15. On deaths, see *The Autobiography of Lincoln Steffens* (New York: Harcourt, Brace, 1931), p. 634. On barrenness, Steffens to Harlow Gale, July 20, 1896, in Ella Winter and Granville Hicks, eds., *The Letters of Lincoln Steffens*, 2 vols. (New York: Harcourt, Brace, 1938), 1:482. On home and wife, Steffens to Laura Suggett, April 11, 1912, Steffens Papers, Columbia University.

16. On deepest desire, Steffens to Suggett, April 16, 1924, *Letters*, 2:641. On Pete, Steffens to Suggett, October 13, 1925, ibid., p. 714, and *Autobiography*, p. 820. In two articles, however, he proclaimed his fatherly pride: "Radiant Fatherhood: An Old Father's Confession of Superiority" (1925), reprinted in *Lincoln Steffens Speaking* (New York: Harcourt, Brace, 1936), pp. 5–6, and "Becoming a Father at Sixty Is a Liberal Education," *American Magazine*, August 1928, reprinted in Ella Winter and Herbert Shapiro, eds., *The World of Lincoln Steffens* (New York: Hill & Wang, 1962), pp. 194–203. I have developed this analysis more fully in "The 'Secret Desire' of Lincoln Steffens," *Harvard Magazine* 88(September–October 1985):72A–72H.

Once again Debs and Steffens follow uncannily parallel lines. Married to a woman who was infertile, Debs in middle age adopted the 10-year-old son of her recently widowed step-brother. The arrangement dismayed Kate, who prided herself on an orderly, spotless house. But Debs welcomed the boy because for 30 years he had longed to be a father (and, one might add, because he did not do the housework). Surprisingly, Salvatore ignores this episode. See Ray Ginger, *The Bending Cross: A Biography of Eugene Victor Debs* (New Brunswick: Rutgers University Press, 1949), pp. 61, 298–299.

17. Justin Kaplan, *Lincoln Steffens: A Biography* (New York: Touchstone, 1974), p. 331, also pp. 302–306. In general, see James Olney, ed., *Autobiography: Essays Theoretical and Critical* (Princeton: Princeton University Press, 1980), esp. Barret J. Mandel, "Full of Life Now," and Olney, "Autobiography and the Cultural Moment."

This discrepancy is more than a matter of genre. It is also a matter of gender. There are female autobiographies and there are male autobiographies, and they show us different parts of the same world. Women, even women who have succeeded in a professional career, tend to write more about siblings, spouses, and children, as well as more about anxieties, fantasies, and love — in sum, more about the private stuff of their lives. In male autobiographies, most of the action takes place in streets and legislatures and other public arenas rather than at home or in the heart. Does this contrast occur, one may ask, because women have undergone more private experience than men? But the answer follows easily. Spouses and children, romances and sorrows, run with equal urgency through the lives of male and female autobiographers. The contrast springs from what the authors choose to tell and what they choose to hide. As it turns out, the choice is governed strongly, almost irresistibly, by gender.[18]

The histories that men have written about themselves, then, contain the same bias as the histories they have written about one another. The three-dimensional man — private, semipublic, and public — is flattened into a masculine stereotype, an image who poses like the Marlboro man on a billboard beside the highway. The task of gender historians is to create a more rounded truth.

"M" AS IN GENDER

Talking about individual men is not equivalent to talking about men. Biographies do not add up to history. A man-by-man analysis marks only the first stage of revisionism, just as a "herstory" of heroines and victims characterized the infancy of female studies. After 20 years of prolific research, women's historians have moved beyond simply discovering female astronomers, architects, and Revolutionary War soldiers (what Gerda Lerner calls "compensatory history"), as well as beyond emphasizing women's role in the labor movement or the New Deal ("contribution history").[19] Instead of changing the pronouns of traditional history, recent scholars have been studying the experiences of women — especially ordinary women — regardless of what men were doing and regardless of traditional notions of significance. From this latest approach, which is basically a female branch of social history, we have learned about women's jobs, friendship, sexuality, and life cycle, just to name a few examples.

Given all this accumulated analysis, a few historians are shifting the frame of reference in order to begin a new, still more ambitious task,

18. Estelle C. Jelinek, ed., *Women's Autobiography: Essays in Criticism* (Bloomington: Indiana University Press, 1980), Intro.
19. Lerner, *Majority*, pp. 145–146.

namely, to reconceptualize the past by understanding how gender has functioned in social, economic, and political developments. Instead of the suffrage movement, for example, one would study gender and power; instead of Victorian women's sexuality, the bourgeois experience. Instead of supplementing the history of men, these gender historians would rewrite it. As Joan Scott explains: "The point is to examine social definitions of gender as they are developed by men and women, constructed in and affected by economic and political institutions, expressive of a range of relationships which included not only sex, but class and power. The results throw new light not only on women's experience, but on social and political practice as well."[20]

The vanguard of women's historians are looking toward gender history, but the gender includes only one sex. Ladies, prostitutes, wives, mothers, and assorted "females" occupy all but a handful of the 150 titles listed in Scott's footnotes. Where are the gentlemen, pimps, husbands, fathers, or simply "males"? They are absent, awaiting gender-conscious historians to bring them back to life.

The situation has begun to improve. Male consciousness has been emerging at a clumsy but quickening pace. Not surprisingly, the forerunners were social psychologists, whose professional training had sensitized them to issues of identity and role. In the 1970s, as the titles of their books announced, they analyzed the "myth" of masculinity, exposing the "hazards" and "paradoxes" that threatened the health and happiness of men, while urging "liberation" from the *macho* straitjacket.[21] Meanwhile, with an illuminating shift of perspective, Daniel Levinson arranged these issues along a life cycle — *The Seasons of a Man's Life* — and thereby fed an already voracious interest in "midlife crisis."[22]

20. Joan Wallach Scott, "Women in History: The Modern Period," *Past and Present*, no. 101(November 1983):153.

21. Leonard Kriegel, *The Myth of American Manhood* (New York: Dell, 1978); Joseph H. Pleck, *The Myth of Masculinity* (Cambridge: MIT Press, 1981); Herb Goldberg, *The Hazards of Being Male: Surviving the Myth of Masculine Privilege* (New York: Nash, 1976); Donald H. Bell, *Being a Man: The Paradox of Masculinity* (Lexington, Mass.: Lewis, 1982); and Warren T. Farrell, *The Liberated Man: Beyond Masculinity* (New York: Random House, 1974). See also Deborah David and Robert Brannon, eds., *The Forty-nine Percent Majority* (Reading, Mass.: Addison-Wesley, 1976); Joseph H. Pleck and Jack Sawyer, eds., *Men and Masculinity* (Englewood Cliffs, N.J.: Prentice-Hall, 1974); and Robert Lewis, ed., *Men in Difficult Times: Masculinity Today and Tomorrow* (Englewood Cliffs, N.J.: Prentice-Hall, 1981).

22. Daniel J. Levinson, *The Seasons of a Man's Life* (New York: Knopf, 1978); George E. Vaillant, *Adaptation to Life* (Boston: Little, Brown, 1977); Roger Gould, *Transformations: Growth and Change in Adult Life* (New York: Simon and Schuster, 1978); Nancy Mayer, *The Male Mid-Life Crisis: Fresh Starts after Forty* (New York: Doubleday, 1978); Gail Sheehy, *Changes: Predictable Crises of Adult Life* (New York: Dutton, 1976); Peter Filene, ed., *Men in the Middle: Coping with the Problems of Work and Family in the Lives of Middle-Aged Men* (Englewood Cliffs, N.J.: Prentice-Hall, 1981).

This awareness was happening not simply on the printed page; it was developing in the minds of men, especially younger and college-educated men. "The criteria for manhood in this society are in a muddied state," Cardol Tavris concluded in 1977 after polling 28,000 readers of *Psychology Today* about their attitudes toward masculinity.[23] Traditional presumptions were being stirred up. Men were the ruling class who penalized women in various ways, but masterhood carried penalities: workaholism, heart attacks, fear of losing control, diminished touch with family and one's own emotions. For those men who deviated from the masculine norm by being homosexual, the penalties were even more tangible: a stigma so ferocious that most gays stayed in the closet of anonymity.

Consciousness went hand in hand with action; the personal became political. If any men in the 1970s were to develop a sense of collective identity and grievances, it would be gay men. And indeed, after the Stonewall Inn riot (1969), when patrons of a Greenwich Village bar resisted a police raid by throwing bricks and trash cans, there emerged a gay rights movement of astonishing magnitude.[24] A men's movement was another matter, though. To be sure, men's centers opened in consciousness-raised cities such as Berkeley and Boston, while countless informal support groups met each week in living rooms across the country, and several hundred men met each year in a national Conference on Men and Masculinity. But these results hardly measured up to announcements of "our own birth as a movement." A network is closer to the truth, a network that in 1983 acquired strength and structure in the form of the National Organization for Changing Men.[25]

While activists worked to organize the present and future, historians have been trying to reorganize the past. A few surveys and a few dozen monographs hardly constitute a discipline or a school or even a trend, but they form a start. One turns attention first to the surveys because they came first, playing the role of (literally) reconnaissance men. Unlike in established fields, where survey's "cover" evidence that has been abun-

---

23. Carol Tavris, "Men and Women Report Their Views on Masculinity," *Psychology Today* 10(January 1977):35. See also Anthony Pietropinto and Jacqueline Simenauer, *Beyond the Male Myth* (New York: Times Books, 1977).

24. John D'Emilio, *Sexual Politics, Sexual Communities: The Making of a Homosexual Minority in the United States, 1940–1970* (Chicago: University of Chicago Press, 1983), chap. 12.

25. Quotation from Sam Julty, "Creating a Movement for Change" (keynote address, Fourth Conference on Men and Masculinity, St. Louis, November 25, 1977, reprinted by *The Malebox* [Ann Arbor] n.d.). See also Robert Brannon, "Inside the Men's Movement," *Ms.* 10(October 1982):40–44; and Alan Gross, "The Men's Movement: Personal vs. Political," in *Social Movements of the Sixties and Seventies*, ed. Jo Freeman (New York: Longman, 1983). Also Men's Studies Newsletter no. 1(January 1984), published by the Men's Studies Task Group of the National Organization for Men.

dantly harvested by generations of scholars, in men's history they have set down a new conceptual framework and, through it, reviewed familiar evidence.

In *Be a Man!* for example, Peter Stearns offered a brisk, bold synthesis of how the roles of lower-class as well as middle-class men have changed in Western Europe and the United States since the eighteenth century. Using a variety of evidence from secondary and some primary sources, Stearns developed the theory that industrialization rigidified the definitions of gender roles and increasingly differentiated "masculine" activities and ideals from "feminine" ones.[26] Joe L. Dubbert performed a similar service in *A Man's Place,* which deftly traced the evolution of masculine stereotypes in the United States since 1830. Like Stearns, Dubbert analyzed the societal expectations that men were supposed to fulfill in their occupations, families, and personal prowess. Without pursuing a single large-scale theory, he continuously located the evolving expectations in a context of economic, political, military, and cultural events. He also tried — less successfully, I think — to explain men's attitudes in terms of their childhood upbringing.[27]

In *Him/Her/Self,* I studied the changing roles of middle-class Americans from 1890 to the present. Family and sexuality, work, war, and reform movements — these are the primary settings in which I analyzed "masculine" behavior and attitudes during the course of a fast-moving century. Along the way I reinterpreted certain events in terms of gender: World War I, for example, as an effort to reclaim "the strenuous life" that had been thwarted by a corporate bureaucratic world. In addition, the binocular focus on both genders created a wider context than simply masculinity, It showed how men performed their social scripts in response to women's scripts, and vice versa — a dialectical drama of the sexes.[28]

Supplementing these overviews, Joseph and Elizabeth Pleck provided two invaluable services by editing *The American Man.* First, they conveniently assembled 16 instructive articles spanning colonial to modern times and ranging from sodomy to Kit Carson to foreign policy. Second, their introduction made that most fundamental of historical revisions, a new periodization. The Plecks proposed dividing American men's history into four eras: agrarian patriarchy (1630–1820), the commercial age

26. Peter Stearns, *Be a Man! Males in Modern Society* (New York: Holmes & Meier, 1979).

27. Joe L. Dubbert, *A Man's Place: Masculinity in Transition* (Englewood Cliffs, N.J.: Prentice-Hall, 1980).

28. Filene, *Him/Her/Self.* (New York: Harcourt Brace Jovanovich, 1975; 2nd ed. 1986, Baltimore: Johns Hopkins University Press). See also Peter Filene, "Between a Rock and a Soft Place: A Century of American Manhood," *South Atlantic Quarterly* 84(Autumn 1985):339–355.

(1820–1860), the strenuous life (1861–1919), and companionate providing (1920–1965).[29]

With large, longitudinal strokes, these surveys have marked the terrain for scholars to explore. They point out private and semipublic sectors — the "secrets" of male experience. They suggest ways to reframe familiar events, such as wars and reform movements, in terms of gender. They speculate on the interaction between men's roles and historical trends, particularly industrialization and the closing of the frontier. Finally, they remind historians that gender involves two sexes, not one, and that the development of each gender's roles interacts with the development of the other's. Such is the agenda of men's history, and during the past decade or so a gratifying number of scholars have begun to put it into practice.

Private History

Attention has focused most fully and fruitfully on the private side of men's lives. Fathers and sons in colonial New England have received careful scrutiny from John Demos and Philip Greven.[30] To meet their southern counterparts, one can accompany Daniel Blake Smith, *Inside the Great House*.[31] For incisive interpretations of southern men's familial roles in the nineteenth century, one turns to studies by Eugene Genovese on slaves, Steven Stowe on planters, and Bertram Wyatt-Brown on the multilayered concept of "honor."[32] In the North, meanwhile, E. Anthony Rotundo read the letters and diaries of 50 middle-class men in order to define the meanings of manhood not only within families but also with respect to friendship, health, and success.[33] As a summary of research thus far and an

29. Elizabeth J. Pleck and Joseph H. Pleck, eds., *The American Man* (Englewood Cliffs, N.J.: Prentice-Hall, 1980).

30. John Demos, *A Little Commonwealth: Family Life in Plymouth Colony* (New York: Oxford University Press, 1970); Philip Greven, *Four Generations: Population, Land, and Family in Colonial Andover, Massachusetts* (Ithaca: Cornell University Press, 1970), and *The Protestant Temperament: Patterns of Child-Rearing, Religious Experience, and the Self in Early America* (New York: Knopf, 1977).

31. Daniel Blake Smith, *Inside the Great House: Family Life in Eighteenth Century Chesapeak Society* (Ithaca: Cornell University Press, 1980).

32. Eugene D. Genovese, *Roll, Jordan, Roll.: The World the Slaves Made* (New York: Pantheon, 1974); Steven Stowe, "The 'Touchiness' of the Gentleman Planter: The Sense of Esteem and Continuity in the Ante-Bellum South," *Psychohistory Review* 8(1979):6–15, and "Mastery and Doubt: Becoming a Man in the Planter Class" (paper delivered at the 74th annual meeting of the Organization of American Historians, Detroit, April 3, 1981), and "'A Deeply Interesting Sphere': Manhood in the Southern Planter Class" (paper delivered at the 99th annual meeting of the American Historical Association, San Francisco, December 28, 1983); and Bertram Wyatt-Brown, *Southern Honor: Ethics and Behavior in the Old South* (New York: Oxford University Press, 1982).

33. Rotundo, "Manhood."

invitation to further work, John Demos has written an invaluable essay on "The Changing Faces of Fatherhood."[34]

Between boyhood and manhood comes a stage that modern Americans have labeled *adolescence*. Joseph Kett has written a fine survey of evolving adolescent ideals and behavior from 1790 to 1970. Choosing a narrower focus and working with gender as a variable, David Allmendinger has portrayed the life within nineteenth-century New England preparatory schools, while Paula Fass has done the same for colleges in the 1920s.[35]

The roles of husbands and wives have been treated not only in the family histories mentioned above but also in books dealing intensively with marriage. John Mack Faragher has drawn on diaries, ballads, folklore, and other materials to create a vivid protrait of marital roles among mid-nineteenth-century farm families. Ellen K. Rothman has provided a sensitive reading of courtship during the past 150 years. At the other end of the cycle, Elaine Tyler May and Robert Griswold have studied divorce cases in the late Victorian era as barometers of male–female expectations and behavior.[36]

The last category of private life includes sexuality and health. Two path-breaking essays on the cultural definitions and functions of men's sexuality during the nineteenth century were written by Peter Cominos and Charles E. Rosenberg.[37] More recently, Peter Gay has published a large volume on sexuality among bourgeois Victorians in Europe and the United States, focusing heavily on women but not neglecting men. Although his Freudian perspective will deter some readers, Gay portrays ideas and feelings with persuasive complexity.[38] Twentieth-century sexu-

34. Demos, *Past, Present, and Personal: The Family and the Life Course in American History* (New York: Oxford University Press, 1986).

35. Joseph Kett, *Rites of Passage: Adolescence in America,1790 to the Present* (New York: Basic Books, 1976); David Allmendinger, Jr., *Paupers and Scholars: The Transformation of Student Life in Nineteenth-Century New England* (New York: St. Martin's Press, 1975); and Paula Fass, *The Damned and the Beautiful: American Youth in the 1920s* (New York: Oxford University Press, 1977).

36. John Mack Faragher, *Women and Men on the Overland Trail* (New Haven: Yale University Press, 1979); Ellen K. Rothman, *Hands and Hearts: A History of Courtship in America* (New York: Basic Books, 1984); Elaine Tyler May, *Great Expectations: Marriage and Divorce in Post-Victorian America* (Chicago: University of Chicago Press, 1980); and Robert L. Griswold, *Family and Divorce in California, 1850–1890: Victorian Illusions and Everyday Realities* (Albany: SUNY Press, 1982).

37. Charles E. Rosenberg, "Sexuality, Class and Role in Nineteenth-Century America," *American Quarterly* 35(May 1973):131–153; Peter T. Cominos, "Late-Victorian Sexual Respectability and the Social System," *International Review of Social History* 8(1963):18–48, 216–250.

38. Peter Gay, *Education of the Senses: The Bourgeois Experience, Victoria to Freud* (New York: Oxford University Press, 1984).

ality still awaits its historian. But homosexuality has emerged from the historical closet, first with two compilations of documents by Jonathan Katz, then with John D'Emilio's thorough monograph covering the homosexual movement since 1940.[39]

Health, illness, and the body have become important topics among women's historians, but the male side of the story has been almost entirely neglected. E. Anthony Rotundo has written an insightful article, Lois Banner has given men a chapter in her book on American beauty, and Nathan Hale discussed men's nervous breakdowns in his monograph on the early years of psychoanalysis.[40]

Semipublic History

Thus far, men's voluntary associations have been discussed in depth by only a few scholars, but their work certainly forms a fine precedent. David Macleod has devised a meticulous, probing study of the Boy Scouts and the YMCA, emphasizing aspects of character building, body building, and work.[41] As part of her complex study of middle-class family life in the mid nineteenth century, Mary Ryan offers important analysis of fraternal organizations and work roles among young men.[42]

Sports have become the subject of several historians lately, although manhood is rarely their explicit focus. Benjamin Rader provides a good survey of two centuries, while Donald Mrozek, Steven Riess, and Steven Gelber restrict themselves to the pre–World War I era. For a theoretical introduction to the cultural meanings of sports, one should consult Allen Guttmann's *From Ritual to Record*.[43]

39. Jonathan Katz, ed., *Gay American History: Lesbians and Gay Men in the U.S.A.: A Documentary Anthology* (New York: Crowell, 1976) and *Gay/Lesbian Almanac: A New Documentary* (New York: Harper & Row, 1983); and D'Emilio, *Sexual Politics*.

40. Rotundo, "Body and Soul: Changing Ideals of American Middle-Class Manhood, 1770–1920," *Journal of Social History* 16(Summer 1983):23–38; Lois Banner, *American Beauty* (New York: Knopf, 1983); and Nathan G. Hale, Jr., *Freud and the Americans: The Beginnings of Psychoanalysis in the United States, 1876–1917* (New York: Oxford University Press, 1971).

41. David I. Macleod, *Building Character in the American Boy: The Boy Scouts, YMCA, and Their Forerunners, 1870–1920* (Madison: University of Wisconsin Press, 1983).

42. Mary P. Ryan, *Cradle of the Middle Class: The Family in Oneida County, New York, 1790–1865* (New York: Cambridge University Press, 1981).

43. Benjamin Rader, *American Sports: From the Age of Folk Games to the Age of Spectators* (Englewood Cliffs, N.J.: Prentice-Hall, 1983); Donald J. Mrozek, *Sport and American Mentality, 1880–1910* (Knoxville: University of Tennessee Press, 1983); Steven A. Riess, *Touching Base: Professional Baseball and American Culture in the Progressive Era* (New York: Greenwood, 1980); Steven M. Gelber, "Working at Playing: The Culture of the Workplace and the Rise of Baseball," *Journal of Social History* 16(Summer 1983):3–22; Allen Guttmann, *From Ritual to Record: The Nature of Modern Sports* (New York: Columbia University Press, 1978).

Public History

The meanings and practice of work — that prime ingredient of manhood —have kept sociologists and psychologists very busy, but historians have thus far tended to neglect it. Daniel T. Rodgers examined *The Work Ethic in Industrial America,* but in terms of class more than gender. For the 1930s generation, and with full attention to gender, Glen Elder has written a path-breaking longitudinal study of lower-class and middle-class *Children of the Great Depression.* For the post-1950 era, we are given contrasting views, one by Joseph Veroff *et al.* looking at *The Inner American,* the other by Barbara Ehrenreich looking into *The Hearts of Men.* Whereas Veroff reported (from 20 years of national polls on work and family) a basic continuity in men's values, Ehrenreich discovered a breadwinners' "flight from commitment." [44]

Masculine images and heroism have stimulated a large number of studies. Two of the best are Theodore Greene's systematic analysis of heroes as portrayed in magazine articles and Joan Mellen's survey of masculinity as projected in Hollywood films. [45]

This rate of publication hardly rivals the avalanche in women's history, and one may suspect it never will. But predictions are risky. Who would have foretold in 1963 that Gerda Lerner would become head of a Ph.D. program in women's studies? Similarly, who can predict the future now that 35 colleges have instituted men's studies courses and, at the University of Southern California, a Program for the Study of Women and Men in Society? [46] Gradually we are unlearning the old past and writing one in which we underline the genders of pronouns and spell out the implications. Her history has been added to his, and slowly his to ours.

44. Daniel T. Rodgers, *The Work Ethic in Industrial America, 1850–1920* (Chicago: University of Chicago Press, 1978); Glen H. Elder, Jr., *Children of the Great Depression: Social Change in Life Experience* (Chicago: University of Chicago Press, 1974); Joseph Veroff, Elizabeth Douvan, and Richard Kulka, *The Inner American: A Self Portrait from 1957–1976 (New York: Basic Books, 1981);* and Barbara Ehrenreich, *The Hearts of Men: American Dreams and the Flight from Commitment* (New York: Doubleday Anchor, 1983).

45. Theodore P. Greene, *America's Heroes: The Changing Models of Success in American Magazines* (New York: Oxford University Press, 1970); and Joan Mellen, *Big Bad Wolves: Masculinity in the American Film* (New York: Pantheon, 1977).

46. *New York Times,* April 15, 1984, sec. 12, pp. 16–17.

5

The Contemporary "Crisis" of Masculinity in Historical Perspective

Michael S. Kimmel

Society is everywhere in conspiracy against the manhood of every one of its members.
— RALPH WALDO EMERSON, 1841

Isn't it time we destroyed the macho ethic? . . . Where has it gotten us all these thousands of years? Are we still going to have to be clubbing each other to death? Do I have to arm wrestle you to have a relationship with you as another male? Do I have to seduce her — just because she's a female? Can we not have a relationship on some other level? . . . I don't want to go through life pretending to be James Dean or Marlon Brando.
— JOHN LENNON, 1980

That men are today confused about what it means to be a "real man" — that masculinity is in "crisis" — has become a cultural commonplace, staring down at us from every magazine rack and television talk show in the country. Not only did Bruce Feirstein's affectionately satiric gloss, *Real Men Don't Eat Quiche,* sell millions of copies and produce several spinoffs, but scores of more serious books have jockeyed for visibility next to books advising women on becoming and remaining thinner, dumping inappropriate partners, and being successful career women. According to these books, American men are increasingly bumping up against the limits of traditional concepts of masculinity, attempting to push beyond the rigid role prescriptions that constrain male behavior and prevent men from more fully expressing intimacy and vulnerability, becoming more devoted and loving fathers, more sensitive lovers, and more compassionate friends to both women and other men.

One reason men are still confused is that these advice manuals and "pop" psychological analyses reproduce precisely the problem they are intended to cure. Most adopt a simplistic formulation of "sex roles" to which males and females are assigned, into which boys and girls struggle to fit, and out of which men and women are trying to break free. But this model implies a vaguely ahistorical inevitability, which is contradicted by its emphasis on cultural relativity; in each culture the researcher can identify a static sex-role container into which all biological males and females are forced to fit. As such, the paradigm ignores the extent to which our conceptions of masculinity and femininity — the content of the male or female sex role — is relational, that is, the product of gender relations that are historically and socially conditioned. Masculinity and femininity are relational constructs; the definition of either depends on the definition of the other. The sex-role paradigm has been critically discussed and evaluated in detail.[1] These writers, though, tend to stress problems with the model as it applies to the study of gender in general, or of women in particular. Little, if any, attention has been paid specifically to men and masculinity as a social scientific problematic, which is my intention here.

The sex-role socialization model is ahistorical in another sense. Almost all sex-role research focuses on attributes, indicating behavioral or attitudinal traits associated with the role. Changes in sex roles thus appear as changes in the list of traits or attitudes associated with masculinity or femininity. But masculinity and femininity are more the products of role *enactments;* instead of specifying traits, one might detail the ways in which people negotiate their roles, the historically fluid and variable enactments of specific role prescriptions. Such a focus on gender relations allows articulation not only of traits at separate times but also the processes by which the changes occur.

The sex-role paradigm also minimizes the extent to which gender relations are based on power. Not only do men as a group exert power over women as a group, but the historically derived definitions of masculinity and femininity reproduce those power relations. Masculinity becomes associated with those traits that imply authority and mastery, femininity with those traits that suggest passivity and subordination. By undervaluing the historical and social bases for gender relations, then, the sex-role paradigm can reproduce the very problems it seeks to understand.

1. See, e.g., J. Gerson and K. Peiss, "Boundaries, Negotiation, Consciousness: Reconceptualizing Gender Relations," *Social Problems* 32, no. 4(April 1985):317–331. M. Gould and R. Kern-Daniels, "Toward a Sociological Theory of Gender and Sex," *American Sociologist* 12(1977):182–189. H. Z. Lopata and B. Thorne, "On the Term 'Sex Roles'," *Signs* 3(1978):718–721. J. Shapiro, "'Women's Studies': A Note on the Perils of Markedness," *Signs* 7(1982):717–721. J. Stacey and B. Thorne, "The Missing Feminist Revolution in Sociology," *Social Problems* 32, no. 4(1985):301–316. D. Tresemer, "Assumptions Made about Gender Roles" in *Another Voice: Feminist Perspectives on Social Life and Social Science*, ed. M. Millman and R. Von Kanter (Garden City, N.Y.: Anchor), pp. 308–339.

An emphasis on gender relations as historically and socially constructed also sheds different light on another problem. The sex-role paradigm posits two fixed, static, and mutually exclusive role containers with no interpenetration. Further, bipolar mutual exclusivity of sex roles reinforces oppositional assumptions about masculinity and femininity; although defined in reference to abstract ideals, sex roles reinforce the popular notions of the "otherness" of the "opposite" sex.

I believe, therefore, that the sex-role socialization model is theoretically inadequate on conceptual grounds. But its explanatory weakness is best revealed when one looks at those historical moments in which gender issues assume a prominent position in the public consciousness, moments of gender confusion and the vigorous reassertion of traditional gender roles against serious challenges to inherited configurations—moments, we might say, of "crisis" in gender relations, historical moments not unlike our own.

In this paper, I examine two such historical eras, two precursors to the contemporary crisis of masculinity, to explicate the larger social and historical field in which such crises develop. By looking at Restoration England, 1688–1714, and the United States two centuries later, 1880–1914, we can identify how historical and social changes create the conditions for gender crisis. To the historical sociologist, these crises occur at specific historical junctures, when structural changes transform the institutions of personal life such as marriage and the family, which are sources of gender identity. As a result, though the battles may be fought out in sexual discourse, ultimately, Smith-Rosenberg reminds us, "social, not sexual disorder lies at the heart of these discourses"; and this because "when the social fabric is rent in fundamental ways, bodily and familial imagery will assume ascendency."[2]

One sociological implication of this gender relations alternative to the sex-role paradigm is that it allows the observer to specify not only the reconstitution of gender over time but also the *directionality* of changes in gender relations. The historical evidence suggests that while both masculinity and femininity are socially constructed within historical context of gender relations, definitions of masculinity are historically *reactive* to changing definitions of femininity. Such a claim runs counter to traditional formulations of gender, such as David Riesman's comment in *The Lonely Crowd* that "characterological change in the West seems to occur first with men."[3] Instead, my argument suggests that since men benefit from inherited definitions of masculinity and femininity, they would be

2. C. Smith-Rosenberg, *Disorderly Conduct: Visions of Gender in Victorian America* (New York: Knopf, 1985), pp. 268, 90.
3. D. Riesman, *The Lonely Crowd* (New Haven: Yale University Press, 1950), p. 18.

unlikely to initiate change. In fact, I would argue that men as a group have benefited from the sex-role socialization *model* that has governed behavioral science's treatment of gender, since it uses masculinity as the normative standard of reference and maximizes the distance between the two genders, while it minimizes the extent to which these definitions reproduce existing power relations, are historically variable, and are therefore open to challenge. The articulation of new versions of masculinity in late-seventeenth- and early-eighteenth-century England and in the late-nineteenth- and early-twentieth-century United States suggests the ways in which larger structural changes set in motion those microsocial processes that led women to redefine their roles, the critical events that provoke the historical "crises" of masculinity.

SOCIAL CHANGE IN RESTORATION ENGLAND, 1688–1714

In the decades following the Glorious Revolution, enormous structural changes, set in motion during the century, began to resonate in the English family and in relations between men and women. Several important, large-scale changes converged on the late-seventeenth-century household, prompting the renegotiation of gender relations, of sexuality and marriage, and a reexamination of the notion of masculinity.

One crucial set of structural changes hinged on the transformation of the economy in general and on the organization of work in particular. Individual handicraft production by independent artisans was declining in the cities, as artisans were "entering upon their long agony in competition with bigger economic units."[4] In the countryside, larger units became increasingly common, as land ownership was consolidated by a new wave of enclosures toward the end of the century. The small, independent farmer, the yeomanry, was "disappearing,"[5] and waves of rural migrants were forced off the land and streamed into London and other cities. "The country is poor, the nation is racked . . . and the humble gentlemen is half-starved," observed Sir Charles Sedley in the House of Commons in November 1691.[6]

Concentration of land ownership and the decline of craft production combined with mercantilist economic doctrines in transforming London

---

4. C. Hill, *The Century of Revolution, 1603–1714* (New York: Norton, 1961), p. 308.
5. Ibid.
6. Cited in J. H. Plumb, *The Growth of Political Stability in England, 1675–1725* (Harmondsworth, England: Penguin, 1967), p. 136.

from a capital city to a "focal point," a "centre of world trade."[7] The ballooning population of the capital was even further exacerbated by late-century changes in the treatment of the poor. Before the Civil War, the Royal Council had often intervened in the localities and provided poor relief and some small measure of security. After 1660, however, "the problem of poverty was left almost entirely to the Justices of the Peace and to private charity,"[8] which meant that the poor were left to fend for themselves. Countless numbers, therefore, descended on London in hopes of finding work, charity, or both.

These economic changes add up to a profound loss of occupational autonomy experienced by a large number of men. Artisans, craftsmen, small shopkeepers, yeomen farmers (copyholders), and other independent tradesmen and professionals suffered a sever erosion of autonomy in the organization of work. This loss of autonomy may have been ironically abetted by ideological changes that stressed the increasing importance of the individual and political changes that enlarged the franchise. The rise of classical liberal theory at the end of the century — especially in the work of Locke, and earlier, Hobbes and Harrington — indicated a shift "from the collectivity, whether kin or nuclear family, to the individual"[9] and provided an ideological grounding for capitalist accumulation, as well as a celebration of individual freedom. Simultaneously, in the late seventeenth century, the "electorate grew very rapidly" so that despite the exclusion of women, children, and the laboring poor — the electorate included less than 1/30 of the population — Plumb claims that "for the first time in English history [an electorate] had come into being."[10]

Even though these changes "brought no widening of the franchise,"[11] it is more important perhaps that contemporaries believed that they augured substantive change. Just when so many Englishmen were losing their economic autonomy, ideological shifts indicated that they had gained increased individual independence. One psychological outcome of such contradictory information was a confused and amorphous self-blaming, in which English men had neither relief nor justification for rebellion. There remained "no political outlet for the passions and resentments of those whom their betters expected to work harder for low wages in deplorable

7. R. Lockyer, *Tudor and Stuart Britain, 1471–1714* (New York: St. Martin's, 1964), p. 435; and Hill, *Century of Revolution*, p. 266.

8. Lockyer, *Tudor and Stuart Britain*, p. 445.

9. L. Stone and J. F. Stone, *An Open Elite? England, 1540–1880* (New York: Oxford University Press, 1984), p. 402.

10. Plumb, *Political Stability in England*, pp. 45, 40.

11. Hill, *Century of Revolution*, p. 297.

living conditions,"[12] and there was no one, it seemed, to blame but themselves.

FAMILY AND GENDER RELATIONS
IN LATE-SEVENTEENTH-CENTURY ENGLAND

These structural changes resonated with changes in social relations, especially relations within the family. The rise of literacy and individualism, and the decline of infant mortality and the traditional patriarchal family, sparked a renegotiation of the relations between women and men. Inspired by individualism, men, at least of the upper classes, "now pleased themselves by marrying later; by marrying brides of their choice . . . by staying unmarried altogether if they were so inclined . . . and by limiting births in order to ease the strain on their wives and to improve the quality of care devoted to their children."[13] Schofield and Wrigley calculate that in the second half of the seventeenth century, as much as 22.9% of the population of both sexes between ages 40 and 44 had never been married.[14]

Even though Protestant doctrine since the Reformation had assigned to the husband the role of spiritual leader of the family — a role that had formerly belonged to the parish priest — which tended to buttress patriarchal authority, Hill also notes that "the close knit patriarchal community was being undermined in the same decades as the patriarchal theory of monarchy collapsed. The wives of the poor were becoming domestic drudges for their absent husbands rather than partners in a family workshop."[15] Women's slow entry into the world of work was also seen as a threat to continued male domination; women's wages "were regarded as a threat to male authority, a temptation to female luxury and indulgence, and an incitement to female independence."[16] Economically, politically, and socially, "women were chipping away at the edges of traditional ex-

12. Ibid.

13. Stone and Stone, *An Open Elite?*, p. 402.

14. R. S. Schofield and E. A. Wrigley, *The Population History of England, 1541–1871* (Cambridge, Ma.: Harvard University Press), p. 176. By the second half of the eighteenth century, less than 9% were unmarried, so the percentages had shifted from 1 in 4 to 1 in 10 in less than a century.

15. Hill, *Century of Revolution*, p. 308.

16. N. McKendrick, "Home Demand and Economic Growth: A New View of the Role of Women and Children in the Industrial Revolution," in *Historical Perspectives: Studies in English Thought and Society in Honour of J. H. Plumb* (London: Europa, 1974), p. 167.

pectations," a process that made men increasingly anxious.[17] Finally, the reign of Queen Anne (1702–1714) may have increased the male–female tension, since Regency governments were often politically vulnerable and brought gender issues into the spotlight.

One ought not be surprised, therefore, to discover a gender crisis in late-seventeenth- and early-eighteenth-century England. A virtual pamphlet war erupted as both men and women attempted to renegotiate the structure of gender relations and develop new definitions of masculinity and femininity.[18] Interestingly, much of this pamphlet war was carried out within a specific form of discourse, the traditional satiric "comforts," "joys," or "plagues" of a particular status, and pamphlets that provide answers to these satires. Satire was "a fertile field for reframing what is most frightening into something comic,"[19] but readers might be misled assuming all are viciously sarcastic, since a few, such as *The Fifteen Comforts of Whoring*, are serious celebrations of the practice.[20]

What were the objects of contention between men and women, the themes of the pamphlet war? For one thing, women were extremely ambivalent about marriage. Marriage provided the only legitimate status for adult women and the foundation of economic activity; "economic organization was domestic organization," writes Laslett.[21] The only question that mattered was that asked of women in the inns of court: "Are you a maid, a

---

17. F. Nussbaum, *The Brink of All We Hate: English Satires on Women, 1660–1750* (Lexington, Ky.: University Press of Kentucky, 1983), p. 9.

18. Earlier pamphlet battles had raised these issues. Jane Anger's *The Protection for Women* (1589), Constantia Munda's *The Worming of a Mad Dog* (1617), and Mary Tattlewell and Joan Hit-him-Home's *The Woman's Sharp Revenge* (1640) are particularly interesting examples of proto-feminist responses to gender relations in the late sixteenth and early seventeenth centuries. Anger insisted on a war between man and women, arguing that "there is a continual deadly hatred between the wild boar and tame hounds; I would there were the like between women and men unless they amend their ways." And both Munda and Tattlewell suggested that women were not only equal to men but superior; Munda notes that woman is "the greatest part of the lesser world," while Tattlewell insists that women are "either men's betters or their equals" (which isn't very difficult, since she claims that men are "lime twigs of lust and Schoolmasters of Folly"). And even in the first part of the century, women were seen as in possession of a sexuality; Newstead implies, in fact, that women's chastity is more commendable than men's, since she is more subject to imperious physical desire, to the "riotous pleasures of their bodies." And Robert Burton asked in 1621, "of woman's unnatural lust, what country, what village, does not complain?"

19. Nussbaum, *Brink of All We Hate*, p. 167.

20. This form of pamphlet has a venerable tradition in England, dating back at least to the translation of Antoine de la Sale's well-known and popular French pamphlet *Quinze Joyes de mariage* (1603), which was translated into English by Thomas Decker as *Bachelor's Banquet* that same year and was continually revised by different authors.

21. P. Laslett, *The World We Have Lost* (New York: Scribner's, 1965), p. 4.

widow, or a wife?"[22] Marriage also increasingly appeared as a form of
sexual slavery, reinforcing economic inequality and denying autonomy to
women. "I fear you would debauch me into that dull slave call'd a Wife,"
observes one character in Aphra Behn's *The Feign'd Courtezans*,[23] while the
anology is made explicit in *An Essay in Defense of the Female Sex* (1696),
whose author suggests that "women, like our Negroes in our Western
plantations, are born slaves, and live prisoners all their lives."

Women suggested several remedies to make marriage more palatable.
Noting a "male shortage" — one observer estimated 13 women for every
10 men in London in 1694 — [24] women insisted that men not delay in
marrying them, and petitioned Parliament in 1693 for an annual tax on all
men who remained single after they turned 21 years old. This disincentive
to bachelorhood, women believed, would encourage men to legitimate
their (women's) economic existence, virtually to call them into being in the
body politic (cf. *The Petition of the Ladies,* 1693). Another pamphlet, in
1690, suggested that the neglect of marriage threatened the destruction of
the nation, since nearly half the population were dying single and a third of
the others marrying far too late. *Marriage Promoted* also supported obligatory marriage for men by age 21.

But the marriage contract these women sought was to be based on new
principles. One pamphlet, *The Duty of a Husband* (1706), written in response to Samuel Johnson's *The Duty of a Wife* (1693), challenged the old
analogy of house and kingdom:

> *Therefore tis plain this mutual love*
> *Commanded is by heaven above*
> *And Man in Duty is Confined*
> By sacred Laws to be more kind
> And not like Tyrant rule his Wife
> As if she was his Slave for Life.

Marriage was like the political nation: If the latter was now governed not
by absolute monarchy but by contract, so too should the former be governed. Marriages ought to be equal, the author argued, "[f]or Woman has
an equal share / At least on what depends on Care / Of household accidental things / Which comfort and relief doth bring." Women were angered
by their second-class status; "[a]s if we were for nothing else designed / But
made, like puppets, to divert mankind," as Lady Chudleigh put it.[25]

22. Cited in A. Fraser, *The Weaker Vessel* (New York: Knopf, 1984), p. 467.
23. Ibid., p. 271.
24. Cf. Nussbaum, *Brink of All We Hate*, p. 9.
25. Fraser, *Weaker Vessel*, p. 328.

Some women saw their slavery in dramatically sexual terms, as in *The Lost Maiden-Head* (1691):

> —*But I forget—too soberly I Rave.*
> *They in their heighth of Pride—*
> *Think Woman only made to be their Slave*
> *The very Sex, a Brothel built by Jove*
> *To hold their superfluitities of Love:*
> *A decent ditch when the Tide runs too high*
> *By prudent nature made to drain it dry*
> *Good serviceable Beasts of Burden, when*
> *The Journey's o're, turn'd out to graze agen.*

The explicitly sexual imagery in this passage is not accidental, for women perceived marriage as the only legitimate source of sexual pleasure, which required greater equality. The author of *An Answer to the Pleasure of the Single Life* (1701) supports marriage precisely because it provides regular sex for women:

> *Thus single Sots, who wedlock vainly fight*
> *Are slaves to Lust, both Morning, Noon, and Night*
> *Ruin their health, their Honour and estate*
> *And buy Repentence at a cursed rate*
> *While lawful wedded couples spend their times*
> *In happy charming Pleasures without crimes . . .*

And women actually enjoyed the sex: "While happy Man and Wife in Love agree / And both unite in Mutual Harmonie." No surprise, then, that one female pamphleteer suggested that "a levelling of Marriages is the most Reasonable Thing in the World" (*The Levellers*, 1703).

Men responded vigorously to women's efforts to renegotiate marriage relationships. Their satires, Nussbaum writes,

assume woman's lust, inconstancy, and vanity; they curse her fecundity, her sexual appetite, and her ability to disrupt men's expectations and illusions, while a simultaneous impulse describes her sexual autonomy and power. The satires deplore women's attractiveness and their ability to feminize men even as they lament men's self-hatred and emasculation. At the same time that the satirist narrator wallows in the satiric myth of impotence as a lover, however, the force of his words creates a potent weapon. . . . The popular satires of the Restoration transfer the responsibility for love to woman, and more and more to the sex as a whole, as an abstraction that can be attacked without so much reference to the male's own feelings of love.[26]

26. Nussbaum, *Brink of All We Hate*, p. 75.

In their responses to the women's petition to Parliament, *A Humble Remonstrance of the Bachelors* (1693?), men accuse women of inversion of the gender hierarchy, as they "not only dispute the Superiority with Men, but even pretend to the right of Conquest over them; for their Grandmother Eve, they say, triumphed over the weakness of our great Grandfather Adam in Paradise." The men claimed they were unwilling to marry because women have become so demanding as to render it economically unwise. One woman pamphleteer noted that "[a] good Estate and Virtue makes a Man Beautiful in any Garb," since "matrimony is become a matter of Money" *(The Levellers)*. One male pamphleteer had a woman admit that "he that bids most shall speed soonest; and so he hath money, we care not a fart for his honesty."[27] Men also accused women, especially widows, of luring men to the altar with their wealth; a contemporary ballad had it that

> *Young maidens are bashful, but widows are bold,*
> *They tempt poor young men with their silver and gold,*
> *For love nowadays for money is sold,*
> *If she be worth a treasure no matter how old.*[28]

To the women's petition, the authors of the bachelors' remonstrance (1693) noted:

> A Courtship, as the Ladies are pleased to order it, is now the greatest
> Pennance any Man in the World can undergo. We must swear as many
> Oaths as would serve one of His Majesties largest garrisons for a
> Twelve-Month, till we are believed. We must treat them like Goddesses,
> lie prostrate at their feet, make Presents so expensive and numerous that
> perhaps the Wife's portion will scarce make amends for what the Mistress
> exorted from us.

Women claimed that men were reluctant to marry when they could always visit prostitutes in the cities:

> I am ashamed and Blush to Speak it how many lewd Creatures there are
> of our Sex both in the Town and Country; were there not so many
> whores there would be more wives. The vicious sort of Men are by them
> kept from Marrying; for 'tis mere Virtue must confine a Man to a
> Married State, where he has an uninterrupted Converse with Womankind
> as Seldom and as often as he pleases, without confinement to any
> particular Person or Temper. *(The Levellers)*

27. Cited in A. MacFarlane, *Marriage and Love in England, 1300–1840* (New York: Blackwell, 1986), p. 162.
28. Ibid.

But, the men counter, they only visit prostitutes because virtuous women resist their sexual advances:

> 'Tis a sad truth, we confess it, the number of these Interlopers is very grievous; and yet tis as sad a truth that the Petitioning Ladies have occassioned it. Let them but leave quarreling about *Jointures* and carry a little more Christian Compliance about them, and the other Fry would disappear in the way of trade, only used for the Convenience of Readier Change. But those obdurate females would have every Person of Quality who keeps it in his own defense, pay a good swinging fine to the government. *(Remonstrance of the Bachelors)*

As is evident in this brief skirmish, much of the war between the sexes in Restoration England was about sexuality. Men frequently wrote eloquent defenses of premarital sex. Since "[t]ravellers, before a Horse they buy / His speed, his Paces and his Temper try" (*The Pleasures of a Single Life*, 1701), why can't men and women sample each other before marriage? One female pamphleteer, at least, seems to be willing; in a rather steamy passage she pines:

> *Ah tis my misfortune not to meet*
> *Any man that would my passion greet*
> *He with balmy kisses stop'd my Breath*
> *In which one could not die a better death*
> *Stroke my Breasts, those Mountains of Delight*
> *Whose very touch would fire an anchorite*
> *Or let your wanton palm a little stray*
> *And dip thy fingers in the milky way:*
> *On having raiz'd me, let me gently fall*
> *The trumpets sound, so Mortal have at all.*
> *Why wish I this bliss? I wish in vain*
> *Of my Plaguy burthen do complain*
> *Sooner may I see whole nations dead*
> *I find one to get my Maidenhead.*
> *(Fifteen Plagues of a Maiden-Head, 1707)*

Later, the author confesses that as soon as she lies down to sleep, "I dream I'm mingling with some Man my Thighs / Till something more than ordinary does rise." And another maiden dreams of sexual gratification in *The Maiden's Dream* (1705), but can obtain it only by being taken duplicitously:

> *Once slumb'ring as I lay within my Bed,*
> *No Creature with me, but my Maidenhead,*

> *Methought a Gallant came, (as Gallants they can do*
> *Much with Young Ladies, and with old ones too)*
> *He woo'd, he Su'd, at length he sped,*
> *Marry'd methought we were, and went to Bed.*
> *He turn'ed to me, got up, with that I squeak'd,*
> *Blush'd, and cry'd oh? and so awak'd.*
> *It wou'd have vexed a Saint, my Flesh did burn,*
> *To be so near, and miss so good a Turn.*
> *Oh! cruel Dream, why did you thus deceive me,*
> *To shew me Heaven, and then, in Hell, to leave me?*

But no sooner do women attempt to claim sexual agency, to seek sexual gratification actively, than they are restrained either by traditional morality—

> *Our thoughts like tinder apt to fire*
> *Are often caught with loving kind desire*
> *But custom does such rigid laws impose,*
> *We must not for our lives the thing disclose.*
> *If one of us a lowly youth has seen,*
> *And straight some tender thoughts to feel begin . . .*
> *Custom and modesty, much more severe*
> *Strictly forbid our passion to declare.*
>
> (*Sylvia's Complaint*, 1688)

—or by men's reversal of the traditional axiom of women's passive asexuality. Women are accused of sexual insatiability. The author of *The Bachelor's Banquet* (1709) suggests that women are both sexual and insatiable, that they "love to sport in Bed"; while the author of *Fifteen Comforts of Matrimony* (1706) insists that their "insatiate fire" leads women to sleep with other men, get pregnant by them, and actively seek sexual gratification where they can find it. The author of *The Fifteen Comforts of a Wanton Wife* (1706–1707) accuses women of draining men both economically and sexually: "Containing an Unequal Dividend / His Business is to get and Hers to spend / If he's unable to supply her lust / She'll take such care of that, another must."

In response, women claimed that they were frequently deceived by men who promised to marry them and then abandoned them after receiving sexual favors. As the author of *The Lost Maiden-Head* (1691) laments:

> *A favour'd Lover who one fatal day*
> *When she and all her Vertue slumbring lay*
> *Stole both her Heart and Maidenhead away*
> *She wak't and found him gone, while shame, disgrace*

> *Vexation and Despair supply'd his place*
> *With Daggers fill'd her Breast, with Blushes fill'd her Face*
> *While he to every Tavern-Friend will boast*
> *How small a Price so great a Conquest cost*
> *How soon, how willingly the Town was lost.*

Men are accused of seduction and then abandonment when the woman becomes pregnant. The author of *The Whores and Bawds Answer to the Fifteen Comforts of Whoring* (1706) writes, for example, that

> *No sooner does the Maid arrive to years*
> *And she the pleasures of Conjunction hears,*
> *But straight her Maidenhead a Tic-Toc runs*
> *To get her like, in Daughters or in Sons;*
> *Upon some Jolly Lad she casts her eye*
> *And with some am'rous gestures by the by;*
> *She gives him great encouragement to take*
> *His fill of Love, and swears that for his sake*
> *She soon shall die, which makes the Youth so hot*
> *To get about the Maiden's Honey pot,*
> *That promising her Marriage and the like*
> *They both a bargain very quickly strike*
> *And Rubbers often take till she does prove*
> *With child, then, then [sic] he bids adieu to love*
> *And ere she's brought to bed away does Creep*
> *For fear he should the Wenches Urchin keep.*

Men's responses often debated the coercive quality of women's claims of rape; while Sylvia is furious after having been raped in *The Lost Maiden-Head*, one response in *Restored Maidenhead* (1691) argues that she really wanted it: "O Crime, abhorred! no sign of discontent / No least effort the Robbery to prevent / Surely he stole her with her own consent."

When women claim equality of desire, men often invert it and turn desire against the women themselves. But even here, women can salvage an angry equality in the spread of sexually transmitted diseases; *The Whores and Bawd's Asnswer* (1706) asserts: "Was only tit for tat, so if the Men / Do Clap the Whores, and Whores Clap them again / Tis only tit for tat; tis very true / What's good for Goose is good for gander too."

MASCULINITY IN CRISIS IN ENGLAND, 1688–1714

Changes in gender relations — efforts to renegotiate marriage, the family, and sexuality — provide the background, the context for a change in the

definition of masculinity in Restoration England. As the structural bases
for gender relations had shifted and were thrown into disarray, the meaning of masculinity itself was brought into question, debated, and in part
redefined. Women's assertion of sexual agency, of an equality of desire,
and of equal rights within the marriage, inspired men to abandon traditional roles within the family, just as changes in the organization of work
and political changes eroded their economic autonomy and the traditional
system of fixed political statuses in precapitalist society. Men's abandonment of their traditional roles, eschewing marriage for example, was the
subject of several satiric pamphlets. But more than simply marriage,
women were concerned that men were abandoning masculinity itself,
becoming soft, urbanized, and weak; in short, women were concerned that
just as they challenged their traditional female roles, men were jumping to
embrace precisely those female roles. One pamphlet (*The Levellers*, 1703)
complains:

> The Men, they are grown full as Effeminate as the Women; we are
> Rivall'd by 'em even in the Fooleries peculiar to our Sex; They Dress like
> Anticks and Stage-Players, and are as ridiculous as Monkeys; they sit in
> monstrous long Periwigs, like so many owles in Ivy Bushes, and esteem
> themselves more upon the Reputation of being a Beau, than on the
> Substantial Qualifications, of Honour, Courage, Learning, and
> Judgment. . . . If you heard 'em talk you'd think yourself at a Gossiping
> at Dover, or that you heard the learned Confabulation of the Boys in the
> Piazzas of Christs Hospital.

One particularly interesting pamphlet, *Mondus Foppensis: or, The Fop
Displayed* (1691), outlines several telling indications of the "feminization"
of late-seventeenth-century English men. While it is impossible to discern
exact numbers of men displaying these behaviors, this and other pamphlets reveal an emergent public discourse on the nature of masculinity and a
concern over men's abandonment of traditionally male behaviors. For one
thing, the pamphlet evidences a concern that men are cross-dressing: "I
could produce ye Emperours/That sate in Women's dress whole hours"
— and wearing makeup:

> *Hard case to blame the Ladies Washes*
> *When Men are come to mend their faces*
> *Yet some there are such Women grown*
> *They cann't be by their faces known.*

And that they are more concerned with hairstyle than substance: "How is the Barber held divine/That can a Perriwig Carine!" The adoption of these traditionally female preoccupations by men is part, the author tells us, of a more general embrace of vanity: "Far must more time Men trifling Wast/E'er their soft bodies can be drest/The Looking Glass hangs just before/And each o'th' Legs requires an hour."

This portrait of the "feminized" man suggests a deep fear of male abandonment of traditional roles. Men were coming to resemble women on the surface, the pamphlet argues, because they were coming to resemble women's sociosexual affective patterns. Men are not only abandoning their roles within the family but are abandoning women altogether. While this fear of male homosexuality simmers below the surface of the entire text, it emerges explicitly in one passage:

> *Ladies this was ill luck, but you*
> *Have much the worser of the two;*
> *The world is chang'd I know not how,*
> *For men Kiss Men, not Women now;*
> *And your neglected lips in vain*
> *Of smuggling Jack and Tom complain:*
> *One Man to lick the other's Cheek;*
> *And only what renews the shame*
> *Of J. the First and Buckingham:*[29]
> *He, true it is, his Wives Embraces fled*
> *To slabber his lov'd Ganimede;*
> *But to employ, those lips were made*
> *For Women in Gomorrha's Trade*
> *Bespeaks the Reason ill design'd*
> *Of railing thus 'gainst Woman-kind:*
> *For those that Loves as Nature teaches,*
> *That had not rather kiss the Breeches*
> *Of Twenty Women, than to lick*
> *The bristles of one Male dear Dick?*

The "new man" of Restoration England was transformed into a feminized, feminine "invert," as vain, petty, and pretty as any woman. Interestingly, accusations of pettiness, vanity, and feminity then became rhetorical weapons of both male and female pamphleteers in the renegotiations of gender relations, just as accusations of "masculinization" also fueled this sexual discourse, as in women accusing men of being sexual brutes and men accusing women of insatiable lust.

29. The reference to James I and Buckingham may be obscure to the contemporary reader, but everyone in late-seventeenth-century England knew of James's promiscuity and sexual orientation, and knew that his relationship with his closest aide was more than platonic.

Contemporary commentators were conscious of how several of the
structural changes in English society had produced the conditions for
these changes, although they did not have the historical distance, perhaps,
to disaggregate these changes into several component parts that we might
identify as causal. To the late-seventeenth-century mind, however, the city
represented, encapsulated, these structural transformations; urbanization
was the consummate expression of structural transformation. For one
thing, the city was the location of vice, uncontrolled and possible
uncontrollable:

> For let the Church be empty as it will
> You'll see the Playhouse and the Tavern fill
> Whole afternoons, whole nights they'll squander there
> Yet can't spare one poor minute on't for Pray'r.
> This is the Sum of a Licentuious town
> Where lewdness is into example grown.
>
> (Fifteen Comforts of Whoring, 1706)

In the city women can seek their pleasures as well as men, and once
tempted, they are unable to resist its magnetic lure. In *The Fifteen Comforts
of a Wanton Wife* (1706–1707), the male writer quotes his wife, who,
caught cheating on him, faces the confrontation with a strong assertion of
her commitment to continue her behavior:

> Of such foul deeds my Conscience now is clear
> But this I tell you for your further ease
> Where I have been, I'll do when'ere I please
> Do you think I'll be kept in like a Drone
> While others reap the pleasures of the Town.

Not only does the city liberate women, turning them into wanton, disre-
spectful, and arrogant wenches, but the city feminizes men, removing
them from the land (the source of productive labor and hence diligence
and masculine discipline) and exposing these rough-hewn rural men to the
effete life of the fop. In part, the city represents other cultures, more
feminized and more refined; travel to other countries, especially France, is
to be shunned. Of course, this provides the occasion for a bit of xenopho-
bic anti-French sentiment to surface, linking feminization to treason and
traditional masculinity to patriotism:

> So strangely does Parisian air
> Change English Youth, that half a year
> Makes em forget all Native Custome

To bring French modes, and Gallic Lust home;
Nothing will these Apostates please
But Gallic health and French disease.
In French their Quarrels and their fears
Their Joys they publish and their Cares
In French they quarrel and in French
Mon coeur, they cry, to paltry Wench.

And France is blamed for gender confusion; *A Satyr Against France* (1691) accused the French of being noisy, talkative, gossipy, and passive:

'Tis to that Fopish Nation that we owe
Those antick Dresses that Equip a Beau:
So many sorts of Riggins dress the Elf
Himself sometimes does hardly know himself.

Such passages bring us full circle, returning to the structural changes that had begun to tear at traditional, precapitalist English society, suggesting that geopolitical tensions increasingly threatened the stability of English society. (England was at war with France for much of the late seventeenth and early eighteenth centuries in the War of the Spanish Succession, and each side indulged in a favorite pastime of rival nations: questioning the virility of the other side.) What we have observed is that structural changes — changes in economic organization, especially in the structure of work, urbanization, political enfranchisement, and other changes — provoked a crisis in gender relations, expressed as protofeminist claims by women to renegotiate marriage and sexuality along new lines and by antifeminist men to retain and preserve traditional gender arrangements. Simultaneously, the reformulation of gender prompted women to challenge men's abandonment of their traditional role and to suggest that men were, in fact, abandoning masculinity in the wake of women's claims. Abandoning masculinity implied sexual treason, which is only a special case of political treason, to these women pamphleteers. If men were feminized, they might as well be French, for they had forsaken their English birthright and their obligations as freeborn English men.

THE CHALLENGE TO MANHOOD
IN LATE-NINETEENTH-CENTURY AMERICA

The early nineteenth century provided a fertile environment for an expansive American manhood. Geographic expansion — the taming of the

West, the "pacification" of its native population, and dramatic urban growth—combined with rapid economic growth, and the development of an industrial infrastructure to fuel a virile optimism about social possibilities. The Jacksonian assault on effete European bankers and the frighteningly "primitive" Native American population grounded identity in a "securely achieved manhood."[30]

By midcentury, though, "the walls of the male establishment began to crack," as masculinity was increasingly threatened by the twin forces of industrialization and the spread of political democracy.[31] The postbellum era witnessed several important structural changes that transformed the social institutions in which gender relations were negotiated and that led of profound changes in the cultural conception of masculinity. For one thing, western expansion came to an end as the frontier closed by the end of the century. The open West had signaled freedom to men:

> The possibilities for men who wanted to experience autonomy, to leave home and go not only to a new place for them but a new place for anyone, were enormous in 19th century America: no checks on movement horizontally and formally, and none vertically for white men, together with a typing of life style that strenuously encouraged motion, from country to town, job to job, ambition to ambition, and the most striking area for this motion was the West.[32]

But that era was over. "For nearly three centuries," wrote Frederick Jackson Turner in 1896, "the dominant fact of American life has been expansion. And now the frontier is gone and with its going has closed the first period of American history."

Rapid industrialization in late-nineteenth-century America radically transformed men's relationship with their work. The independent artisan, the autonomous small farmer, the small shopkeeper were disappearing. Before the Civil War, 88% of American men were farmers or self-employed businessmen; by 1870, that figure had dropped to 2 out of 3 men; and by 1910, less than one-third of all American men were so employed.[33] Increased mechanization and the routinization of labor accompanied industrialization; individual workers were increasingly divorced from control over the labor process, as well as dispossessed of ownership. Thus Henry George wrote in *Social Problems* (1883) that labor-saving devices result in "positive evils" for the working man, "degrading men into the

30. M. Rogin, *Fathers and Children* (New York: Pantheon, 1975), p. 162.

31. J. Dubbert, "Progressivism and the Masculinity Crisis," in *The American Man*, ed. E. Pleck, and J. Pleck (Englewood Cliffs, N.J.: Prentice-Hall, 1980), p. 307.

32. G. J. Barker-Benfield, *The Horrors of the Half Known Life: Male Attitudes Toward Women and Sexuality in Nineteenth-Century America* (New York: Harper & Row, 1976), p. 13.

33. Today, one-tenth of all American men are self-employed.

position of mere feeders of machines."[34] Machines, he claimed, were "absolutely injurious," rendering the workman more dependent; depriving him of skill and of opportunities to acquire it; lessening his control over his own condition and his hope of improving it; cramping his mind, and in many cases distorting and enervating his body."[35]

In such an atmosphere, the dramatic international economic collapse of 1873 took on especially pointed dimensions. The Wall Street crash triggered a series of bankruptcies, bank failures, and foreclosures that shook the nation's economic foundations. Six thousand businesses closed in 1874 alone, and in some months in 1878, 900 businesses closed. Political conflict was virtually inevitable. In the South, Midwest, and Southwest, dispossessed farmers fought back against big capital through the Farmers Alliance and the Populist movement, perhaps America's only genuine mass political movement. In the cities, a "widening class rift" led to increasing class-based hostility, which erupted in 1877 in strikes and political revolts that brought the nation to the brink of armed insurrection. "Sudden as a thunderburst from a clear sky the crisis came upon the country," wrote the journalist Dacus in 1877.[36] "It seemed as if the whole social and political structure was on the very brink of ruin."

And indeed it was. Efforts to revive masculinity were often embedded in a larger critique of American culture. A convulsively antimodernist sentiment captured the imagination of many groups across the nation. Although this sentiment was often expressed in contradictory ways, each of its manifestations had important consequences for the redefinition of masculinity. For some, antimodernism glorified individual achievement, reviving a martial ideal of heroic individuals battling faceless bureaucrats, and celebrating the charismatic cult of the warrior confronting bourgeois conformity. For most, antimodernism revealed a desperate longing for community. A resurgent medievalism, a fascination with oriental cultures, and a revived religious fundamentalism (especially Catholicism) proclaimed the annihilation of the ego, the destruction of the self and its immersion into a transcendent mythic community, an "oceanic feeling of oneness with the universe."[37] For others, antimodernism did not involve a thoroughgoing critique of industrial society but a simple addition to the prevailing culture, as in the spectacular bicycle boom of the 1890s and the dramatic increase in interest in sports and health. Serious intellectuals extolled nature's tonic freshness and its virile impetus, "an indispensable

34. Cited in A. Trachtenberg, *The Incorporation of America: Culture and Society in the Gilded Age* (New York: Hill and Wang, 1982), p. 43.

35. Ibid.

36. Ibid., pp. 70–71.

37. T. J. Lears, *No Place of Grace* (New York: Pantheon 1982), p. 230.

remedy for the artificiality and effeteness" of late-nineteenth-century urban life.[38] The Country Life Movement elevated naturalism to a transcedent category, seeking "to preserve traditional agrarian ideals in the face of industrialism."[39]

A profound rejection of the industrial city was woven into this antimodernist critique. The city was the breeding ground for both "idleness" and "vicious classes," according to reformer Wendell Phillips;[40] the city was the "storm center" of civilization to Josiah Strong in 1886, and its "most serious menace."[41] Frank Lloyd Wright's tirade against New York captures part of this antiurbanism; he wrote in *The Future of Architecture:*

> A place fit for banking and prostitution and not much else . . . a crime
> of crimes . . . a vast prison . . . triumph of the herd instinct . . .
> outgrown and overgrown . . . the greatest mouth in the world . . .
> humanity preying on humanity . . . carcass . . . parasite . . . fibrous
> tumor . . . pig-pile . . . incongruous mantrap of monstrous
> dimensions. . . . Enormity devouring manhood, confusing personality by
> frustration of individuality. Is this not anti-Christ? The Moloch that
> knows no God but *more?*[42]

To others, the city was less a sinkhole of vice and violence than an enervating seductress, skillfully sapping men of their virility. In contrast to the frontier, "the city represents civilization, confinement, and female efforts to domesticate the world,"[43] and its effect, as Ernest Thompson Seton put it, was to make Americans "degenerate. We know money grubbing machine politics, degrading sports, cigarettes . . . false ideals, moral laxity, and lessening Church power, in a word 'City rot' has worked evil in the nation."[44] The city was cast as cultural villain, either because of its effete, feminine, refinement or for the ominous danger lurking in the rows of working-class tenements that housed the unwashed immigrants. Each strain threatened traditional masculinity.

38. J. Higham, *Strangers in the Land: Pattern of American Nativism, 1860–1925* (New York: Atheneum 1971), p. 81.

39. W. L. Bowers, *The Country Life Movement in America 1900–1920* (Port Washington, N.Y.: Kennikat Press, 1974).

40. Cited in W. Leach, *True Love and Perfect Union: The Feminist Reform of Sex and Society* (New York: Basic Books, 1980), p. 334.

41. Cited in Trachtenberg, *Incorporation of America*, p. 102.

42. F. L. Wright, *The Future of Architecture* (New York: Dover, 1970).

43. D. Pugh, *Sons of Liberty: The Masculine Mind in Nineteenth Century America* (Westport, Conn.: Greenwood, 1983), p. 150.

44. Cited in D. Macleod, *Building Character in the American Boy: The Boy Scouts, YMCA, and Their Forerunners, 1870–1920* (Madison: University of Wisconsin Press, 1983), p. 32.

FAMILY AND GENDER RELATIONS IN FIN-DE-SIÈCLE UNITED STATES

Against this background of dramatic structural change, the family and relations between women and men were undergoing similar upheaval in the late nineteenth century. Rapid capitalist industrialization "increasingly subverted the older sexual division of labor [and] created conditions favorable to the emergence of women into the public realm with men." [45] Women were involved in arenas that directly touched the lives of men:

in temperance, social science, and moral education; in the reforms . . . of the marriage laws . . . that legally permitted women to transact their own business, keep their own separate earnings, and retain ownership of their separate estates; in the reform of many state laws . . . that sanctioned the rights of women, whether married or single, to employment in the professions; and in the growing employment of large numbers of women in the industrial sector of the economy and . . . in the professions, especially medicine, journalism, and education. [46]

Increased public presence was buttressed by changes in the family, such as shrinking family size, increasing nuclearization of family structure, and a clear demarcation between workplace and household as separate units of production and consumption. Motherhood was even more seen as a calling, a "profession"; everywhere, "motherhood was advancing, fatherhood was in retreat." [47]

Such changes placed contradictory demands on a woman; she was to be both the True Woman, "emotional, dependent, and gentle — a born follower," and the Ideal Mother, "strong, self-reliant, protective, an efficient caretaker in relation to children and home." [48] By "combining piety and domesticity with submissiveness and passivity," the notion of the True Woman "controlled women and narrowed their options." [49] But both Ideal Mothers and True Women were confined to the home and other arenas of social reproduction, so culture became "increasingly the sphere of women, of ladies of charity as well as schoolteachers and librarians." [50] That American culture was increasingly "feminized" became a dominant theme in the discourse between women and men.

The separation of work and home, the privatization of family life, and other changes meant that childhood socialization was increasingly the

45. Leach, *True Love and Perfect Union*, p. 123.
46. Ibid.
47. E. A. Rotundo, "Body and Soul: Changing Ideas of American Middle Class Manhood, 1770–1920," *Journal of Social History* 16, no. 4(1983):30.
48. Smith-Rosenberg, *Disorderly Conduct*, p. 199.
49. C. Degler, *At Odds: Women and the Family in America from the Revolution to the Present* (New York: Oxford University Press, 1980), pp. 26–27.
50. Trachtenberg, *Incorporation of America*, p. 145.

work of women—as mothers, schoolteachers, and Sunday school teachers.[51] By the late nineteenth century, "women were teaching boys to be men,"[52] which caused both women and men to maneuver against perceived constraints.

Several social changes—the rise of women's colleges, increased literacy, delayed age of marriage, an ideology of upward mobility, and capitalist development—gave rise to the New Woman, a single, highly educated, economically autonomous woman who "challenged existing gender relations and the distribution of power."[53] Since, as Sarah Norton observed in 1870, the "inequality of women finds its origins in marriage," and in order to make political equality possible, "social equality of the sexes must precede it,"[54] the New Woman eschewed marriage and "fought for professional visibility, espoused innovative, often radical economic and social reforms, and wielded real political power."[55] The New Woman was an avowed feminist who campaigned for suffrage and asserted her autonomy in the world of men.

Thus the stage was set for a new "crisis of masculinity." Structural changes had transformed the structure of gender relations, and both men and women struggled to redefine the meanings of masculinity and femininity; the "real gender drama in this period involve[d] the changes in men's lives and their reactions to them."[56] Writers acknowledged that "their readership was hungry to be told of what true manhood and true womanhood consisted," and though they often "flew to the simplest, most extreme kind of definitions,"[57] a serious reexamination was also under way. Men felt themselves beseiged by social breakdown and crisis, as "the familiar routes to manhood [became] either washed out or road-blocked,"[58] and male anxieties intensified by democracy and industrialization:

> Men . . . were jolted by changes in the economic and social order which made them perceive that their superior position in the gender order and their supposedly "natural" male roles and prerogatives were not somehow rooted in the human condition, that they were instead the result of a complex set of relationships subject to change and decay.[59]

51. Cf. A. Douglas, *The Feminization of American Culture* (New York: Knopf, 1977).
52. Rotundo, "Body and Soul," p. 32.
53. Smith-Rosenberg, *Disorderly Conduct*, p. 245.
54. Cited in Leach, *True Love and Perfect Union*, p. 190.
55. Smith-Rosenberg, *Disorderly Conduct*, p. 245.
56. M. Hartman, "Sexual Crack-Up: The Role of Gender in Western History" (unpublished paper, Rutgers University, 1984), p. 13.
57. Barker-Benfield, *Horrors of Half Known Life*, p. 210.
58. Hartman, "Sexual Crack-Up," p. 13.
59. Ibid.

At both the textual and the institutional levels—in works of fiction, sermons, and scientific tracts, as well as in public policy and voluntary associations—the late-nineteenth-century crisis of masculinity revealed three important reactions to the perceived feminization of American culture. First, there was a considerable antifeminist backlash, which cast women as the source of men's troubles and sought to reestablish a perceived erosion of male dominance. Second, a "promale" backlash sought vigorously to reassert traditional masculinity, especially as a cultural and political ethos, against social and political trends of which feminism was but a symptom, not a cause. Finally, a small but important group of men openly embraced feminist ideas and ideals as the signposts pointing toward a radically different future.

MASCULINITY IN CRISIS IN THE UNITED STATES, 1880–1914

The Antifeminist Backlash

> *I reckon I got to light out for the Territory ahead of the rest, because Aunt Sally she's going to adopt me and civilize me, and I can't stand it.*
> — HUCK FINN

For some men, the need to redefine masculinity was caused by women's ill-advised challenge to their traditional role; if masculinity was in crisis, it was women's fault, and the solution to the crisis was the revival of a hypermasculine subordination of women. A strongly misogynist current runs through a number of religious tracts, medical treatises, and political pamphlets of this period, as the assault against women's gains came largely from the religious and medical spheres, and from opposition to women's suffrage. All three discourses resorted to a revivified emphasis on the "natural" differences between men and women as the basis for social differentiation; opponents of increasing economic, political, and social equality between men and women almost always resort to arguments about the "natural order of things" as counters to progressive social trends.

For example, pamphlets about women and sexuality by women and clergy "played with stereotypic sex distinctions," providing "a testament of sexual tension, of covertly stated hatred of women by men and the reverse."[60] A new "muscular Christianity" hailed a remasculinized Jesus:

60. Douglas, *Feminization of American Culture*, p. 228.

He was "no dough-faced, lick-spittle proposition," proclaimed Billy Sunday, but "the greatest scrapper who ever lived."[61] And the Right Reverend John L. Spalding, Catholic bishop of Peoria, fused political repression and sexual repression of women when he wrote:

> Sensuality and love, though mysteriously related, are contrary as religion and superstition. The baser passion grows upon the grave of the finer virtue. Woman, like religion, appeals to what is highest in man. Her power over him is that of sentiment, and to seek to place her in rivalry with him in the rude business of life is an aim worthy of an atheistic and material age.[62]

Men's antisuffrage organizations sprang up around the nation to rally men behind the masculine cause. Suffrage was seen as the "ultimate invasion of the male domain by women in their drive to save the Republic."[63] To oppose women's suffrage was a patriotic act: "The American Republic stands before the world as the supreme expression of masculine force," claimed the Illinois Association Opposed to Women's Suffrage in 1910. And those who supported women's advance, or progressive reformism generally, were less than American, hence less than real men:

> Reformers and genteel intellectuals who stood above party battles invited the scorn of the regulars, a scorn couched frequently in images fusing anger at feminizing culture with sexual innuendo, and manly braggadocio of the stalwarts: "political hermaphrodite," "miss-Nancys," "man-milliners," Nonpartisans were a "third sex," "the neuter gender not popular in nature or society."[64]

Medical texts reveal the twin terrors of sexuality and women's advances, and many manuals conflated their effects, casting women as both lustful temptresses and the pious guardians of home and hearth. The male response to the New Woman underscores how scientific discourse came to dominate the arguments over women's equality. While men first attacked the New Woman for her rejection of motherhood, by the turn of the twentieth century, armed with new medical "evidence," she was attacked for her rejection of men. The New Woman was a third sex, an intermediate sex, a "mannish lesbian." By linking social protest to biological differences, male antifeminists could claim that this war against gender was really a war against nature:

61. Ibid., p. 327.
62. Cited in P. Gardella, *Innocent Ecstasy* (New York: Oxford University Press, 1984), p. 116.
63. Dubbert, *Man's Place*, p. 86.
64. Trachtenberg, *Incorporation of America*, p. 163.

Men's growing sense of vulnerability after the Civil War—their notion of social crisis and the concomitant gynecological crescendo—cannot be disassociated from the increasing vociferousness of women at the same time, most noticeably on the suffrage front. Doctors like other men also displayed persistent anxiety over the growing numbers of the new, conspicuously consuming, fashionable life style of city women, their style dangerously attractive to all women.[65]

From this growing fear came an episode of reactionary myth making; commentators "clothed gender distinctions specific to late 19th century industrial countries in the unchangeability of human biology," making the social appear natural and immutable.[66]

On the other side, physicians warned against feminized boys and spent tremendous energy in advising parents on proper socialization to manhood. Alfred Stille, president of the American Medical Association in 1871, warned that "a man with feminine traits of character or with the frame and carriage of a female is despised by both the sex he ostensibly belongs to and that of which he is at once a caricature and a libel."[67] And Augustus Kinsley Gardner stressed the imperative of different childrearing techniques for boys and girls. His extensive consideration of male masturbation in *Our Children* (1872) led him to recommend against featherbeds for boys because "the very softness is not desirable, while the very excess of heat conduces to a frame of mind not desirable, engenders and ferments lascivious thoughts in the adolescent, and is otherwise very objectionable."[68] Parents had an enormous responsibility, and manuals proliferated to help them guide their children through the perilous journey to maturity. Several cautioned against dancing, book learning, and even fraternities, since they would corrupt the young.[69] Barely concealed were views of children, especially young boys, as increasingly impressionable and vulnerable to feminine wiles, and of women as dangerous and tempting threats to masculinity. The separation of boys from girls became "a kind of mania"; in some libraries, it was the rule to segregate volumes authored by men from those authored by women.[70] Male antifeminists were wary of the feminizing clutches of mothers and teachers, whose refined civility would be the undoing of American masculinity, and sought to push women out of the public domain and return them to the home as passive, idealized figurines, so their influence could no longer sap the vitality of the nation.

65. Barker-Benfield, *Horrors of Half Known Life*, p. 123.
66. Smith-Rosenberg, *Disorderly Conduct*, p. 289.
67. Barker-Benfield, *Horrors of Half Known Life*, p. 86.
68. Ibid., p. 232.
69. Cf. W. McKeever, *Training the Boy* (New York: Macmillan, 1913).
70. Hartman, "Sexual Crack-Up," p. 11.

Nowhere is the male antifeminist backlash better expressed than in Henry James's novel *The Bostonians* (1886), whose hero, dashing Basil Ransom, is afraid that the natural masculinity of political leaders would be rendered impotent by meddling, aggressive women; he "projects his anxiety onto women and provides . . . an explicit literary example of the castration complex."[71]

> The whole generation is womanized; the masculine tone is passing out of the world; it's a feminine, nervous, hysterical, chattering canting age, an age of hollow phrases and false delicacy and exaggerated solicitudes and coddled sensibilities, which, if we don't soon look out, will usher in the reign of mediocrity, of the feeblest and flattest and most pretentious that has ever been. The masculine character, the ability to dare and endure, to know and yet not fear reality, to look the world in the face and take it for what it is . . . that is what I want to preserve, or rather . . . recover; and I must tell you that I don't in the least care what becomes of you ladies while I make the attempt![72]

Not long thereafter, asked if he regards women as "quite inferior," Ransom replies: "For public, civic uses, absolutely—perfectly weak and second rate."[73] The assertion of masculinity required the resubordination of women.

The Promale Backlash

Other men were equally anxious and distressed about masculinity but saw solutions to gender crisis in a vigorous reassertion of traditional masculinity in other, more public domains. Women were not the enemy; women's increased power was but symptomatic of cultural changes that had reduced the importance and visibility of masculinity. Masculinist sentiments countered feminization as a cultural process, not women either as a group or as individuals. Several well-known authors jumped on the masculinist bandwagon. Melville argued that masculinity was a "resistance to sentimentalism," and "effort at a genuinely political and philosophical life,"[74] and Harvard senior John Dos Passos complained to a friend in 1917:

> I think we are all of us a pretty milky lot, don't you? With our tea table convictions and our radicalism that keeps up so consistently within the bounds of decorum. . . . And what are we to fit when they turn us out of Harvard? We're too intelligent to be successful businessmen and we haven't the sand or the energy to be anything else?[75]

71. Pugh, *Sons of Liberty*, p. 109.
72. H. James, *The Bostonians* (New York: Modern Library, 1965), p. 343.
73. Ibid., p. 348.
74. Douglas, *Feminization of American Culture*, p. 294.
75. Cited in P. Filene, "Between a Rock and a Soft Place: A Century of American Manhood" (ms., University of North Carolina, 1984), p. 10.

William James wrote that there was "no more contemptible type of human character than that of the nervous sentimentalist and dreamer, who spends his life in a weltering sea of sensibility and emotion, but who never does a concrete manly deed."[76]

Several antidotes to this perceived feminization were offered, antidotes that would increase male fellowship and instill those masculine virtues that could rescue an enfeebled nation. James prescribed a stiffening of American ideals with the tonic of the common laborer's "sterner stuff of manly virtue." Such an infusion of masculinity into the predominantly feminine precincts of refinement would allow the entire society to "pass toward some newer and better equilibrium."[77] And Senator Albert Beveridge of Indiana counseled, in his *Young Man and the World* (1906) that the male youth "avoid books, in fact avoid all artificial learning for the forefathers put America on the right path by learning from completely natural experience."[78]

This compulsive reassertion of traditional masculinity resonated with the reactivated martial ideal that characterized a strain of antimodernist sensibility at the turn of the century and pushed the nation even closer to war. If, as Maurice Thompson wrote in 1898, "the greatest danger that a long period of profound peace offers to a nation is that of [creating] effeminate tendencies in young men,"[79] then war could be sensible policy for the nation and a remedy for feminized men.

The building of empire through military domination was fueled by an emotional fervor to prove masculinity; thus, according to the *Washington Post* in 1898:

A new consciousness seems to have come upon us — the consciousness of strength, and with it a new appetite, a yearning to show our strength. . . . Ambition, interest, land-hunger, pride, the mere joy of fighting, whatever it may be, we are animated by a new sensation. . . . The taste of empire is in the mouth of the people, even as the taste of blood in the jungle.[80]

General Homer Lea linked the two explicitly when he noted that "manhood marks the height of physical vigor among mankind, so the militant

---

76. Cited in R. Bellah *et al., Habits of the Heart* (Berkeley: University of California Press, 1985), p. 210.

77. Trachtenberg, *Incorporation of America*, pp. 141–142.

78. Cited in Dubbert, "Progressivism and Masculinity Crisis," p. 310.

79. M. Thompson, "Vigorous Men, a Vigorous Nation," *Independent*, September 1, 1898, p. 610.

80. Cited in J. Booth, *The End and the Beginning: The Nicaraguan Revolution* (Boulder, Colo.: Westview, 1982), p. 27.

successes of a nation mark the zenith of its physical greatness."[81] Perhaps no one better captures this militarist strategy than Theodore Roosevelt, who elevated compulsive masculinity and military adventurism to the level of national myth. Roosevelt's triumph over his youthful frailty and his transformation into a robust, vigorous man served as a template for a revitalized American social character. Roosevelt's foreign policy was military expansion, his style hypermasculine, proven in imperial adventures in the Caribbean and the Philippines. "The nation that has trained itself to a cancer of unwarlike and isolated ease is bound, in the end, to go down before other nations which have not lost *the manly and adventurous virtues,*" he thundered.[82] "There is no place in the world for nations who have become enervated by the soft and easy life, or who have lost their fibre of vigorous hardiness and masculinity," he inveighed. A Kansas newspaper editor hailed Roosevelt's "hard muscled frame" and his "crackling voice" as a model for Americans.

The masculinist response to the crisis of masculinity also manifest less bellicose institutional responses, such as the founding of the Boy Scouts of America in 1910. Boy Scouts celebrated a masculinity tested and proven against nature and other men, removed from the cultural restraints of home, hearth, school, and church. If "spectatoritis" had "turned robust manly, self-reliant boyhood into a lot of flat-chested cigarette smokers with shaky nerves and doubtful vitality," according to Chief Scout Ernest Thompson Seton in his *The Boy Scouts of America* (1910), then the BSA could counter the forces of feminization and maintain traditional manhood.[83] Americans found in the BSA "an institutional sphere for the validation of masculinity previously generated by the flow of daily social life and affirmed in one's work."[84] Here was the place to re-create an ideal boyhood and its natural small-town setting, masculine preserves against the urban world of enfeeblement, refinement, civility and women. To the BSA fell the "noble ideal of restoring the primitive past."[85] resolving a cultural Oedipal angst by removing boys from mothers and reinserting them into nature with the band of brothers, the primal horde, re-created in the American small town.

Such organized "primitiveness" requires quotation, because the goal of the BSA was hardly to encourage political rebellion against an enervating

81. Cited in T. Roszak and B. Roszak, *Masculine/Feminine* (New York: Harper & Row, 1975), p. 92.

82. Ibid.

83. Cited in Macleod, *Building Character in American Boy*, p. 49.

84. J. P. Hantover, "The Boy Scouts and the Validation of Masculinity," in *The American Man*, ed. E. Pleck and J. Pleck (Englewood Cliffs, N.J.: Prentice-Hall, 1980), p. 299.

85. Dubbert, *Man's Place*, p. 156.

culture but to redirect male anxieties, to reassert a traditional masculinity, but all within the bounds of an extended complacency and obedience to the emerging industrial order. Anthony Baden-Powell, founder of the Boy Scouts in England, understood this campaign for moral redemption well; England was "shamed by the Boer War, concerned about the vulnerability of its vast empire and the specter of social unrest among its own laboring classes," [86] when Baden-Powell wrote that the brotherhood of scouts consisted of: "real *men* in every sense of the word . . . they understand living out in the jungles, and they can find their way anywhere . . . they know how to look after their health when far away from any doctors, are strong and plucky, and ready to face any danger, and always keen to help each other." [87]

But this does not suggest anarchy, or even autonomous individualism, for scouting's cult of masculinity requires that they "give up everything, their personal comforts and desires, in order to get their work done. They do not do all this for their own amusement, but because it is their duty to their king, fellow country-men, or employers." [88] In the United States as well, the goal of all this "stodgy fun" was therapeutic, to turn boys into docile middle-class workers, tuned to middle-level occupations, with some responsibility, but subordinate and able to take commands from superiors. [89] If boys were provided a place away from the city, from women, and from culture — where they "could be boys" — then they would surely become the "real men" required by early-twentieth-century industrial capitalism.

Profeminist Men

The world is oppressed by masculinity.
— MARY HUBBARD, 1873

Although fewer in number and less influential institutionally, a significant group of American men openly embraced feminist principles as a potential solution to the crisis of masculinity. Inspired by women's increasingly visible public presence (in reformist movements such as abolition,

86. Cited in M. Rosenthal, "Recruiting for Empire: Baden-Powell's Boy Scout Law," *Raritan* 4, no. 1(Summer 1984):46.
87. Cited in ibid.
88. Cited in ibid., p. 45.
89. Macleod, *Building Character in American Boy;* see also Rosenthal, "Recruiting for Empire."

populism, and labor, and socially redemptive groups such as the WCTU and the Social Purity movement), many men believed that women's political participation, to be symbolized by the extension of suffrage to women, would be a significant gain for all Americans, male and female. Other men supported feminist women's goals to revolutionize the relations between men and women in the family and in sexuality. Still others maintained a firm belief in the division of the sexes, but argued that increased feminization might prove a palliative to the dangers of compulsive masculinity.

Male support for women's public participation came first from the founders and early leaders of the newly opened women's colleges. Matthew Vassar, William Allan Neilson and Joseph Taylor (both of Smith), and Henry Durant (Wellesley) championed women's citizenship. Durant wrote that "the real meaning of the Higher Education for women" was "revolt":

> We revolt against the slavery in which women are held by the customs of society — the broken health, the aimless lives, the subordinate position, the helpless dependence, the dishonesties and shams of so-called education. The Higher Education of Women . . . is the cry of the oppressed slave. It is the assertion of absolute equality . . . it is the war of Christ . . . against spiritual wickedness in high places.[90]

Vassar President Henry Noble MacCracken instituted the first Euthenics program under feminist reformer Julia Lathrop, a program that represented, he believed, the "socialization of the curriculum."[91] MacCracken also chartered trains to transport Vassar students to the great suffrage demonstrations in New York where — to jeers from the crowd — he would proudly lead the college's contingent and hold one end of the Vassar College Suffrage Association banner.

The movement for coeducation was also promoted by antisexist men, whose political views were often fueled by scientific advances. John Vleck, for example, who presided over Wesleyan's experiment with coeducation, believed that "egalitarian coeducation represented the true index of the scientific advancement of the race."[92] And Burt Green Wilder, a scientist at Cornell, condemned the "barbaric cruelty" and "repression" that had "crushed" women's spirit and transmuted sexual "equivalence" into sexual disequilibrium. "The real creed of the future," he wrote in the *Atlantic Monthly*, "is equal but not identical; diverse yet complementary; the man for the woman, and the woman for the man."[93]

90. Cited in H. L. Horowitz, *Alma Mater: Design and Experience in the Women's Colleges from Their Nineteenth Century Beginnings to the 1930s* (New York: Knopf, 1984), p. 44.
91. Ibid., p. 297.
92. Cited in Leach, *True Love and Perfect Union*, p. 73.
93. Ibid., p. 49.

Men also directly supported women's suffrage, believing with Charles Taylor that the repression of women was "the greatest evil of modern society,"[94] and that political equality might relieve the world of oppressively masculine politics. The Men's League for Women's Suffrage had both English and American branches; in the United States, Greenwich Village radical Max Eastman was its guiding light. His pamphlet *Is Woman Suffrage Important?* linked a socialist economic critique of the leisured class with an analysis of the social construction of gender differences; these combine to turn women's "enforced feebleness into a holy thing."[95]

Men participated regularly in suffrage demonstrations. An editorial from *La Follette's* in May 1911 praises the 85 "courageous and convinced men" who marched in a demonstration, among them John Dewey, Hamilton Holt, Oswald Garrison Villard (editor of the *New York Evening Post*), and Edward Markham. Although "hooted and jeered" and "guyed in the streets," one counted being "booed and hissed down the Avenue . . . a very thrilling and inspiring experience. . . . I am determined," he continued, "that if I can help to that end, there shall be a thousand men in line next year." He was not very far off target. An editorial in *the New York Times* the next year predicted 800 men would march in a suffrage demonstration the next day, and suggested, somewhat smugly, these "courageous" men would face an "unsympathetic multitude" as they stood publicly for what they believed.

But suffrage was but a public expression of a deeply social challenge that feminists had issued to the social order that bound them to unattainable ideals and repressive social conditions. "Woman's suffrage is not primarily a political but a social question," wrote Jesse Jones, a Boston Unitarian minister in *Woman's Journal*, "and means a profounder revolution in the whole structure of society than many advocates seem ever to have dreamed of."[96] Within the personal sphere, men sought to resolve the crisis of masaculinity by supporting women's claims for autonomy, both within the family and marriage and in their demands for sexual freedom.

Many men supported feminists' repudiation of the traditional hierarchal principles of patriarchal authoritarianism. "For them personal love was the determinant factor in marrying. The problem for them was how to transform sexual love into an egalitarian relation while at the same time preserving social order and community."[97] The Reverend Jesse Jones championed the notion of divorce, "so far as women take the initiative in

94. Cited in Degler, *At Odds*, p. 256.
95. Cited in S. Strauss, *Traitors to the Masculine Cause: The Men's Campaign for Women's Rights* (Westport, Conn.: Greenwood, 1983), p. 229.
96. Cited in Leach, *True Love and Perfect Union*, p. 15.
97. Ibid., p. 126.

it" as "one phase of the revolt of women against the harem idea." Although it seemed "corrupting", he wrote in *Woman's Journal*, it was "a movement for good, for it is a movement to escape out of tyranny into freedom." [98] Many men followed Henry Blackwell's earlier admonitions that women maintaining careers after marriage was essential to the survival of their equal union. [99] In the language of late-nineteenth-century magazines, the profeminist man married neither "drudge nor ornament." He would not try to transform his wife into a woman chained to "sexual servitude or bodily toil" or to conditions in which "her mind rises no further than the roof that shelters it." [100] And birth-control reformer Margaret Sanger's husband, William, actively supported her participation in the public sphere. "You go ahead and finish your writing," she quotes him as saying, "and I'll get the dinner and wash the dishes." [101]

The sex radicals who clustered around Greenwich Village in the first two decades of the twentieth century supported women's sexual equality while they challenged traditional notions of masculinity and wrestled with issues of equality and autonomy in their own lives. They believed that sexual repression was an essential underpinning of capitalism and based their critiques on socialist politics and scientific advances, both of which posited an equality of sexual desire between women and men. Sex radicals tried to transform the entire sexual relation between men and women. Denlow Lewis wrote in 1900 that "the sexual act must be performed with satisfaction to both participants in the conjugal embrace." [102] Ben Reitman, a Village bohemian and long-time lover of Emma Goldman, supported her work in birth-control reform and was well identified with the feminist cause. On trial, one prosecutor denounced him as "an Anarchist, who comes to our fair city to defy our laws. . . . If you will let him break the law on birth control, our property and our wives and daughters will not be safe [from their] dirty, filthy, stinking birth control literature." [103] And Floyd Dell, who believed that feminism was the only antidote to ruling-class pretense and materialistic value culture, also claimed that men were "tired of the subservient woman — the pretty slave with all the slave's subtlety and cleverness." [104] The liberation of women from the oppressive bonds of traditional femininity — women were "world builders" to Dell

98. Ibid., p. 145.

99. Cf. ibid., p. 196.

100. Ibid., p. 30.

101. Cited in M. Forster, *Significant Sisters: The Grassroots of Active Feminism* (New York: Knopf, 1985), p. 252.

102. Cited in Degler, *At Odds*, p. 274.

103. Cited in C. Falk, *Love, Anarchy, and Emma Goldman* (New York: Holt, Rinehart and Winston, 1985), p. 254.

104. Cited in Strauss, *Traitors to Masculine Cause*, p. 249.

—implied the liberation of men from the restrictive moorings of traditional masculinity. In a 1914 essay, "Feminism for Men," Dell made this connection explicit:

The home is a little dull. When you have got a woman in a box, and you pay rent on the box, her relationship to you insensibly changes character. . . . it is in the great world that a man finds his sweetheart, and in that narrow little box outside of the world that he loses her. When she has left that box and gone back into the great world, a citizen and a worker, then with surprise and delight he will discover her again and never let her go.[105]

These three responses to the late-nineteenth- and early-twentieth-century crisis of masculinity—antifeminist, promale, and profeminist—sought to resolve the crisis in different ways; but all agreed that masculinity was not to be defined in social isolation, as a "sex role," but as part of the problematic of gender relations. Masculinity was a relational construct and was to be reconstructed, reasserted, or redefined in relation to changing social and economic conditions and the changing position of women in society. It is hardly surprising that today, in the wake of transformations of work, the closing of the imperial frontier, and new gains for women, we again find these three responses to the crisis of masculinity. Groups of men suggest a return to traditional gender differences (through a distortion of "scientific" evidence of "natural" differences); others seek a reinvigorated masculinity and support for wounded men (as well as antifeminist challenges to divorce, alimony, child custody and abortion rights); and an increasing number of men are recognizing the ways in which their ability to transform masculinity is inspired by, and made possible by, the women's movement, and have begun the difficult and painful process of dismantling masculinity in order to implement a vision of sexual equality and gender justice.

Author's Note: Much of the research on late-seventeenth- and early-eighteenth-century English pamphlets was made possible by a Visiting Fellowship to the William Andrews Clark Memorial Library and a Summer Faculty fellowship from Rutgers University. I am grateful to the library for its generosity and hospitality. Portions of this paper were presented in the seminar on The Psychology of Love at Rutgers University in April 1986. I am grateful to seminar organizer Carol Gilligan, and also Laura Benkov and Celeste Schenck for their comments and support at that presentation. This paper was also presented at the convention of the American Sociological Association, New York, August 1986. Finally, I am grateful to Jeff Beane, Harry Brod, Martin Duberman, Kate Ellis, Janet Goldstein, Margaret Hunt, Barbara Laslett, Joe Pleck, several anonymous reviewers, and especially Carol Briggs for support and criticisms.

105. Cited in E. K. Trimberger, "Feminism, Men, and Modern Love: Greenwich Village, 1900–1925," in *Powers of Desire: The Politics of Sexuality* (New York: Monthly Review Press, 1984), p. 136.

6

Surviving the Institutional Decimation of Black Males: Causes, Consequences, and Intervention

Clyde W. Franklin II

BLACK MALES AND INSTITUTIONAL DECIMATION

A quiet, almost invisible tragedy is unfolding in contemporary America and only rarely is it discussed outside the black community, black studies courses, black publications, and the like. Nevertheless, the tragedy is real, frightening, and devastating for black America. What is this phenomenon, and what are its consequences? Beyond a shadow of doubt, being black and male in the United States is hazardous to one's health because black males in America continue to face disproportionate dangers — both outside and within the black community — well into the 1980s. In some literary and academic circles, black males have even been referred to as an endangered species.[1]

The problem has been called "the institutional decimation of Black males." Stewart and Scott define this concept as "the coordinated operation of various institutions in American society which systematically remove Black males from the civilian population."[2] They note that the concept of institutional decimation had been derived from *(a)* a historical definition of the term "decimation" (meaning the selection by a lot of every tenth man to be put to death, as a punishment in cases of mutiny or other offenses by a body of soldiers);[3] and *(b)* an emphasis on societal

1. See, e.g., W. Leavy, "Is the Black Male an Endangered Species?" *Ebony*, August 1983, pp. 41–46; and Society for the Study of Social Problems, "Black Males and Gender Roles" (Session 79 of a meeting held at the Shoreham Hotel, Washington, D.C., August 26, 1983).

2. J. B. Stewart and J. W. Scott, "The Institutional Decimation of Black Males," *Western Journal of Black Studies* 2, no. 2 (1978): 82–91.

3. The concept used by Stewart and Scott is based on a meaning of *decimation* found in *The Oxford English Dictionary*: "For he divided his men by legions and then of them he put the tenth legion to death." See Stewart and Scott, "Institutional Decimation."

"systems which directly reduce the black male population and those which contribute to the decimation process in an indirect manner" (such systems involve, according to Stewart and Scott, the penal correction system and the military indirectly, as a result of black male responses to economic frustrations; and crime and vice, and educational and health-care institutions directly).

Stewart and Scott suggest that while the decimation process for a cohort of black males generally is full blown by age 45 (in terms of relative decimation, their data showed that "there are ten percent fewer non-white male survivors than white male survivors by age 45 and by age 65, twenty percent fewer non-white survivors, and by age 75, thirty percent fewer"[4]), the entire process begins at birth. Moreover, they contend, the decimation process seems to be functional for those interested in reducing the probability of black male survival compared with nonblack male survival.

Pointing out that while the decimation process is not aimed at total removal of black males from society because most remain functional to the economic system by providing a potential source of cheap labor, Stewart and Scott suggest three major ways in which the decimation process is beneficial for a society that discriminates: (a) "It serves to contain pressures in Black communities in which the potential for violent uprisings exists; (b) it serves to maintain a balance between the number of black and white males, counteracting the disproportionate number of black male births in comparison with white male births; and (c) it promotes social instability in black communities by stimulating increased competition for available black males."[5]

In reporting their findings, Stewart and Scott also emphasize that the sex ratio among blacks fell by aproximately 10% between 1920 and 1970. They warn that another decimation will occur over a much shorter period, unless steps are taken to counteract the problem. Given the continued black-on-black violence, generally involving only males (homicide is the leading cause of death among black males age 15 to 24), and the high rates of black male incarceration, along with the "disintegration of the black nuclear family,"[6] it is obvious that Stewart and Scott's warnings are not being heeded.

4. Ibid., p. 83.
5. Ibid.
6. K. S. Jewell, "Use of Social Welfare Programs and the Disintegration of the Black Nuclear Family," *Western Journal of Black Studies* 8, no. 2 (1984): 192–198.

Deviance and Black Men's Plight

Walter Leavy defines an endangered species as "one which suffers a serious reduction in its population and faces the threat of extinction because of its exposure to unfavorable social and environmental conditions."[7] In the case of the black male, there is a long list of societal conditions that, in one way or another, removes him from the civilian population.[8]

To the skeptic, this may seem to be only a rationale for many black men's failures "to incorporate societal definitions of appropriate role behavior into self and to internalize as salient identities given social positions and their accompanying expectations" — both of which effectively control the individual.[9] Put simply, this perspective suggests that the black male's plight is the result of his deviance — the fact that instead of seeking confirmation or validation of legitimate identities by behaving in societally appropriate ways, many behave in ways that elicit validating responses from deviant others and thus conform to the expectations of deviant others. Black men's identities, according to this view, are premised on definitions that lie outside, or in direct opposition to, society. These definitions, in turn, produce deviant behavior. Moreover, because self-esteem is related to behaving in conforming ways that elicit validation from others, many black men's deviant behaviors actually may result in feelings of high self-esteem for them. This view, held by some, is consistent with the observations of Oliver, who suggests that lower-class black men frequently adopt a compulsive masculinity alternative in order to mitigate low self-esteem and negative feelings that emerge from their inabilities to enact traditional masculine roles.[10] Also emphasized by Oliver is intrablack male sex-role socialization that teaches toughness, sexual conquest, manipulation, and thrill seeking — all of which inform many black male youth that they must engage in "deviant" behaviors in order to feel good about themselves.

In practical terms, what does all this mean? It means that black men's deviance should be held responsible for the fact that the homicide rate for black males is 60 per 100,000, a rate that is higher than those of white males, white females, and black females combined; that the leading cause of death among black males age 15–24 is homicide; that black men account for approximately 50% of all persons in state prisons in the United States (170,453 out of 345,960); that the black male suicide rate has more

7. Leavy, "Black Male an Endangered Species?"

8. Ibid., p. 41.

9. S. Stryker, *Symbolic Interactionism: A Structural Version* (Menlo Park, Calif.: Cummings, 1980).

10. W. Oliver, "Black Males and the Tough Guy Image: A Dysfunctional Compensatory Adaptation," *Western Journal of Black Studies* 8, no. 2 (1984): 199–203.

than doubled in the past 12 years; that the black male life expectancy is roughly 13 years less than the white female, 9 years less than the black female, and 5 years less than the white male; that the black male infant mortality rate is more than double that of black females.[11]

Black males also are blamed for some other statistics, which include the following: nationally, 33% of black children lived in homes headed by black women in 1983 (in Chicago, for example, the percentage in 1983 was 66%, a 33% increase over 1970). In addition, over 50% of the black children born nationally in 1983 were born to unmarried mothers (in Chicago, the comparable percentage was 75%, up 29% from 1970).

The Children's Defense Fund that released the study "Black and White Children in America: Key Facts" on June 3, 1985 essentially found that black children have been sliding "backward." An example: In 1977, black and white high school graduates were almost equally likely to go to college (50% for blacks; 51% for whites). By 1982, 52% of white high school graduates were going to college, compared with 36% of black high school graduates. According to the report, poverty is the key factor. Households headed by women correlate highly with poverty.

Combined with over 50% of black children nationally born to unmarried mothers is the poverty rate for all families headed by black women: 63.7% and a whopping 85.2% when the women are under age 25.

William Wilson of the University of Chicago concludes that "the shrinking pool of marriageable Black men seems a likely explanation for at least some of the increase in out-of-wedlock births and single-parent households among Blacks."[12] Who is responsible for this shrinking pool?

Social Structure and Black Men's Plight

Concentrating on a role-taking socialization, psychological explanation, I contend, axiomatically leads to a blame-the-victim explanation of the growing disappearance of black men in America, which may not be entirely accurate. Furthermore, such an emphasis may inhibit positive intervention. But we do not need to remain totally psychological in our analysis. This is certainly the case if "patterned regularities that characterize most human interaction"[13] are legitimate units of analysis to use in investigations of social phenomena. This also is the case if we believe in the concept of the "social person." The concept focuses on the ways in which the

11. Leavy, "Black Male an Endangered Species?", p. 42.
12. W. J. Wilson, *The Declining Significance of Race* (Chicago: University of Chicago Press, 1980).
13. Stryker, *Symbolic Interactionism*, p. 65.

individual comes to have a self and to define situations. It is thought that these ways are functions of social interaction that result in people "incorporating societal and/or subcultural definitions of appropriate role behavior into self and in internalizing as salient identities given social positions and their accompanying expectations."[14] From this perspective, then, some portion of the blame for the disappearance of black men must lie with the social structure, which, in part, creates the black "social" male.

Given that the social person exists and is shaped by interaction, it is possible to say that social structure (patterned regularities) shapes the *possibilities* for interaction and, ultimately, *the person*. The social person *can*, however, creatively alter patterns of interaction. These patterns can in turn change social structure. In the following discussion, I concentrate on how the social structure affects black men's possibilities for interaction and, ultimately, black men as social beings. I also indicate how I feel black men can creatively alter the social patterns of interaction and ultimately change the social structure.

SOCIAL STRUCTURE, BLACK MEN, AND SOCIAL INTERACTION

The concept of social structure refers to groups, organizations, communities, and other aspects of social life in which subsets of persons are tied together in patterned interactions and are separated from other persons.[15] Stryker, in discussing this concept, says that people simply are not distributed randomly throughout the system, nor do they have opportunities for interaction or interact randomly. Instead, the social structure shapes the possibilities for interaction and ultimately the person, as stated earlier. I contend that many black men's social structures are constructed in manners that portend ultimate decimation for the group.

Typically, black men live in and interact in three groups that provide "the point of articulation between the larger social system and themselves as social beings."[16] In other words, many black men interact within the boundaries of three groups that not only impact on the larger social system but also affect the probabilities that they come into contact with particular kinds of persons and that their interaction takes particular forms and contents.[17] A brief description of the three groups and the consequences of within-group interaction for black men follow.

14. Ibid., p. 64.
15. Ibid., p. 66.
16. Ibid., p. 69.
17. Ibid.

The Black Man's Peer Group and Black Men's Interaction

I call the first group the "black man's peer group." For a particular black male, the black man's peer group *consists of from 2 to n black males roughly similar to him in terms of education, occupation, income, values, aspirations, and the like*. The importance of this particular group to a given black male seems to increase with decreases in his socioeconomic status. In other words, the lower the socioeconomic status, the greater the influence of the black man's peer group on the lives of black men and, conversely, the higher the socioeconomic status, the lesser the influence of the black man's peer group on the lives of black men.

While the above propositions may sound provocative, what do they mean? What is the nature of the influence of the black man's peer group? First, the black man's peer group is a kind of misogynist adaptation some black men have made to a racist American society and can result in behaviors that range from ritualistic to innovative. Norms for the black man's peer group include *(a)* maintaining proper sexist attitudes toward women and femininity in general; *(b)* little tolerance for nonaggressive solutions to disputes (therefore having the proper in-group hatred and antagonism — especially toward other black men); *(c)* having sufficient *contempt* for societal nonmaterial culture and appropriate respect for societal material culture; *(d)* support for the heterosexual sexual script (objectification, fixation, and conquest of women);[18] and *(e)* a firm belief that equality for women begins and ends with a considerable amount of "role overload" for women.

If the black man's peer group assumes an influential role in the life of a black male, it is likely that the larger society plays a much lesser role in terms of defining the inventory of the kinds of persons black males can possibly become. After all, one cannot become a soccer player in America if the society does not provide that opportunity.

If the black man's peer group's definition of the "inventory" of possible positions for black males indicates limited numbers of positions, and that only a few of these positions are important and/or worthy of holding, then black men's efforts to attain these positions will be negatively affected (they will *not* try to attain them). This group, as complicated as it may seem,

18. Jack Litewka describes what can be called a sexual handicap that many American men bring with them into the heterosexual arena. This sexual handicap is a "socialized penis" that is taught to perform only if the man can objectify females, fixate on their body parts, and, ultimately, conquer them. This is the traditional heterosexual script equated with maleness and masculine ego, and seems essential for many males' sexual functioning. See J. Litewka, "The Socialized Penis," in *For Men against Sexism: A Book of Readings*, ed. J. Snodgrass (New York: Times Change Press, 1977).

is not the only influential element. Black men also must negotiate with another group, one that I call the "subcultural reference group" (the black community).

The Subcultural Reference Group and Black Men's Interaction

The "subcultural reference group" for black men in America is a complex structure that nevertheless connects with the black man's peer group on certain issues and departs significantly on others. I believe this group has been under significant attack for some time in America; and only recently has this group shown signs of growing weary. It is the group that has survived hundreds of years of social and political discrimination; physical violence where its women were raped, men killed, and children enslaved, only to repeat the cycle all over again.

The group nevertheless remained strong primarily (I am convinced) because it minimized the polarization of sex roles. In fact, scholars such as Lewis, Young, Peters and deFord, Hill, Billingsley, and Noble have spoken of the role flexibility and interchange that characterized black families.[19] This led to the contention that traditional sex roles were much too simplistic to use in examining black families. But, as I have stated elsewhere,[20] this rather progressive view regarding the polarization of sex roles may have begun to dissipate during the late 1960s civil rights movement; and according to more recent writings, this view has continued to dissipate.[21]

Still, black men generally are expected by the black community to assume a sex role that is not as extremely traditional as the societally sanctioned one. This expectation is held by many within the black subcultural reference group. Consider the following statement, which comes from a black woman who feels that black men "want it both ways" and send out mixed signals to black women:

19. D. K. Lewis, "The Black Family: Socialization and Sex Roles," *Phylon* 36, no. 3 (1975): 221–237; V. H. Young, "Family and Childhood in a Southern Negro Community," *American Anthropologist* 72 (1970): 269–298; M. Peters and C. deFord, "The Solo Mother," in *The Black Family: Essay and Studies*, ed. R. Staples (Belmont, Calif.: Wadsworth, 1978); R. Hill, *The Strength of Black Families* (New York: Emerson Hall, 1972); A. Billingsley, *Black Families in White America* (Englewood Cliffs, N.J.: Prentice-Hall, 1968); and W. Nobles, "Toward an Empirical and Theoretical Framework for Defining Black Families," *Journal of Marriage and the Family* 40 (1978): 679–690.

20. C. W. Franklin II, "Black Male–Black Female Conflict: Individually Caused and Culturally Nurtured," *Journal of Black Studies* 15, no. 2 (1984): 139–154.

21. M. Wallace, "A Black Feminist's Search for Sisterhood," in *All the Blacks Are Men, All the Women Are White, but Some of Us Are Brave*, ed. G. T. Hall *et al.* (Old Westburg, N.J.: Feminist Press, 1982); and B. W. Baye, "You Men Want It Both Ways," *Essence*, July 1985, p. 62.

Black women, like their counterparts of other races, are liberating their minds and their bodies from the shackles of the past. Increasingly, women are refusing to waste their lives trying to decode men's mixed messages and buying into some man's macho fantasies. Instead, many women who are or want to be high achievers are accepting the fact that the price of success may be temporary loneliness. And even that loneliness is relative, since many of us have learned that having a man isn't all there is to life"[22]

Even Nikki Giovanni, the paragon of revolution during the early 1970s, says she is proud to be a BUMP (Black Upwardly Mobile Professional) in 1985.[23]

More than this, however, is the fact that aside from the historical emphasis on minimum sex-role polarization in the black community, few black women seem willing to assume the servile role that white women assumed in the past. A quote from Baye illustrates this reluctance:

A friend of mine got married a few years ago to a man she'd been dating for more than a year. This was a marriage made in heaven, or so she and we thought. Both she and her husband were talented go-getters who seemed to want the same things out of life. When they first met, she says, he told her he didn't dig her just for her body but also for her sharp mind. Before long, however, it became clear that the only thing he wanted to do with her mind was to cause her to lose it. She says he wanted her to be dynamic by day and servile by night. Finally, after much verbal and physical abuse, she split.[24]

Magazine articles, workshops, and conferences frequently recount similar stories with similar endings, all suggesting support among black women for a more liberal perspective on sex roles. Michele Wallace is perhaps the most often cited person on the topic of crises in black male – black female relationships, and according to her, black men raised the expectations of black women but could not deliver: "When she stood silently by as he [the black male] became a man, she assumed that he would finally glorify and dignify black womanhood just as the white man had done for white women."[25] Wallace concludes that the black man did not deliver.

For some, because of their unfamiliarity with the history of black people in America regarding minimum sex-role polarization, black women's responses to the very real fact that black men did not become their Prince Charmings and they are not Black Cinderellas mean black women have become evil stepmothers and stepsisters. The "Prince Charming" concept, refers to *the philosophical belief that being a responsible, mature male is to*

22. Baye, "Men Want It Both Ways," p. 70.
23. Quoted in *Essence*, May 1985, p. 60.
24. Baye, "Men Want It Both Ways," p. 70.
25. M. Wallace, *Black Macho and the Myth of the Superwoman* (New York: Dial, 1979); and Wallace, "All the Blacks Are Men."

assume a protective, condescending, providing and generally patriarchal role toward one's female mate and women in general. The Prince Charming ideal is complementary to Collette Dowling's "Cinderella Complex" which is characterized as *female dependence, irrational fears and a deep wish to be taken care of by others.*[26] Because some black women have recognized that few, if any, black men can assume a Prince Charming role, they have become relatively independent. Staples has pointed out that in recent times, black women have used higher education as a vehicle for upward mobility to a much greater extent than black men.[27] The result has been that, in 1982, for example, there were 52,000 eligible black women with five years or more of college but only 15,000 such eligible black men. Black men, in increasing numbers, seem appalled by black women's independence. Consider the following quote:

> One of my own former girlfriends told me that she was having a difficult time deciding on what to do with her new status. She had recently passed the New York Bar and had gotten a new job. "I don't know what I should be: a socialite, a hard-boiled attorney; or sort of work out a blend of my professional and social life," she mused. Curiously, none of the choices included me, so I asked, "where do I fit in?" She stared blankly for a moment, as though she'd come home and discovered she'd forgotten to buy catsup. Then she said: "You know, Donald, sometimes I think you really have a place in my life, and sometimes I think if you walked out the door and never came back, it wouldn't faze me at all."[28]

Why Singletary found his woman friend's statement so appalling is difficult to understand, unless it is because many black men, since the revolutionary days of the 1960s, have actually bought into a sex-role ideology that was archaic when Stokely Carmichael suggested it and, even more important, unworkable, because of *(a)* the social–psychological makeup of black men; and *(b)* structural constraints inhibiting black men's assumption of a Prince Charming role. Here is a social-psychological example of what eligible black men are saying these days: "While women are in their twenties, they party like crazy and tell you not to pressure them into relationships. Then all of a sudden they hit 30 and *whee-oh!* Everybody races the clock to get married and make that baby. What are we, sperm factories? I'm supposed to get married so *you* can have cut crystal?"

In a very real sense, then, black men do not expect to assume a traditional male sex role; more likely, they expect black women to assume multiple roles: to combine a traditional female sex role with other sex

26. C. Dowling, *The Cinderella Complex* (New York: Harper & Row, 1981).
27. D. Singletary, "You New Women Want It All," *Essence*, July 1985, p. 67.
28. Ibid., p. 68.

roles. This message is given to black youth in barbershops, reference peer-group encounters, and other informal socialization settings. The difference between the prescribed androgyny for black males and females this time around is that the minimization of sex-role polarization was emphasized from a position of black unity before the 1960s. Today the minimization of sex-role polarization is emphasized from the perspective of conflict between the black sexes.

The Societal Reference Group and Black Men's Interaction

The larger social system is a third group in which black men participate: the "societal reference group." Unfortunately for black men, this often is the most influential group in their lives. Moreover, black men's participation in this group frequently is constrained or limited. In addition, this group is likely to be "out of sync" with the other two groups in which black males participate. What is this group for black men? Ordinarily, the societal reference group influences individual role strain and role conflict either by increasing it or, more positively, decreasing it.

For black males, the societal reference group often is the catalytic agent for role strain and increases role strain where the seeds of it exist. The Prince Charming ideal is alive, if faltering, in the United States. Consider the amount of retrenchment throughout the 1980s, legislatively and socially, that supports the Prince Charming ideal—a set of attitudes and behaviors that facilitates females being emotionally, physically, psychologically, and in other ways dependent on men and that result in males behaving toward women in so-called protective, condescending, and generally patriarchal ways; and that also supports the Cinderella Complex—"a network of largely repressed attitudes held by women toward the full use of their minds and creativity . . . that psychology dependency—the deep wish to be taken care of by others."[29] There are countless societal examples of present-day support for these two conceptions of sex roles, which occur in both the most conservative and most liberal groups in America. That black men hear and often internalize these conceptions of sex roles should be a foregone conclusion. Interestingly, this is the point where the societal reference group and the black man's peer group intersect. It is also the point when black male pathology begins. Illustratively: "Black women think they're badder than us. They think they're men. Always running their fat mouths . . . telling us what we ain't doing. Always putting us down. I know if another one of them jumps up in my face, I'm gonna choke her."[30]

29. Dowling, *Cinderella Complex.*
30. S. Taylor, "Black Love under Siege," *Essence,* July 1985, p. 62.

Given the above quote, is there any doubt that at least one aspect of traditional masculinity is internalized by black men: violence toward women? Yet, despite the fact that black men attempt to emulate white men in some areas, they still fall victim to society's barriers to full male traditional sex-role assumption, and this prevents them from enacting the Prince Charming ideal. Susan Taylor, editor-in-chief of *Essence*, calls attention to what she calls a chilling report about black men: "Recently, the National Urban League released a chilling report on black men in America. It confirms that life for our men in this country is still a dangerous, perilous thing — an ordeal that leaves them 'wounded and crippled,' if not physically, then most assuredly mentally and spiritually. It is an ordeal that is 'life-stunting and life-threatening.'"

The report, authored by James McGee, recounts the statistics discussed earlier, as well as reporting high unemployment rates among black males and relative high admissions of black men to mental hospitals (black men are admitted at a rate twice that of white men and the typical client in drug-treatment centers is "a 27-year-old black male who has not completed high school, and who began using drugs regularly in his middle teen years"). McGee notes: "The wonder is not that so many [black men] are wounded and crippled . . . but that so many survive with their minds healthy and their souls intact."[31]

Taylor suggests that the alarming statistics portend a dismal future for black males and the entire black community, and so black love is under siege. I believe that she is right. I have argued that the three most influential groups that together make up black men's social structure are the black man's peer group, the black subcultural reference group, and the societal reference group. Before the civil rights movement, the black men's subcultural reference group and the black man's peer group *both* emphasized exchanging instrumental and expressive functions among the sexes as one way to adapt to the social and economic demands of American life. This was deemed necessary because of societal limitations on black men's abilities to assume a traditional American male sex role. Frequently, it was necessary for black women to be breadwinners, and while black men may have been depicted in the media as shiftless, lazy, henpecked, spineless, etc., black women *and* black men knew the score — *they knew that role exchange was the key to black survival.* Not only was this information imparted in various ways by the subcultural institution but it was also part of black men's peer-group socialization of its younger members. Thus, while society indeed affected the kinds of roles black men and women could assume, black people did not live under the illusion that they could emu-

31. Ibid., p. 64.

late the white family; instead, they embraced workable alternatives. Thus, while the societal reference group existed for a few blacks as one to be emulated, most blacks recognized the group as an unworkable alternative.

The seeds of change in the black man's peer group were sown during the late 1960s and early 1970s when increasing numbers of black men began to buy the idea that black women were largely responsible for the plight of black men because of women's aggressive stances and the fact that they did not assume a sex role similar to the one assumed by white women.[32] While this change in the black man's peer group has meant that now there is greater consistency between it and the societal reference group, the price has been very high for black men. It has meant that black men have found their numbers dwindling at an alarming rate.

When black men in the early 1970s in many ways embraced America's ideas about masculinity (e.g., competitiveness, aggressiveness, violence, sufficient distance from femininity — and this is certainly apparent in the 1980s), the decimation of black men and the destruction of the black family intensified.

The societal reference group did not reshape its "oughts," "shoulds," and "musts" for black men — it has not changed sufficiently those norms defining the reciprocal rights and duties of black men as functioning members of the system. The societal reference group has not removed those barriers to upward mobility that relegate most black men to pitiful positions in America. Yet this same structure continues to emphasize learning the traditional ways to achieve in America; and also to tell black men that if they have not achieved, it must be the result of some defect in their character. Why? *Because anybody in America can be what he wants to be!* Never mind that the black male unemployment rate for those age 20+ hovers around 13.6%, while the rate for white males of the same age is 5.2%; and the rate for black males age 16–19 is much higher.[33]

Certainly there is a relationship between these structural barriers to black men's advancement and the increasing decimation of black men, especially when black men believe the societal reference group socialization message exhorting them to adopt the Prince Charming ideal with little possibility for enactment. Certainly these experiences for many black men result in alarming drug addiction rates, dramatic increases in black male admission to mental hospitals, appalling black male incarceration rates — and the list goes on. But what can we do about it?

32. In many ways this was a critical aspect of D. Moynihan, *The Negro Family: The Case for National Action* (Washington, D.C.: Department of Labor, Office of Planning and Research, 1965).

33. U.S. Bureau of Labor Statistics figures, May 1985.

CONSEQUENCES OF BLACK MEN'S INSTITUTIONAL DECIMATION

The consequences of black men's memberships in groups that make up their social structures are decidedly pathological. That black men experience role strain is to be expected, as it is for most people who face distracting and often conflicting role expectations. What happens for many others that does not happen for black men is that the larger social system (the societal reference group) intervenes and reduces role strain to tolerable levels. In the case of black men, all too often, the societal reference group intervenes and *increases* role strain to intolerable levels. Being a "good" father means setting positive social–behavioral examples, meeting job obligations, earning a decent salary, participating in child care and child-rearing activities. When the societal reference group encourages and supports policies that allow only a few black men to be able to participate in fatherhood, that group must bear part of the blame for black men's intolerable levels of role strain. After all, roles are structurally linked, which means that structural blockage of role assumption in any one or more roles will have consequences for other role assumptions. I submit that this has been, and is, the case for black males in America.

When black males are unable to assume those roles prescribed by society, the subcultural reference group no longer wields the influence on black males that it once did. No longer does this group provide the needed refuge for black men — the needed support for minimum sex-role polarization because of the conflict between black men and black women, and because of the tendency for black men and black women today to eschew the historical example of cooperation between the sexes in an effort to build a unified racial minority. The result is predictable: The black man's peer group, no longer adaptive, has become a pathological clone of archaic traditional *machoism*, leading some to suggest that many black men, like their white brothers, have destructive, sexist attitudes. The subcultural reference group gradually seems to be deteriorating into a war zone where black men and black women battle for limited resources at the expense of black children — the next generation. The societal reference group that underwent change 15 years ago from a black male perspective has regrouped and is reappearing as inflexible and insensitive to black men's problems as ever, while continuing to espouse a male socialization process that is dysfunctional for black men and that results in such pathological response as violence, crime, and other asocial behaviors once black men become aware of the futility of attempting to assume such a role.

SOME SOLUTIONS TO THE INSTITUTIONAL DECIMATION OF BLACK MEN

Since the early 1980s, the societal reference group has in many ways reneged on implicit promises made to black men — in fact, to black people

—during the late 1960s and early 1970s when the threat of a full-scale black male revolution seemed imminent. Before the 1980s, the societal reference group made great strides toward creating equal opportunities in educational and economic institutions. Since then, many would argue that there has been enormous retrenchment. Consider that corporations are given extended amounts of time before penalties are assessed for sex discrimination and race discrimination, and in some instances, no penalties are levied at all. Also, school districts are allowed to integrate their schools gradually before harsh penalties are extended for segregation, and some districts are now allowed to return to the "neighborhood" school model. Even more debilitating for black males is the relatively stable unemployment rates black males face because of job scarcity. I believe it is reasonable to expect, in fact to demand, that the societal reference group respond in more sensitive ways to black men's unemployment problems, which result in the removal of many black men from the civilian population.

Just as critical for intervention purposes as changes in the societal reference group's response to black males is change in the black man's peer group. This means, essentially, the development and nurturing of black men's peer-group norms that stress the inappropriateness of violent youth gangs, drug cultures, and teenage fatherhood.

Intervention is absolutely essential if the black family is to survive. I am not referring to federal or state government intervention. I *am* referring to alterations in the black man's peer group. Given the very high percentage of black children being reared in single, female-headed households, it is not feasible to expect that changes in parents' childrearing strategies alone can change the course of black family and black male destruction. The attempt to alter black male decimation and black family deterioration must be a black men's community effort. Black males must develop a functional message for black male youth and other black males and black females — a message that essentially calls for a return to more peaceful and productive relations between black men, and between black men and black women. This means that tacit approval – support can no longer be given to black men's violence with themselves, with one other, with black women, and with others.

A socialization message for black male youth must be constructed that includes the above and that says it is highly unmanly, irresponsible, and "uncool" to father children who cannot be provided for. A part of this message also must be devoted to emphasizing intra- and intergroup respect and intra- and intersex respect. This is the kind of message that black men and black male youth must hear in barbershops and bars, on street corners, and in similar informal sex-role socialization settings. Succinctly, the black man's peer group must once again be aligned with the subcultural reference group. Such an alignment means that black male pioneers in this effort will likely be questioned regarding motives, and perhaps even ridiculed. In fact, this is to be expected if Emihovich, Gaier, and Cronin's conclusion from their white father – son study has any general applicability to the strategy I am proposing.[34] They concluded that fathers' beliefs and expectations clearly influenced sons' beliefs and that drastic change in adolescent boys' gender beliefs should not be expected unless there was "father support" for the change. Moreover, despite the fact that the fathers in the father – son pairs studies were well educated, they were nevertheless quite traditional in sex-role expectations for their sons, suggesting, as men did during the Plecks' "strenuous life" period, that boys were becoming "too feminized" and that they were in danger of forgetting what it means to "act like a man."[35]

Because so many black male youth in all likelihood spend little time with their biological fathers and much more time with older, unrelated males, where a compulsive masculinity alternative is stressed, the likelihood of altering black male decimation in the near future does not seem high. Given today's continued increases in black male youth violence, especially in urban areas, dramatic increases in black teenage pregnancy, and the continual rise in black male teenage and young adult crime, abatement of the institutional decimation of black males is not in sight. Indeed, a drive within the subcultural reference group, based in black subcultural institutions such as the church, major economic institutions, and most important, informal socializing structures and institutions, must be made if black men are to survive and if the black family is to regain its strength, its vitality, its unity, and its health.

34. C. A. Emihovich, C. A. Gaier, and N. C. Cronin, "Sex-Role Expectation Changes by Fathers for Their Sons," *Sex Roles* 11 (1984): 861–869.

35. E. H. Pleck and J. H. Pleck, *The American Man* (Englewood Cliffs, N.J.: Prentice-Hall, 1980).

III

Work and Play

Do men work at establishing their masculinity through their play? Do they play-out internal psychic dramas through their work? In this section Richard Ochberg and Michael Messner demonstrate that boundaries between work and play, inner and outer dimensions of men's experience, and public and private roles are more permeable than we have been led to believe. One way the preceding section can inform this one is to understand the peculiar impersonal personableness of modern business life as resulting from a transition from the demands of "character" to those of "personality" that accompanied the shift from nineteenth- to twentieth-century codes of masculinity.

"The Male Career Code and the Ideology of Role" investigates, through case studies, how men "lose themselves" in their work. Conflicting needs to integrate and separate the spheres of home and work create psychodynamic tensions in men's experiences of themselves as performers in various roles, leading to anxiety, stress, and a discomfiting internal self-vigilance. Unresolved intergenerational identifications and intragenerational competitions may also mold career paths.

"The Meaning of Success: The Athletic Experience and the Development of Male Identity" explores the social–psychological relationship of "masculinity" with organized sports in a life-course perspective. It examines men's interactions with sports in terms of their initial boyhood attraction to sports, how notions of "success" in sports connect with a developing sense of male identity, and how relationships to work and other people change after the sports career ends, often precipitating a "disengagement crisis." Young males' ambivalent gender identities predispose them to experience the rule-bound structure of sports as a "safe" place to seek connection with others and validation of self. But as the boy becomes an "athlete" and attempts to succeed within the competitive, hierarchic sports world, he often develops an increasingly instrumental personality that has a negative impact on his self-image and his ability to develop intimate relationships. Such findings have implications for understanding the contradictions of nonathlete men's lives as well.

7

The Male Career Code and the Ideology of Role

Richard L. Ochberg

One of the more popular lines of contemporary social criticism holds that the impersonality of male career culture deadens the inner world of working men. Attractive as this thesis may be to some scholars, it does justice to neither the ambivalence within career culture nor the psyches of the men who serve it. The culture of upper-middle-class careers is not now — if indeed it ever was — monolithically impersonal. Certainly, the corporate world, to take the best-studied subculture, expects men to divulge little of their personal lives and to hold in check whatever personal sentiments, especially affection, they may feel toward their colleagues.[1] At the same time, since at least Riesman's famous reappraisal,[2] that world also has demanded that men perfect a form of businesslike glad-handedness, that they be sufficiently affable to be part of the team. (Whyte makes a similar observation.[3]) In fact, the balance between detached, self-interested calculation and disingenuous affection is one of the formative tensions built into the fabric of the business world. Sutton remarks:

> Salesmen assume a cheery enthusiasm and friendliness; the clerks in women's stores behave with saccharine familiarity. . . . Assumed friendliness has an even more obvious significance in the problem of initiating business relationships. . . . Outgoing "friendliness" in this sense has obvious functional importance in a dynamic, progressive economy. . . . It also gives rise to considerable strain. . . . Where narrow self-

1. R. M. Kanter, *Men and Women of the Corporation* (New York: Basic Books, 1977); C. Sofer, *Men in Mid-Career* (Cambridge, England: Cambridge University Press, 1970); and W. E. Henry, "The Business Executive: The Psychodynamics of a Social Role," *American Journal of Sociology* 54 (1949):286–291.
2. D. Riesman, *The Lonely Crowd* (New Haven: Yale University Press, 1950).
3. W. H. Whyte, *The Organization Man* (New York: Simon and Schuster, 1956).

oriented relationships are clothed in the forms of intimate relationships, suspicions about sincerity can hardly be avoided.[4]

For many men, this social tension resonates with a private conflict. Men are no more perfectly dispassionate than the culture within which they serve; many men long to establish personal relationships with their colleagues, yet fear that any overture of affection will leave them vulnerable. Thus a harmony of mutually exacerbating ambivalence exists—a tension constructed on one side by conflicting social demands and on the other by conflicting personal desires.

As might be expected, the culture of careers suggests something of a solution, at least for the social problem. Men who face these contradictory social demands—that they be both collegial and dispassionate—often describe their sense of "acting in role." That is, they reveal something of their personal lives, but only to the degree that the job requires. Their personalism is part of the professional act; it departs from the official code of impersonality by as small and calculated a fraction as wearing Nikes to the office. This strategy of being personal within the limits of role has a further use. It can be deployed to solve not only the social problem but the psychodynamic one as well. It allows men to be as affectionate with each other as they dare while reassuring them that they will not go overboard.

Partly, my intention in this chapter is to describe the interaction of these social and psychodynamic problems, and their simultaneous solution by the formula that "role" provides self-consciousness. However, I have a second purpose, which takes as its point of departure the similarity between the way these men, and we in the academy, use the term *role*.

Men's studies, of course, has a major interest in roles. A leading collection of essays and a prominent journal bear the title *Sex Roles*; the term might serve as a shorthand description of our discipline. Eventually I argue that these men use the idea of role to misconstrue themselves, at the cost of self-denial. Of course, these men are not academicians; they use the term in ways we might not. Still, there are similarities. To the degree that their self-conception of acting in role degrades their subjectivity, it points out a risk that we should avoid in our academic usage.

I begin by presenting two men—Don and Ken—whom I interviewed for about 5 hours each in the course of a larger study on men's careers.[5] These two cases may not satisfy the expectations of social scientists—who will want to know how representative they are of men in general—or

4. F. X. Sutton, *The American Business Creed* (Cambridge: Harvard University Press, 1956).

5. R. Ochberg, *Middle-aged Sons and the Meaning of Work* (Ann Arbor: UMI Research Press, 1987).

clinicians—who will want much more individual detail. But my intention is neither to claim that these men are typical (although the things they say about their world, and their place in it, are certainly familiar) nor to provide a thorough clinical analysis. My aim is to show the conceptual limits of a particular interpretive perspective—classic role theory—which for the moment may appear to us not an interpretive perspective at all.

DON

For the past 10 years, Don has been a psychologist with the Jackson State Penitentiary. Six months ago, he was appointed director of two new projects within the penal system: an alcohol treatment center and a half-way house for men newly released from prison. Although both programs are running successfully, in our conversations Don's focus was on the strain he felt administering programs that were still in the chaotic first stages of getting established. He remarked, "We are starting something and creating it at the same time . . . ideologically I disagree with that. I'm the sort of person who has to plan through a thing to some degree before I do it."

It soon emerged that Don's discomfort with hectic disorganization is far more general than these particular jobs. Don prepares carefully for each day. Two hours before leaving home in the morning, he lays out his goals for the day and the amount of time each should consume. He explained that without this sort of advance planning, work would take over his life. Should he feel overly stressed during the day, he will pause to meditate or leave the building for a walk. Once home, he attempts to put work entirely out of mind.

> I always make a clear separation out [of work], so that I am not still
> processing it . . . I try to leave it so when I walk in the door I am ready
> to deal with the dog, my wife and the kids, and not force them to deal
> with me. That is a high priority for me, one of my highest values. When I
> go home I am available, not demanding . . . I try not to be a burden, as
> much as humanly possible.

This passage suggests several ideas, which on further exploration turned out to be pervasive themes in Don's life. One is his concern with being helpful, an idea that Don associates with being available, wholly present, engaged. There is a corollary to this idea, which in a curious way is its exact opposite. Don feels that in order for him to be wholly engaged

with his family he must, in another sense, be wholly detached. He must rid
himself of the workday's residue of agitation. He accomplishes this by
"separating out" — consciously shifting his attention from work to home.
He explained, "I shift roles — theological, naval, mental health, and personal roles. I consciously move from one to another, and behave differently in each." A bit later he explained,

> If I can't, as a husband and father, be available to my family in the limited
> time I have, then I am cheating them. The primary responsibility is to
> shift roles, to be available to my client, to [my boss], to my wife. I try to
> be a helpful person.
>   When I come home I don't want the rest of the world to intrude.
> Right now I am on back-up. . . . If the phone rings, then I'll deal with it.
> But if I don't deny, project, compartmentalize to some degree, then every
> time the phone rings I flinch, and I can't give my attention to the kids
> doing their homework, whatever.

At first glance, Don seems concerned about distinguishing his work life
from his family, but his language suggests something more. The way he
uses the term *role*, especially his idea of a *personal* role, hints that he is not
merely separating work and family, but personal involvement and effective helpfulness. Even at home, where we might expect him to be personal,
Don describes himself in curiously impersonal images. At one point he
remarked, "Lately one of my highest priorities is to help the children with
their homework. I am good at algebra and literature; my wife at grammar.
Between us we have a lot of the skills; we can transfer that to the kids."

Parenting, in this account, becomes the transfer of skills: an oddly
technical description of fatherhood, shorn of emotion. Don suggests an
image of himself as technically appropriate but perhaps never entirely
expressive. Viewed this way, life becomes a series of tasks, each requiring a
clear head, unemcumbered by the leftovers of the hour before. Don is not
unemotional; certainly no one would accuse him of being cold. Yet when
he says his highest value is to be available, he seems to wish he were an
instrument of service, purified of any personal neediness.

Don's preoccupation with carefully controlled boundaries suggests an
underlying anxiety. What would he risk if his own feelings intruded on his
"role" performance? Here, he describes the danger of allowing personal
feelings to invade work:

> You know how in power plants they have those bubbling power gauges?
> The bubble goes out of range when the pressure goes up, or it
> drops . . . it really goes out of sight. Clinically, when I lose the bubble I
> have lost my sense of . . . where I am, where the client is. . . . Where

you really lose the bubble is where you become part of the problem; the countertransference gets out of whack and you get hooked into it.

Countertransference is, of course, a legitimate preoccupation of anyone who works in the counseling professions, but Don has felt this concern at other, less conventional times. When he was a chaplain in the Navy, Don felt, "I had to know certain things about how the ship was set up so that if there was an emergency, you couldn't be a liability." Here again his concern seems to be that he might damage someone else in a moment of crisis by getting in the way. He might, as he puts it, "become part of the problem."

Don's conception of himself as an emotionally detached, efficient provider is, of course, not his invention. He is speaking a language here that we all know by heart: It is the code of masculinity, with all its limitations and — I would insist — its own honor. Yet there is a more idiosyncratic side to this story, to which we must now turn.

Don was born with a twin brother who died 12 days after birth. The umbilical cord became twisted around the brother's neck so that oxygen was cut off. Although Don obviously was not able to recall his childhood feelings about his brother's death, it is a reasonable guess that he harbors some sense of guilt. Don may have felt then — and unconsciously still — that his presence was part of the problem that killed his brother. This thought would draw added power from the fact that the brother received the name picked in advance — he was named for the father — while Don was named for the doctor. The history of names could add to a child's thought: "He was the real baby; I wasn't supposed to be there, and that is what killed him."

Seven years later, Don's father died of a heart attack.

We had just gotten through with the tug-of-war [at a picnic]. My father's side had won, and we were all excited. I remember being on the bench, hanging on to him, trying to get on to his shoulders or something, and he was saying, "I'm tired, just bug off." Something to that effect. And as it turned out he was having a heart attack. And then he got up and collapsed a few feet away. A lot of people came around and I was excluded. . . . They put him in an ambulance and we followed, being helpless and cut off, the adults taking over, that whole sense of being detached.

Here, again, is the implication that Don caused a death by his intrusive presence. He was "part of the problem" — with lethal results. Less obviously, the opposite sentiment is also represented. In each event Don also pictures his own exclusion. The brother, not Don, was the expected child. Immediately after the father's heart attack, Don was "cut off," "detached." As Don recalls those events he underscores both his deadly intrusiveness and simultaneously his sense of being left out.

In the years after his father's death the family moved to a new town. Don's mother and older sister grew closer, with the result that Don came to feel less engaged within what remained of his family. Relief came from the families of his school chums. He recalled, "Some of the fathers of the other kids would include you, take you fishing. You'd feel included. 'Gee, Don, I'm really glad you could come.'" When I asked what it was about him that other children's fathers liked, he replied,

> As an adult and as a kid, I'm a nice guy. I am not mean. I heard someone say . . . that a gentleman is someone who never intentionally hurts another person. That sort of captures me in a way. I will certainly unintentionally hurt people; we all do. But I always consciously try to be a positive influence, not something that drags things down or is negative.

One more time, the themes of not being a hurtful person and being included come together.

These themes are still active in Don's adult life. Both at work and with his family he remains preoccupied with not being hurtful. (To return to where we began: The problem with stress, Don explained, is that it makes him testy with his employees.) Don's dilemma is to find a way of being helpfully engaged yet sufficiently detached to avoid imposing on others. His solution is a highly self-conscious sense of acting in role. Acting in role — as therapist, administrator, naval officer or parent — Don can be wholly and *helpfully* engaged and at the same time detached enough to protect those he loves from his destructive intrusiveness.

The only problem is that the strategy never completely works. No matter how careful Don is, his sense of danger never disappears. At work, he is constantly aware of his susceptibility to agitation. Although he attempts to separate his personal and work lives, his early-morning listmaking brings work intrusively into his home. Thus, in the classic manner of an obsessive–compulsive neurosis, Don surreptitiously infiltrates the danger he fears through the back door, in the very act of barricading the front. Perhaps most significantly, no matter how much time Don manages to spend with his family, he remains emotionally distant. His own careful "niceness" contributes to his isolation. He is cut off, not from the physical presence of others, but from deeply felt emotional contact.

KEN

Ken, who at age 37 holds a high-level management position in a small industrial company, begins from a premise exactly opposite Don's.

Where Don emphasizes the importance of keeping work and home separate, and avoiding the intrusion of personal sentiment into one's work, Ken pictures himself as deliberately personal. He describes his managerial style as that of a "coach," and explains that a small company like his cannot be run by an impersonal director. He actively courts the loyalty of his employees with dinners, invitations to his home, and an interest in their families.

> You have to take a key employee to dinner with his wife . . . and try to engender support in her, because if you don't have both people you will never be effective. You don't want her complaining [when he has to work late]. You have to sit down with his wife and explain your feelings about her husband: how important he is and how much you rely on him.

Yet it soon became apparent that Ken's personal managerial style has distinct limits. The invitations to dinner at his home are strictly in the interests of promoting business harmony. There is no question of real friendship. In a remarkably candid passage he described the limits that his own power places in the way of genuine friendship with his employees.

> It is not a standoffish kind of relationship; we get into good discussions and understand each other, and talk very frankly about certain issues, but there is still a natural barrier that inhibits it. . . . It can't become [a friendship] because I am in a control position. I have got too much influence on their normal sphere of life, and that kind of relationship doesn't work.

Over the course of several interviews, this theme — the balance between genuine intimacy and detached collegiality — emerged as a preoccupation in Ken's life. His brother and his father were bad managers because they were too standoffish; Ken admired his father-in-law, who taught him to be a good listener. He had quarreled with an old friend whose management style was more impersonal; in contrast, he had fired a subordinate who, Ken felt, abdicated authority by becoming too personal with his workers.

By good fortune, the period when I interviewed Ken coincided with a moment in his career that dramatically highlighted the issue of detached collegiality. Ken had just been promoted to chief of sales. His first major act on assuming his new position was to hire a professional business consultant, who prepared a psychological report on each of Ken's employees. Partly, Ken wanted to evaluate his staff, but he also saw the evaluation as a means of building team spirit. The idea was that employees would share their psychological profiles with one other. This would enhance mutual understanding and team productivity. An unforeseen consequence of the

evaluation was the discovery that a junior colleague, who had been Ken's
protégé, was thoroughly incompetent, disliked by his colleagues, and suspected of favorable treatment because he was Ken's friend. Ken's reaction
to the whole affair was complicated.

The relationship with his protégé had been an exception to Ken's managerial philosophy. The two men had been friends outside of work; Ken had
been a confidant during his protégé's divorce; against his own best judgment, Ken had offered the man a second and then a third chance to reform
his work habits. Now Ken felt betrayed and humiliated.

> The feeling is extreme disappointment on my part. He doesn't either
> respect me or care enough about me to do his job. . . . Instead of saying,
> "Ken, I will do twice as good this time, for you, because you are giving
> me this chance," he takes it as a sign of weakness: "That means I can
> screw off even more." . . . I treated him as a friend, not as an employee,
> and as a friend he has disappointed me miserably, miserably. I guess that
> is why it gets me. I have given so much and gotten so little in return.

The notable point about Ken's reaction was the way he felt victimized.
Ken felt he had allowed himself to be drawn beyond his own careful
boundaries into a personal, emotional relationship. He experienced this as
consciously manipulative on his protégé's part, and degrading. Over the
course of several interviews, Ken's concern with emotional manipulation
became obvious. At one point he described his experience in dealing with
the union: "The union reps work like classical debate guys. They will
antagonize you intentionally to get you to say something that they can pick
up on" Another time, he described his antipathy to playing golf with
colleagues whose good offices he needed: "I hate the goddamn game. Why
should I put myself into such frustration because some guy I am selling to
happens to enjoy that kind of masochistic game?" Finally, there is this
passage, in which Ken describes his style of dealing with the people from
whom he buys parts:

> I deal with a lot of machinery salesman, and they are really aggressive
> guys. It is a rough business; steel and machinery are like that. And they
> are professionals at dominating a sales meeting: Sign up, sign up, do this,
> do that. So what I like to do is encroach on their so-called perimeter,
> really cut their defenses down. I play the body language thing [here he
> pulled his chair very close to mine and leaned forward], get really close,
> until the guy is uneasy, the sweat is pouring out of him and he doesn't
> know what the hell is going on. Pretty soon he is totally out of control, he
> is so anxious to get out of there. . . . And I found that once you pull that
> type of thing, all of a sudden your relationship changes. Next time, it will

be more as if I were a peer and not some guy where you have to put the move on him.

What stands out in each of these passages is Ken's sense of being manipulated into losing emotional control or personal distance, and thereby losing power. As always, his language tells the story: Another man will "put the move on him"; he will be forced to play a "masochistic" game. He is sensitive to a particularly degrading sense of powerlessness.

If the theme of emotional manipulation recurred constantly in Ken's description of work, its meaning did not become clear until we turned to his history. Unlike Don, with Ken there were no sharp, unambiguously traumatic incidents. Instead, Ken recounted a history of continual, accumulating stress. His father had a violent and unpredictable temper, yet his storms would pass abruptly.

> He yells, blows up, calls you every name in the book, then ten minutes later gives you a hug and says, "Why are you so upset?" You are ready to kill him at that point, and he can't understand it. "What's the matter, got a chip on your shoulder?" After he has totally abused you. . . . He is just vicious when he goes on the attack. [And then an hour later] he'd say that I am carrying a grudge, you know without an apology or discussion. It was just expected to be dropped.

Ken came to feel that these explosions were an almost deliberate strategy on his father's part to manipulate control: "He controls situations by being inconsistent. His emotions are inconsistent. He has to be right, and how he approaches being right could be anything from calling you a son of a bitch to overwhelming you with affection."

When Ken was a child, most of his father's rage was vented on Ken's older brother. Ken became the exemplary child; an Eagle Scout, an honors student, an athlete who eventually won scholarships to colleges around the country. Ken avoided his brother's rowdy excesses, spent as much time as he could outside the house, and largely escaped his father's rage. And then a curious thing happened.

Sometime in college, Ken discovered that neither his strategy of being the exemplary child nor of absenting himself from home was working. He began to notice his father's habit of belittling his achievements while lauding his brother for much smaller victories. Ken cited a string of examples: The father boasts about Ken's brother, who had graduated from Ohio State, but never mentions the MA Ken earned at Michigan. A tool the brothers invented together (Ken thought it was mostly his idea) is credited solely to the brother. The brother's leadership on civic committees is a source of family pride; Ken's position on a governor's task force is never mentioned.

More painful was Ken's growing realization that for all their fighting, his brother and father were much closer to each other than either was to him. For years, Ken and his brother had a tradition of staying up all night, drinking and talking. Sometimes their father joined them. Occasionally, when Ken was not around, his brother and father stayed up alone. One year, Ken asked his father to stay up alone with him.

> He wouldn't do it. Not with me. And I asked him, "You've done this for years with Jack, why won't you stay up and—" "Well, I'm getting too old for that." He didn't really want me to know him the way that Jack knew him, or something.
>
> The thing that will always bother me as long as I live is never having had my Dad say I have done a good job with the business. And he never will say that, I guarantee it, until the day he croaks. . . . To the day I die it is going to bother me. It is just like the play, "I never sang for my father."

Against this background, Ken's relationship to his employees, and the particular insult of his protégé, begin to make sense. In effect, Ken has become to his employees what his father could never be to him. Where his father was emotionally distant, Ken is personal and caring. Where his father exploited emotional volatility as a form of manipulation, Ken is detached. Of course, the balance Ken needs to strike is delicate. Much as Ken wants to be the "coach" to his employees, personal engagement always threatens to go too far. At those moments, Ken loses his own boundaries; he is drawn into emotionally roiled waters. He feels himself manipulated and demeaned, just as he did as a child. For Ken to be to his employees the good father he himself misses, he must tread a narrow line between engagement and dispassion. This is the source of his obsessive allegiance to his difficult managerial philosophy of detached collegiality. It also explains his sense of injury at the hands of his protégé.

The way Ken safeguards himself is to say, "I care about my employees, but only in a professional way." It is exactly what he says about dinner invitations. This is not real friendship, not the kind of out-of-control emotion that can get you humiliated; it is kept within harmless bounds by the recognition, on both sides, that this sort of friendship is only business. His protégé broke the code. He acted as if the friendship were real. The insult—because Ken feels insulted—is not that the protégé was wrong but that he was right. In a sense, Ken keeps his emotional balance by pretending to pretend. He says, in effect, "I may seem to be friendly, but make no mistake: This isn't real friendship, it is a calculated business policy." The trouble is that every once in a while, Ken loses track of who is fooling whom. The friendship with the protégé was real. Robbed of his usual pretense of detachment, Ken ultimately felt manipulated and demeaned.

Ken's reaction to what he perceived as his protégé's affront was immediate and unequivocal. He immediately demoted the protégé to a front-line sales position at half his previous salary (although commissions might restore part of the balance). When I asked Ken why he did not offer the man a bit more security—given his decision not to fire him outright—Ken explained:

> Let's say he could live with $25,000 a year, is he going to be an effective
> salesman? I don't know. In that case I am stuck with an ineffective
> salesman and he is bitter at that point. [This way] he can walk away or
> say, "I don't like it, but I think I can do it, and I am going to give it a shot."

Ken's business logic is impeccable, but the words he chooses catch our attention. Ken does not want to be "stuck" with a "bitter" subordinate. This idea, like his concern about emotional manipulation, is a repeated motif in Ken's description of how he conducts his adult life, and what he had been unable to do as a child. Speaking of a different skirmish in his organization that he nipped in the bud, Ken said, "If you don't squelch it right away it will fester; go down the ladder [of the company organization] and all of a sudden you have a real serious problem." Or again, describing a battle with his brother about how to exploit their joint invention:

> I am not prepared to put up with it again. I would force the issue next
> time. Just continue antagonizing the issue until a decision would have to
> be made. . . . I would rather fight it as hard as I can, with everything I
> have, than sit back and say, "This is how it will be forevermore." That
> would tear me up. . . . It would bother me less to lose my brother's
> friendship as a result of going on the attack to straighten up the situation.

In each of these recountings, we hear echoes of Ken's childhood experience. At that time, he had been left smoldering, while his father blithely sailed on. As an adult, he is determined to root out festering rancor everywhere he suspects it—in himself, in his organization, and in his chastised protégé's heart. One other point about Ken's reaction must be mentioned. Although Ken did acknowledge how personally he felt his protégé's rebuff, he did so only once, in our final interview. More often, he described his reaction as that of a manager who has discovered a crack in the corporate machine. Speaking in this vein, he drew an odd connection between the affair with his protégé and his new policy of managerial self-revelation:

> People expect this situation [with the protégé] to be resolved in a
> legitimate manner. . . . We are going through an awful lot of changes

right now, with people exposing themselves. . . . It isn't strickly personal,
there is a much bigger picture in here. . . . You know, if they are going
to expose themselves, and try to make a contribution, the company is
going to have to make a contribution too, and do it in a forthright, honest
manner.

The connection between punishing his protégé and encouraging his employees to share their profiles is not apparent. A different manager might
have noticed that his employees would be all the more frightened by the
protégé's example: After all, the consultant's investigation had exposed his
incompetence. If Ken's favorite could not count on protection when damaging secrets came to light, who could? Ken did not see it this way, and that
is interesting.

His logic seems to have been something like this: Demoting his protégé
reestablished the damaged boundary between friendship and businesslike
collegiality. This, in turn, made it once again safe for Ken's junior managers to share their psychological profiles. In effect, Ken says, "The profiles are safe because they are not really personal. There is no room in this
company for that kind of personalism. I guarantee it; punishing my protégé is proof. So come on in, let your hair down, join the team. It is only
business." Of course, we may wonder whose doubts are being allayed, but
that is a different matter.

ROLE AS A SOCIAL AND A PSYCHODYNAMIC SOLUTION

Clearly, Don and Ken start from different—nearly opposite—premises.
Don begins by describing his need to separate sharply his life at home and
at work. Ken starts from the opposite point: his conviction that "team
spirit" is possible only if the manager and his players socialize after-hours.
On closer examination, these men have more in common than either
might recognize. Each is struggling with the boundary between private
and public life; each is highly ambivalent.

The two men describe their solutions in curiously similar terms. Each
describes his sense of acting in role. This idea allows each man to address
both the social and the psychodynamic problem he faces. Socially, the
sense of acting in role allows Don and Ken to give as much of themselves as
the job demands yet retain the distinction between work life and private
life. Don trades roles—minister, social worker, husband—and in this way
leaves the cares of each occupation safely outside the door of the next. Ken
invites his employees home, yet never loses track of the difference between
colleagues and friends.

Psychodynamically, the sense of acting in role promises each man a resolution to his ambivalent wish to be wholly engaged and at the same time safely dispassionate. Don gets to feel that he can be wholly available (to his boss, his wife, his children) without worrying that his own private turmoil will invade the relationship and make him "part of the problem." Ken gets to socialize with his employees in the brotherly (or fatherly) fashion he longs for, without worrying that he will be drawn in too far, forced to lose his cool, and humiliated.

Yet if *role* promises to address both the social and psychodynamic problem, it succeeds unequally. Ken and Don manage the contradictory demands of public life with considerable agility. Operating as a manager, Ken can be both unusually personal and completely detached. Similarly, Don in his capacity of counselor, chaplain, (or his "role" of father), feels he can be wholly present yet unintrusive. The curious fact is that neither seems wholly convinced by his own success. Each man remains leery, watching over his own shoulder lest private feeling suddenly, and damagingly, intrude. Don remains continually anxious at work. He experiences this anxiety primarily in somatic terms, as stress. He is reluctant to consider the unconscious, interpersonal meaning that hides behind his somatic experience. The price he pays is that he must be eternally, and only half successfully, on guard against tension. Ken, for his part, seems to invite his favored lieutenants—and perhaps now his whole staff—to more-than-usual intimacy; then he feels humiliated. At this point, social reality enters the equation: Don is a middle-level manager; Ken is now the chief administrator of his division. Partly for this reason, Don pays the cost of his neurosis personally, while Ken takes his vengeance out on his subordinates.

Now this is something to wonder at. Why, we might ask, are Ken and Don not reassured by their own success? We might put the matter in developmental terms. Both men have had difficult childhoods, which have left them anxious and vulnerable. Each has overcome his handicap enough to manage—with some facility—the contradictary demands of public life. In their private experience, however, each remains plagued by the anxieties of childhood. It is as if development has proceeded on separate tracks. The maturation of the public man has left the private one untouched. (Or, more formally, neither man has internalized into his ego the *savoir faire* of his own public persona).

The explanation, of course, lies in the idea of role as a form of self-experience. Out of concern that private, unruly emotion will disrupt their public functioning, these men have drawn a distinction between their roles and their selves. Because of the sharpness with which this boundary is maintained, the public person never has a chance to reeducate the private one. The problem bears an interesting resemblance to one described by Selma Fraiberg in the psychoanalysis of children.[6] With small children, who have not yet developed the capacity for self-reflection, play therapy often centers on imaginative dramas peopled by fictional naughty children and disapproving adults. The analyst understands these ostensibly fictional characters to represent the young patient and his or her family. But unless the therapist can make the patient aware of the connection between play and self-experience, therapy is likely to remain only marginally effective. Fraiberg remarks:

> Somehow I have got to get that fictional bad boy and his accusers back into [the patient's] ego or he will never be obliged to acknowledge that the impulses arise from within him and that the punishments derive from his own conscience . . . [Otherwise] we may find that some small benefits have come to the patient as the result of the *fictional* small boy's analysis, but there are no fundamental changes in the patient himself.[7]

Ken and Don obviously do not separate their roles and selves as rigorously as Fraiberg's five-year-old analysands; the developmental problem they face, however, is similar. Because the imaginary character — or role —is distinguished from self, curing the role may leave the ego unimproved.

The result is a curious form of dual existence. These men have two lives, and they come to reside more and more in the public one. In times of stress, this is where they retreat. So, for example, when Ken felt manipulated by friendship with his protégé, he restored impersonality by escaping into role. He did this in two senses. In the public arena of work, Ken imagined that he was restoring safe impersonality by demoting his protégé. This demonstrated that theirs was only a professional relationship and, by a not completely logical extension, that the intrusive psychological profiles were safe. This social act was also a psychodynamic restoration: Ken disavowed *to himself* his sense of humiliation, by escaping into his public persona.

The problem with this strategy is twofold. First, as I have been saying, it undermines the way social experience ordinarily fosters psychological development. Second, it disavows the importance of private feelings.

There seems to be no way to approach this latter point without admitting it as an *a priori* value. We can concede that by experiencing themselves as actors in roles, Don and Ken improve their ability to function publicly. We can even concede the possibility — in this case, untrue — that role experience allows these men to defend against privately experiencing their

    6. S. Fraiberg, "A Comparison of the Analytic Method in Two Stages of a Child Analysis," *Journal of the American Academy of Child Psychiatry* 4 (1965):387–400.
    7. Ibid., pp. 394–396.

anxieties. (For Don and Ken, role experience seems to provide only a leaky psychodynamic defense. Don is obsessed about stress and never notices its interpersonal meaning, while Ken oscillates between defensive aggression and his unadmitted fear of humiliation.) Even if experiencing self-as-role resulted in thoroughly successful social adaptation and psychic defense, we might yet object that this form of self-experience reduces men. The trouble is that in experiencing their selves as roles, both men escape a more private experience of selfhood.

We can understand their reasons. Don, for example, fears that he harbors within himself a degree of agitation that will destroy those he loves. By acting in role, Don gets away from himself altogether so that he can be with people without damaging them. What is worrisome about this maneuver is that Don and Ken renounce the legitimacy of private experience. They take up a position from which their own passions are disqualified from subjective consideration. They experience themselves in terms of their value to others. They evade the difficulty of their own private being by escaping into their public personas. However difficult these private passions are, the solution — to abandon one's private selfhood in favor of self experienced and valued as if from the outside — seems an abdication.

This brings me to the theoretical point I mentioned at the start of this discussion. If Don and Ken use role as a defensive form of self-representation — one that ultimately degrades their subjectivity — we must also be wary of what academic theories we use to describe the relation between public roles and private reasons.

ROLE AS SELF-CONSCIOUSNESS AND AS THEORY

The emerging discipline of gender studies, whether it examines men's or women's experience, has a strong commitment to the idea of role as a theoretical optic. Role allows gender studies to explore the idea that images of feminity and masculinity are not neutral, objective descriptions but culturally contingent constructions. Further, role theory allows us to examine the way cultural norms are internalized into subjective experience. Finally, the theoretical language of role appears to lend itself to the cause of liberation. This point bears examination.

Men are not alone in adopting the imagery of self-in-role. Don's comments, for example, have a great deal in common with what has become a popular image among women; a similar criticism may be relevant. The dilemma of women who seek careers is not simply the burden of multiple commitments on their time and energy; it is that the domains of career and family require different combinations of aggressive competence and nurturance. The imagery of self-in-role allows women to claim — as a host of television commercials, ever our best index of popular self-imagery, promise — that they can be as tough as men in the office from nine to five, and seductively gentle after-hours. The idea of switching temperament from role to role allows women to claim they can be all things to all partners. But is this really a liberating idea? From the dominant male perspective, women have always been viewed as partners — and have in turn so viewed themselves. The imagery of self-in-role promises them greater efficacy in this endeavor. But does it not do so at the price of reinforcing their status as nothing but counterplayers?

Much the same point applies to Don. In choosing to describe himself (and, more important, experience himself) from the perspective of acting in role, Don has taken up a point of view outside himself. He experiences himself in terms of his value to others, but renounces the legitimacy of his own private cares. This perspective diminishes him; it makes him into nothing but an eternal partner. (Don, of course, would protest. He feels that he is most fully realized as a partner. But we notice how much he pushes his own concerns underground, and at what cost.)

Don and Ken direct us to consider a problem that usually slips beneath theoretical observation. Although gender studies are often critical of the current content of gender roles, theory takes as axiomatic the idea that *some* sort of self-in-role experience must exist. Self-experience is always conditioned by public demands and by the subjective experience of one's public reception. From this theoretical point of departure, the idea of criticizing role experience per se seems nonsensical. What Don and Ken call to our attention is that experiencing oneself as an actor in role is a form of self-consciousness, created by particular cultural conditions, donated to the partial alleviation of social and psychodynamic stress, and bearing a substantial price tag. Our ability to examine these issues depends on our theoretical point of departure.

Social–psychological theory can be divided — with some heuristic exaggeration — into different conceptions of how public roles and private subjectivity are related. In its simplest, most radically sociological form, role theory provides an account that dispenses altogether with private self-experience. Thus Becker, toward the end of an essay on how social structure accounts for personal change and stability in adult life, remarks:

> The processes we have considered indicate that social structure creates the conditions for both change and stability in adult life. . . . They enable us to arrive at general explanations of personal development in adult life *without requiring us to posit unvarying characteristics of the person, either elements of personality or of "value structure."*[8]

8. H. Becker, "Personal Change in Adult Life," *Sociometry* 27 (1964):40–53. Emphasis added in quote.

In this passage, Becker makes clear the advantage he foresees in a purely sociological account of adult development. It will allow us to avoid speculating about anything that has to do with "personality" or "value structure," that is, anything not given by the social situation. There is an interesting parallel between the advantages Becker foresees and the use to which Don, for example, puts a similar, informal theory of himself. Don too would like to dispose of any personal baggage that encumbers his public performance. I have tried to show that he cannot, and that the idea that he should do so diminishes him. Becker, whose conception of role theory takes for granted the repudiation of private motive to which Don aspires, is not likely to appreciate the renunciation implicit in this self-representation.

Fortunately, this is not the only possible account of the relationship between public and private self-experience. Erikson — who is often one-sidedly misquoted by psychologists and sociologists to effect each other's erasure — describes identity as the joint product of self experienced in role and the self of private experience. "The conscious feeling of having a *personal identity*," Erikson says, "is based on two simultaneous observations: the immediate perception of one's selfsameness and continuity in time, and the simultaneous perception of the fact that others recognize one's sameness and continuity."[9] And, "We deal with a process "located" in the core of the individual and yet also in the core of his communal culture, a process which establishes, in fact, an identity of those two identities."[10]

If we confine ourselves to the pure role position Becker advocates, then the kind of escape that Don and Ken attempt — from selfhood into persona — becomes conceptually invisible. Only from a position such as Erikson's, in which there exists the conceptual possibility of distinguishing private self-experience and the experience of self-in-role, can we notice what Ken and Don are doing. In viewing themselves from the perspective of their public roles these men disqualify the private aspect of their self-experience. They sever half of what Erikson means by identity.

But although Erikson's perspective is, for our purpose, an improvement, there is a problem here as well. In his insistence on the "simultaneity" of public and private self-experience, Erikson does not tell us which experience predominates. He encourages the conclusion that, in identity, the subjective experience of individuality and public role are equally salient. But this is not the story we have heard. Don does not experience

9. E. Erikson, "Ego Development and Historical Change," *The Psychoanalytic Study of the Child*, 2 (1946):359–396.

10. E. Erikson, *Identity: Youth and Crisis* (New York: Norton, 1968).

himself "simultaneously" as a private person and a public actor; he has subjugated the private man to the public one. It is as if he were trying to escape the experience of his private life by fleeing into the imagined security of his public persona. Were we to construct a psychosocial account of career culture on the Eriksonian principle of giving equal weight to private and public self-experience, we would be inaccurate. The more accurate account must show how men's private experience of themselves has been submerged beneath their experience of themselves as public actors.

At first glance, this might seem to return us to Becker's position. Perhaps Erikson is wrong; perhaps all we need know to appreciate the experience of identity is the actor's public role. But no, this is not quite the case. Identity, experienced solely in terms of public role, is a diminishment of what Erikson has in mind. Erikson is speaking about an ideal of identity (and often sounds as if he imagines that ideal were contemporary reality). Role theory, in its pure sociological form, has taken the reduction of that ideal as its point of conceptual departure. It does seem to be the case that men who follow the career code view themselves as if they were nothing but public actors. But this is not a way of talking that we should accept at face value. It is not a neutral fact about oneself, like one's height or age. It is a form of self-consciousness, a decision to describe selfhood in half the tones that might be available, serving the ends of psychodynamic conflict, and donated to this service by our particular culture.

These considerations have special relevance to men's studies. Men live large portions of their lives in public arenas. Their public image, especially their work image, forms a large part of their private self-conception. Men's studies has often been critical of the specific content of various public images. Few studies have investigated the relationship between public and private experience (except by assuming their isomorphism). We have left unexplored the possibility suggested here: that men may attempt to escape their private troubles by migrating — like souls fleeing diseased bodies — from their private lives into public ones.

Seen from this angle, *role* is not simply a neutral, scientific term. It is also a form of self-consciousness, which has a basis in our contemporary social structure — the demanding relationship between private and public life — and specific, subjectively damaging consequences.

Our ability to view these consequences rests on what theoretical choices we make. Men's studies has taken as part of its disciplinary mandate the critique of cultural forms that diminish male subjectivity. Toward this end, it should hold up for our inspection the language in which we explain ourselves. In particular, it should point out the conventions by which we disguise ourselves from ourselves; the public formulas that save us — to our greater loss—from looking at what we prefer not to see. But any academic discipline can reveal the unspoken in public culture only if it does not already contain the same silences within itself. Theory can illuminate the world only through the conceptual lenses that are available to it, and neither role theory nor Eriksonian psychosociology are likely to serve this cause. *Identity* envisions no conflict, while role theory has eliminated one of the contestants.

Ideally, cultural criticism should enlarge public discourse. If the rationalizations of career culture obscure what we are able to acknowledge of our lives, critical interpretation should expose the reasons and strategies through which that obscurity operates. Individuals, and the career culture within which they operate, are all too ready to suppress the private man in favor of the public actor. It should be our task—those of us who study men's lives and the culture in which we find ourselves—to point out the reasons and tactics of that reduction. Our aim, as catalysts of social discourse, should be to raise the problem of work—and more generally, of lives lived in the medium of any less-than-fulfilling cultural vehicle—to the level of public visibility and debate. How we study this territory, what conceptual choices we make, will determine our ability to comment on this suppression or find ourselves its unwitting partner.

8

The Meaning of Success: The Athletic Experience and the Development of Male Identity

Michael Messner

Vince Lombardi supposedly said, "Winning isn't everything; it's the only thing," and I couldn't agree more. There's nothing like being number one.
— JOE MONTANA

The big-name athletes will get considerable financial and social remuneration for their athletic efforts. But what of the others, the 99% who fail? Most will fall short of their dreams of a lucrative professional contract. The great majority of athletes, then, will likely suffer disappointment, underemployment, anxiety, or perhaps even serious mental disorders.
— DONALD HARRIS AND D. STANLEY EITZEN

What is the relationship between participation in organized sports and a young male's developing sense of himself as a success or a failure? And what is the consequent impact on his self-image and his ability to engage in intimate relationships with others? Through the late 1960s, it was almost universally accepted that "sports builds character" and that "a winner in sports will be a winner in life." Consequently, some liberal feminists argued that since participation in organized competitive sports has served as a major source of socialization for males' successful participation in the public world, girls and young women should have equal access to sports. Lever, for instance, concluded that if women were ever going to be able to develop the proper competitive values and orientations toward work and success, it was incumbent on them to participate in sports.[1]

1. J. Lever, "Sex Differences in the Games Children Play," *Social Problems* 23 (1976).

In the 1970s and 1980s, these uncritical orientations toward sports have been questioned, and the "sports builds character" formula has been found wanting. Sabo points out that the vast majority of research does *not* support the contention that success in sports translates into "work success" or "happiness" in one's personal life.[2] In fact, a great deal of evidence suggests that the contrary is true. Recent critical analyses of success and failure in sports have usually started from assumptions similar to those of Sennett and Cobb and of Rubin:[3] the disjuncture between the *ideology* of success (the Lombardian Ethic) and the socially structured *reality* that most do not "succeed" brings about widespread feelings of failure, lowered self-images, and problems with interpersonal relationships.[4] The most common argument seems to be that the highly competitive world of sports is an exaggerated reflection of advanced industrial capitalism. Within any hierarchy, one can actually work very hard and achieve a lot, yet still be defined (and perceive oneself) as less than successful. Very few people ever reach the mythical "top," but those who do are made ultravisible through the media.[5] It is tempting to view this system as a "structure of failure" because, given the definition of *success*, the system is virtually rigged to bring about the failure of the vast majority of participants. Furthermore, given the dominant values, the participants are apt to blame themselves for

2. D. Sabo, "Sport Patriarchy and Male Identity: New Questions about Men and Sport," *Arena Review, 9,* no. 2 1985.

3. R. Sennett and J. Cobb, *The Hidden Injuries of Class* (New York: Random House, 1973); and L. B. Rubin, *Worlds of Pain: Life in the Working Class Family* (New York: Basic Books, 1976).

4. D. W. Ball, "Failure in Sport," *American Sociological Review* 41 (1976); J. J. Coakley, *Sports in Society* (St. Louis: Mosby, 1978); D. S. Harris and D. S. Eitzen, "The Consequences of Failure in Sport," *Urban Life* 7 (July 1978): 2: G. B. Leonard, "Winning Isn't Everything: It's Nothing," in *Jock: Sports and Male Identity,* ed. D. Sabo and R. Runfola (Englewood Cliffs, N.J.: Prentice-Hall, 1980); W. E. Schafer, "Sport and Male Sex Role Socialization," *Sport Sociology Bulletin* 4 (Fall 1975); R. C. Townsend, "The Competitive Male as Loser," in Sabo and Runfola, eds., *Jock;* and T. Tutko and W. Bruns, *Winning Is Everything and Other American Myths* (New York: Macmillan, 1976).

5. In contrast with the importance put on sports success by millions of boys, the number who "make it" is incredibly small. There are approximately 600 players in major-league baseball, with an average career span of 7 years. Approximately 6–7% of all high school football players ever play in college. Roughly 8% of all draft-eligible college football and basketball athletes are drafted by the pros, and only 2% ever sign a professional contract. The average career for NFL athletes is now 4 years, and for the NBA it is only 3.4 years. Thus the odds of getting anywhere *near* the top are very thin—and if one is talented and lucky enough to get there, his stay will be brief. See H. Edwards, "The Collegiate Athletic Arms Race: Origins and Implications of the 'Rule 48' Controversy," *Journal of Sport and Social Issues* 8, no. 1 (Winter–Spring 1984); Harris and Eitzen, "Consequences of Failure," and P. Hill and B. Lowe, "The Inevitable Metathesis of the Retiring Athlete," *International Review of Sport Sociology* 9, nos. 3–4 (1978).

their "failure." Schafer argues that the result of this discontinuity between sports values – ideology and reality is a "widespread conditional self-worth" for young athletes.[6] And as Edwards has pointed out, this problem can be even more acute for black athletes, who are disproportionately channeled into sports, yet have no "social safety net" to fall back on after "failure" in sports.

Both the traditional "sports builds character" and the more recent "sports breeds failures" formulas have a common pitfall: Each employs socialization theory in an often simplistic and mechanistic way. Boys are viewed largely as "blank slates" onto which the sports experience imprints values, appropriate "sex-role scripts," and orientations toward self and world. What is usually not taken into account is the fact that boys (and girls) come to the sports experience with an *already gendered* identity that colors their early motivations and perceptions of the meaning of games and sports. As Gilligan points out, observations of young children's game-playing show that girls bring to the activity a more pragmatic and flexible orientation toward the rules — they are more prone to make exceptions and innovations in the middle of the game in order to make the game more "fair" and maintain relationships with others.[7] Boys tend to have a more firm, even inflexible orientation to the rules of a game — they are less willing to change or alter rules in the middle of the game; to them, the rules are what protects any "fairness." This observation has profound implications for sociological research on sports and gender: The question should not be *simply* "how does sports participation affect boys [or girls]?" but should add "what is it about a developing sense of male identity that *attracts* males to sports in the first place? And how does this socially constructed male identity develop and change as it interacts with the structure and values of the sports world?" In addition to being a social – psychological question, this is also a *historical* question: Since men have not at all times and places related to sports the way they at present do, it is important to explore just what kinds of men exist today. What are their needs, problems, and dreams? How do these men relate to the society they live in? And how do organized sports fit into this picture?

THE "PROBLEM OF MASCULINITY" AND ORGANIZED SPORTS

In the first two decades of this century, men feared that the closing of the frontier, along with changes in the workplace, the family, and the schools,

6. Schafer, "Sport and Male Sex Role," p. 50.
7. C. Gilligan, *In a Different Voice: Psychological Theory and Women's Development* (Cambridge: Harvard University Press, 1982); J. Piaget, *The Moral Judgment of the Child* (New York: Free Press, 1965); and Lever, "Games Children Play."

was having a "feminizing" influence on society.[8] One result of the anxiety men felt was the creation of the Boy Scouts of America as a separate sphere of social life where "true manliness" could be instilled in boys *by men*.[9] The rapid rise of organized sports in roughly the same era can be attributed largely to the same phenomenon. As socioeconomic and familial changes continued to erode the traditional bases of male identity and privilege, sports became an increasingly important cultural expression of traditional male values — organized sports became a "primary masculinity-validating experience."[10]

In the post-World War II era, the bureaucratization and rationalization of work, along with the decline of the family wage and women's gradual movement into the labor force, have further undermined the "breadwinner role" as a basis for male identity, thus resulting in a "problem of masculinity" and a "defensive insecurity" among men.[11] As Mills put it, the ethic of success in postwar America "has become less widespread as fact, more confused as image, often dubious as motive, and soured as a way of life [Yet] there are still compulsions to struggle, to 'amount to something'."[12]

How have men expressed this need to "amount to something" within a social context that seems to deny them the opportunities to do so? Again, organized sports play an important role. Both on a personal – existential level for athletes and on a symbolic – ideological level for spectators and fans, sports have become one of the "last bastions" of traditional male ideas of success, of male power and superiority over — and separation from — the perceived "feminization" of society. It is likely that the rise of football as "America's number-one game" is largely the result of the comforting *clarity* it provides between the polarities of traditional male power, strength, and violence and the contemporary fears of social feminization.

But these historical explanations for the increased importance of sports, despite their validity, beg some important questions: Why do men fear the (real or imagined) "feminization" of their world? Why do men appear to need a separate male sphere of life? Why do organized sports appear to be such an attractive means of expressing these needs? Are males

8. P. G. Filene, *Him / Her / Self: Sex Roles in Modern America* (New York: Harcourt Brace Jovanovich, 1975).

9. J. Hantover, "The Boy Scouts and the Validation of Masculinity," *Journal of Social Issues* 34 (1978): 1.

10. J. L. Dubbert, *A Man's Place: Masculinity in Transition* (Englewood Cliffs, N.J.: Prentice-Hall, 1979).

11. A. Tolson, *The Limits of Masculinity* (New York: Harper & Row, 1977).

12. C. W. Mills, *White Collar* (London: Oxford University Press, 1951).

simply "socialized" to dominate women and to compete with other men for status, or are they seeking (perhaps unconsciously) something more fundamental? Just what is it that men really *want?* To begin to answer these questions, it is necessary to listen to athletes' voices and examine their lives within a social–psychological perspective.

Daniel Levinson's concept of the "individual life structure" is a useful place to begin to construct a gestalt of the life of the athlete.[13] Levinson demonstrates that as males develop and interact with their world, they continue to change throughout their lives. A common theme during developmental periods is the process of individuation, the struggle to separate, to "decide where he stops and where the world begins."

> In successive periods of development, as this process goes on, the person forms a clearer boundary between self and world. . . . Greater individuation allows him to be more separate from the world, to be more independent and self-generating. But it also gives him the confidence and understanding to have more intense attachments in the world and to feel more fully a part of it.[14]

This dynamic of separation and attachment provides a valuable social–psychological framework for examining the experiences and problems faced by the athlete as he gropes for and redefines success throughout his life course. In what follows, Levinson's framework is utilized to analyze the lives of 30 former athletes interviewed between 1983 and 1984. Their *interactions* with sports are examined in terms of their initial boyhood attraction to sports; how notions of success in sports connect with a developing sense of male identity; and how self-images, relationships to work and other people, change and develop after the sports career ends.

BOYHOOD: THE PROMISE OF SPORTS

Given how very few athletes actually "make it" through sports, how can the intensity with which millions of boys and young men throw themselves into athletics be explained? Are they simply pushed, socialized, or even *duped* into putting so much emphasis on athletic success? It is important here to examine just what it is that young males hope to get out of the athletic experience. And in terms of *identity*, it is crucial to examine the ways in which the structure and experience of sports activity meets the developmental needs of young males. The story of Willy Rios sheds light

13. D. J. Levinson, *The Seasons of a Man's Life* (New York: Ballantine, 1978).
14. Ibid., p. 195.

these needs are. Rios was born in Mexico and moved to the United States at a fairly young age. He never knew his father, and his mother died when he was only 9 years old. Suddenly he felt rootless, and at this time he threw himself into sports, but his initial motivations do not appear to be based upon a need to compete and win.

> Actually, what I think sports did for me is it brought me into kind of an instant family. By being on a Little League team, or even just playing with all kinds of different kids in the neighborhood, it brought what I really wanted, which was some kind of closeness.

Similar statements from other men suggest that a fundamental motivational factor behind many young males' sports strivings is a need for connection, "closeness" with others. But why do so many boys see *sports* as an attractive means of establishing connection with others? Chodorow argues that the process of developing a gender identity yields insecurity and ambivalence in males.[15] Males develop "rigid ego boundaries" that ensure separation from others, yet they retain a basic human need for closeness and intimacy with others. The young male, who both seeks and fears attachment with others, thus finds the rulebound structure of games and sports to be a psychologically "safe" place in which he can get (nonintimate) connection with others within a context that maintains clear boundaries, distance, and separation from others. At least for the boy who has some early successes in sports, some of these ambivalent needs can be met, for a time. But there is a catch: For Willy Rios, it was only after he learned that he would get attention (a certain kind of connection) from other people for being a good athlete — indeed, that this attention was *contingent* on his *being good* — that narrow definitions of success, based on performance and winning, became important to him. It was years before he realized that no matter how well he performed, how successful he became, he would not get the closeness that he craved through sports.

> It got to be a product in high school. Before, it was just fun, and having acceptance, you know. Yet I had to work for my acceptance in high school that way, just being a jock. So it wasn't fun any more. But it was my self-identity, being a good ballplayer. I was realizing that whatever you excel in, you put out in front of you. Bring it out. Show it. And that's what I did. That was my protection. . . . It was rotten in high school, really.

15. N. Chodorow, *The Reproduction of Mothering* (Berkeley: University of California Press, 1978).

This conscious striving for successful achievement becomes the primary means through which the young athlete seeks connections with other people. But the irony of the situation, for so many boys and young men like Willy Rios, is that the athletes are seeking to get something from their success in sports that sports usually cannot deliver — and the *pressure* that they end up putting on themselves to achieve that success ends up stripping them of the ability to receive the one major thing that sports really *does* have to offer: fun.

ADOLESCENCE: YOU'RE ONLY AS GOOD AS YOUR LAST GAME

Adolescence is probably the period of greatest insecurity in the life course, the time when the young male becomes most vulnerable to peer expectations, pressures, and judgments. None of the men interviewed for this study, regardless of their social class or ethnicity, seemed fully able to "turn a deaf ear to the crowd" during their athletic careers. The crowd, which may include immediate family, friends, peers, teammates, as well as the more anonymous fans and media, appears to be a crucially important part of the process of establishing and maintaining the self-images of young athletes. By the time they were in high school, most of the men interviewed for this study had found sports to be a primary means through which to establish a sense of manhood in the world. Especially if they were good athletes, the expectations of the crowd became very powerful and were internalized (and often *magnified*) within the young man's own expectations. As one man stated, by the time he was in high school, "it was *expected* of me to do well in all of my contests — I mean by my coach and my peers, and my family. So I in turn expected to do well, and if I didn't do well, then I'd be very disappointed."

When so much is tied to your performance, the dictum that "you are only as good as your last game" is a powerful judgment. It means that the young man must continually prove, achieve, and then *reprove, and reachieve* his status. As a result, many young athletes learn to seek and *need* the appreciation of the crowd to feel that they are worthy human beings. But the internalized values of masculinity along with the insecure nature of the sports world mean that the young man does *not* need the crowd to feel *bad* about himself. In fact, if one is insecure enough, even "success" and the compliments and attention of other people can come to feel hollow and meaningless. For instance, 48-year-old Russ Ellis in his youth shared the basic sense of insecurity common to all young males, and in his case it was probably compounded by his status as a poor black male and an insecure family life. Athletics emerged early in his life as the primary arena in which he and his male peers competed to establish a sense of self in the world. For Ellis, his small physical stature made it difficult to compete successfully in most sports, thus feeding his insecurity — he just never felt as though he belonged with "the big boys." Eventually, though, he became a top middle-distance runner. In high school, however:

> Something began to happen there that later plagued me quite a bit. I started doing very well and winning lots of races and by the time the year was over, it was no longer a question for me of *placing*, but *winning*. That attitude really destroyed me ultimately. I would get into the blocks with worries that I wouldn't do well — the regular stomach problems — so I'd often run much less well than my abilities — that is, say, I'd take second or third.

Interestingly, his nervousness, fears, and anxieties did not seem to be visible to "the crowd":

> I know in high school, certainly, they saw me as confident and ready to run. No one assumed I could be beaten, which fascinated me, because I had never been good at understanding how I was taken in other people's minds — maybe because I spent so much time inventing myself in their regard in my own mind. I was projecting my fear fantasies on them and taking them for reality.

In 1956 Ellis surprised everyone by taking second place in a world-class field of quarter-milers. But the fact that they ran the fastest time in the world, 46.5, seemed only to "up the ante," to increase the pressures on Ellis, then in college at UCLA.

> Up to that point I had been a nice zippy kid who did good, got into the *Daily Bruin* a lot, and was well-known on campus. But now an event would come up and the papers would say, "Ellis to face so-and-so." So rather than my being *in* the race, I *was* the race, as far as the press was concerned. And that put a lot of pressure on me that I never learned to handle. What I did was to internalize it, and then I'd sit there and fret and lose sleep, and focus more on not winning than on how I was doing. And in general, I didn't do badly — like one year in the NCAA's I took fourth — you know, in the *national finals*. But I was focused on winning. You know, later on, people would way, "Oh wow, you took fourth in the NCAA? — you were *that good*?" Whereas I thought of these things as *failures*, you know?

Finally, Ellis's years of training, hopes, and fears came to a head at the

1956 Olympic trials, where he failed to qualify, finishing fifth. A rival whom he used to defeat routinely won the event in the Melbourne Olympics as Ellis watched on television.

> That killed me. Destroyed me . . . I had the experience many times after that of digging down and finding that there was infinitely more down there than I ever got—I mean, I know that more than I know anything else. Sometimes I would really feel like an eagle, running. Sometimes in practice at UCLA running was just exactly like flying—and if I could have carried that attitude into events, I would have done much better. But instead, I'd worry. Yeah, I'd worry myself sick.

As suggested earlier, young males like Russ Ellis are "set up" for disappointment, or worse, by the disjuncture between the narrow Lombardian definition of success in the sports world and the reality that very few ever actually reach the top. The athlete's sense of identity established through sports is therefore insecure and problematic, *not simply* because of the high probability of "failure," but also because *success* in the sports world involves the development of a personality that *amplifies* many of the most ambivalent and destructive traits of traditional masculinity. Within the hierarchical world of sports, which in many ways mirrors the capitalist economy, one learns that if he is to survive and avoid being pushed off the ever-narrowing pyramid of success, he must develop certain kinds of relationships—to himself, to his body, to other people, and to the sport itself. In short, the successful athlete must develop a highly goal-oriented personality that encourages him to view his body as a tool, a machine, or even a weapon utilized to defeat an objectified opponent. He is likely to have difficulty establishing intimate and lasting friendships with other males because of low self-disclosure, homophobia, and cut-throat competition. And he is likely to view his public image as a "success" as far more basic and fundamental than any of his interpersonal relationships.

For most of the men interviewed, the quest for success was not the grim task it was for Russ Ellis. Most men did seem to get, at least for a time, a sense of identity (and even some happiness) out of their athletic accomplishments. The attention of the crowd, for many, affirmed their existence as males and was thus a clear motivating force. Gary Affonso, now 42 years old and a high school coach, explained that when he was in high school, he had an "intense desire to practice and compete."

> I used to practice the high jump by myself for hours at a time—only got up to 5'3"—scissor! [*Laughs*] but I think part of it was, the track itself was in view of some of the classrooms, and so as I think back now, maybe I did it for the attention, to be seen. In my freshman year, I chipped my two

front teeth in a football game, and after that I always had a gold tooth, and I was always self-conscious about that. Plus I had my glasses, you know. I felt a little conspicuous.

This simultaneous shyness, self-consciousness, and conspicuousness *along with* the strongly felt need for attention and external validation (attachment) so often characterize athletes'descriptions of themselves in boyhood and adolescence. The crowd, in this context, can act as a distant, and thus nonthreatening, source of attention and validation of self for the insecure male. Russ Ellis's story typifies that what sports seem to *promise* the young male—affirmation of self and connection with others—is likely to be *undermined* by the youth's actual experience in the sports world. The athletic experience also "sets men up" for another serious problem: the end of a career at a very young age.

DISENGAGEMENT TRAUMA: A CRISIS OF MALE IDENTITY

For some, the end of the athletic career approaches gradually like the unwanted houseguest whose eventual arrival is at least *known* and can be planned for, thus limiting the inevitable inconvenience. For others, the athletic career ends with the shocking suddenness of a violent thunderclap that rudely awakens one from a pleasant dream. But whether it comes gradually or suddenly, the end of the playing career represents the termination of what has often become the *central aspect* of a young male's individual life structure, thus initiating change and transition in the life course.

   Previous research on the disengagement crises faced by many retiring athletes has focused on the health, occupational, and financial problems frequently faced by retiring professionals.[16] These problems are especially severe for retiring black athletes, who often have inadequate educational backgrounds and few opportunities within the sports world for media or coaching jobs.[17] But even for those retiring athletes who avoid the pitfalls of financial and occupational crises, substance abuse, obesity, and ill health, the end of the playing career usually involves a crisis of identity. This identity crisis is probably most acute for retiring *professional* athletes, whose careers are coming to an end right at an age when most men's careers are beginning to take off. As retired professional football player Marvin Upshaw stated,

   16. Hill and Lowe, "Metathesis of Retiring Athlete," pp. 3–4; and B. D. McPherson, "Former Professional Athletes' Adjustment to Retirement," *Physician and Sports Medicine,* August 1978.
   17. Edwards, "Collegiate Athletic Arms Race."

You find yourself just scrambled. You don't know which way to go. Your light, as far as you're concerned, has been turned out. You miss the roar of the crowd. Once you've heard it, you can't get away from it. There's an empty feeling — you feel everything you wanted is gone. All of a sudden you wake up and you find yourself 29, 35 years old, you know, and the one thing that has been the major part of your life is gone. It's gone.

High school and college athletes also face serious and often painful adjustment periods when their career ends. Twenty-six-year-old Dave Joki had been a good high school basketball player, and had played a lot of ball in college. When interviewed, he was right in the middle of a confusing crisis of identity, closely related to his recent disengagement from viewing himself as an athlete.

These past few months I've been trying a lot of different things, thinking about different careers, things to do. There's been quite a bit of stumbling — and I think that part of my tenuousness about committing myself to any one thing is I'm not sure I'm gonna get strokes if I go that way. [*Embarrassed, nervous laugh.*] It's scary for me and I stay away from searching for those reasons . . . I guess you could say that I'm stumbling in my relationships too — stumbling in all parts of life. [*Laughs.*] I feel like I'm doing a lot but not knowing what I want.

Surely there is nothing unusual about a man in his mid 20s "stumbling" around and looking for direction in his work and his relationships. That is common for men of this age. But for the former athlete, this stumbling is often more confusing and problematic than for other men precisely because he has lost the one activity through which he had built his sense of identity, however tenuous it may have been. The "strokes" he received from being a good athlete were his major psychological foundation. The interaction between self and other through which the athlete attempts to solidify his identity is akin to what Cooley called "the looking-glass self." If the athletic activity and the crowd can be viewed as a *mirror* into which the athlete gazes and, in Russ Ellis's words, "invents himself," we can begin to appreciate how devastating it can be when that looking-glass is suddenly and permanently *shattered,* leaving the young man alone, isolated, and disconnected. And since young men often feel comfortable exploring close friendships and intimate relationships only *after* they have established their separate work-related (or sports-related) positional identity, relationships with other people are likely to become more problematic than ever during disegagement.

WORK, LOVE, AND MALE IDENTITY AFTER DISENGAGEMENT

Eventually, the former athlete must face reality: At a relatively young age, he has to start over. In the words of retired major league baseball player Ray Fosse, "Now I gotta get on with the rest of it." How is "the rest of it" likely to take shape for the athlete after his career as a player is over? How do men who are "out of the limelight" for a few years come to define themselves as men? How do they define and redefine success? How do the values and attitudes they learned through sports affect their lives? How do their relationships with friends and family change over time?

Many retired athletes retain a powerful drive to reestablish the important relationship with the crowd that served as the primary basis for their identity for so long. Many men throw themselves wholeheartedly into a new vocation—or a confusing *series* of vocations—in a sometimes pathetic attempt to recapture the "high" of athletic competition as well as the status of the successful athlete in the community. For instance, 35-year-old Jackie Ridgle is experiencing what Daniel Levinson calls a "surge of masculine strivings" common to men in their mid 30s.[18] Once a professional basketball player, Ridgle seems motivated now by a powerful drive to be seen once again as "somebody" in the eyes of the public. When interviewed, he had recently been hired as an assistant college basketball coach, which made him feel like he again had a chance to "be somebody."

> When I say "successful," that means somebody that the public looks up to just as a basketball player. Yet you don't have to be playing basketball. You can be anybody: You can be a senator or a mayor, or any number of things. That's what I call successful. Success is recognition. Sure, I'm always proud of myself. But there's that little goal there that until people respect you, then—[*Snaps fingers.*] Anybody can say, "Oh, I know I'm the greatest thing in the world," but *people* run the world, and when *they* say you're successful, then you *know* you're successful.

Indeed, men, especially men in early adulthood, usually define themselves primarily in terms of their position in the public world of work. Feminist literature often criticizes this establishment of male identity in terms of work–success as an expression of male privilege and ego satisfaction that comes at the expense of women and children. There is a great deal of truth to the feminist critique: A man's socially defined need to establish himself as "somebody" in the (mostly) male world of work is often accompanied by his frequent physical absence from home and his emo-

18. Levinson, *Seasons of a Man's Life.*

tional distance from the family. Thus, while the man is "out there" establishing his "name" in public, the woman is usually home caring for the day-to-day and moment-to-moment needs of her family (regardless of whether or not she also has a job in the paid labor force). Tragically, only in midlife, when the children have already "left the nest" and the woman is often ready to go out into the public world, do some men discover the importance of connection and intimacy.

Yet the interviews indicate that there is not always such a clean and clear "before–after" polarity in the lives of men between work–success and care–intimacy. The "breadwinner ethic" as a male role *has* most definitely contributed to the perpetuation of male privilege and the subordination and economic dependence of women as mothers and housekeepers. But given the reality of the labor market, where women still make only 62 cents to the male dollar, many men feel very responsible for providing the majority of the income and financial security for their families. For instance, 36-year-old Ray Fosse, whose father left his family when he was quite young, has a very strong sense of commitment and responsibility as a provider of income and stability in his own family.

> I'm working an awful lot these days, and trying not to take time away
> from my family. A lot of times I'm putting the family to sleep, and
> working late hours and going to bed and getting up early and so forth.
> I've tried to tell my family this a lot of times: The work that I'm doing
> now is gonna make it easier in a few years. That's the reason I'm working
> now, to get that financial security, and I feel like it's coming very
> soon . . . but, uh, you know, you go a long day and you come home,
> and it's just not the quality time you'd like to have. And I think when that
> financial security comes in, then I'm gonna be able to forget about
> everything.

Jackie Ridgle's words mirror Fosse's. His two jobs and strivings to be successful in the public world mean that he has little time to spend with his wife and three children.

> I plan to someday. Very seldom do you have enough time to spend with
> your kids, especially nowadays, so I don't get hung up on that. The wife
> do sometimes, but as long as I keep a roof over their heads and let 'em
> know who's who, well, one day they'll respect me. But I can't just get
> bogged down and take any old job, you know, a filling station job or
> something. Ah, hell, they'll get more respect, my kids for me, right now,
> than they would if I was somewhere just a regular worker.

Especially for men who have been highly successful athletes (and never have had to learn to "lose gracefully"), the move from sports to work–

career as a means of establishing connection and identity in the world is a "natural" transition. Breadwinning becomes a man's socially learned means of seeking attachment, both with his family and, more abstractly, with "society." What is salient (and sometimes tragic) is that the care that a woman gives her family usually puts her into direct daily contact with her family's physical, psychological, and emotional needs. A man's care is usually expressed more abstractly, often in his absence, as his work removes him from day-to-day, moment-to-moment contact with his family.

A man may want, even *crave,* more direct connection with his family, but that connection, and the *time* it takes to establish and maintain it, may cause him to lose the competitive edge he needs to win in the world of work — and that is the arena in which he feels he will ultimately be judged in terms of his success or failure as a man. But it is not simply a matter of *time* spent away from the family which is at issue here. As Dizard's research shows clearly, the more "success oriented" a man is, the more "instrumental" his personality will tend to be, thus increasing the psychological and emotional distance between himself and his family.[19]

CHANGING MEANINGS OF SUCCESS IN MIDLIFE

The intense, sometimes obsessive, early adulthood period of striving for work and career success that we see in the lives of Jackie Ridgle and Ray Fosse often begins to change in midlife, when many men experience what Levinson calls "detribalization." Here, the man

> becomes more critical of the tribe — the particular groups, institutions, and traditions that have the greatest significance for him, the social matrix to which he is most attached. He is less dependent upon tribal rewards, more questioning of tribal values. . . . The result of this shift is normally not a marked disengagement from the external world but a greater integration of attachment and separateness.[20]

Detribalization — putting less emphasis on how one is defined by others and becoming more self-motivated and self-generating — is often accompanied by a growing sense of *flawed* or *qualified* success. A man's early adulthood dream of success begins to tarnish, appearing more and more as an illusion. Or, the success that a man *has* achieved begins to appear hollow and meaningless, possibly because it has not delivered the closeness he

19. J. E. Dizard, "The Price of Success," in *Social Change in the Family,* ed. J. E. Dizard (Chicago: Community and Family Study Center, University of Chicago, 1968).

20. Levinson, *Seasons of a Man's Life,* p. 242.

truly craves. The fading, or the loss, of the dream involves a process of mourning, but, as Levinson points out, it can also be a very liberating process in opening the man up for new experiences, new kinds of relationships, and new dreams.

For instance, Russ Ellis states that a few years ago he experienced a midlife crisis when he came to the realization that "I was never going to be on the cover of *Time*." His wife had a T-shirt made for him with the message *Dare to Be Average* emblazoned on it.

> And it doesn't really *mean* dare to be average—it means dare to take the pressure off yourself, you know? Dare to be a normal person. It gets a funny reaction from people. I think it hits at that place where somehow we all think that we're going to wind up on the cover of *Time* or something, you know? Do you have that? That some day, somewhere, you're gonna be *great*, and everyone will know, everyone will recognize it? Now, I'd rather be great because I'm *good*—and maybe that'll turn into something that's acknowledged, but not at the headline level. I'm not racing so much; I'm concerned that my feet are planted on the ground and that I'm good.

> [It sounds like you're running now, as opposed to racing?]

> I guess—but running and racing have the same goals. [*Laughs, pauses, then speaks more thoughtfully.*] But maybe you're right—that's a wonderful analogy. Pacing myself. Running is more intelligent—more familiarity with your abilities, your patterns of workouts, who you're running against, the nature of the track, your position, alertness. You have more of an internal clock.

Russ Ellis's midlife detribalization—his transition from a "racer" to a "runner"—has left him more comfortable with himself, with his abilities and limitations. He has also experienced an expansion of his ability to experience intimacy with a woman. He had never been very comfortable with the "typical jock attitude" toward sex and women,

> but I generally maintained a performance attitude about sex for a long time, which was not as enjoyable as it became after I learned to be more like what I thought a woman was like. In other words, when I let myself experience my own body, in a delicious and receptive way rather than in a power, overwhelming way. That was wonderful! [*Laughs.*] To experience my body as someone desired and given to. That's one of the better things. I think I only achieved that very profound intimacy that's found between people, really quite extraordinary, quite recently. [*Long pause.*] It's quite something, quite something. And I feel more fully inducted into the human race by knowing about that.

TOWARD A REDEFINITION OF SUCCESS AND MASCULINITY

"A man in America is a failed boy," wrote John Updike in 1960. Indeed, Updike's ex-athlete Rabbit Angstrom's struggles to achieve meaning and identity in midlife reflect a common theme in modern literature. Social scientific research has suggested that the contemporary sense of failure and inadequacy felt by many American males is largely the result of unrealistic and unachievable social definitions of masculinity and success.[21] This research has suggested that there is more to it than that. Contemporary males often feel empty, alienated, isolated, and as failures because the socially learned means through which they seek validation and identity (achievement in the public worlds of sports and work) do not deliver what is actually craved and needed: intimate connection and unity with other human beings. In fact, the lure of sports becomes a sort of trap. For boys who experience early success in sports, the resulting attention they receive becomes a convenient and attractive means of experiencing attachment with other people within a social context that allows the young male to maintain his "firm ego boundaries" and thus his separation from others. But it appears that, more often than not, athletic participation serves only to exacerbate the already problematic, insecure, and ambivalent nature of males' self-images, and thus their ability to establish and maintain close and intimate relationships with other people. Some men, as they reach midlife, eventually achieve a level of individuation — often through a midlife crisis — that leads to a redefinition of success and an expansion of their ability to experience attachment and intimacy.

Men's personal definitions of success often change in midlife, but this research, as well as that done by Farrell and Rosenberg,[22] suggests that only a *portion* of males experience a midlife crisis that results in the man's transcending his instrumental personality in favor of a more affective generativity. The midlife discovery that the achievement game is an unfulfilling rat race can as easily lead to cynical detachment and greater alienation as it can to detribalization and expanded relational capacities. In other words, there is no assurance that Jackie Ridgle, as he ages, will transform himself from a "racer" to a "runner" as Russ Ellis has. Even if he does change in this way, it is likely that he will have missed participating in the formative years of his children's lives.

Thus the fundamental questions facing future examinations of men's lives should focus on building an understanding of just what are the keys to

21. J. H. Pleck, *The Myth of Masculinity* (Cambridge: MIT Press, 1982); Sennett and Cobb, *The Hidden Injuries of Class*; Rubin, *Worlds of Pain*; and Tolson, *Limits of Masculinity*.
22. M. P. Farrell and S. D. Rosenberg, *Men at Midlife* (Boston: Auburn House, 1981).

such a shift at midlife? How are individual men's changes, crises, and relationships affected, shaped, and sometimes contradicted by the social, cultural, and political contexts in which they find themselves? And what *social* changes might make it more likely that boys and men might have more balanced personalities and needs at an *early* age?

An analysis of men's lives that simply describes personal changes while taking social structure as a given cannot adequately *ask* these questions. But an analysis that not only describes changes in male identity throughout the life course but also critically examines the socially structured and defined meaning of "masculinity" can and must ask these questions.

If many of the problems faced by all men (not just athletes) today are to be dealt with, class, ethnic, and sexual preference divisions must be confronted. This would necessarily involve the development of a more cooperative and nurturant ethic among men, as well as a more egalitarian and democratically organized economic system. And since the sports world is an important cultural process that serves partly to socialize boys and young men to hierarchical, competitive and aggressive values, the sporting arena is an important context in which to begin to confront the need for a humanization of men.

Yet, if the analysis presented here is correct, the developing psychology of young boys is predisposed to be attracted to the present structure and values of the sports world, so any attempt *simply* to infuse cooperative and egalitarian values into sports is likely to be an exercise in futility. The need for equality between men and women, in the public realm as well as in the home, is a fundamental prerequisite for the humanization of men, sports, and society. One of the most important changes that men could make would be to become more equally involved in parenting. The development of early bonding between fathers and infants (in addition to that between mothers and infants), along with nonsexist childrearing in the family, schools, and sports would have far-reaching effects on society: Boys and men could grow up more psychologically secure, more able to develop balance between separation and attachment, more able at an earlier age to appreciate intimate relationships with other men without destructive and crippling competition and homophobia. A young male with a more secure and balanced personality might also be able to *enjoy* athletic activities for what they really have to offer: the opportunity to engage in healthy exercise, to push oneself toward excellence, and to bond together with others in a challenging and fun activity.

IV
Social and Biological Bonding

Can a man's best friend be another man? How can men's bonds be explained? In this section Drury Sherrod, Dorothy Hammond and Alta Jablow, and Perry Treadwell attempt to answer such questions through social psychology, anthropology, and biosociology.

"The Bonds of Men: Problems and Possibilities in Close Male Friendships" examines the social psychology of men's friendships. Research reveals that men and women cite about the same number of friends, but "friendship" means something different to men and women. Men follow a different path to intimate friendships than women do, and as a result are less likely to achieve and maintain intimate friendships. The chapter reviews four theoretical explanations for men's relative lack of intimate friends: (a) a biological one, emphasizing the effects of male hormones on aggressiveness and competition; (b) a psychoanalytic one, tracing differential ego boundaries to early mother–infant attachments; (c) a socialization one, explaining behavior as influenced by social conditioning; and (d) an economic–historical one, viewing social roles as products of technology, labor, and family organization. Close male relationships may change in response to changing gender roles.

"Gilgamesh and the Sundance Kid: The Myth of Male Friendship" traces the history of a persistent, conventionalized image of male friendship through the western literary tradition. All the narratives portray friends as male peers, engaged in agonistic activities, in a relationship of lifelong loyalty and devotion. In earlier societies the stereotype validated aristocratic male roles and alliances, but the structure of contemporary society obviates such a function. Anthropological evidence is at such variance with the myth that its persistence must be explained by its providing the stable ideology and values for the labile and socially unstructured role of "friend" in modern society.

"Biologic Influences on Masculinity" examines the data on whether relative quantities of testosterone and estrogen in an individual influence the expression of masculinity. The paper concludes that these hormones affect the brain structure before birth and influence aggressiveness as demonstrated in sports prowess, military success, and criminal behavior during life. Such hormonal influence does not support biological determinism but does suggest the creation of a wide diversity of potential physiologic responses that are influenced by social environments. The openness of the hormonal system to the influence of the environment implies that sports and military training select individuals already "at risk" of reacting to social environments more stereotypically and enhance the physiologic response of aggressiveness: increased testosterone. Biosociological research can elucidate the reciprocal interactions in biology and environment in determining masculinities.

9

The Bonds of Men: Problems and Possibilities in Close Male Relationships

Drury Sherrod

In a scene from Sam Shepard's play *True West,* two clashing brothers halt their fighting long enough to hammer out a screenplay about two feuding men who chase each other across an empty western night. A scene in the brothers' screenplay mirrors their own predicament, and that of many men:

> So they take off after each other straight into an endless black prarie.
> The sun is just comin' down and they can feel the night on their backs.
> What they don't know is that each one of 'em is afraid, see. Each one
> separately thinks that he's the only one that's afraid. And they keep ridin'
> like that straight into the night. Not knowing. And the one who's chasin'
> doesn't know where the other one is taking him. And the one who's being
> chased doesn't know where he's going.[1]

There is an altogether different scene in D. H. Lawrence's *Women in Love,* a scene that reflects an opposite pole of men's relationships. From his sickbed, a man talks with his best friend, and their conversation drifts from business to women to fear of dying. Finally, the sick man confesses his feelings for his friend:

> Suddenly he saw himself confronted with another problem—the problem
> of love and eternal conjunction between two men. Of course this was
> necessary—it had been a necessity inside him all his life—to love a man
> purely and fully. "You know how the old German knights used to swear a
> *Blutbruderschaft* . . . swear to be true to each other, of one blood, all

---

1. S. Shepard, *True West,* in S. Shepard, *Seven Plays* (New York: Bantam, 1981).

their lives? That is what we ought to do . . . we ought to swear to love
each other, you and I, implicitly, and perfectly, finally, without any
possibility of going back on it. . . . Not sloppy emotionalism. An
impersonal union that leaves one free."[2]

These two scenes reveal the apparent contradictions in close relationships between men: a dark struggle for dominance that separates one man
from another versus the desire for a perfect, nonemotional union that
bonds together two men in one blood. How these contradictions arise, how
they are manifested, and how they might be resolved are the questions of
this essay. For answers, I turn to psychological research and theory on the
nature of close, nonsexual relationships between men. This literature
addresses the problems of intimacy between men and speaks to the possibilities of intimate male bonds.

The essay has three parts. Part 1 examines social–psychological research on men's friendships in order to determine the nature and extent of
intimacy in close male relationships. Part 2 looks at several alternative
explanations for the kind of intimacy — or lack of intimacy — that generally characterizes male relationships. And Part 3 suggests some reasons
why male relationships may be forced to take on new forms, and how
these changes may be achieved.

This review will provide ammunition for both sides of the dialogue with
which Lawrence closes his book *Women in Love:*

> "Did you need Gerald?" she asked one evening.
> "Yes," he said . . .
> "Having you, I can live all my life without anybody else, any other sheer intimacy.
> But to make it complete, really happy, I wanted eternal union with a man too: another
> kind of love," he said.
> "I don't believe it," she said. "It's an obstinacy, a theory, a perversity."
> "Well—" he said.
> "You can't have two kinds of love. Why should you!"
> "It seems as if I can't," he said. "Yet I wanted it."
> "You can't have it, because it's false, impossible," she said.
> "I don't believe that," he answered.[3]

THE BEST OF FRIENDS: ON THE NATURE OF MALE RELATIONSHIPS

Our culture has traditionally viewed male friendship as embodying the
ideals of comradeship and brotherhood. Men have buddies, pals, lifelong
ties — bonds of unspoken, unshakeable commitment — the kind of friends

2. D. H. Lawrence, *Women in Love* (New York: Penguin, 1976).
3. Ibid., p. 198–199.

for whom one would "lay down one's life." Yet surveys find most men today name their wife as their closest friend.[4] And the psychiatrist Daniel Levinson concluded in *The Seasons of a Man's Life* that "close friendship with a man or woman is rarely experienced by American men."[5] Much research supports Levinson's conclusion, but thorny questions plague our interpretation of the research.

A difficulty in evaluating research on men's friendships is the question of an appropriate standard of intimacy. Should male intimacy be compared to female intimacy in its form, style, and goals? Or should the unspoken commitments of typical male friendships be evaluated by different standards than the easy verbal and physical intimacies of women's relationships? If male intimacy exists largely as an implicit untested "feeling" —the assumption that a friend will be there when you need him—how can this perception of available friendship be ranked alongside the lived daily connectedness of women's ties? Is a perceived bond the same thing as an actual bond? And what is the real-life basis for men's perceptions of an intimate bond? If few specific behavioral and verbal intimacies can be identified in male friendships, how can we be sure the perceived bond is no more than an illusion? Before grappling with these questions directly, it will be helpful to look at the research on men's and women's friendships.

Numbering Friends

The simplest comparison between men's and women's friendships is to ask, "Who has more friends, men or women?" When the question is framed this way, the answer is deceptively simple. Sociologists have conducted several large surveys recently in different parts of America, and the number of friends claimed by men and women is fairly even. When all the categories of people—young and old, working and not working, blue collar and white collar—are taken together, men and women report roughly the same number of friends. For example, in a survey conducted in Nebraska, men and women each counted about 3 people among their closest friends.[6] In the San Francisco Bay area, women claimed slightly more than 6 close friends apiece, while men reported about 5.[7] Across northern California, the average man named 11 nonkin persons he could

---

4. R. Bell, *Worlds of Friendship* (Beverly Hills, Calif.: Sage, 1981).

5. D. Levinson, *The Seasons of a Man's Life* (New York: Ballantine, 1978).

6. A. Booth, "Sex and Social Participation," *American Sociological Review* 37(1972):183–192.

7. M. Lowenthal, M. Thurner, and D. Chiriboga, *Four Stages of Life* (San Francisco: Jossey-Bass, 1975).

call on for help and advice, while the average woman cited 10.[8] And among college students at the University of California, Los Angeles, young men and women said they had between 3 and 4 intimate friends each, and about 6 to 8 casual friends apiece.[9]

Some gender differences emerge in these friendship surveys, but they are small, and they tend to reflect the different number of social contacts that age and occupation provide to men and women. For example, young working men sometimes report slightly more friends than women report, apparently because young working males have more opportunity for social contacts than nonworking women. In contrast, older retired males usually report slightly fewer friends than older women, as males lose access to their work-related contacts, while women retain their social networks with age.[10] But, overall, as far as numbers go, both sexes report about equal numbers of friends. Both men and women name between 3 to 6 people they consider close friends, and up to 10 or 11 people they can call on for help and advice. The meaning of these numbers is unclear, however, because men and women seem to define friendship in very different terms.

The Meaning of Friends

Robert Bell is a sociologist who has interviewed almost 200 men and women in the northeastern United States about their friendships. His interviews give us some idea of what friendships mean to men and women. For example, a 45-year-old woman described her friendships with women in the following way:

> In my close friendships there is a high degree of giving and receiving. What I mean is that things that are important to each of us are expressed and reacted to by each of us. If I am really troubled or upset I can unload on my friends and they will understand and give serious consideration to my problems. Because we can deal with the really significant things in our lives our friendship is complete and revealing.[11]

A 38-year-old man experienced his friendships in quite a different way:

---

8. C. Fischer, "A Research Note on Friendship, Gender, and the Life Cycle," *Social Forces* 62(1983):124–133.

9. M. Caldwell, and L. A. Peplau, "Sex Differences in Same-Sex Friendship," *Sex Roles* 8(1982):721–731.

10. Fischer, "Friendship, Gender, and Life Cycle."

11. Bell, *Worlds of Friendship.*

I have three close friends I have known since we were boys and they live here in the city. There are some things I wouldn't tell them. For example, I wouldn't tell them much about my work because we have always been highly competitive. I certainly wouldn't tell about my feelings of any uncertainties with life or various things I do. And I wouldn't talk about any problems I have with my wife or in fact anything about my marriage and sex life. But other than that I would tell them anything.[12]

These quotations sound extreme, but they accurately mirror the meaning of same-sex friendships to men and women. In a study conducted in St. Louis, young adult men and women held very different criteria for what made someone a best friend. Women sought a friend who could be a confidante, a friend who would help them "grow as persons." Men were more likely to seek a friend with similar interests, someone "to have fun with."[13]

Young men and women in southern California showed the same differences in their expectations of friends. Here Mayta Caldwell and Anne Peplau asked almost a hundred young adults detailed questions about their friendships. What do friends do when they are together? What do they talk about? What is the real basis of best friendships? Virtually all the subjects —men and women— said they wanted intimate friendships, but males and females held different notions of what constituted intimacy. When they were given the choice between "doing some activity" or "just talking" with their best friend, almost twice as many men than women chose the activity, while over three times as many women than men preferred just to talk. Consistent with these preferences, the majority of young men sought a best friend who "likes to do the same things" rather than a friend who "feels the same way about things." In contrast, the majority of young women wanted a friend who shared the same feelings. Furthermore, when these individuals listed three things that formed the basis of the relationships with their best friend, men were more likely to list some activity rather than talking; women more frequently mentioned talking than an activity.[14]

Anecdotal observations and research findings demonstrate that men and women, on the whole, define friendship in different ways. Women seem to look for intimate confidantes, while men seek partners for adventure.

12. Ibid.
13. G. Ho-Yoon, "The Natural History of Friendship: Sex Differences in Best-Friendship Patterns" (Ph.D. dissertation, St. Louis University, 1978).
14. Caldwell and Peplau, "Sex Differences."

Measuring Male Intimacy

We generally think of close friendships as involving a good deal of disclosure about the intimate details of our lives. After all, a best friend is someone who accepts us as we are. Yet in the same way that men and women disagree about the meaning of close friendship, they also differ in the amount and kind of personal information they disclose to close friends. A striking example of the limits on self-disclosure among men is seen in David Michaelis's book *The Best of Friends,* subtitled *Profiles of Extraordinary Friendships.* Michaelis describes two middle-aged best friends who met as college athletes at Yale, later sailed a 20-foot boat across the North Atlantic, and have remained competitive yet committed friends for more than 20 years. Over the years, they evolved an unwritten code, a gentleman's agreement that their competition should never result in an affront to their friendship. As one of them observed:

> I often wonder why our friendship continues to bounce along the way it is, but I'm not going to try and alter it to serve some other god such as "progress-in-a-relationship" or what one calls "growth." This friendship is not trying to produce a family. This is not trying to satisfy the various ego needs of the participants, though it may do that anyway. It simply satisfies some sort of ultimate human regard: That you are highly regarded and that you regard another with the highest esteem. But I don't know if friendships do progress anywhere. I've often wondered, why do he and I find it perfectly comfortable to continue playing these roles that have been comfortable for so long. I guess we return to that mode because it seems natural to both of us. . . . Plenty of serious discussions go on. But even those discussions are guided by the same limits. There definitely are limits.[15]

A considerable body of research confirms the limits on self-disclosure in most close male friendships. In the typical research paradigm men and women fill out a "self-disclosure questionnaire," which asks them to rate on a scale from 1 to 5 the degree of information they have revealed about themselves in their most intimate conversations on a variety of topics. The topics range from trivial items, such as hobbies and favorite sports, to extremely intimate topics such as sexual fantasies, guiltiest secrets, and inferiority feelings. Women usually disclose significantly more intimate information about themselves than men do, regardless of age, region of the country, or social class. When the most intimate questions are analyzed separately, men disclose much less than women.[16] Furthermore, when the

15. D. Michaelis, *The Best of Friends* (New York: Morrow, 1983).
16. B. S. Morgan, "Intimacy of Disclosure Topics and Sex Differences in Self-Disclosure," *Sex Roles* 2(1976):161–166.

recipient of information is considered, men reveal much more about themselves to their closest female friend — usually a wife or girlfriend — than to their closest male friend.[17]

The content of men's conversations has been studied explicitly by Caldwell and Peplau. When men and women listed the kinds of things they talked about with their same-sex close friends, many more women than men said they talked about feelings, problems, and people. When unacquainted pairs of men and women role-played a conversation with a close friend, men expressed less enthusiasm, offered less support, talked less about relationships, and asked much less about feelings than women.[18]

Other research supports these consistent gender differences. A recent study in New Brunswick, New Jersey, examined the communication styles of men and women in their 20s and 30s. The subjects supplied detailed accounts of what they talked about with their best friends and how they related to each other. Consistent with other findings on self-disclosure, the New Jersey men talked with each other mainly about topical issues, such as work, sports, movies, or politics. The women talked about these issues too, but they were also just as likely to talk about personal problems, as well as their relationship with each other. Despite these major differences in men's and women's relationships, both sexes felt they were completely open and trusting with their best friend. As one of the men said about his best friend. "We are pretty open with each other, I guess. Mostly we talk about sex, horses, guns, and the army."[19]

The same disparity between actual disclosure and perceived intimacy has been found in studies of adolescent boys and girls. At a stage when friendships are crucially important to both males and females, both sexes say that they feel equally free to reveal personal information to their same-sex best friends, and both sexes believe they know their best friends intimately. Furthermore, both sexes are equally accurate in the extent of intimate information they are able to report about their best friends. Yet when adolescents are asked how much they actually disclose to one another, girls usually reveal much more intimate information than boys.[20]

17. M. Komarovsky, "Patterns of Self-Discolure of Male Undergraduates," *Journal of Marriage and the Family* 36(1974):677–686.

18. Caldwell and Peplau, "Sex Differences."

19. L. R. Davidson and L. Duberman, "Friendship: Communication and Interactional Patterns in Same-Sex Dyads," *Sex Roles* 8(1982):809–822.

20. R. M. Diaz and T. J. Berndt, "Children's Knowledge of a Best Friend: Fact or Fancy? *Developmental Psychology* in press; R. Sharbany, R. Gershoni, and J. H. Hofman, "Girlfriend, Boyfriend: Age and Sex-Differences in Intimate Friendships," *Developmental Psychology* 17(1981):800–808; D. Eder and M. T. Halinan, "Sex Differences in Childrens' Friendships," *American Sociological Review* 43(1978):237–250; and T. J. Berndt, "The Features and Effects of Friendship in Early Adolescence," *Child Development* 53(1982):1447–1460.

The same differences repeatedly emerge in patterns of male and female self-disclosure, regardless of age, region of the country, or type of measure. In general women talk much more intimately with their friends than men do.

Friendship and "Inferred Intimacy"

So far, we have seen that men and women claim about the same number of friends, that both sexes desire intimate friendship, and that both sexes describe friends as equally important in their lives. Also, both feel they are open and trusting with their friends, and among older adolescents, males seem to know at least as much about their best friends as females know about their best friends. Yet the meaning and content of male and female friendships are vastly different, on the whole: Men prefer activites over conversation, and men's conversations are far less intimate than women's conversations.

How do these disparate facts about men's friendships fit together? How can we reconcile men's assertions that they value and enjoy close friendships with the fact that they seldom reveal much about themselves to friends? There are two possibilities: Either men communicate intimacy in different ways than women, and male intimacy should not be measured in terms of self-disclosure; or, perhaps men's friendships are in fact less intimate than women's, and men are satisfied with "low intimacy" friendships. Let us consider the former possibility first.

It is difficult to assess a perception of intimacy that seems to exist without verbal and behavioral referents, and few researchers have probed the more ephemeral side of male intimacy. Yet some researchers have attempted to measure the "tone" or "style" of interactions of groups of males as compared to groups of females. Elizabeth Aries set up several discussion groups composed of college men and women at Yale University. Some groups were all male, some all female, and some mixed; and all groups met for five sessions of 90 minutes each. Marked differences characterized the all-male and all-female groups. Early in the sessions, the men developed a stable dominance hierarchy so that the same men always talked the most in all the sessions. In contrast, the women never established a dominance pyramid, and different women held forth on different occasions. Males made their points to the group as a whole, as if to command attention, while women talked more to each other, as equals. Males said little about themselves, while the women revealed much about their feelings, homes, and families. Males did considerable testing and sizing each other up, through sarcasm, putdowns, and laughter. Males often told stories of superiority and aggression, of riots, pranks, and humiliations.

Females stuck to the topic longer and talked more intimately.[21] Patterns similar to these have also been noted in naturally occurring groups of teenage boys.[22]

Other research strategies have assessed the "style" of male friendships more directly, by asking men how much they relied on nonverbal cues in order to understand a friend. In the New Jersey study mentioned above, the researchers asked men and women, "Do you and your friend seem to understand each other with a minimum of talking, using mostly gestures and facial expressions?" To this question 82% of the women said they frequently relied on nonverbal cues in understanding their friends, compared to only 28% of the men. As one man said about his best friend, "We don't have any special gestures or ways of communicating. Still, I think we understand each other with little talking because we are both intelligent and have similar interests.[23]

A simpler way of assessing the quality of male intimacy is to ask men directly about their experience of friendship. In my own research with several hundred college students in the Northeast, my colleagues and I asked our subjects to rate their close friendships on several dimensions, and we found striking differences between men and women. Although both sexes named an equal number of close friends, women felt they could count on their friends for much more support than men could. Women also said they were more satisfied with their friendships, and they rated their friendships considerably more positively than males did.[24]

If males generally fail to communicate intimacy with other males, are less satisfied with their friendships than women, and perceive less support from their friends than women do, may we conclude that men's friendships are less intimate than women's friendships? From one perspective, the answer is clearly yes: on behavioral and perceptual measures, men experience less intimacy in their same-sex friendships than women. But from another perspective, the question itself may be inappropriate. For most men, most of the time, the dimension of intimacy in friendships with other men may be irrelevant to their lives. According to the research, men seek not intimacy but companionship, not disclosure but commitment. Men's friendships involve unquestioned acceptance rather than unre-

21. E. Aries, "Interaction Patterns and Themes of Male, Female, and Mixed-Sex Groups," *Small Group Behavior* 7(1976):7–18.

22. G. A. Fine, "The Natural History of Preadolescent Male Friendship Groups," in *Friendship and Social Relations in Children*, ed. H. C. Foot, A. J. Chapman, and J. R. Smith (Chichester, England: Wiley, 1980).

23. Davidson and Duberman, "Friendship."

24. D. Sherrod, S. Cohen and M. Clark, "Social Suppport, Gender, and Friendship" (manuscript. Scripps College, Claremont, Calif., 1985).

stricted affirmation. When men are close, they achieve closeness through shared activities, and on the basis of shared activities, men infer intimacy simply because they are friends. Yet, there are times when a man becomes aware that something is lacking. Inferred intimacy seems to work well until a disturbing problem demands more from the relationship than unquestioned acceptance. At that point, many men find themselves without the kind of friend on whom they can rely. This perspective on male intimacy is consistent with the observations of psychiatrist Daniel Levinson, in his study of men's lives:

> [Close friendship] is not something that can be adequately determined by a questionnaire or mass survey. The distinction between friend and acquaintance is often blurred. A man may have a wide social network in which he has amicable, "friendly" relationships with many men and perhaps a few women. In general however, most men do not have an intimate male friend of the kind they recall fondly from boyhood or youth.[25]

If most men cannot claim an intimate male friend, and if intimacy with another man is not an important dimension in most men's lives, what accounts for this predicament? In the next section, we look at several explanations of why intimacy is not a more important dimension in men's relationships with other men.

THE TIES THAT BIND: INFLUENCES ON MALE RELATIONSHIPS

Men's inability to relate intimately with other men has been explained in various ways. In this section we consider four different explanations for males' difficulties in expressing intimacy. Each explanation focuses on a different level of analysis. Although the four approaches may be complimentary, each has been advanced independently to account for male behavior in intimate relationships. The four approaches are the psychoanalytic, the biological, the socialization, and the economic–historical perspectives.

The Psychoanalytic Perspective

Differences between men's and women's experience of intimate friendships can be traced to the psychodynamics of early childhood. Freud's original explanation of sex typing — the process by which boys and girls

25. Levinson, *The Seasons of a Man's Life.*

become psychological males and females — centered on the Oedipus complex and its resolution. While this explanation accounts for children's identification with male and female sex roles, feminist critics argue that traditional Freudian theory does not adequately explain the development of male and female sex roles in the first place. Why are women more nurturant than men, for example? And why is "mothering" almost exclusively a female activity? Critics such as Nancy Chodorow and Dorothy Dinnerstein have reinterpreted male and female Oedipal conflicts in light of the mother–child relationship, and their perspective speaks directly to men's and women's experience of friendships.[26]

According to Chodorow, girls' and boys' gender identities develop at three crucial stages: (a) the pre-Oedipal stage, when mothers relate to boys and girls in distinctly different ways; (b) the Oedipal stage, when boys and girls encounter different kinds of Oedipal conflicts; and (c) the post-Oedipal stage, when males and females resolve their Oedipal conflicts in different ways. Because of the differences at these three stages, Chodorow argues, girls develop more permeable, less rigid ego boundaries than boys. Chodorow concludes: "The basic feminine sense of self is connected to the world, the basic masculine sense of self is separate."[27]

Chodorow's formulation begins with the pre-Oedipal period and focuses on the distinctly different relationship that mothers forge with their infant daughters as compared to their infant sons. Because mothers and daughters are the same gender, mothers "overidentify" with their daughters and feel a strong sense of oneness and continuity with a female child. In contrast, mothers see their sons as a male opposite, a definite "other." As a result, mothers bond less tightly with their sons, and boys pass through the Oedipal period more quickly than girls. As a defense against the precipitous loss of the pre-Oedipal relationship with their mothers, boys begin to develop firmer, more differentiated ego boundaries than girls. In contrast, because of a girl's lack of separateness between self and mother, girls begin to develop more permeable, less rigid ego boundaries than boys. Consequently, girls emerge from the pre-Oedipal period with a built-in basis for empathy that boys lack, since a girl's boundary diffusion between self and mother provides her with a stronger basis for experiencing another's needs and feelings as her own.

Girls not only remain in the pre-Oedpial period longer than boys, but when girls enter the Oedipal stage they encounter different kinds of conflicts than boys. When boys enter the Oedipal phase, they switch their

26. N. Chodorow, *The Reproduction of Mothering* (Berkeley, Calif.: University of California Press, 1978); and D. Dinnerstein, *The Mermaid and the Minotaur: Sexual Arrangements and Human Malaise* (New York: Harper & Row, 1976).
27. Ibid., p. 169.

identification rather completely from mother to father in order to ward off the father's threatened castration. In contrast, girls never quite surrender their mothers as an internal love object, even as they come to prefer their father and his penis. Because a father is usually not a primary caretaker, a father is a less satisfying love object for a young girl than is a mother. Consequently, girls tend to oscillate between mother and father as love objects. Furthermore, because separation between mother and daughter is less complete than separation between mother and son, a girl's defenses against the anxiety of separation are less complete than a boy's defenses. Thus, masculine development depends on the denial of a boy's relationship with his mother in favor of identification with a rather distant father, whereas feminine development incorporates relationships with both mother and father. As a result, Chodorow claims, girls develop a more complex inner relational world than boys, and women retain an emotional attachment to other women even as they develop a sexual attachment to men.

Finally, girls do not resolve their Oedipal conflicts as thoroughly as boys do. A boy's love for his mother is an extension of the initial mother – infant bond and is more intense, overwhelming, and threatening to his ego than is a girl's love for her father. Because a boy's Oedipal conflict is more intense than a girl's, boys have a greater need to repress their Oedipal conflicts and turn outward to the nonfamilial world. In contrast, because a girl's Oedipal conflict is weaker than a boy's, girls do not surrender or repress their Oedpial attachments to their mothers and fathers as completely as do boys. According to Chodorow, a girl's less complete resolution of the Oedipal conflict helps account for the female's sense of connectedness between her own ego and the external world. Meanwhile, a boy's more complete Oedipal resolution tends to leave him with firmer, more differentiated ego boundaries. In other words, women remain preoccupied with ongoing relationship issues, while men tend to deny relationships and connections, preferring instead a more fixed and simpler world.

Chodorow's extension of psychoanalytic theory helps explain the differing styles of men and women in close relationships. Preoccupied with relationship issues, as females are thought to be, women invest considerable time and energy in developing, maintaining, and affirming intimate ties, especially with other women. Consequently, women are vulnerable, disclosing, and attentive in their same-sex friendships. In contrast, males, concerned as they are with separateness, distinctness, and individuation, invest less time and energy in developing, maintaining, and affirming intimate relationships, particularly with other men. Instead, when men form intimate bonds with other males, they prefer simply to live these bonds as unquestioned, unemotional commitments. According to the psychoanalytic perspective, these differences reflect the distinctly different psychodynamics of boys' and girls' development, as shaped by early relationships with their mothers and fathers.

The Biological Perspective

Evidence from many sources suggests that the male hormone testosterone may influence males to behave more aggressively than females, especially toward other males. If males in fact have some biologically determined tendency to behave aggressively toward other males, then this tendency could help account for men's behavior in same-sex friendships. Yet several problems cloud our interpretation of research on testosterone and male aggressiveness.[28] First is simply defining what constitutes aggression. In research on animals, aggression is defined as fighting; in research on children, aggression is loosely defined as "rough and tumble play"; and in research on adults, particularly prisoners, aggression has been defined as "violent crimes." Exactly how these diverse criteria relate to competitiveness and dominance in male relationships is debatable. Second, much of the testosterone research has been conducted on rats and monkeys, species whose behavior is more directly controlled by hormones. Third, when research on human beings appears to link hormones with aggression, the samples have been small and observations have sometimes been potentially biased. Finally, even if clear links could be established between testosterone and aggression in humans, it is still the case that human behavior is more controlled by culture and cognition than by hormones.

Despite these caveats, evidence from animal experiments, human behavior, and cross-cultural observations suggests that males are more aggressive than females and that male aggression may be rooted in male biology. As Maccoby and Jacklin concluded in their comprehensive review of the sex-difference literature on aggression, "There is a sex-linked differential readiness to respond in aggressive ways to the relevant experiences [of males and females]."[29] If so, the male predisposition toward aggression may help explain men's behavior in same-sex relationships.

In their review of research on the biogical basis of male aggression, Maccoby and Jacklin cite three kinds of evidence linking male hormones to aggressive behavior.[30] This is not the place to review the research in detail,

28. R. Bleier, *Science and Gender: A Critique of Biology and Its Theories on Women* (New York: Pergamon, 1984). See also A. Fausto-Sterling, *Myths of Gender* (New York: Basic, 1985); and C. Tavris and C. Wade, *Sex Differences in Perspective* (San Diego: Harcourt, 1984).

29. E. E. Maccoby, and C. N. Jacklin, *The Psychology of Sex Differences*. (Stanford: Stanford University Press, 1974).

30. Ibid., p. 243.

but samples of the findings are helpful in understanding the position of Maccoby and Jacklin.

The first kind of research links prenatal levels of male hormones with aggressive behavior after birth. For example, when pregnant monkeys were given testosterone, their female offspring had masculinized genitalia and played in a rougher way than offspring of monkeys who did not receive the hormone. Similarly, when human females are born with adrenal gland malfunctions that produce higher levels of male hormones, their parents report that the girls play more like boys than like other girls.

The second kind of research links postnatal administration of male hormones to aggressive behavior in animals. When researchers gave female monkeys testosterone treatments for 8 months, the females became dominant over a group of male monkeys to whom they had previously been submissive.

The third kind of research seeks to correlate high levels of male hormones and high levels of aggressive behavior. For example, a study of male monkeys found the more dominant animals to have higher levels of male hormones than the less dominant animals. Among imprisoned criminals, men with higher testosterone levels have committed more violent crimes. But the research is complex, for animal studies have also shown that aggressive behavior itself produces higher levels of testosterone in males. And among humans, high testosterone levels have been associated with some forms of aggression and not others, and among younger men but not older men.

In addition to the biological research, the case for male aggression is supported by observations of male behavior in nonhuman primates and across a variety of human cultures. For example, among monkeys and apes in the wild, adolescent females usually remain close to home, often in the company of adult females rather than peers, helping to care for the young. In contrast, adolescent males spend most of their time jockeying for dominance over peers at the periphery of the larger group.[31] The same patterns are found in many human cultures. In traditional African societies, for example, groups of young boys hunt small game and play imaginary war games. In Mongolia, boys pretend to go on long caravans, steal cattle and sheep, and build separate shelters away from adults. Native American boys also went on imaginary war parties and wandered in the forest for days at a time before returning home. Girls' roles in traditional cultures are generally quite different. Girls traditionally remain within the household, learning adult roles from their mothers and older women, and playing in pairs and small groups rather than in gangs, as boys do.[32]

31. R. C. Savin-Williams, "Social Interactions of Adolescent Females in Natural Groups," in Foot *et al.*, eds, *Friendship and Social Relations.*
32. Fine, "The Natural History of Preadolescent Male Friendship Groups."

If male sex hormones predispose males to behave aggressively toward other males, then male biology may contribute to the competitive nature of male relationships. Male hormones may help set the conditions under which young boys learn to relate to other boys. In an atmosphere of competition and dominance, boys are unlikely to learn skills of intimacy, vulnerability, and self-disclosure. Thus men's difficulty with intimate friendships may reflect the influence of male biology.

The Socialization Perspective

Appropriate behavior for males and females is heavily controlled by social institutions. Parents, teachers, peers, media, and even children's games teach boys and girls to adopt different styles of relating to the world and to each other. Socialization influences begin in the earliest months of life and continue throughout child and adolescent development, and they offer an alternative explanation for the behavior of males and females in intimate relationships.

Research on socialization of sex-differentiated behavior has been reviewed by Jeanne Block, who asserts that our social institutions encourage boys to develop "wings," while we expect girls to put down "roots." Wings without roots, she says, can lead males to become "unfettered, adventurous souls — free spirits who, however, may lack commitment, civility, and relatedness." In contrast, roots without wings can produce females who are "prudent, dependable, nurturing, but tethered individuals — responsible beings who may lack independence, self-direction, and a sense of adventure."[33]

How can childhood socialization produce such far-reaching effects on the behavior of women and men? To understand this process, we can look at examples from four categories of research: parents' attitudes and values; parents' behavior; teachers' behavior; and children's games.

PARENTS' ATTITUDES AND VALUES

When parents are asked to describe their approach to childrearing, boys' parents — mothers and fathers — endorse statements that emphasize achievement and competition. For example, "I feel it is good for a child to play competitive games" or "I encourage my child to control his – her feelings at all times." In contrast, girls' parents endorse statements that emphasize warmth and closeness. For instance, "I express affection by

33. J. Block, "Psychological Development of Female Children and Adolescents," in *Women: A Developmental Perspective*, ed P. W. Berman and E. R. Ramey (Bethesda, Md.: National Institutes of Health, 1982).

hugging and holding my child" or "I don't go out if I have to leave my child with a sitter he – she does not know."[34] Similarly, surveys of parents' attitudes find that parents expect their sons to be independent, self-reliant, ambitious, and strong willed, among other traits, while daughters are expected to be unselfish, loving, well mannered, and kind.[35]

PARENTS' BEHAVIOR

Parents not only expect different behaviors from their sons and daughters but they bring their expectations to life through differential treatment of male and female children. Almost from birth, boys are held more, aroused more, and given richer, more varied stimulation than girls. Such stimulation may predispose boys toward a more active engagement with the world at a later age. Furthermore, mothers and fathers react more contingently to the behavior and vocal cues of infant boys than of girls, which may encourage boys to develop a stronger sense of self-efficacy than girls.[36] Moreover, boys' independence is reinforced by the greater variety of toys, and toys with more inventive possibilities, than those provided for girls.[37] Again and again, studies find that parents — particularly fathers — give boys more freedom and less supervision, set higher standards, encourage greater achievement, and provide different kinds of reinforcements than for girls.[38] As a result, boys and girls grow up in systematically different social environments, which leave girls more embedded in social and familial networks, and send boys out into the world to develop competence and mastery.

TEACHERS' BEHAVIORS

Schools help maintain the sex differences that parents engineer. Several studies have found that nursery school teachers give boys more attention, both positive and negative, than girls. Other studies find that teachers not

34. J. Block, "Another Look at Sex Differentiation in the Socialization Behavior of Mothers and Fathers," in *Psychology of Women: Future Directions of Research,* ed. J. Sherman and F. K. Denmark (New York: Psychological Dimensions, 1979).

35. L. W. Hoffman, "Changes in Family Roles, Socialization, and Sex Differences," *American Psychologist* 32(1977):644–657.

36. G. Margolin and G. R. Patterson, "Differential Consequences Provided by Mothers and Fathers for Their Sons and Daughters," *Developmental Psychology* 11(1975):537–538.

37. H. L. Reingold and K. V. Cook, "The Content of Boys' and Girls' Rooms as an Index of Parents' Behavior," *Child Development* 46(1975):459–653.

38. S. Saegert and R. Hart, "The Development of Sex Differences in the Environmental Competence of Children," in *Women in Society,* ed. P. Burnett (Chicago: Maaroufa Press, 1976).

only respond more to boys than to girls but they also respond in more encouraging ways to boys. And more than one study reveals teachers to be particularly discouraging in their responses to high-achieving girls. This pattern of discouragement and negative reinforcement for females' intellectual activities may help account for males' consistently greater confidence in school settings, higher self-concepts, and greater mastery of problem-solving behaviors.[39]

CHILDREN'S GAMES

Even children's games help shape differences in boys' and girls' behavior. Boys' games typically occur in larger groups, have more rules, are more complex, require more player interdependence, feature explicit goals, and are more competitive. Team sports account for many of these differences, but even sedentary games differ for each sex. For example, boys play competitive board games or race cars; girls play cooperative fantasy games such as school or house. Overall, 65% of boys' games have been rated as competitive, compared to only 37% of girls' games.[40]

In light of the diverse evidence supporting the existence of sex-differentiated socialization at home, at school, and on the playground, it is not surprising that males and females grow up in very different experiential environments. In Jeanne Block's metaphor of "wings" and "roots," these different environments provide males with wings "which permit leaving the nest, exploring far reaches, and flying alone." In contrast, they provide females with roots "which anchor, stabilize, and promote growth." Like the psychoanalytic perspective, the socialization perspective sees females as embedded in family and social networks, whereas males are propelled onto an independent path beyond the family where they are less bound by social ties. Through the countless small processes of socialization, the average male becomes competitive and distant with other people, and these traits are exaggerated in relationships between men.

The Economic – Historical Perspective

A fourth perspective on male and female friendships looks not at psychodynamic residues, biological programming, or socialization practices but emphasizes instead the effect of economic and historical forces. This comparative historical perspective focuses on the behavior of men and women in different historical periods and considers what forces may have altered

39. Block, "Psychological Development of Female Children and Adolescents."
40. J. H. Lever, "Sex Differences in the Complexity of Children's Play and Games," *American Sociological Review* 43(1978):237–250.

social and sexual roles over time. Unfortunately, it is difficult to compare the quality of men's and women's friendships over time, for unlike bonds of marriage, birth, and kinship, friendships were not documented in courthouse files, village records, or family Bibles. As a result, there is no social history of friendship comparable to the social histories of marriage and the family. Yet literature, philosophy, poetry, and individual diaries speak frequently of friendships. Our historical knowledge of the institutions of work and marriage also allows certain inferences about the forms of friendship in earlier periods. As a result, it is possible to reconstruct a view of friendships in different historical periods, although with few exceptions these friendships occurred between men, for women's friendships were so little noted that women's ties remained obscure until very recent times.[41]

Friendship was particularly important in the writings of two historical periods. During the Classical Age of Greek society, and during the European Renaissance, male friendships were considered the highest form of love. Among the Greeks, bonds between men were celebrated in philosophy, literature, poetry, and art. Male relationships ranged from overtly homosexual relationships to a "platonic" love of soul for soul.[42] And in outposts where female society flourished, such as Sappho's school for girls on the island of Lesbos, women's friendships appear to have been as passionate as men's.[43] In classical Greece the most significant human bonds occurred not between husbands and wives but within the sexes, in relationships between men, and probably in relationships between women as well.

A similar degree of same-sex closeness can also be seen in Renaissance and post-Renaissance Europe. For example, the prolific sixteenth-century French essayist Michel Montaigne wrote little about his wife and family but produced a classic essay "On Friendship," in which he described his bond with his best male friend as "souls that mingle and blend with each other so completely that they efface the seam that joined them."[44] During the same period in England, male friendships were celebrated from the stage and in literature in terms of similar intimacy, as "one soul in bodies twain."[45] And at least one English woman, Katherine Phillips, published poetry that

41. A. M. Seiden and P. B. Bart, "Woman to Woman: Is Sisterhood Powerful?" in *Old Family/New Family*, ed. N. Glazer-Malbin (New York: Van Nostrand, 1975).

42. K. J. Dover, *Greek Homosexuality* (New York: Vintage, 1978). See also R. J. Hoffman, "Some Cultural Aspects of Greek Male Homosexuality," *Journal of Homosexuality* 5(1980):217–226.

43. L. Bernikow, *Among Women* (New York: Harper & Row, 1980).

44. M. Montaigne, "On Friendship," in *Selected Essays*, trans. W. J. Black (New York: Donald France, 1943).

45. L. J. Mills, *One Soul in Bodies Twain: Friendship in Tudor Literature and Stuart Drama* (Bloomington, Ind.: Principia, 1937).

protrayed women's friendships in the same way, as "love refin'd and purg'd from all its dross."[46] Based on literary sources, we can assume that educated Europeans 500 years ago, like educated Greeks 2500 years ago, held a high regard for intimate friendships. For both men and women, same-sex friendships apparently embodied a rich emotional tone and occupied a central role in everyday life.

The same case can be made for traditional people in contemporary non-Western cultures. The anthropologist Robert Brain has written a moving portrayal of friendship and its rituals among the tribal people of Africa, South America, and Oceania.[47] Here, where social roles are rigidly defined by gender, both men and women expect significant social bonds to develop within the sexes as well as across the sexes. Time and again, Brain describes cultures in which males ceremonially formalize their friendship bonds as lifetime comrades, blood brothers, or even symbolic "spouses." Yet in contemporary Western cultures, there are virtually no formal rituals to celebrate friendship, and few bonds — especially among men — publically affirmed as "one soul in bodies twain."

What happened in Western society to alter so drastically the meaning of same-sex friendships, and why did the changes affect men more strongly than women? I believe that two kinds of changes helped produce the "low intimacy" friendships that characterize men's relationships in America today. One change erected barriers between men, and came to limit the emotional intimacy of male friendships. The other change removed barriers between men and women, and came to increase the emotional intimacy between husbands and wives. These changes gradually reshaped the nature of male friendships, as well as the nature of marriage. Friendships between women were less affected by these changes because the daily lives of women were less affected. Both changes stemmed from the industrial revolution, which replaced old, traditional patterns of social relationships with new patterns to which men and women are still adjusting.

The first set of changes affected men's friendships by changing the nature of men's work. When economic production shifted away from the home and family farm and into cities and factories, male labor moved along with it. Families migrated to the new cities, where they were cut off from the kinship–friendship networks of their rural villages. In the new industrial world, men competed directly with other men for work, wages, and worth. Personal relationships came to reflect the new economy. Men no longer shared a common fate with village kin and friends. Instead, they worked for wages, competing head to head. In the new climate of competi-

---

46. Bernikow, *Among Women.*
47. R. Brain, *Friends and Lovers* (New York: Basic Books, 1976).

tion, intimate friendships began to give way to the more superficial ties of modern working men.[48]

The industrial revolution also set in motion another set of changes that altered the nature of marriage and changed the relationship between husbands and wives. Historically, marriage had been a practical arrangement to meet mutual needs, as it provided for procreation and helped build family lands and wealth. But spouses hardly expected to be each other's friends. Friends, after all, were people like oneself — people with the same social role, status, job, and sex. Although Enlightenment thinkers had begun to argue a case for individuality and individual happiness, it took the new industrialism to create a middle class. For the first time, a large number of people could afford privacy and leisure. People began to expect a right to happiness and self-fulfillment. They also expected more from marriage, and they expected that husbands and wives might actually offer each other emotional satisfaction in addition to a practical solution of life's basic needs.[49]

Affectionate marriages were not enough to make husbands and wives the best of friends, however, even as late as the nineteenth century. But the new marriages allowed men to rely on women for emotional support, at the same time that the changing nature of work was making it harder for men to receive that support from other men. Thus the industrial revolution set the stage for the twentieth-century social arrangement that typifies the lives of most American males — marriage as best friendship.

Relationships among women were less affected by the economic and social changes that altered men's work and changed the nature of marriage. From the early days of industrialism to the present, women's labor was less valued than the work of men. Even as marriages became more equal and more affectionate, wives were still subordinate to their husbands. Men accepted the emotional support of their wives, but usually offered little in return. In their relative powerlessness and need for support, women had nowhere to turn but to other women. To each other they offered a rich emotional bond, according to historian Carol Smith-Rosenberg. Based on women's diaries and letters in nineteenth-century America, Smith-Rosenberg concludes that women's lives were organized not only around their husbands and families but also, and perhaps more important, around a separate network of women's friendships. Bound together by the biological realities of pregnancy, childbirth, nursing, and menopause, women supported each other with a constant ritual of letter

48. I. Illich, *Gender* (New York: Pantheon, 1982).

49. L. Stone, *The Family, Sex, and Marriage in England: 1500–1800* (New York: Harper & Row, 1977).

writing, visiting, and mutual aid. Such support is reflected in a New York woman's letter to her best friend, assuring her friend of uninterrupted devotion on the occasion of her friend's marriage: "I wanted so to put my arms round my girl of all the girls in the world and tell her I love her as wives do love their husbands, as friends who have taken each other for life—and believe in her as I believe in my God."[50]

If these sentiments sound extreme, Smith-Rosenberg assures us that they are representative of thousands of other letters between women in nineteenth-century America. Such sentiments echo Montaigne's writings about this best male friend in sixteenth-century France, and of a tribal man about his blood brother in traditional Africa, but they are very much unlike what one man would say to another in contemporary America.

Four Perspectives: An Overview

We have considered four explanations for the lack of intimacy in male relationships. The psychoanalytic perspective argues that men's and women's differential pattern of social relationships reflects different kinds of "ego boundaries." As a result of early experiences with their mothers, girls develop more permeable ego boundaries, which leave them open to intimate ties with others, while boys form more rigid boundaries, which cause them to be relatively closed to others. The biological perspective asserts that male hormones predispose males to greater aggression than females, particularly toward other males. By setting the stage on which boys learn competition and dominance with other boys, male hormones may help to limit emotional vulnerability between men. The socialization perspective points out that boys and girls are treated differently by their parents almost from the moment of birth, and parents' attitudes and responses are augmented by schools, media, and other social institutions. Consequently, boys and girls grow up in functionally different social environments, which promote independence and self-determination in boys and cooperation and connectedness in girls. Finally, the economic–historical perspective shows how men's and women's social roles have been shaped by technological and economic forces. The industrial revolution turned male labor into a competitive market commodity and erected barriers to male intimacy, while the same economic forces encouraged greater leisure and helped remove barriers to emotional intimacy between spouses.

50. C. Smith-Rosenberg, "The Female World of Love and Ritual: Relations between Women in Nineteenth-Century America," *Signs: Journal of Women in Culture and Society* 1(1975):1–29.

At the risk of considerable speculation, I believe it is possible to weave together these four perspectives to account for the differences in contemporary men's and women's relationships. When economic forces released by the industrial revolution required male competition rather than cooperation, the nature of male relationships began to shift from "high" to "low" intimacy. New values arose regarding appropriate male behavior, and these values were gradually incorporated into childrearing practices, resulting in different developmental environments for boys and girls. The developmental environment of boys reinforced male biological predispositions toward intrasexual aggression and competition. The same environment also intensified and accelerated the process through which boys detach from primary bonds with their mothers and come to identify with their fathers. But fathers' relative absence from childrearing, combined with their nonnurturant behavior, served to deprive boys of a male model of closeness and intimacy. As a result, the typical male develops an interpersonal style characterized by separation and individuation, as opposed to the female's style of connection and social embeddedness.

If economic forces released by the industrial revolution resulted in a radical transformation of men's friendships, then current economic forces may once more be transforming the landscape of men's relationships. But today's economic forces are having a greater impact on the lives of women, and it is this impact that may indirectly affect the lives of men. In the next section, we consider how relationships between men may change as a result of changes in the lives of women.

THE BONDS REBOUND: THE FUTURE OF MALE RELATIONSHIPS

America today is in the midst of a new economic and social revolution. Since 1979, more than half of the adult women in the United States have been employed outside their homes. So many mothers with small children work that only 5% of America's households fit the mold of a working father, a mother at home, and minor children. In America's cities, the divorce rate hovers around 50%. More Americans are delaying marriage, never marrying, and living alone than ever before.[51] The structure of the family has been so stretched and torn by dual careers, divorce, and single life styles that the family may no longer be a reliable source of intimacy and emotional support for either men or women. Since many more men than women rely on their spouses for the intimate support of a best friend, the

51. S. J. Diamond, "Women's Work," *Los Angeles Times*, September 9, 1984, Sec. 1, p. 1.

transformation of the family may have a profound effect on men's relationships. Quite simply, men may no longer be able to look to their wives for a best friend, for their wives may be physically and emotionally unavailable. For their part, women may have to forge new styles of friendship more compatible with the competitive career roles that they now share with men. One option for both men and women will be intimate, nonsexual friendships with the opposite sex. But our focus here is neither the future of cross-sex friendships nor of women's friendships, but the effects of sweeping economic and social changes on men's relationships with other men.

How might men respond to a social environment in which they must look beyond their wives as their primary and often sole source of emotional support? There are several options. Some men may withdraw from intimacy altogether, retreating into the narcissistic self-preoccupation of the "new male" described by Barbara Ehrenreich.[52] Other men may slump into the depression of the disconnected. But neither of these options satisfies the human need to be known and valued by another person. For this essential human link, many men, I believe, will look to other men. Here, in a shared sense of "maleness," men may find the kind of emotional support and intimacy from a male friend that men have traditionally enjoyed in other times and other cultures.

Assuming that men may turn once again to other men for intimate friendship, how successful will men be in forging intimate bonds with other men? Can men successfully escape the bonds of biology, socialization, and economic competition? And what forms might male intimacy take? Will men's friendships mimic women's friendships in physical and emotional closeness, or will men follow uniquely male pathways? The answers to these questions are speculative, but our speculation can be informed by three different sources of data. First, several recent anecdotal accounts of important male friendships point to some likely issues in male relationships; second, observations in other cultures suggest that men's ties can be as emotionally significant as any human bond; and third, limited research suggests that variations in child rearing and educational practices can result in novel patterns of male behavior.

One man who set out to find a close male friend was Stuart Miller, who recorded his experiences in *Men and Friendship*.[53] The book begins with the author's lament that he has no male friends who are equivalent to his wife's close women friends. For months, Miller tried to identify potential candidates for the sort of friend he wanted, but over and over he encoun-

52. B. Ehrenreich, *The Hearts of Men* (New York: Doubleday Anchor, 1983).
53. S. Miller, *Men and Friendship* (Boston: Houghton Mifflin, 1983).

tered barriers to his search. The men he approached were uninterested or unavailable or afraid. At the conclusion of the book, the author had not found the friend he sought, but he learned some lessons from his search, and he was optimistic for the future. To men who seek close male friends, Miller urges a willingness to give of oneself in countless minor ways; to be deliberate and persistent in the pursuit of friendship; to ask for friendship and cultivate it; to admit one's loneliness; and to allow the possibility of being hurt. Even then, the forces that divide men will make the search difficult. But as more and more men decide to establish close male friendships, Miller is convinced, their collective efforts will produce change.

More encouraging examples of male friendships are found in David Michaelis's *The Best of Friends,* subtitled *Profiles of Extraordinary Friendship.*[54] What is striking about these extraordinary friendships, however, is the uniquely male nature of the relationships. These committed friends are not the kind of men who "wear their hearts on their sleeve," as one naval officer said about his long-time friendship with another officer. Yet he is eloquent about their friendship:

> I can't imagine going through life and not having someone like Mike. I don't know what those people who don't have a friend like Mike do. I almost find it hard to believe that everybody doesn't. I mean you gotta have somebody. And I mean a nonsexual friend. There's only so much that you'll tell your whoever, and at that point you need that kind of guy with whom you can just really be yourself. That's the purest kind of relationship. There's nothing asked, nothing expected, nothing to cloud it up. . . . I accept him as he accepts me.

Stuart Miller's personal search for friendship and Michaelis's profiles of best friendships demonstrate that many men feel a need for an intimate bond with another man, even though the forms of such a bond may be difficult to achieve. For many males, the path to intimacy with another man leads through a series of tests and challenges. Intimacy often grows through shared pursuits and shared risks, rather than the shared disclosures of women. Repeatedly, men have described their own friendships to me as "different" from the friendships of their wives or girlfriends. As one man said, about his best male friend, "We don't act the same way my wife acts with her friends, but it doesn't mean we don't care. It's just different. We express a lot through racquetball."

The problem with the male path to friendship is not so much its peculiarly male destination but its rocky, winding, lonely route. Without the

54. Michaelis, *Best of Friends.*

direct access of intimate disclosure, emotional catharsis, or physical affirmation, male friendships progress slowly and haltingly toward the goal of
intimacy. If men are to offer each other the kind of emotional support they
have previously obtained from their wives, I believe males will have to
adopt more direct avenues to emotional intimacy. To do so, men will have
to learn skills that their culture has not necessarily provided but that still
exist in many of the world's traditional cultures.

Numerous cultures socialize their young males to seek and court a best
friend in the same way American youths pursue a girlfriend. In the Kanuri
tribe of Nigeria, every young boy has a "secrets man" who shares his most
intimate thoughts. Among the Bangwa of the Cameroon, adolescent males
form best friendships that last a lifetime, and Bangwa folktales include dire
warnings about the calamaties that befall a man who has no friend. In the
sexually open culture of the Trobriand Islands, adolescent males use the
same word to describe their best friend as they use for their female lover.[55]

Other cultures have exclusive rituals and ceremonies to celebrate best
friendships among men. The Azande people, who live in the upper Nile
basin, cement male friendships with an elaborate blood-brother ritual
before the whole community. Two men cut each other's chest and arms
and smear their blood on little stubs of wood. Each man swallows the wood
covered with his friend's blood and swears an oath to his friend's essence,
now inside his own body. Afterward, the two men spend most of their time
together. In southern Ghana, men who are best friends in the Nzema tribe
hold a different sort of ceremony. They "marry" each other, and share the
same bed, although each man keeps a harem of wives for sex. The two men
offer bridal presents to each other's parents and call each other's wives
"my rivals." Somewhere between the blood brothers of the Azande and
the male wives of the Nzema are the intense *camarada* friendships of the
Chinautleco Indians of Guatemela. Here, almost all young males have a
special friend from whom they are inseparable. To the public at large,
these friendships are treated almost like a marriage. Sometimes the
friendships last a lifetime, and sometimes they burn out like a love affair.[56]

Our own culture also offers some exceptions to the typical male friendship patterns we have described earlier. Just as traditional schools and
games help maintain stereotyped male behavior, so can alternative social
structures encourage alternative behavior in children and adolescents. For
example, in one nursery school, teachers broke down the pattern of competitive, sex-segregated play by reinforcing children whenever boys and
girls played together cooperatively. As a result, cooperative cross-sex play

55. Brain, *Friends and Lovers.*
56. Ibid.

increased from about 5% of the time to 25% of the time. Though cross-sex play fell back to the old rate when the two weeks of reinforcement discontinued, the study shows that situational factors can alter traditional patterns of children's play.[57]

Another study of children's friendships found the traditional gender differences in five out of six fifth-grade classrooms surveyed. The one nonconforming group was an open classroom that allowed more social interaction outside of highly structured team sports. Other factors may have affected this classroom as well, but the study demonstrates that alternative patterns of friendship are possible in nontraditional settings.[58] Among older students, factors such as school size and curricular tracks also affect the kinds of friendships reported by boys and girls.[59]

These few studies offer meager support for the possibility of new forms of male relationships, but they offer hope. As evidence from other cultures shows, males are not necessarily destined by biology and developmental psychodynamics to lives of emotional distance from other men. Men's search for intimacy with other men will be difficult, and the forms of close male relationships will probably differ from the forms of women's relationships. But if the need is great enough, men can learn new and more direct styles of relating to one other. By acknowledging their need for intimacy, and risking the pursuit of friendship, men can begin to achieve the kind of closeness that males have known in other times and other cultures.

I believe the years ahead will see a resurgence of friendship and intimacy among men. The impetus is present in the economic and social changes that are reshaping the lives of women and altering the nature of the family. I believe these changes will force men to forge new bonds with one another.

Having begun this essay with examples of male friendship from English and American literature, I want to close with an example from my own life. I have a best friend of more than 20 years' standing. Although he lives across the country we manage to stay in regular touch. Several weekends a year we visit each other's homes, and each summer we have a tradition of camping in the mountains. We talk openly about our lives, and we spend a lot of time playing, appreciating our shared sense of humor. Over the years, we have accepted our friendship as a bond of love, distinct from

57. L. A. Serbin, I. J. Tonick, and S. H. Sternglanz, "Shaping Cooperative Cross-Sex Play," *Child Development* 48(1977):924–929.

58. Eder and Hallinan, "Sex Differences in Children's Friendships."

59. N. Karweit and S. Hansell, "Sex Differences in Adolescent Relationship: Friendship and Status," in *Friends in School,* ed. N. Karweit and S. Hansell (New York: Academic Press, 1983).

romantic and familial love, but equally important. If our relationship is unusual in light of the research cited in this essay, it is not because we ourselves are unique, but because we have made an unusual commitment to our friendship. We have invested time, energy and resources; and we have made ourselves vulnerable and acknowledged our need for one another. In the same way, other men, too, can commit themselves to close male relationships. With commitment and persistence, men can learn to break through the bonds that confine them and rebuild the bonds that unite them.

10

Gilgamesh and the Sundance Kid: The Myth of Male Friendship

*Dorothy Hammond
and Alta Jablow*

Until recently, anthropological studies of society, like those of all the social sciences, have been almost exclusively male oriented. Contemporary studies of women's roles have shown that this orientation yielded only a partial, and hence distorted, view of society. Generalizations about the institutions and culture of any society from the prefeminist perspective not only ignored the roles of women but undoubtedly skewed the descriptions of men's roles as well. It has become imperative to rethink the public roles of men, formerly so stressed in ethnographies. In the public sphere, men must cooperate to achieve their personal and institutional goals. Their cooperation has been attributed not only to its practical necessity but as fulfillment of a need perceived as intrinsic to males. That it is in the nature of men to bond with one another has become a truism that shaped the thinking of anthropologists as separate in generation as Schurtz and Tiger.[1] Tiger goes so far as to attribute the dominance of men in the public sphere directly to their unique capacities for bonding.[2]

That men bond to form friendships is an ideal that derives less from the work of scholars than from an overriding cultural assumption. This cultural article of faith is expressed in an elaborate stereotype of men and a related stereotype of friendship as the special proclivity and province of men. The stereotype idealizes men's capacities for loyalty, devotion, and self-sacrifice. It further implies men's potential for commitment to larger causes and their readiness to fight for them. The image totally excludes women and the domestic sphere. Men are most manly when they are fighting side by side in a world without women.

1. H. Schurtz, *Alterklässe und Männerbunde* (Berlin, 1902); and L. Tiger, *Men in Groups* (New York: Random House, 1969).
2. Tiger, *Men in Groups*, pp. 132–155.

A contrary, and indeed, pejorative stereotype exists about women. They are presumed to be unable to form loyal friendships. As young, unmarried women, they are rivals for men's attentions; as married women, they are committed to their families and absorbed in the daily round of domestic life.

The stereotype of male friendship has been made familiar through repetition in a large body of literary materials from modern Western cultures and their antecedents. No such narratives exist about women. Only under the stimulus of the feminist movement have women's friendships been discussed or even acknowledged.

The image of male friendship closely parallels that of romantic love. Both idealize a dyadic relationship and set expectations of undying loyalty, devotion, and intense emotional gratification. Twelfth-century narratives established the theme of romantic love, which has predominated in most fiction up to the present. The theme is not merely a literary convention; romantic love became a social convention, as the only desirable basis for sexual relations between men and women, and as the prime motive for marriage. Lacking institutionalization, friendship is more private, less open to scrutiny than courtship and marriage. There are no rituals to describe and no statistics to report.

Our concern in this paper is with the content and persistence of the stereotype of male friendship and its relation to the realities of modern life. A review of anthropological studies of friendship in modern Western societies, which we include here, presents a picture so at variance with the literary and popular stereotypes that its viability seems even more remarkable. It constitutes, in essence, a myth of male friendship. Admittedly, we are stretching the definition of *myth* to include a wide variety of literature —a necessity for literate societies. All the pertinent literature buttresses and reflects the popular stereotype to create a coherent myth.

The Malinowskian axiom that myth is a charter for institutions is not applicable to friendship, since it is hardly a concrete institution in Western society. Nevertheless, Malinowski's theoretical position also encompasses the idea that myth serves as a charter for values, and this is the relevant factor in the persistent stereotype of friendship.[3]

We therefore hypothesize that the myth persists because it provides an ideology that enhances the idea of friendship between men. The myth is so pervasive that we cannot cover all the pertinent literature. We analyze the content of the relevant major epics, ancient legends and stories, and a sampling of contemporary materials.

3. B. Malinowski, "The Psychological Function of Myth," in *Magic, Science and Religion* (Garden City, N.Y.: Doubleday, 1954).

ANTHROPOLOGICAL APPROACHES

The study of friendship in Western societies challenges the concepts of anthropology because they have been shaped by the institutionalized forms of friendship in non-Western societies: blood brotherhood, trade friends, and bond friends. These relationships all entail clearly defined rights and obligations that have jural sanction and ritual validation. They are, as well, fully integrated into the overall social structure. For anthropologists, the difficulties of studying Western friendship are inherent in its very nature. Friendship in Western society, for the most part, lacks formal structure; it is based on individual volition and mutual affection, and is interstitial in the social structure. Friends establish their own terms for the relationship in which there are no obligations except those freely embraced, no rights except those freely given. Nadel recognizes the unstructured quality of Western friendships as having "general coordination of behaviour whose precise aim content is mostly indeterminate, in other words, friends will act as such, assisting and showing their regard for one another on almost any occasion, no activity being excluded or specifically referred to in the relationship formula."[4] Elsewhere, Nadel states that "friend" can be described only as a "quasi-role."[5] The fluidity of the concept can encompass relationships in which roles are not socially defined, and in which expectations are set by the participants rather than by the formal structure of society. So amorphous a relationship, however important to the individual participants and the society, tends to escape the anthropological mesh.

Anthropologists have attempted in various ways to deal with what is for them refractory material. Brain affirms the affective nature of friendship. He contrasts friendships in the Western world with the highly structured friendships in the Cameroons and concludes that, lacking the support of formal organization, Western friendship can be only a fragile relationship. He calls for legal and ritual institutionalization to buttress a relationship that, otherwise, would seem to be floating in social midair.[6]

Eisenstadt and Pitt-Rivers also stress sentiment as the essential core of the relationship. Eisenstadt, however, views the private dyad of friendship as potentially oppositional to the values of the total society.[7] Pitt-Rivers, in

4. S. F. Nadel, *The Foundations of Social Anthropology* (London: Cohen and West, 1951), p. 91.

5. S. F. Nadel, *The Theory of Social Structure* (London: Cohen and West, 1957), p. 28.

6. R. Brain, *Friends and Lovers* (New York: Basic Books, 1976).

7. S. N. Eisenstadt and L. Roniger, *Patrons, Clients and Friends: Interpersonal Relations and the Structure of Trust in Society* (Cambridge, England: Cambridge University Press, 1984), pp. 282–283.

contrast, indicates that the practical realities of Andalusian life are antago-
nistic to the maintenance of the *simpatia* required of the relationship.[8]
While recognizing the ideal of affect, both authors predicate an inevitable
tension between society and friendship.

Certain studies of friendship in small, closed communities in Newfoundland and Ireland, minimize the issue of sentiment.[9] They fail to
confront the lack of institutional forms inherent in the relationship by
asserting that friendship is an institution "with a force and vitality of its
own."[10] Their analyses set out institutional parameters in which friendship
serves as the basis for recruitment of fishing crews or drinking partners,
settlement patterns or political and economic alliances. They are, per-
force, focussed on the transactions between and among friends, rather
than with the nature of the relationship itself.

Other anthropologists have dealt with modern friendship in purely
theoretical terms, creating conceptual structures where there is no social
structure. Du Bois, Cohen, and Wolf have developed typologies of friendship based on a scale from "affective" to "instrumental" or "expedient,"
rephrasings of the Aristotelian distinction between "good" and "useful"
friends.[11] Du Bois includes several more parameters: intimacy and muta-
bility. Cohen distinguishes four levels of friendship ranging from inalien-
able to expedient, linking each to a particular kind of community: inalien-
able to maximally solidary; close to solidary–fissile; casual to
nonnucleated; and expedient to individuated. Wolf reverts to the Aristotelian twofold category: the expressive or emotional friendship and the
instrumental. Like Cohen, he links the expressive kind to solidary social
units and the instrumental to individuated societies.

However neat these linkages seem, the actual correlations are suspect
because the institutionalized friendships of solidary societies, expressive or
not, are often highly instrumental. For instance, in Melanesian societies
where trade is conducted through friends, they are far more concerned
with the unimpeded exchange of trade goods than with sentiment. Close,

8. J. A. Pitt-Rivers, *The People of the Sierra* (New York: Criterion, 1954), pp. 137–160.

9. R. Schwartz, "The Crowd: Friendship Groups in a Newfoundland Outport," in *The Compact: Selected Dimensions of Friendship*, ed. E. Leyton, Newfoundland Social and Economic Papers No. 3(Toronto: University of Toronto Press, 1974); E. Leyton, "Irish Friends and 'Friends': Friendship, Kinship, and Class in Aughnaboy," in Leyton, ed., *Compact*.

10. Leyton, "Irish Friends," p. 104.

11. C. Dubois, "The Gratuitous Act: An Introduction to the Comparative Study of Friendship Patterns," in Leyton, ed., *Compact*; Y. A. Cohen, "Patterns of Friendship," in *Social Structure and Personality*, ed. Y. A. Cohen (New York: Holt, Rinehart and Winston, 1961); and E. Wolf, "Kinship, Friendship and Patron–Client Relationships in Complex Societies," in *The Social Anthropology of Complex Societies*, ed. M. Banton (London: Tavistock, 1966), pp. 3–27.

affective friendships are not lacking in contemporary Western individuated societies. Commerce is impersonal and contractual; friendship is a relationship of "mutual liking . . . mutual service . . . mutual confidence."[12]

Although the typologies recognize a continuum between the polarities of affective and instrumental friendship, the poles are seen as distinct types. Both are, however, components of any friendship. Aristotle was right to add to his typology that even perfect friendship retains some element of the useful and that the moral imperative of sentiment colors even the highly expedient friendship.

THE LITERATURE

The large body of literary materials about friendship in the Western world includes novels, films, songs, and even opera, along with myth and legend. Despite the variety in form and content, all reiterate similar themes concerning friendship. A persistent literary tradition has developed from pre-Babylonian times, appearing among ancient Semites, pagan Greeks, medieval Christians, and the modern secular West. The tradition always dramatizes the devotion between male friends, usually a dyad, forged in an agonistic setting.

The earliest recorded version of the myth is in the Gilgamesh epic, but it was unknown to the modern West until the cuneiform tablets from the royal library in Ninevah were excavated and decoded in the late nineteenth century. This was the literary version of Akkadian myths and legends of a much earlier period. Similarly, the story of David and Jonathan, as we know it from the Bible, and the story of Achilles and Patroclus in the Iliad, had much earlier oral antecedants. Although the myth thus exhibits long historical continuity, the classical Greek narratives were probably the model for all later narratives.

All the variants of the myth, over more than 3000 years, retain the essential core despite drastic changes in culture and society. With the exception of imperial Rome, earlier societies share characteristics that contrast with modern industrial society. Early Sumer, ancient Greece, and medieval Europe were all small-scale polities engaged in endemic warfare; they were socially stratified with a small, literate upper class at the apex. In all of them, membership in the extended kin determined rank and wealth. A man without kin had, at best, little place in society and, at worst, small

12. Pitt-Rivers, *People of Sierra*, p. 139.

chance of survival. What, then, would be the place of an ideal friendship in such a society? The kin group was undoubtedly supportive, but membership in it entailed obligations and constraints that could be very onerous. Aries points out that the extended kin line was the primary unit of loyalty but functioned "without regard to the emotions engendered by cohabitation and intimacy."[13] Friendship, in contrast, provided a volitional alternative source of support without the restrictions of kinship and may well have given more emotional gratification than the obligatory amity of kin.

In such societies, marriages were arranged with an eye to considerations of property and useful alliance; emotional attachment between spouses was not essential. All the more reason to value the affection of a chosen friend. Women's roles, even in the upper classes, were confined to the household, but there the women were in control. A man's place in his home was honorific but involved little participation. A man who limited himself to home and hearth was considered less than a man.

The public domain was the province of men where their participation made men's relationships with one another politically significant. A friend was also an ally. In the Greek city-states, every citizen (citizenship was limited to men of the upper stratum) was expected to be a warrior. Warfare was the quintessential form of political action. War not only separated men from their families but thrust them into dependent and sometimes long-lasting relationships. Warfare is the prime setting for the drama of male friendship.

With hindsight, the narratives of friendship seem to be political propaganda for abrogating familial ties in favor of male solidarity. In them friendship was idealized, war glorified, and the warrior the ideal man.

The conventions of the myth express an ideology upholding the moral worth of friendship and the social premium placed on it. The myth is retained in form and content even in societies such as Rome and the modern West, which are mass societies, where the soldier replaces the warrior, bureaucracy dominates political and economic life, and loyalty to the state supersedes loyalty to kin. The myth could not be impervious to such radical change if it did not evoke a positive emotional response. Changed contexts, however, base that response on different values and needs.

The literary epic of Gilgamesh, dating from approximately 1600 B.C., combines what were probably separate narratives, from earlier oral traditions. The episode of Gilgamesh and Enkidu in the early part of the epic contains the basic themes of ideal friendship between two men. The gods, having determined that Gilgamesh, king of Uruk, suffered from loneli-

13. P. Aries, *Centuries of Childhood* (New York: Vintage, 1965), p. 356.

ness, pitied him and created Enkidu to be his friend, one "who can measure up to him and give him companionship."[14] The gods, interestingly
enough, chose to provide a friend rather than a wife and family to assuage
loneliness. Enkidu, an artifact of the gods, was a total isolate. Without kin
or community, he could be absolutely committed to his friend and con-
comitantly became the instrument that prevented Gilgamesh's marriage.
Gilgamesh and Enkidu first met as Gilgamesh was about to be married, but
Enkidu barred access to the bride's house. They engaged in a hand-to-
hand fight in which Enkidu defeated Gilgamesh and then said, "'Gilgamesh, you have proved full well that you are the child of a goddess and that
heaven itself has set you on your throne. I shall no longer oppose you. Let
us be friends.' And raising him to his feet, he embraced him."[15] Gilgamesh's heart was won, and forgetting about the marriage, he embraced
Enkidu as his true friend. Together they went on to have many heroic
adventures. Their final exploit so seriously offended the gods that they
caused Enkidu's death, leaving Gilgamesh inconsolable.

> *Enkidu, whom I love dearly*
> *Whoever went through all hazards with me,*
> *The fate of man has overtaken him.*
> *All day and night have I wept for him,*
> *And would not have him buried.*
> . . .
> *Since he is gone I can no longer comfort find.*
> *Keep roaming like a hunter in the plains.*[16]

This story is exceptional only in the divine creation of a special friend;
otherwise, it conforms to all the narratives of heroic friendship that follow.
All make high drama of the relationship, endowing it with glamour and
beauty. The friends are heroes: aristocratic, young, brave, and beautiful.
In their free and wholehearted response to one another, they openly
declare their affection and admiration. They engage in many adventures
and battles, sharing danger, loyal to the death. Throughout life, they
remain devoted and generous to each other.

The heroes value their friendship above all other relationships. Some of
the heroes may actually have been kinsmen, but the family ties are totally
overshadowed by the friendship. The fact that Achilles and Patroclus were
cousins, and Castor and Pollux half-brothers, is not important. Wives and

14. T. Jacobsen, *The Treasures of Darkness* (New Haven: Yale University Press, 1976), p.
196.

15. T. H. Gaster, *The Oldest Stories in the World* (Boston: Beacon, 1952), p. 55.

16. Jacobsen, *Treasures of Darkness*, pp. 203–204.

lovers recede into the background, often a very remote one. Family relationships are secondary if mentioned at all. When kinsmen play a significant role in the narrative, it underlines the primacy of the friendship.
Jonathan actually defied his father, King Saul, to protect David. In the
Verdi opera, Don Carlos rejected his royal father out of love for his friend.
Achilles spurned his mother's attempts to comfort him at his friend's
death. Amile was willing to sacrifice his own children for the sake of his
friend. This is probably the most drastic expression of rejection of kin to
reaffirm the intensity of the bond between friends.

The spiritual bond achieves its most poignant expression in the laments
at the death of one of the pair. In the *Iliad*, when Patroclus was killed by
Hector, Achilles, in an agony of grief, threw dust on his face and tore his
hair. He lamented:

> My dearest friend is dead, Patroclus, who was more to me than any other
> of my men, whom I loved as much as my own life. . . . I have lost
> Patroclus. . . . I have no wish to live and linger in the world of men,
> unless before all else, Hector is felled by my spear and dies, paying the
> price for slaughtering Patroclus. . . . [17]

The death of one friend and the overwhelming grief of the survivor is a
theme that occurs frequently in the heroic tales. It is an essential element,
not only in Gilgamesh and the *Iliad*, but also in the tales of David and
Jonathan, Theseus and Pirithous, Castor and Pollux, Hercules and Hylas,
and Roland and Oliver. Such great heroes were bound to have short lives.

The stories all have an agonistic setting. Confrontation with extreme
danger heightens and proves the essential quality of friendship. In the
Gilgamesh epic, the heroes overcame monsters; Damon and Pythias were
subject to political tyranny; Orestes and Pylades braved the savagery of the
Taurians. Achilles and Patroclus were fighting the Trojans as Roland and
Oliver fought together against the Saracens. The heroes were warriors
whose major goal was personal and everlasting fame gained on the field of
battle.

Love between friends was expressed in words and deeds. The men
embraced, exchanged vows of undying affection and loyalty. Pylades supported Orestes in the dreadful matricide of Clytemnestra. Friends were
willing to die for each other. Castor and Pollux symbolized the ideals of
friendship to the Greeks. Of the two, Pollux alone was immortal, but he so
loved his friend that he bestowed half his immortality on Castor at his
death. To this day, the familiar legend of Damon and Pythias epitomizes
ideals of loyalty. Pythias, condemned to death by the ruler of Syracuse, was

17. *The Iliad*, trans. E. V. Rieu (Harmondsworth, England: Penguin, 1950), p. 330.

granted leave to set his affairs in order on Damon's pledge of his own life. The equally loyal Pythias returned to redeem the pledge, and the tyrant, moved by the generosity of their love, released them both.

In Greek literature, the image of friendship is elaborated and repeated over and over again. It is a stock subject for myth, legend, drama, and philosophy. The *Symposium* and *Phaedrus* expressed Plato's deep interest in the subject, and Aristotle wrote *the book* on friendship, establishing the canons still relied on by anthropologists.

"The Greeks gave to friendship the attachment and loyalty which elsewhere accompany the love of women."[18] In Classical times, homosexuality was openly practiced, but the theme of male friendship was distinct from that of homosexuality. Lovers were expected to be a youth and an older man who would also serve as his mentor.[19] Friends, in contrast, were always peers, and their equality was an important component of the stereotype. But the friends were not sexual lovers. We cannot evaluate the extent to which these stories express latent homosexuality. There is no direct evidence of overt homosexuality between the friends; the narratives, on the contrary, provide ample indication of their sexual interest in women. Patroclus and Achilles took Trojan women as spoils of war, and when Achilles was forced to return one of his female captives, he withdrew from the war in resentment. Only his rage to avenge the death of Patroclus induced him to take up arms once again. David's love for Jonathan in no way distracted him from his career as a lover of women, a career that scarcely needs recapitulation. Both Castor and Pollux were married; Pylades married the sister of his friend, Orestes; Theseus, that much-married hero, once attempted to abduct the beautiful Helen. The climax of the adventures of Theseus and Pirithous was the hare-brained scheme to abduct Persephone from Hades to give Pirithous a second wife.[20] Not all the stories mention love affairs or marriages, but when they do, it is clear that relationships with women were of minor importance. Most of the heroes would have agreed with David that the love of his friend "was wonderful, passing the love of women."[21] Although Plato reinterpreted the *Iliad* to reflect the homosexuality prevalent in his own times, he did consider that friendship at its best consisted of a spiritual rather than a sexual bond.

Distinctively Roman narratives about friendship seem to be lacking for possibly two reasons. First, the Romans adopted as their own the literature of Greece. Virgil's depiction of friendship in the *Aeneid* was obviously

18. C. M. Bowra, *The Greek Experience* (New York: Mentor, 1957), p. 39.
19. K. J. Dover, *Greek Homosexuality* (Cambridge: Harvard University Press, 1978).
20. E. Hamilton, *Mythology* (New York: Mentor, 1940).
21. 1 Sam. 11.

based on the Homeric model. Second, as Grant points out, Roman myth underwent continuous revision in the direction of political and familial values.[22] Roman armies were not made up of aristocratic Bronze Age warriors but of soldiers drawn from all ranks of society, subjected to an iron military discipline. Save for the generals, there was little room for individual exploits in quest of personal glory. "They want centurions to be not rash fire eaters, but born leaders, steady, and of strong personality, who will stand firm in the pinches and die, rather than surrender."[23] The Roman ideal of loyalty was patriotism, not friendship.[24]

Post-Roman times were characterized by the absence of strong central governments, and major political loyalties were those between lord and vassal. Warfare became again, as in the Homeric epics, a matter of heroes —nobles and knights-at-arms. Accounts of medieval warfare thus hark back to the earlier aristocratic tradition, and the battlefield once more becomes the setting for the grand display of heroic action.

Most medieval literature concerns themes of romantic love and religious devotion. There are, however, two outstanding legends of male friendship: the eleventh-century *Song of Roland* and the thirteenth-century tale of Amis and Amile, which appears in many versions. The protagonists of the Classical myths and epics were not exemplars of moral virtue, other than their loyalty to one another. It was enough that they were highborn, brave, and beautiful. In the medieval narratives, however, the heroes epitomize Christian virtues of piety, charity, and humility; they were as noble in character as they were in social rank.

Roland and Oliver were two of the Twelve Peers who composed the elite warrior band around Charlemagne, archetypal feudal knights defending their emperor and their God against the infidel Saracens. Their friendship began when they were boys sent to the court of Charlemagne. Together the youths were trained in the arts of war and the code of chivalry. Roland and Oliver became devoted friends and, fighting side by side, gained fame as warriors. They exemplified all the renewed pre-Roman ideals of friendship, and as in the earlier stories, the death of one evoked an impassioned lament by the other. Roland thus grieved for Oliver, "Sir, my companion, woe worth your valiant might! Long years and days have we lived side by side, ne'er didst thou wrong me nor suffer wrong of mine. Now thou art dead, I grieve to be alive."[25]

22. M. Grant, *Roman Myth* (London: Weidenfeld and Nicolson, 1971), p. 229.
23. Polybius, *Histories* 6, in *The Roman Mind at Work*, trans. P. MacKendrick (New York: Van Nostrand, 1958).
24. E. Hamilton, *The Roman Way* (New York: Norton, 1932), p. 114.
25. *The Song of Roland*, trans. D. Sayers (Baltimore: Penguin, 1957), p. 129.

Domination of the Christian ethos over medieval literature is obvious in the historical discrepancy in the *Song of Roland*. The legend describes the Battle of Roncevaux, in which both heroes met their deaths, as a fight against the Muslim Saracens. In reality, Charlemagne and the Saracens were allies at Roncevaux, fighting against the Christian Basques. As ever, legend brings history into line with ideology.

In the tale of Amis and Amile, the eponymous knights were also brothers-in-arms in Charlemagne's elite band. They were born at exactly the same time and were taken by their fathers to Rome for baptism by the pope. Their equality was affirmed by Amis's father. "Are you not alike in all things — in beauty, in comeliness and in strength, so that whoever sees you thinks you to be sons of one mother?"[26] The basic thread of the tale is heroic self-sacrifice. Amis, defying custom and God, took Amile's place in a trial by combat in which Amile, guilty of the charge, would surely have been slain. Punished by God, Amis became a leper, and Amile, loyal in his turn, took him into his own home and healed him. Under instruction from the angel Rafael, Amile beheaded his own children, using their blood to restore the health of his friend.

Although shocking to modern sensibilities, the willing sacrifice of one's children was probably less so to medieval audiences, since it was a sacrifice dictated by God. It had a biblical precedent in Abraham's willingness to sacrifice Isaac. The episode in the legend expresses not only the devotion of friends but also the strength of medieval religious faith. Moreover, according to Aries, relationships within the medieval family tended to lack significant emotional force or great intimacy.[27]

The final episode, Charlemagne's campaign against the Lombards, depicted the heroes fighting valiantly in the battle of Belle-Forêt. "There, too, on that field died Amis and Amile, for as it had pleased God to make their lives lovely and pleasant together, so in their deaths they were not divided."[28] They lay together in the same sarcophagus, just as the ashes of Achilles and Patroclus were joined in the same burial urn. Burial together, rather than family interment, indicates the social approval bestowed on such devoted friendships.

In the medieval period, tales of unequal friendship mirror the relationships of lord and vassal or knight and squire. In these variants of the major theme, one of the pair is adjunct to the other and in some way inferior. He may be junior in age or rank or less gifted. This theme of friendship

---

26. *Aucassin and Nicolette and Other Medieval Romances and Legends*, trans. E. Mason (London: Dent, 1910), p. 175.

27. Aries, *Centuries of Childhood*, pp. 355–356.

28. *Aucassin and Nicolette*, p. 193.

becomes as persistent as the theme of friendship between equals. For example, in the *Beowulf* epic, the hero was aided and supported by his devoted and loyal young vassal and kinsman. According to legend, Richard the Lion-Hearted was ransomed from captivity only because of the single-minded zeal of his friend and minstrel, Blondel. El Cid and Alvar Fañez, knights and vassals of Alfonso of Castile, were best friends. El Cid, however, was a figure of such heroic dimension that Fañez inevitably played a supporting role as his aide. In *Don Quixote*, Cervantes parodied this theme; the nobly born knight was a figure of pathos and comedy, and his squire a low-born peasant, devoting his life to the extrication of his lord from one self-inflicted predicament after another.

A related theme, but even earlier in origin, tells of a band of intrepid men, usually led by a great hero. The band, engaged in war or adventure, proved a fertile ground for the formation of close friendships. These dyads created an infrastructure for the band itself, providing it with an emotional quality beyond the *ésprit de corps*. The loyalties of the friends intensified loyalty within the band itself and to the leader. Such a theme is prefigured in the adventures of Jason and his brave band of Argonauts. It is restated more fully in the *Aeneid* where the loving friendship between Nissus and Euryalus elicited a corresponding emotional reaction from the other members of the Aeneadae. It is, as well, a theme in the tales of Arthur and his Knights of the Round Table, Robin Hood and His Merry Men, and is most striking in the legends surrounding the Twelve Peers of Charlemagne. Each one of this elite band had a special friend in the group.[29] Group bonds based on a loyalty to a cause and to a leader continue as an ideal in subsequent literature. It affects most obviously accounts for warfare, outlawry, and pioneering, and is a tangential theme to that of the basic dyadic relationship.

Despite variations in theme, and the great differences in religion and culture, the narratives through medieval times project and validate the earlier ideals of friendship. The stories belong to a tradition that was about and for aristocrats. The major change in modern versions of the myth is the loss of the aristocratic tradition. The class structure of the modern Western world, along with much else, has been revolutionized, but the ideals of friendship have not undergone radical change. They persist in modern popular literature and films that depict situations of danger and isolation. The modern protagonists, often heroes in spite of themselves, are usually of the lower class: common soldiers, seamen, prospectors, cowboys, criminals, and policemen. Their dangerous occupations provide the arena for the drama of friendship.

29. *Song of Roland*, p. 37.

Warfare, the typical context for earlier tales of friendship, gave purpose to the lives of the earlier heroes. They welcomed it for the opportunity to gain personal honor and fame, unlike the modern conscript for whom warfare is a hell to be endured. His goal is to survive and return to civilian life. Sharing the danger, hardships, and boredom with a special friend enables a modern soldier to retain his sanity and identity in the dehumanizing bureaucracy of the army.

The classic novels and films of World War I — *All Quiet on the Western Front, What Price Glory?* and *A Farewell to Arms* — all contain a friendship between two men as an important element. Nothing so sentimentalizes the wartime friendships as the then-popular song *"My Buddy,"* an almost classic lament for a dead friend. World War II fiction contains many friendships: the imprisoned aviators of *The Purple Heart*, the infantrymen in *A Walk in the Sun*, the naval officers in *The Cruel Sea* and *Mr. Roberts*. The same themes are repeated in *MASH*, about the Korean war, and in *The Killing Fields*, a book and documentary film about the Vietnam war. In none of the narratives is war glorified, but the friendships portrayed are so positive an element that the miseries of war are reduced to setting — the stark contrast to the heartwarming friendship.

Men in other dangerous or isolated situations form friendships like those of soldiers. Henry Lawson, "The Poet of the Outback," eulogized the "mateship" of Australian gold prospectors: "Mateship began with the mutual regard and trust between men working together in the lonely bush . . . there grew up the idea of a kind of a holy grail, the 'Bonanza' which helped bind men together in a mystical friendship . . . continued, ideally, until death."[30] A recent travel book by Ted Simon repeats the "mateship" theme in the description of Australian long-distance truck drivers. "They were truckies, and in Australia that was tantamount to being an outlaw. . . . They were mates, of course, which is a powerful enough bond."[31]

Frontier America is an appropriate setting for tales and legends to grow around the tradition of friendship, whether as dyadic relationships, hero and sidekick, or the loyal band. The tradition followed the moving frontier in time and space from James Fenimore Cooper's *Leatherstocking Tales* to long-running television epics such as *Gunsmoke*. The Lone Ranger and Tonto, and Wyatt Earp and Doc Holliday, are archetypes for the stock figures of sheriffs and their loyal deputies in the narratives. On the other side of legality, the Wild West produced its share of outlaws to whom organized society was the enemy. The Dalton Boys, the Youngers, and the Jesse James band live on in American folklore.

30. Brain, *Friends and Lovers*, p. 68.
31. T. Simon, *Jupiter's Travels* (Garden City, N.Y.: Doubleday, 1980), 327.

Two films elevated a pair of small-time bandits to the status of mythic heroes. Butch Cassidy and the Sundance Kid were, in reality, none-too-successful bank robbers whose brushes with the law eventually forced them to flee the country. The films depicted them as inseparable friends. Their loyalty, tested in adversity, withstood their attachment to the same woman and remained intact throughout their lives. They died together in a shootout with South American lawmen. This poignant death scene is pure fiction, but it brings the story into strict conformity with the mythic tradition. One can almost assume that they would have been buried in the same grave if that last adventure had ever taken place. *Butch Cassidy and the Sundance Kid* was so successful as a movie that it inspired a sequel about the pair's earlier adventures. The extent of the popular response to the films, especially the first one, demonstrates that the theme of friends, loyal to the death, still pulls at modern heartstrings.

The urban counterpart of frontier narrative is most prevalent in the form of detective and police stories. The most familiar are British: Arthur Conan Doyle's Sherlock Holmes and Dr. Watson, Agatha Christie's Poirot and Hastings, Dorothy Sayers's Lord Peter Wimsey and Bunter (his valet), and Ngaio Marsh's Superintendant Roderick Alleyn and Inspector Fox. It is, perhaps, characteristic that the British tend to maintain the aristocratic tradition, at least in some of this literature. There are innumerable, if not as memorable and certainly not aristocratic, American versions. Television has shown us many pairs of friends: Starsky and Hutch, the Rookies, Rockford and his policeman friend. Captain Kirk and Mr. Spock have extended the image into outer space.

The model has even served to depict the friendship between two police-women in *"Cagney and Lacey."* It departs from the model in that the heroines, though devoted to each other, are not detached from kin or the world of men. Lacey is provided with a husband and children whom she loves dearly. Cagney, unmarried and a more aggressive and committed policewoman, is nonetheless devoted to her father. This popular television series thus makes its obeisance to the domestic feminine stereotype.

MYTH AND REALITY

The narratives of male friendship define the role of friend not only in terms of expectations and attitudes but also in terms of status and code of behavior. Friends are described as male peers cooperating in a hazardous venture, whether it is robbing a bank or slaying monsters. They support each other throughout a life of adventure and danger, in which they exhibit great courage and fortitude. Mundane affairs such as marriage, making a living, or having a family, which make up the lives of other men, do not concern them. The emotional bonds between them are stronger than any other, even ties to wives, children, or kinsmen. Their prime attachment is to each other, expressed in open affection and lifelong loyalty. If they do not die together, the death of one strikes to the heart of the other.

Much of this definition of the role lacks relevance to modern times. Heroic action, mutual self-sacrifice, and loyalty to the death are anomalous in a bureaucratized world. Aubert and Arner found that "the social structure of the Norwegian Merchant Marine includes a near taboo on personal friendships."[32] The ship is a tightly integrated bureaucratic institution in which work roles predominate and status in the structure precludes the formation of close dyads. Similarly, bureaucracy, along with its promotion of competitiveness, inhibits the formation of friendships in the appropriately agonistic settings described in the training of the first astronauts[33] and the designing of a new microcomputer.[34]

The agonistic drama of the mythic tradition of friendship is likewise incongruous in modern society. The men engaged in dangerous occupations rarely dramatize their jobs. Most men work within corporate structures whose goals are mainly financial, and success is achieved through individual competition rather than dyadic or group bonding. Men's lives are constrained by the institutional framework of society, and the routines of daily life hardly provide an arena for the heroic exploits of devoted friends. Agon gives way to anxiety.

The open avowals of devotion or physical expressions of affection prevalent in the early literature are considered embarrassing behavior for men in this society.[35] Emotional restraint is the general rule among male friends: " . . . love between men that is neither romantic nor sexual is terribly hard for most men to acknowledge to one another."[36] The behavior patterns in the literature do not serve as a model for men in modern society.

The value of male solidarity and the definition of manliness implicit in the myth have lost much of their force for modern society. The myth contains the message that a man should hold himself aloof from the world

32. Quoted in O. Ramsøy, "Friendship," in *International Encyclopedia of the Social Sciences*, 1968, 6:14.
33. T. Wolfe, *The Right Stuff* (New York: Farrar, Straus and Giroux, 1979).
34. T. Kidder, *The Soul of a New Machine* (Boston: Atlantic-Little, Brown, 1981).
35. R. R. Bell, *Worlds of Friendship* (Beverly Hills: Sage, 1981), pp. 77–84.
36. E. G. McWalter, "Hitting the Road," *New York Times Magazine*, May 27, 1984, p. 46.

of women. His loyalties should be to other men: friends, political leaders, and his fellows in the group. Overinvolvement with a wife, children, or kin inhibits a man's wholehearted participation in the male world. In modern society, the dichotomy between the worlds of men and women is no longer so clearly drawn. Men are not considered unmanly for their participation in the domestic sphere, and women are active outside it. Marriage and the creation of a nuclear family are now volitional. Unlike earlier societies, in which marriages were arranged, men and women seek fulfillment of their emotional needs in the family. It is here that the most intense relationships exist, and friendship plays a secondary role.

Solidarity among men is peripheral to the major concerns of the individual man and interstitial in the functioning of society. Political life in Athens involved the active participation of every citizen; it is now reduced to the yearly visit to the voting booth. Work may require that men cooperate, but it does not require solidarity or loyalty. On every level of economic and political life, bureaucracy sets the terms for cooperation, and those terms exclude emotional affect. In the myth, friends are partners whose whole lives are inextricably intertwined. In modern society, work and friendship belong to distinct compartments. The place of friends is limited to leisure activities.

The myth has always expressed the fulfillment of a wish. In the past, the wish may have been release from the obligations imposed by the lineage, desire for the emotional warmth to be found neither in lineage nor family, and the hunger for fame and glory. Now the wish may involve escape from the hothouse intensity of the nuclear family and its disappointments, the dull routines of work, or the frustrations of living in a mass society. The fantasy of an ideal friendship is a response to whatever specific discontents a particular society induces.

The myth persists, not because it instructs the specifics of conduct, but because it still promotes and legitimizes a code of values. The ideology of friendship—affection, loyalty, and trust—has never gone out of style. The affirmation of these values elicits a positive response, perhaps even more now than in the past. Urbanization and bureaucratization, social and geographical mobility, all may foster instrumental and expedient relationships, but they surely induce a sense of individual isolation. All forms of permanent affiliation, even the bonds of kinship, are attenuated. The human need for enduring, emotionally satisfying relationships often remains unfulfilled. The hunger for affiliation is certainly one of the major factors accounting for the viability of the myth of friendship. The search for a "best friend" begins in the playground, often at the urging of adults, who believe that having friends is a necessary socializing experience. And Ramsøy points out that, throughout life, to lack friends is a source of

shame.[37] Even without the formal social organization to define relationships and instruct them, people often make enduring and gratifying
friendships.[38] Both old and contemporary versions of the myth offer the
image and promise of true friendship.

The myth conveys other messages as well. Shifting focus away from the
affective core of bonding, we perceive an all-too-familiar image of men:
the traditional stereotype, in which men are dominant, independent of
women but sexually exploitative of them, and their manliness is expressed
through violence. The myth especially exaggerates male aggressiveness
and the value placed on combat. The heroes are always fighters and the
settings always agonistic.

In the narratives, the behavior of the heroes is often socially irresponsible, so centered are they on each other, ego and alter ego. Wives, children,
kin, society at large, and even the gods are disregarded. Ordinary life is
tame and dull compared to the high-pitched quality of their adventurous
careers. The image is thus implausibly youthful, and, literally, the heroes
die young, obviating any need to come to terms with maturity. Such an
image is wholly antithetical to the realities of society where men must meet
the responsibilities of ongoing life. No matter how preposterously distorting, the myth is legitimized in the beautiful name of friendship.

CONCLUSION

In sociology and anthropology, studies of friendship are based on the
assertion that it is an institution and, as such, open to investigation. The
institutional aspects of friendship are its recurrence and its social importance. But contemporary Western friendship lacks other defining characteristics of an institution: regularity and consistency of behavior, clear-cut
definition of roles, and jural or ceremonial status. The patterns of behavior in friendship vary from one set of friends to another. Mutual habitua-
tion defines its unique roles and creates its own structures, its own rituals
and styles of communication. In the face of such discrepancy, social scientists tend to retreat by qualifying the term; Ramsøy calls friendship a
"vague institution," and Paine describes it as an "institutionalized non-in-
stitution."[39] It is, at best, a quasi-institution, as friend is a quasi-role.

37. Ramsøy, "Friendship," p. 14.
38. Bell, *Worlds of Friendship;* and M. B. Parlee *et al.*, "The Friendship Bond," *Psychology Today* 13, no 4(1979):42–54, 113.
39. Ramsøy, "Friendship," p. 13; and R. Paine, "In Search of Friendship: An Explor-
atory Analysis in 'Middle-Class' Culture," *Man*, December 1969, p. 514.

We must first loosen the nexus between institution and role to comprehend fully the nature of friendship in Western society. The process of self-definition of the role is the point at issue. Other prevalent dyadic relationships exhibit the same lack of institutionalization. Couples of the same or opposite sex form households without marriage, without models for behavior or even standard terminology for the relationships. These pairs must also make their own rules and set their own terms. In our rapidly changing society, roles, even in as formal an institution as marriage, are subject to individual definition. Women in the business and professional world have just begun to reject the male model for their conduct and dress to redefine their roles. Despite the fluidity of roles and their definitions, ideology remains intact. Professional women still are achievement oriented and ascribe to the competitive ethos. Sex or marital partners retain the belief in love and stability of the relationship. Friendships are still maintained on the basis of loyalty, trust, and mutuality. Ideology thus seems to be the stable element in "quasi-institutions."

We therefore chose to focus on the ideologically stable core of friendship between men. To this purpose, we turned to the literary sources to trace the historical development of what we have chosen to call the myth of friendship, finding its first and full-blown formulation in the earliest recorded epic of Gilgamesh. The essential content of the myth remained notably unchanging throughout the vagaries of different times and different cultures. It has persisted, despite its present incongruity, as a charter for the values of male friendship.

11

Biologic Influences on Masculinity

Perry Treadwell

> *To cast in my lot with Jekyll was to die to those*
> *appetites which I had long secretly indulged and*
> *had of late begun to pamper. To cast it in with*
> *Hyde was to die to a thousand interests and*
> *aspirations, and to become at a blow and forever,*
> *despised and friendless.*
> — *STEVENSON,* The Strange Case of
> Dr. Jekyll and Mr. Hyde

To consider masculinity as dependent on innate biologic factors is to misunderstand the basis of genetics. But to consider masculinity as a purely social construct with no physiologic basis is scientifically dangerous. In the Spring 1977 issue of *Daedalus*, the sociologist Alice Rossi dropped an academic bomb in the middle of women's studies with her article "A Biosocial Perspective on Parenting."[1] It was her intent to pave the way for biosocial investigation: discovering the "influence of physiological factors in interaction with social and cultural factors" on human behavior. Two years later, *Signs* reported a portion of the controversy surrounding the Rossi article. In it, Martha McClintock accused Rossi of evoking "innate behaviors" and taking "essentially a biologically deterministic approach."[2]

The hyperbole expressed by some sociobiologists explaining much of human behavior as genetically programmed certainly has made many social scientists biology-shy. Janet Sayers documents the use that has been made of biology in supporting white male domination.[3] Hughes and Lambert argue that the functionalists (the social Darwinists) miss the importance of structure,[4] and Lewontin and his colleagues answer the sociobio-

1. A. Rossi, "A Biosocial Perspective on Parenting," *Daedalus* 166(Spring 1977):1–31.
2. M. McClintock, "Considering a Biosocial Perspective on Parenting," *Signs*, 4(1979), pp.703–710.
3. J. Sayers, *Biological Politics* (New York: Tavistock, 1982).
4. A. J. Hughes and D. M. Lambert, "Functionalism, Structuralism and 'Ways of Seeing,'" *J. Theoretical Biology* 111(1984):787–800.

logists by emphasizing that behavior is a meld of diverse physiologies and environments not so easily reduced to components as the sociobiologists would have us believe.[5] It is the interactive rather than the reductive approach to masculinity that I wish to emphasize in this chapter.

Rossi replied to her detractors with a most prescient statement:

> Research in areas like neuroendocrinology and brain neurochemistry may come up with evidence in the coming decade that feminists will have to absorb, some of which I predict will show additional evidence of fundamental differences in brain structure laid down during early fetal development which may carry consequences for sex differentiation during childhood and adolescent development.[6]

I develop this perspective and its consequences for men's studies in the following pages.

This chapter presents the basis for understanding the male brain and its connections to the body, and reflects on some physiologic origins for the diversity of male behavior. A concomitant feature of this study is developing a sense of masculinity, used here to connote the mosaic of attitudes that influence male behavior. I focus on studies on brain–hormonal influences on human male aggression. Although animal, and particularly primate, research may point the way toward human studies, they cannot be extrapolated to the psychosocially complex human. As I demonstrate, there is a rich literature of human studies that should provoke the necessary biosocial research. I conclude with a model for studying physiologic contributions to behavior. I wish to be counted a member of the *wake*, celebrating the death of the nature versus nurture controversy.[7]

PART I. THE MALE BRAIN

Let me begin with a brief refresher on male hormones and the human brain.[8] The brain and body communicate back and forth through a complex neurochemical network using neurons, neurochemicals, and hor-

5. R. C. Lewontin, S. Rose, and L. J. Kamin, *Not in Our Genes* (New York: Pantheon, 1984).

6. A. Rossi, *Signs*, Summer 1979, pp. 712–717.

7. J. Archer and B. Lloyd, *Sex and Gender* (New York: Cambridge University Press, 1985); R. A. Gorski, "Sexual Differentiation in the Brain: Possible Mechanisms and Implications," *Canadian Journal of Physiological Pharmacology* 63(1985):577–594; P. F. Brain and D. Benton, *The Biology of Aggression* (Rockville, MD.: Sigthoff & Noordhoff, 1981).

8. S. H. Snyder, "The Molecular Basis of Communication between Cells," *Scientific American* 253(October 1985):132–141; and J. P. Changeux, *Neuronal Man: The Biology of Mind* (New York: Pantheon, 1985).

mones. Neurons consist of a cell body, many dentrites, and one axon. At least 60 neurotransmitters have been identified, such as norepinephrine, serotonin, dopamine, endorphins. Hormones may be chains of amino acids such as AdrenoCorticoTrophic Hormone (ACTH) or steroids such as testosterone. All these inputs arrive in the brain presenting an apparent confusing array of messages of which the brain must make some sense. The electrical messages travel along the neurons through the first filtering system, the hind brain (or so-called reptilian brain) into the limbic system (or part of the primitive mammalian brain). Here messages may go on to the neocortex (the primate brain), which in turn may modify the limbic response. Hormones and neurotransmitters reach the brain at a much slower rate through the bloodstream.

For example, consider an athlete beginning a rowing competition. His internal and external environments warn him to produce maximum effort. Electrical signals tell the hypothalamus, residing in the limbic system, to release a host of neurotransmitters, including gonadotrophin-releasing hormone (also known as Luteinizing Hormone Releasing Hormone, LHRH). These neurotransmitters travel in the blood a few millimeters to the pituitary gland where the LHRH causes the release of Luteinizing Hormone and Follicle Stimulating Hormone. These travel through the blood to the testes and adrenal where they cause testosterone release and further production. Soon, along with growth hormone, adrenaline, endorphins, and several other chemicals, the concentration of testosterone increases in the blood. Arriving back at the hypothalamus, the testosterone can regulate further LHRH release. Other hormones, such as endorphins, can mitigate this release. This feedback system is reproduced in several other brain–body control systems.

It is also worth pointing out the metabolic relationships between the steroid hormones. Cholesterol is the source of the steroid hormones. In the testes and adrenal glands it is first changed to intermediates, then dehydroepiandrosterone (which may remain in the adrenal as a testosterone-like hormone) and then progesterone (which in the adrenal can become cortisone, regulating glucose metabolism, or aldosterone, regulating salt balance). In the testes, progesterone becomes testosterone, which can be altered further to estradiol or dihydrotestosterone. The significance of these changes will be clear later in the chapter. The testosterone-like hormones are called *androgens*, while the estradiol-like hormones are called *estrogens*. The whole array of steroid hormones is like a clan of cousins, some "kissing," with similar jobs, and some second cousins with totally different jobs.

These hormones must be differentiated as they circulate through the blood. This is done with receptors that recognize the slightly different chemical structure, as a lock does a key. Receptors, on or within a cell, bind the hormone, or neurotransmitter, and the receptor–chemical complex causes the release of a preformed chemical or the production of more of the same chemical. For example, preformed testosterone will be released and more testosterone will be made following LH and FSH stimulation. Many of these chemicals are packaged in vesicles within the cell and, in fusing with the cell membrane, dump their contents into the circulation, creating the dramatic peaks and valleys when these are assayed throughout the day.

Returning to the evidence for sex differences in the brain, it is clear that Rossi's prediction has been more than satisfied. In 1981, the editors of *Science* devoted an issue to "The Dimorphic Brain"[9] and in 1984, *Progress in Brain Research* considered "Sex Differences in the Brain: The Relation Between Structure and Function."[10] It is obvious from reading these reports that the human brain is dimorphic; what is decidedly not clear is how this influences behavior. The anthropologist Melvin Konner subtitles the book in which he begins to approach the problem of physiologic influences "Biological Constraints on the Human Spirit."[11] The idea that there are biological constraints to human behavior would appear to be anathema to Lewontin and his cohorts.

First, consider recent discoveries in brain structure. Toran-Allerand documents sex differences in structure in *(a)* numbers and size of neurons; *(b)* dendritic spines and length of branching; *(c)* numbers, types, and organization of synapses; *(d)* regional nuclear volume; and *(e)* volume of neural structures.[12] Many of these differences occur in the limbic system, predominantly in the preoptic area and amygdala. Differences in numbers and kinds of androgen receptors also are seen in these areas in monkeys.[13]

9. F. Naftolin, ed., "The Dimorphic Brain," *Science* 211(1981):1263–1324.

10. G. J. De Vries *et al.*, eds., *Sex Differences in the Brain: The Relation Between Structure and Function*, Progress in Brain Research, vol. 61 (New York: Elsevier, 1984). See also I. J. Wundram, "Sex Differences in the Brain: Implications for Curriculum Change," in *Feminist Visions: Toward a Transformation of the Liberal Arts Curriculum*, ed. D. Fowlkes and C. McClure (University, Ala: University of Alabama Press, 1984), pp. 158–169; and M. Hines and R. A. Gorski, "Hormonal Influences on the Development of Neural Asymmetries," in *The Dual Brain*, ed. F. Benson and E. Zaidel (New York: Guilford, 1985), pp. 75–96.

11. M. Konner, *The Tangled Wing: Biological Constraints on the Human Spirit* (New York: Holt Rinehart & Winston, 1982).

12. C. D. Toran-Allerand, "On the Genesis of Sexual Differentiation of the Central Nervous System: Morphogenetic Consequences of Steroidal Exposure and Possible Role of Alpha-Fetoprotein," in De Vries, *et al.*, eds., *Sex Differences*, pp. 63–98.

13. B. S. McEwen *et al.*, "Steroid Hormone Receptors, Brain Cell Function, and the Neuroendrocrine System," *Advances in Biochemical Psychopharmacology* 21(1980):383–90; H. Rees and R. Michael, "Brain Cells of the Male Rhesus Monkey Accumulate ³H-Testosterone or Its Metabolites," *Journal of Comparative Neurology* 206(1982):273–277; and *Life Sciences* 30(1983):2087–2093.

Hemispheric differences are also accepted, which are made even more dramatic using Positron Emission Tomography (PET). (PET is a method of viewing the metabolism of the brain as it functions.)

Reviewing the accepted human embryology, each embryo starts on its trek toward maturity with the beginnings of female characteristics. Only if it has the Y chromosome does it begin to modify itself toward a male anatomy and physiology. About the second month of gestation, the fetal gonads become testes and begin to produce testosterone and related androgens. These hormones change the physical anatomy and, most important, create a male brain. Differences in male and female brain structure can be observed at least 3 months before birth.

Roger Gorski summarizes the data: "In general, the sex differences occur in regions known to be associated with sexually dimorphic functions such as gonadotropin secretion and sexual behavior. In addition the sex differences are susceptible to alteration by manipulations of the neonatal hormonal environment."[14] It appears that the masculinization and feminization of the brain depends on the interaction of hormone-dose response.[15] Increasing concentrations of estrogen and testosterone determine the numbers, connections, and sensitivity to stimuli of many nerve-cell groups. The effect of the two hormones is mitigated by alpha fetoprotein, acting as a biological filter binding estrogen, thus preventing some estrogen but allowing all testosterone access to the neurons. While there may be estrogen receptors on cell membranes partially controlling its access into the cell, testosterone depends on diffusion to enter the cell. Within the cell, several enzymes may change testosterone's structure before it finds the appropriate intracellular receptor and enters the nucleus, where it controls nucleic acid formation. Thus an overabundance of estrogen reaching the cell membrane or an excess of testosterone converted to estrogen within the neuron may have the same effect. Geschwind speculates that high levels of testosterone delay left-hemisphere development in the fetus, causing left-handedness and its attendant problems such as higher frequencies of allergy, migraine, and dyslexia.[16]

14. R. A. Gorski, "Long Term Modulation of Neuronal Structure and Function," in *The Neurosciences: Fourth Study Program*, ed. F. Schmitt and F. Worden (Cambridge: MIT Press, 1979), pp. 969–982.

15. N. J. MacLusky and F. Naftolin, "Sexual Differentiation of the Central Nervous System," in Naftolin, ed., "Dimorphic Brain," pp. 1294–1303; K. D. Dohler et al, "Participation of Estrogens in Fetal Sexual Differentiation of the Brain," in De Vries *et al.*, eds., Sex Differences, pp. 99–117. See also note 11.

16. N. Geschwind, "Cerebral Dominance in Biological Perspective," *Neuropsychologia* 22(1984):675–683.

The Brain as a Computer

For a clearer picture, then, visualize the brain as a computer.[17] The hard-wired brain is manufactured during growth within the mother. The wiring and the internal program are influenced by the embryo's immediate environment and chemicals passing from mother to child. At birth, this brain – computer has wiring that is mostly in place and an internal program (response patterns) that will be modified, improved, and tested through interaction with the external environment. Any input will pass through an internal environment to reach the computer and produce a response — a picture on the brain's video screen, if you will. Of course, there is no cathode tube located at some specific locus that the brian views. The brain itself acts like a holographic plate.

The child is born, not with a *tabula rasa* on which to write, but with a three-dimensional network of fibers already in place, to be stimulated by a highly complicated internal and external environment. Only the chemicals we smell react directly with neurons of the brain. All other inputs are filtered through nonneurological receptors and chemical transmitters. As a first approximation, it may be helpful to continue the computer analogy. Each neuron is an off – on switch that is similar to an off – on gate on a computer chip. A chip may contain as many as 1000 gates, and the chips can be "stacked" together to perform a program-like memory. A stack could be considered similar to a brain locus or area such as the hypothalamus. Thus both computers use a binary — off – on — communication language.

But our computer analogy soon breaks down. The human brain is several orders of magnitude more complex:

1. While the number of neurons, about 100 billion, is fixed at birth, the hard wiring through dendritic connections, as many as 100,000 per neuron, continues to expand at least to age 15. Environmental stimulation (e.g., learning) increases the dendritic mass.
2. Neurons are not directly connected as gates are, but separated by a synapse. The electrical message — the action potential — is transferred across the synapse by neurotransmitters reaching their receptors.
3. Neurons transmit a message depending on the number and rate of messages they receive; they are modulating off – on switches. Thus each brain response pattern is influenced by the magnitude of input,

17. R. Restak, *The Brain* (New York: Bantam, 1984); for a picture of nonlinear functions of computers simulating similar brain processing, see W. Allman, "Mindworks," *Science 86* (May):23 – 31.

the concentration of neurochemicals — many drugs alter this — and the number of receptors.

4. Finally, there is tremendous redundancy built into the human brain, not available in any computer.

Although it is theoretically possible to build these four modifications into computers, it would take several times more than 100 billion gates. But thinking about computer models of the brain may help us envision brain physiology in the way that artificial intelligence helps understand the mind. Similar to the human brain, the new generation of computers process complex problems in parallel rather than in series. If the male brain processes environmental information slightly differently from the female brain, it is worth discovering how it affects male behavior.

PART II: PHYSIOLOGY OF MALE BEHAVIOR

Prenatal Influences

When pregnant women are treated with medroxyprogesterone (a drug that reduces the effect of testosterone and also is used for chemical suppression of testosterone production in sex offenders) to maintain pregnancy, their children are judged "less aggressive" than paired controls.[18] The tendency to timidity is greater in girls than boys. I suspect it is easier to reduce testosterone levels chemically in female than male fetuses, since much lower levels occur throughout gestation (see below).

The most dramatic influences of testosterone occur when the female fetus's adrenal glands produce too much testosterone or the male fetus fails to change testosterone into dihydrotestosterone. In the first case, even when the condition is corrected at birth, the girls are judged "tomboys" when compared to matched controls in blind studies. Fetal treatment with diethylstilbestryl (DES) causes similar behavioral changes including an ear preference in hearing more like that in males.[19] In the second case, the boys are born with female-like genitalia and are raised as "girls" until puberty when the surge of testosterone changes the genitals and creates masculine secondary sex characteristics. These men then take on male gender roles, albeit with some psychologic difficulty.

18. H. Meyer-Bahlburg, "Psychoendocrine Research on Sexual Orientation: Current Status and Future Options," in De Vries *et al.*, eds., *Sex Differences*, pp. 375–398.

19. Hines and Gorski, "Hormone Influences."

Conversely, males with the genetic disease Tfm lack the receptors for testosterone in their cells. Although appearing as males, their "sex-role preference" is feminine.[20] When the male embryo is subjected to higher-than-normal levels of testosterone (adrenal hyperplasia), the boys also have been judged as more active than paired controls.[21] Carol Nagy Jacklin and her coworkers correlate timidity in 6- to 18-month-old boys with low levels of testosterone and progesterone in their umbilical cord blood at birth.[22] No correlation is seen in girls. While the effect of opposite-sex twinning on each sex has been known in animals (freemartin in calves where the female is sterile), a recent study indicates such human twin relationships where hormones may be shared protect both from fetal abnormalities and death.[23]

Highly controversial is the suggestion that testosterone levels influence male homosexuality.[24] Mothers' overactive adrenal glands during pregnancy may cause homosexuality in their sons, according to Günter Dörner. Under stress conditions, chemicals produced by the adrenals can inhibit testosterone production. Dörner reported that injection of estrogen in homosexuals caused a decrease of Luteinizing Hormone (LH) and an increase in prolactin, just as in women. In women and homosexual men, the LH increased to 120% of original level at 96 hours. At the same time, LH levels remained below baseline in heterosexual males. Dörner's experimental protocol and results have been questioned by Meyer-Bahlberg and Archer and Lloyd, among others. However, Dörner's observations on the LH response have been confirmed and extended by Gladue and his associates.[25] Dörner correlates his results with his finding significantly more homosexual German men born during World War II than in the 6 years

20. B. S. McEwen, "Gonadal Steroid Influences on Brain Development and Sexual Differentiation," *International Review of Physiology* 27(1983):99–145.

21. J. M. Reinish and S. A. Sanders, "Prenatal Gonodal Steroidal Influence on Gender Related Behavior," in De Vries *et al.*, eds., *Sex Differences*, pp 407–416.

22. C. N. Jacklin, E. E. Maccoby, and C. H. Doering, "Neonatal Sex-Steroid Hormones and Timidity in 6-18-Month-Old Boys and Girls," *Developmental Psychobiology* 16(1983):163–168.

23. C. Boklage, "Interactions between Opposite-Sex Dizygotic Fetuses and Assumptions of Weinberg Difference Method Epidemiology," *American Journal of Human Genetics* 37(1985):591–605.

24. G. Dörner, "Hormones and Sexual Differentiation of the Brain," in CIBA Foundation Symposium, *Sex, Hormones and Behavior* (Amsterdam: Excerpta Medica, 1979), pp. 81–101; G. Dörner, "Sex Hormones and Neurotransmitters as Mediators for Sexual Differentiation of the Brain," *Endokrinologie* 78(1981):129–138; and G. Dörner "Neuroendocrine Aspects in the Etiology of Sexual Deviations in *Medical Sexology*, ed. R. Forleo and W. Pasini (Littleton, Mass.: PSG Publications, 1980), pp. 190–209.

25. B. Gladue, R. Green, and R. Hellman, "Neuroendocrine Response to Estrogen and Sexual Orientation," *Science* 225(1984):1496–1499.

before or after the war. Interviews with some of the men confirmed that their mothers suffered bereavement, divorce, rape, or severe anxiety during pregnancy.

In spite of conflicting data, I must tentatively conclude that there is a biological component to homosexuality in at least some males. My reasons for this conclusion will become clear later in this chapter when Gladue's results are discussed in detail. Dörner can correlate structural changes in the different areas of the hypothalamus (an area of the brain involved in male or female mating behavior) with hormone treatment of rat embryos. We must tentatively conclude that lack of sufficient testosterone during a critical period of brain development allows the brain to remain more feminized. I warn the reader not to conclude that homosexuals are not male or masculine. At best, we might say they are not average. I have more to say about averages later. What "more feminized" may mean biologically is there are fewer brain cells with testosterone receptors or fewer testosterone receptors or differences in enzyme concentrations in the brain. Unfortunately, the descriptive words *feminized* and *masculinized* have been used with little thought to the sociologic meaning. "Femalized" and "malized" would be correct, although awkward.

Whatever terms are used, the spectrum of sexual choice demands more understanding and biosocial study. Frederick Whitam concludes that homosexuality is a "fundamental form of human sexuality" in all cultures at all times.[26] A large proportion of homosexual men recall a feminine gender role preference during childhood, but are defeminized by adulthood.[27] Meyer-Bahlberg concludes that a biological basis for homosexuality is not proved and is more complicated than simply different testosterone levels. He favors a multifactorial explanation.[28]

In summary, hormones can influence sexually differentiated behavior in at least three ways: *(a)* those that undergo differentiation under the influence of hormones and are also activated by hormones; *(b)* those that undergo differentiation independently of the influence of hormones but are activated by hormones; and *(c)* those that are influenced by hormones during differentiation but are not activated by hormones.[29]

26. F. L. Whitam, "Culturally Invariable Properties of Male Homosexuality: Tentative Conclusions from Cross-Cultural Research," *Archives of Sexual Behavior* 12(1983):207–226.

27. J. Harry, "Defeminization and Adult Psychological Well-Being among Male Homosexuals," *Archives of Sexual Behavior* 12(1983):1–19.

28. Meyer-Bahlburg, "Psychoendocrine Research."

29. B. S. McEwen, "Neural Gonadal Steroid Actions," in Naftolin, ed., "Dimorphic Brain," pp. 1302–1312.

Testosterone and Male Behavior

If we accept the evidence that males and females are working with two slightly different computers, what does this mean behaviorally? Will identical environments produce different readouts? I focus on aggression because most agree there is a slight but significant sex difference.[30] Masculinity is associated with aggression. I take the broad view of aggression that it is a desire to overwhelm by any means rather than limit it to physical domination, realizing the energy spent on defining aggression has produced no consensus.[31] Using this criterion, at least 50% of the masculine attributes designated by Bem in her Sex Role Inventory are aggressive.[32] For a further inspection of this definition, see "The Tyranny of Averages" later in this chapter.

As we have seen, the male fetus will have higher levels of unbound testosterone than in any other time of life. At birth the level of testosterone decreases to about 5 nanograms/100 ml plasma. Gender differences in aggressiveness are reported almost at birth. Archer and Lloyd ask how testosterone can cause such differences in behavior in 3-year-olds whose testosterone levels have not begun to increase. I suggest a productive area of research would be studying the influence of adrenal androgens. The more active boy's androgen levels may feed back to brain changes, as well as muscle growth. Thus slight differences in brain structure could be enhanced by behavior.

By the second grade, boys begin to bond and become more disruptive.[33] Boys with adrenal hyperplasia (resulting in increased androgen) show an increased energy expenditure in play and sports and less parenting rehearsal. As early as the fourth grade, some boys will signal beginning of puberty with sperm in their urine.[34] As puberty begins, FSH and LH increase, testosterone binding affinity decreases, and the 14-year-old will have nearly adult levels.[35]

Young men average about 600 nanograms of testosterone/100 ml of

30. Archer and Lloyd, *Sex and Gender*, pp. 25–29.

31. J. R. Durant, "The Beast in Man: An Historical Perspective on the Biology of Human Aggression," in Brian and Benton, *Biology of Aggression*, pp. 17–46.

32. S. Bem, "Gender Schema Theory: A Cognitive Account of Sex Typing," *Psychological Review* 88(1981):354–364; idem, "The Measurement of Psychological Androgeny," *Journal of Consulting Clinical Psychology* 42(1974):155–162.

33. J. Pfeiffer, "Gender and Talking: Girl Talk–Boy Talk," *Current* 272(May 1985):8–11.

34. R. V. Short, "Comments," in CIBA Foundation, *Sex, Hormones and Behavior* p. 206.

35. R. G. Wieland, S. S. C. Yen, and C. Pohlman, "Serum Testosterone Levels and Testosterone Binding Affinity in Prepubertal and Adolescent Males; Correlation with Gonadotropins," *American Journal of Medical Science* 259(1970):358–360.

blood-serum with a range from about 300 to 1200 (see Fig. 1). Less than 10% of the hormone is free in the blood. Some authors claim a circadian rhythm in hormone levels—maximum 6–7 A.M. and minimum 6–8 P.M. A 20- to 30-day rhythm, a fall peak corresponding to an increase in FSH, and a spring trough are also reported. As a man reaches further maturity his levels of testosterone decrease slowly, but the free testosterone and the adrenal androgen drop back to prepubescent levels. The over-40 male has much less testosterone-mediated activity than his son.

After inspecting many of the reports, I find it difficult to compare absolute testosterone levels. Many averages do not coincide. The one common factor is the broad variability between individuals (see Fig. 1). Dai and coworkers, viewing similar confusing data, conclude, "Clearly much of the variance in testosterone levels may be genetically determined and environmental variables explain only a small part of the variance."[36] This is important to remember when we try to talk about the "average" male.

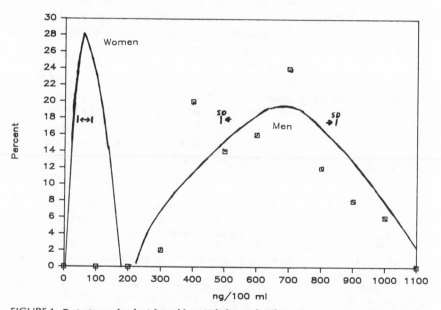

FIGURE 1. **Testosterone levels. Adapted from Kolodny et al., "Plasma Testosterone and Semen Analyses in Male Homosexuals,"** New England Journal of Medicine **285(1971):1170–1174. The range and diversity are confirmed by several subsequent reports.**

36. W. S. Dai et al., "The Epidemiology of Plasma Testosterone Levles in Middle-Aged Men," American Journal of Epidemiology 114(1981):804–816.

Aggression

SPORTS

Aggressiveness and winning have been linked to testosterone levels in wrestling,[37] hockey,[38] tennis,[39] and long-distance running,[40] to mention a few.

It is difficult to determine what the dependent and independent variables are in these studies. Does initial testosterone level determine winning? Does winning determine the final testosterone level? Is the magnitude of change important? When, "fit" and "unfit" men were tested for their testosterone levels, the unfit had significantly lower amounts. After 4 months of exercise, testosterone levels in the unfit were unchanged. The fit personalities were judged as more unconventional, adventurous and trusting.[41]

One study in 1973 showed a significant increase in testosterone when varsity rowers were exercising maximally but not when they were just working out.[42] Both testosterone and growth hormone increased in these men, varsity swimmers, and students on exercise cycles — in the last within minutes after beginning exercise. Although woman swimmers had about 10% testosterone levels compared to the males, they also showed significant increases in testosterone on exercise. More interesting was the observation that baseline testosterone values of the rowers averaged 690 ng/100 ml, while those of the swimmers averaged 1020 ng/100 ml, correlating with a different physiogomy.

A 24-week study of power lifters showed their testosterone levels increased significantly as their ability increased, then went down when their lifting ability plateaued.[43] Testosterone and its cousins have been used for

37. M. Elias, "Serum Cortisol, Testosterone, and Testosterone Binding Globulin Response to Competitive Fighting in Human Males," *Aggressive Behavior* 7(1981):215–224.

38. T. Scaramella and W. Brown, "Serum Testosterone and Aggressiveness in Hockey Players," *Psychosomatic Medicine* 40(1978):262–265.

39. A. Masur and T. A. Lamb, "Testosterone, Status, and Mood in Human Males," *Hormones and Behavior* 14(1980):236–246.

40. A. Dessypris, K. Kuoppasalmi, and H. Adlercreutz, "Plasma Cortisol, Testosterone, Androstenedione and Luteinizing Hormone (LH) in a Non-Competitive Marathon Run," *Journal of Steroid Biochemistry* 7(1976):33–37.

41. R. J. Young and A. H. Ismail, "Ability of Biochemical and Personality Variables in Discriminating between High and Low Physical Fitness Levels," *Journal of Psychosomatic Research* 22(1978):193–199.

42. J. R. Sutton *et al.*, "Androgen Responses during Physical Exercise," *British Medical Journal* (1973):520–522.

43. K. Hakkinen *et al.*, "Serum Hormones during Prolonged Training," *European Journal of Applied Physiology* 53(1985):287–293.

some time in sports, particularly in weight lifting. Conservatively, more than a million American athletes are using anabolic steroids, according to William Taylor.[44] Like the examinations for sex chromatin a few years ago, Olympic athletes are now being tested for the presence of synthetic derivatives of testosterone, which can last as long as 6 months in the body. Taylor reports anabolic steroid use increases self-esteem, sex drive, appetite, explosive hostility and violence, mental intensity, energy, tolerance to pain, and desire to train intensely.

Power lifters, when administered the anabolic steroids (31 mg/day) and testosterone (averaging 478 mg/week), became much stronger than matched controls over a 24-week training period.[45] If the body normally manufactures about 10 mg/day, at least six times this amount was used by these men.[46]

When these steroids are withdrawn, the person shows increases in depression, listlessness, and apathy, and shows a desire for the drug, while the behaviors seen earlier decrease and the ability to remain in control of behavior intensifies, according to Taylor. Continued use of these steroids can cause atrophy of the testes, decrease in sperm production (a feedback inhibiting LH and FSH release), increased risk of cardiovascular disease and liver tumors, and increased acne and baldness. Such anecdotal reporting supports the linkage between testosterone and aggressive behavior. Few studies have compared testosterone levels in professional athletes to the normative.

Dorthy Harris reports that women athletes of all kinds judge themselves (on a Bem-like scale) as less feminine than nonathletes.[47] Distance runners are more undifferentiated, while the others are more androgynous.

One study of male marathon runners showed their testosterone levels normally go up (7 of 11) in the afternoon without running.[48] After the race, 12 of 13 runners showed a decrease in testosterone levels below their normal afternoon levels. The only man showing an increase was the one with the shortest running time. No other difference was obvious.

44. W. N. Taylor, *Hormonal Manipulation: A New Era of Monstrous Athletes* (Jefferson, N.C.: McFarland, 1985); see also *Psychology Today*, May 1985, pp. 63–66.

45. M. Alen, K. Hakkinen, and P. V. Komi, "Changes in Neuromuscular Performance and Muscle of Elite Power Athletes Self-Administering Androgenic and Anabolic Steroids," *Acta Physiologica Scandinavia* 122(1984):535–544.

46. H. Persky, K. D. Smith, and G. K. Basu, "Relation of Psychologic Measures of Aggression and Hostility to Testosterone Production in Man," *Psychosomatic Medicine* 33(1971):265–277.

47. D. V. Harris, "Femininity and Athleticism: Conflict or Consonance?" in *Jock: Sports and Male Identity*, ed. D. Sabo and R. Runfola (Englewood Cliffs, N.J.: Prentice-Hall, 1980), pp. 222–239.

48. Dessypris, Kuoppalsolmi, and Adlercreutz, "Plasma Cortisol."

Sports medicine can contribute much more to understanding the correlation of hormones and behavior. The hypothesis that sports selects a subpopulation that responds differently to vigorous physical challenge should be tested rigorously. It would appear that, at least for some males, the body can be trained to produce more testosterone. More testosterone means better physical performance, which leads to a greater chance of winning the competition. This in turn can train the body to produce more testosterone in anticipation of the next conflict.[49]

MILITARY

Sports may be the functional equivalent of war. Men use the military to define their masculinity. Mark Gerzon proposes that we need new heroes against whom young men can test their masculinity.[50] The military may also select those with the best hormone response. In 1978, Holger Ursin and his colleagues reported changes in testosterone levels in young recruits at a Norwegian Army Parachute Training School.[51] After the first week of training, the testosterone levels had dropped significantly and the adrenaline levels increased. As training continued, testosterone levels rose above the value before training began, and adrenaline dropped. Low levels of testosterone correlated with failures and self-assessments as having a more feminine personality. High levels were seen in men who performed for the "thrill and adventure." Men coping successfully with the stress reported strong feelings of relief and joy (the euphoria of success), "displaying the smile of control and mastery." The effect of stress was less dependent on the amount endured than the ability to cope. Similar results were reported for Finish Army recruits in both their plasma testosterone and androstenedione, with the well conditioned showing a greater increase.[52] In contrast, when young men are stressed during 5 days of simulated combat without sleep, their testosterone levels dropped to about one-sixth normal.[53]

49. F. H. de Jonge and N. E. van de Pol, "Relationships between Sexual and Aggressive Behavior in Male and Female Rats: Effects of Gonadal Hormones" in De Vries et al., eds., Sex Differences, pp. 283–302.

50. M. Gerzon, A Choice of Heroes (Boston: Houghton Mifflin, 1982).

51. H. Ursin and E. Baade, eds., Psychobiology of Stress: A Study of Coping Men (New York: Academic Press, 1978).

52. K. Remes, K. Kuopposalmi, and H. Adlercreutz, "Effect of Long-Term Physical Training on Plasma Testosterone, Androstenedione, Luteinizing Hormone and Sex-Hormone-Binding Globulin Capacity," Scandinanvian Journal of Clinical Laboratory Investigation 39(1979):743–749.

53. A. Aakvaag et al., "Hormonal Changes in Serum in Young Men during Prolonged Physical Strain," European Journal of Applied Physiology 39(1978):283–291.

CRIMINALITY

If men facing combat in sports or war show changes in testosterone levels, then men involved in crimes of violence should show similar correlations. After reading several reports, I can only say that the results are provocative. Although adolescent aggressiveness, particularly in prisoners age 30 or younger, correlated with testosterone levels, several researchers have not been able to confirm these prison studies.[54] Wilson and Hernstein conclude from an extensive survey of twin studies that a genetic component places some boys more at risk of becoming criminals.[55] Viewed in retrospect, the misconducting boy in the third grade may be the criminal at age 18.

Lee Bowker notes that while 16-year-old boys and girls report nearly the same frequency of nonaggressive acts (runaway, truancy, fraud, trespass, drinking), the girls commit much fewer aggressive acts (property destruction, theft, assault, carrying a concealed weapon).[56]

Recently, saliva has been shown comparable to plasma as a source of testosterone, simplifying and enhancing researcher's ability to correlate endocrine activity with behavior.[57] Studying 18- to 23-year-old boys in a youth authority prison, Dabbs and his colleagues confirmed and extended the Kreuz and Rose findings.[58] The researchers found significantly higher levels of free testosterone in the saliva of those convicted of violent crimes, of those dominant in a mildly active dorm, but not in "wild"—less controlled—living conditions, and of those judged by parole board assessments of those convicted of nonviolent crimes as most likely to commit violent crimes on release. The authors point out that testosterone levels

54. L. Kreuz and R. Rose, "Assessment of Aggressive Behavior and Plasma Testosterone in a Young Criminal Population," in *Physiology of Aggression and Implications for Control: An Anthology of Readings*, ed. K. E. Moyer (New York: Raven Press, 1976), pp. 219–230; The Persky Report (see note 47) seems comfirmed by Olweus and colleagues who find a positive correlation between testosterone level and aggression, lack of frustration tolerance or impatience. Ake Mattsson *et al.*, "Plasma Testosterone, Aggressive Behavior, and Personality Dimensions in Young Male Delinquents," *Journal of American Academy of Child Psychiatry* 19(1984):476–490.

55. J. Q. Wilson and R. J. Herrnstein, *Crime and Human Nature* (New York: Simon and Schuster, 1985), pp. 91–95.

56. L. Bowker, *Women, Crime and the Criminal Justice System* (Lexington, Mass.: Lexington Books, 1978), p. 17.

57. D. Riad-Fahmy, G. B. Read, and R. F. Walker, "Salivary Steroid Assays of Assessing Variation in Endocrine Activity," *Journal of Steroid Biochemistry* 19(1983):265–272; see also G. F. Read *et al.*, eds. *Ninth Tenovus Workshop: Immunoassays of Steroids in Saliva* (Cardiff, Wales: Alpha Omega, 1984).

58. J. M. Dabbs, *et al.*, "Saliva Testosterone and Criminal Violence in Young Adult Prison Inmates," *Psychosomatic Medicine*, in press.

may be correlated with one's "strength, impulsiveness, and adventurousness." Particular social environments may direct the individual toward socially appropriate or inappropriate behavior. This is discussed further in this chapter in "Testing Biosocial Relationships."

Testosterone Reduction

These reports raise the question of using chemicals or surgery to change behavior. Rubin reports low levels of testosterone correlate with less aggressiveness and a double dose of the Y chromosome with increased aggressiveness.[59] The correct description may be "more impetuous."[60] In treating antisocial men with antiandrogens, Rubin reports the levels of testosterone must be reduced by 50–75% before there is a behavioral improvement. Money and his coworkers found drastic testosterone reduction and psychotherapy helped sex offenders, but not antisocial offenders (primarily robbery and destructiveness), to regulate their behavior.[61]

In spite of this controversy, surgical castration or chemical reduction of testosterone is being used throughout the world in treating sociopaths. Reay Tannahill summarizes the recent history:

> In San Diego, California, between 1955 and 1975, 397 sex offenders chose to be castrated rather than serve a long jail sentence. In Denmark between 1929 and 1959 300 prisoners or detainees made the same choice. In Britain chemical suppressants of the sex urge are preferred. The World Health Organization strongly opposes the whole idea.[62]

Fred Berlin of Johns Hopkins University screens sex offenders carefully before he treats them with medroxyprogesterone and intensive psychotherapy.[63] Berlin says both the Scandinavian orchectomy studies and his antiandrogen studies show a 1–2% repeater rate, making "a conclusive statement about the role of testosterone in sexually dangerous behavior."

59. R. T. Rubin, J Reinish, and R. Haskett, "Postnatal Gonadal Steroid Effects on Human Behavior," in Naftolin, ed., "Dimorphic Brain," pp. 1318–1324.

60. E. B. Hook, "Behavioral Implications of the Human XYY Genotype," *Science* 179(1973):39–150; see also S. J. Gould, *The Mismeasure of Man* (New York: Norton, 1981), pp. 144–145.

61. J. Money *et al.*, "47, XYY and 46, XY Males with Antisocial and/or Sex-Offending Behavior: Antiandrogen Therapy Plus Counseling," *Psychoneuroendocrinology* (1975): 165–178.

62. R. Tannahill, *Sex in History* (Briarcliff Manor: Stein & Day, 1981), p. 247n.

63. F. Berlin, *Time*, December 12, 1983, p. 70; *Atlanta Journal and Constitution*, January 15, 1983, p. 13b. Upon castration, the androgen receptors disappear quite rapidly from the anterior pituitary and hypothalamus, while the estrogen receptors remain a long time. M. Motta, *Endocrine Functions of the Brain* (New York: Raven, 1976), p. 66.

Berlin also suggests "that non-learned biological as well as learned environmental factors may play an etiological role in development of sexually deviant behaviors."[64] He has recently found that paedophils have a LH response to LHRH different from other paraphils or controls.[65]

Michael and Zumpe, analyzing the uniform crime statistics for 21 regions of the United States, find that assaults and rapes increase to a peak in the late summer, between July 7 and September 8, but not robbery or murder.[66] Inspection of these figures suggest that the curves for robbery and murder were flatter and more diffuse but did peak in October and November. There was no difference in the curves no matter the location, latitude, or annual mean temperature. While serious crime continues to decrease, the rate of forcible rape and aggravated assault continues to increase in the United States. Investigators have found that, on the average, men's testosterone levels increase in the fall.[67] Is a man more susceptible to environments that may elicit an aggressive response the higher his effective testosterone level?

Although I have focused on testosterone's influence on aggressive behavior, I do not wish to create the impression that other metabolic factors are not important. Hypoglycemia and vitamin and trace-element imbalance have also been implicated in aggression.[68]

Related Brain Studies

A study of English prisoners judged as habitually aggressive showed abnormal electroencephalograms (EEG) in 75% with the likely location of the disturbance in the limbic system in most.[69] Even when those prisoners with histories of epilepsy, brain injury, or reduced mental capacity were excluded, 60% of the habitually aggressive still showed abnormal EEGs, whereas only 12% of the other prisoners were abnormal (the same percentage as in the general population). Tavris reports that violence in boys

64. F. S. Berlin and C. F. Meinecke, "Treatment of Sex Offenders with Anti-Androgenic Medication: Conceptualization, Review of Treatment Modalities, and Preliminary Findings," *American Journal of Psychiatry* 138(1981):601–607.

65. G. R. Gaffney and F. S. Berlin, "Is There Hypothalamic-Pituitary-Gonadal Dysfunction in Paedophilia? A Pilot Study," *British Journal of Psychiatry* 145(1984):657–660.

66. R. Michael and D. Zumpe, "Sexual Violence in the United States and the Role of Season," *American Journal of Psychiatry* 140(1983):883–886.

67. A. G. N. Smals, P. W. C. Kloppenborg, and T. J. Benroad, "Circannual Cycle in Plasma Testosterone Levels in Man," *Journal of Clinical Endrocrinologic Metabolism* 42(1976):979–982.

68. A. Dorfman, "The Criminal Mind," *Science Digest,* October 1984, p. 44.

69. D. Williams, "Neural Factors Related to Habitual Aggression," in *Psychopharmacology of Aggression,* ed. M. Sandler (New York: Raven Press, 1979), pp. 111–121.

can be predicted using neuropsychological testing.[70] Many of these boys at risk show abnormal EEGs. One wonders, Why not girls also? Are they never brain damaged, or don't they manifest brain damage with violence? I suggest that physiologic factors might create some individuals more susceptible to environmental stressors. In other societies the ritual rites of passage may have integrated the "at risk" into the culture better than the anonymity of this society.

Assigning a direct relationship between male hormones and behavior is complex and difficult. Only in cases where a profound defect in a nerve track or hormone pattern is identified can a direct relationship be inferred. We are much more complex than "one track minds." It helps to see our reactions, not as a single pattern with variations, but as several patterns that appear grossly the same. The patterns are complicated by several levels of feedback, like a game-playing computer program with several feedback loops at each step.

One cannot ignore the effects of adrenaline (epinephrine), the opioid peptides (enkephalins and endorphins), and drugs on the physiologic and psychologic states. I cite the following as suggestive of the need for further correlations: Viveros has localized enkephalin at the very core of the cerebral hemispheres connecting the limbic system with movement.[71] Cicero, studying the effect of alcohol on males, finds serum testosterone levels are reduced during acute or chronic alcohol use by speeding up its breakdown and reducing its production in the gonads.[72] Essman reports that alcohol, marijuana, apomorphine, and digoxin can change the levels of neurotransmitters like serotonin, levels of testosterone, and levels of brain testosterone receptors.[75] Some men report that using alcohol reduces the pain, meaning their psychologic pain — their anxiety. The animal tranquilizer

70. C. Tavris, *Anger: The Misunderstood Emotion* (New York: Simon and Schuster, 1983), p. 73. She refers to D. O. Lewis, *Vulnerabilities to Delinquency* (New York: Spectrum, 1981), and unpublished material by A. Berman.

71. O. H. Viveros and S. P. Wilson, "The Adrenal Chromaffin Cell as a Model to Study the Co-Secretion of Enkephalins and Catecholamines," *Journal of Autonomic Nervous System* 7(1983):41–58; O. H. Viveros, A. J. Daniels, and E. J. Diliberto, Jr., "Co-secretion of Catecholamines, Opioid Peptides, Ascorbate, and Other Secretory Products from Multiple Compartments within Adrenomedullary Chromation Cells," in *Coexistence of Neuroactive Substances*, ed. V. Chan-Palay and S. L. Palay (New York: Wiley, 1983).

72. T. Cicero, "Alcohol-Induced Deficits in the Hypothalamic-Pituitary-Lutenizing Hormone Axis in the Male," *Alcoholism: Clinical and Experimental Research* 6(1982):207–215.

73. W. B. Essman, "Drug Effects upon Aggressive Behavior," *Aggression and Violence: A Psycho/Biological and Clinical Approach*, ed. L. Valzelli and L. Morgese (Saint Vincent: Edizioni, 1981), pp. 150–171.

PCP (street name "Angel Dust") disconnects the limbic system from the cortical control much like hypoglycemia.

Biosocial investigation of male aggression might focus on the role of neurotransmitters and hormones. What are the gender implications, not only for violent crime, terrorism, and military aggression, but also for the brinkmanship of nuclear stockpiling? Are our political leaders chosen for their virile ability to play a perversely grand poker game? I suspect that the authors of A Sexual Profile of Men in Power would answer yes.[74]

Love and Aggression

One would not suspect that love would have any connection with aggression. But neurophysiologically there may be sufficient similarity to subject the love emotion/behavior to as exhaustive scrutiny as aggression. Of course, "love" is a dumping ground for every emotion from lust and passion to bonding and companionship. Many of the same hormones involved in aggression also increase dramatically during human love. Male and female libido is related to testosterone levels. Some cases of male impotency can be treated with testosterone or LHRH.[75] Liebowitz argues in The Chemistry of Love that much of the emotional component of love has chemical bases, one being neurotransmitter phenyl ethyl amine.[76] (PEA has a similar effect and structure to amphetamines and is diminished during chronic depression.) Variations in hormone levels during attraction, attachment, passion, and commitment phases of the love complex are reasonable expectations. Persky reports couple interaction depends on testosterone levels along with affective and social interactive determinants.[77] Liebowitz, in reporting sex differences, recognizes that his observations on chemical–psychiatric treatment of patients with behavior problems associated with love relationships are anecdotical and pleads for controlled studies. The human sense of smell, influenced by testosterone, may control our love behavior more than we realize.[78] Space does not allow examination of gender differences in the biologic parameters of love in this essay, as interesting as such differences may be.

74. S. Janus and B. Bess with C. Saltus, A Sexual Profile of Men in Power (Englewood Cliffs, N.J.: Prentice-Hall, 1977).

75. Restak, The Brain, pp. 123–126; R. Bahr reviews testosterone treatment in The Virility Factor (New York: Putnam's, 1976).

76. M. B. Liebowitz, The Chemistry of Love (Boston: Little, Brown, 1983).

77. H. Persky, "Determinants of Human Sexual Adjustment," in Fifth World Congress of Sexology (Princeton, N.J.: Excerpta Medica, 1981), pp. 28–36.

78. J. Hopson, Scent Signals (New York: Morrow, 1979); G. Beauchamp, K. Yamazaki, and E. Boyse, "The Chemosensory Recognition of Genetic Individuality," Scientific American 253(July 1985);86–92.

PART III. PUTTING IT TOGETHER

The Tyranny of Averages

If we test a large population of men and women for a wide spectrum of
traits and plot the scores against numbers of people having that same score,
we would see a typical broad-based, bell-shaped curve. Money's gender-
derivative roles,[79] verbal ability, strength, gender-associated adjectives, or
spacial performance[80] could be selected for such an analysis. If we plotted
the ratings for women and men separately for several of these attributes,
we would see two bell-shaped curves with quite an overlap (Fig. 2). This
means that there will be a few women scoring equal or better than most
men on one end of the scale and a few men scoring equal or better than
most women on the other end of the scale. For example, in studies of
spacial performance, 25% of the women scored better that 50% of the
men, while 10% of the men scored better than all the women. There is a

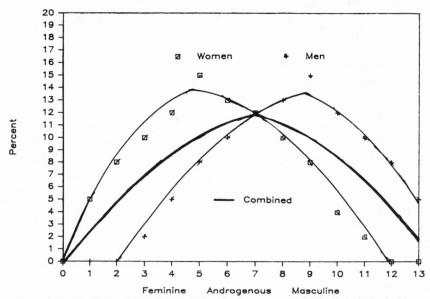

FIGURE 2. Idealized femininity and masculinity scores from Bem's Sex Role Inventory, adapted from S.
Bem "The Measurement of Psychological Androgeny," *Journal of Consulting Clinical Psychology*
42(1974):155–162.

79. J. Money, "Introduction," in *Men in Transition: Theory and Therapy*, ed. K. Solomon
and N. Levy (New York: Plenum Press, 1982), pp. 1–4.
80. Archer and Lloyd, *Sex and Gender*, p. 7.

strong indication that cognitive spatial ability is partly genetic and correlated with a sex-linked recessive gene.[81]

But averages are not biological realities; they are mathematical constructs and do not determine the validity of any behavior. In the past, the male end would have been considered more important than the female end. Today, it is not the difference in gender characteristics that is important, but the wide degree of variation within each gender and the area of overlap.[82] On the average, we are not dealing with polarities but small percentage differences. For example, Reinish and Sanders[83] found no difference between male and female college students in first choice of verbal aggressive response to a conflict situation. But men chose physical aggression significantly more than women as a second choice. Stated differently, 70% of the males but 30% of the females were above the group median for choice of physical aggression. Of course, a person's position on the scale for one attribute may or may not correlate with the position for another attribute. It is the scientist's role to discover the dependent and independent variables in the relationships between physiology and behavior.

Does such a broad diversity imply that we could selectively breed aggressiveness in humans as we do with animals: "brave bulls," fighting cocks, pit bulldogs? No, there is too much genetic variance, environmental variance, and social influence to make eugenics anything more than dangerous science fiction, despite "master race" attempts. One may see the futility of human eugenics by viewing "domestication" of the Yanomano (the "Fierce People" of the Amazon) or the arming of the "benign" !Kung San of the Kalahari Desert within a single generation. (The San even learned to put locks on their doors.)

The broad range in testosterone levels in men indicates that there is not one "natural" level of the hormone but possibly several: the genetic variance Dai suggests. The range of genetic variance is next influenced by an internal brain-hormone feedback system and further modified by the external environment: the environmental variance that has been described here. There is greater danger that social institutions will choose from the large diversity those individuals whose behavior fit their goals: in this society, the more aggressive.

81. R. Sperry, "Consciousness, Personal Identity, and the Divided Brain," in *Two Hemispheres—One Brain, Functions of the Corpus Callosum*, ed., F. Lapore, M. Pitito, and H. Jasper (New York: Alan R. Liss, 1986), pp. 3–20.

82. See Archer and Lloyd, *Sex and Gender*, Fig. 1. See also R. Grant, "A Meta-Model for Male/Female Differences," in Solomon and Levy, eds., *Men in Transition*, Fig. 1.

83. J. Reinish and S. Sanders, "A Test of Sex Differences in Aggressive Response to Hypothetical Conflict Situations," *Journal of Personality and Social Psychology* 50(1985):1045–1049.

The Harvard educator Carol Gilligan proposes that women see life through different eyes and describes that life in *In a Different Voice*.[84] Men, as a class, see life as a process of separation, of individualistic achievement, absolute and hierarchical. Women tend to see life as attachment — related, interdependent, part of a web, caring. Gilligan is quick to warn that the apparent difference "is characterized not by gender but theme." Evelyn Fox Keller supports Gilligan when she notes how a masculine view of scientific investigation has influenced our views of nature.[85] She posits different styles of male and female scientific research that would support Ludwik Fleck's observation that scientific "fact" has a social basis.[86]

Returning to our computer analogy, as the result of the relative doses of estrogen and testosterone, the male computer is built with a decided skew toward individual rights and responsibilities — justice. Let me call it *separation* oriented rather than masculine. The estrogen dose and low testosterone level skew the female computer toward *attachment* — caring. But each computer also contains generous doses of the other principle: the male with attachment, the female with separation. The social environment can stifle attachment in boys and separation in girls, making the melding of the two principles into a whole person much more difficult.

Similarly, the scientific establishment can select those individuals, usually male, who fit the image of a scientist dominating nature. Whether one calls the two principles male and female (which persuades some to ignore the concept altogether), *yin* and *yang*, individualistic and relative, etc., the dilemma remains — balancing these principles. Before a person can be truly human he or she must integrate the two principles (a Jungian idea).

Averages tend to be looked at as polarities, particularly if a statistically significant difference between them can be demonstrated. The degree of overlap is disregarded. It seems reasonable to hypothesize that slight differences in brain structure produce equally slight differences in female and male perceptions and responses to environmental stimuli, what I call *skew*. Societal expectations can enhance these differences. For example, Gilligan's differences in moral reasoning have been questioned. When

84. C. Gilligan, *In a Different Voice* (Cambridge: Harvard University Press, 1982), p. 2; see also J. Spence, who considers masculine and feminine as two independent dimensions in "Changing Concepts of Men and Women: A Psychologist's Perspective," in *A Feminist Perspective in the Academy: The Difference It Makes*, ed. E. Langland and W. Gove (Chicago: University of Chicago Press, 1981), pp. 130–148.

85. E. F. Keller, *Reflections on Gender and Science* (New Haven: Yale University Press, 1985).

86. L. Fleck, *Genesis and Development of a Scientific Fact*, ed. T. Trenn and R. Merton, trans. F. Bradley (Chicago: University of Chicago Press, 1979).

college students were asked to examine their moral response to a personal dilemma, men chose a justice solution, while women chose a caring solution more often.[87] But the difference was not statistically significant. Men scoring high on a femininity scale chose caring more frequently, but the reverse was not true. Similarly, 3- to 5-year-old girls showed significantly more altruism than boys,[88] but the difference was much less than peers and teachers suspected. The skew model means that it is more productive not to view men and women as separate classes but to view individuals within each gender as more or less vulnerable to environmental manipulation depending on the particular behavior in question (see below).

Testing Biosocial Relationships

How can one integrate the physiologic parameters with the environmental input? I propose models of testing physiologic responses to social challenge much like physicians test a persons's cardiovascular response to stress. From the biomedical community has come the concept of *at risk*. The treadmill may produce signs in the EKG of potentially fatal flaws, assessing the risk. Medical students are taught the importance of family and employment history in assisting diagnosis and prognosis. Insurance underwriters assign the risk factors to a battery of behaviors, as well as to physiologic condition. With the exception of certain genetic diseases, all illnesses have a multitude of causes. For example, of those infected with the Epstein–Barr virus, only persons under sufficient stress to cause a reduction in T-lymphocytes will have infectious mononucleosis.

Stress-test models may be conceived for many social situations. In considering sports, military, and criminal behavior as stressors, absolute levels of testosterone were not found necessarily predictive of behavior, yet the weight of these reports infers some connection. When relative response to a stressor was examined, differences in fit and unfit athletes and long-distance runners were found. The observation that the testosterone levels of the "unfit" could not be raised suggests that the hormone has little to do with fitness or that there are some individuals genetically predisposed to a physiologic-social designation of unfit.

To explore this model further I choose to examine a most controversial line of research. Rossi chose parenting for her model of biosocial interaction. I single out sexual choice (preference, orientation). We have seen that

87. M. R. Ford and C. R. Lowery, "Gender Differences in Moral Reasoning: A Comparison of the Use of Justice and Care Orientations," *Journal of Personality and Social Psychology* 50(1986):777–783.

88. L. L. Girch and J. Billman, "Preschool Children's Food Sharling with Friends and Acquaintances," *Child Development* 57(1986):387–395.

the physiology of homosexuals (and, by inference, heterosexuals) has been subjected to extensive study with much confusion and little conclusion.

Responding to Dörner's suggestive reports of differences in lutinizing hormone response to estrogen, Green and his colleagues designed their own study.[89] Of 150 volunteers, 90 were selected after health and drug-use screening; 70 agreed, 55 participated, but only 43 were included in the report. According to the authors, "Several were excluded from statistical analysis because of abnormal baseline hormone concentrations." This explains why the average testosterone levels for both homosexuals and heterosexuals showed much less deviation than expected (see Fig. 1). The importance of this study lies as much in the careful selection and identification of the volunteers as in the careful collection of physiologic data.

When these volunteers — 12 heterosexual women, 17 heterosexual men, and 14 homosexual men (classified 5 or 6 according to Kinsey's scale) — were injected with an estrogen derivative and the LH response normalized to baseline levels, three distinct curves resulted. All levels dropped below 75% within 24 hours. By 48 hours, the female response was 120% above baseline and remained 200% at 72 and 96 hours. The male heterosexual response remained at least 80% of baseline for the whole period of study. The homosexual response was intermediate between the two and significantly different from both heterosexual women and men. Differences in absolute levels of LH were also found.

The three groups also differed in their testosterone response. Although injection of estrogen caused little change in testosterone levels in the women, the men showed a drop to 60% of baseline — negative feedback. The heterosexuals showed a more rapid climb to baseline (still not reached in 96 hours), differing significantly from the homosexuals at 72 and 96 hours. The authors note that there was much more variation within the male homosexual group than either heterosexual group, indicating that some did not show an "average" homosexual response. The authors are careful to conclude: "Since we may have measured an adult hormonal correlate of sexual orientation that is causally independent of sexual differentiation, a causal relation should not be inferred." But the weight of other studies linking hypothalamic differentiation to fetal testosterone levels makes such a relation more acceptable.

The authors were reprimanded not on the scientific quality of their study but on media impact: Was society prepared to accept gay men as biologically different, or would this report be used to "reinforce popular prejudice"?[90] The authors responded that "many lesbians and gay men

89. Gladue, Green, and Hellman, "Neuroendocrine Response."

90. G. M. Herek, "Values, Research Questions, and the News Media," Letter to *Science* 226(1984):1142; Answer by Gladue *et al.* ibid., p. 1142.

have applauded our report of a biological correlate of homosexual orientation. We understand that they see it as an inroad against the vicious attacks [condemning] homosexual orientation as purely willful, sinful, and objectionable." Homosexuality may be shown to be a natural variant, like left-handedness. The authors also observe, "If people are willing to accept that heterosexuality is already determined, why not homosexuality?"[91]

Thus a biologic stressor, estrogen, caused different physiologic responses in the two sexes and also differed between sexual choice, considered a behavioral preference. Using similar challenge protocol, testing the LH response to LHRH, differentiated paedophils from other men.[92] Seyler and colleagues report that female transsexuals respond differently to a similar challenge.[93]

Using the concept of *at risk* in a biosocial context would picture some people more vulnerable to a physical or psychological stress than others. Anthony developed the image of children at risk into "the vulnerable child" in order to explain why the same environments produced different responses in children.[94] Similar examples of vulnerability can be cited for manic depression,[95] crime,[96] and the disruptive child. As I have reported in the section on criminality, early behavior and testosterone levels seem to indicate the child at risk of becoming a criminal. The ability to predict, with reasonable accuracy, the behavior of an individual creates a dilemma for the social scientist. How can one ethically identify the vulnerable individual in order to reduce the risk?

CONCLUSIONS

There can be no average man or average woman on whom we must fit our gender roles. Diversity is the watchword for our lives and for the survival of the species, as it always has been. Rossi's perspective was not to evoke instinct as an explanation of behavior but to increase the number of significant variables to include physiologic ones. She reminds us to consider

91. *Science 84* (December) quotes Gladue *et al.* p. 8.
92. Gaffney and Berlin, "Is There Dysfunction?"
93. L. E. Seyler, Jr., *et al.*, "Abnormal Gonadotropin Secretory Responses to LRH in Transsexual Women after Diethylstilbesterol Priming," *Journal of Clinical Endocrinologic Metabolism* 47(1978):176–183. This study has not been confirmed. See De Vries *et al.*, eds., *Sex Differences*, pp. 399–406.
94. E. J. Anthony, ed., *The Child in His Family*, vol. 4, *Vulnerable Children* (New York: Wiley, 1978), p. 3.
95. J. Alper, "Depression at an Early Age," *Science* 86(May):45–50.
96. Taylor, *Hormonal Manipulation;* and J. Page, "Inside the Criminal Mind," *Science 84* (September):84–85.

"diversity as a biological fact and equality as a political and social precept."

Male and female brains differ structurally. The structures can be modified by different levels of hormones in the fetal environment. Imposed on the structural differences is a whole pharmacopoeia of chemicals that alter behavior. The physiologic parameters of aggression have been examined. Evidence suggests that a physiologic component to aggression be considered for its contribution to masculinity. Maccoby and Jacklin were severly criticized for this conclusion in 1974.[97] The weight of the evidence presented here continues to support them.

Men's studies must take into consideration that (a) testosterone levels are associated in some way with aggression; (b) men have a broad range of biologically determined testosterone levels; and (c) these levels can be enhanced or reduced by social environment.

None of this implies that humans are captives of their physiology. The forebrain can still mitigate the limbic system's emotional outbursts, albeit at times with much difficulty. Dr. Jekyll can control Mr. Hyde if he chooses. (Possibly it was PCP that Dr. Jekyll discovered, unhooking his forebrain from his limbic system.) Some men may be physiologically more at risk than others to environments that stress their control mechanisms. Like modern Jekylls, we subject our biologic system to a trampoline effect of highs, lows, and rebounds, having no idea what profound effects these large fluctuations in hormones may have on our behavior, moods, and libido.

I hope I have added to the demise of the "sterile debate on the nature/nurture 'problem,'" as Paul Brain calls it. Those "classical ethologists" who would evoke "innate" characteristics to explain human aggression or other emotional behaviors create a pessimism about humanity's future. Those sociologists who invoke nurture may also be pessimists; some would manipulate social environments globally. But those who see human behavior as the result of interactions with physiology and environment in a continuous and expanding series of feedback loops seem to be optimists: Intervention becomes individual, immediate, and possible.

Interaction between the individual and the social environment can be demonstrated using masculinity as an example. Joseph Pleck conceives of masculinity as a purely social construct.[98] However, it was developed over millennia as an interactive process between what males were capable of doing and what males as a class determined they should do. Men's concept

97. E. E. Maccoby and C. N. Jacklin, *The Psychology of Sex Differences* (Stanford: Stanford University Press, 1974); a summary of the criticism in T. Tieger, "On the Biological Basis of Sex Differences in Aggression" *Child Development* 51(1980):943–963, and the authors' reply in ibid., pp. 964–980.

98. J. Pleck, *The Myth of Masculinity* (Cambridge: MIT Press, 1981).

of what was feminine also entered into the construct. When this generic concept is imposed on the individual boy, his masculinity will depend on how well he physiologically and psychologically fits the masculine mold. Thus a male's concept of his masculinity has a biologic component.

Just as there is an interaction between the physiologic substrate and the environmental stressor, interaction between the biologist and the social scientist must occur. Each can keep the other honest. The tendency of the biologist to expect single or simple causes of behavior—the infectious disease paradigm—equals the social scientist's body–mind dichotomy: the Judeo-Christian body–soul paradigm. Discovering the interactions without reductionism will be hard work requiring intimate collaboration between the sciences.[99] Men's studies can take advantage of its newness in forming these alliances. Deaux, in "Sex and Gender," recognizes the association of psychological features with biological states and concludes: "Sex and gender is an area of research whose time has come. . . . What one may wish as a feminist is not necessarily what one sees as a scientist."[100]

This preliminary survey of the possible biologic contributions to gender is anecdotal, contradictory, and selective in that I have chosen not to be encyclopedic where one reference is sufficient and earlier controversy is resolvable. But this chapter indicates the state of the art and should suggest directions for study and a need for rigorous experimental design to include biological parameters. It is intended to provoke a dialogue between biology and sociology. It is also a plea that the biosociology of gender be an integral part of men's studies.

99. S. Parker, "Cultural Rules, Rituals, and Behavior Regulation," *American Anthropologist* 86(1984):584–600.

100. K. Deaux, "Sex and Gender," *Annual Review of Psychology* 36(1985):49–81. See also J. Shapiro, "Anthropology and the Study of Gender," in Langland and Gove, eds., *Feminist Perspective*, pp.112–125.

V

Literary Passions

How are texts sexed? In this section James Riemer, John Crowley, and Louis Crompton review various literary works and the men who wrote them through the lens of men's studies to reveal significant and subtle meanings and masks of masculinities.

"Rereading American Literature from a Men's Studies Perspective: Some Implications" argues that men's studies perspectives enable one to read a significant portion of American literature as social documents reflecting changing ideals of masculinity and variations in male roles and manly ideals according to social, economic, and racial–ethnic backgrounds. Such perspectives concretize literary criticism, lead to a greater understanding of male characters, and reveal the effects of manly ideals. Men's studies demonstrates how evaluations of writers identified strongly with ideals of masculinity, such as Ernest Hemingway, have been distorted by critics' acceptance of patriarchal values.

"Howells, Stoddard, and Male Homosocial Attachment in Victorian America" investigates the close professional and personal relationship between W. D. Howells and Charles Warren Stoddard, two American writers of the late nineteenth century, as a representative case of male homosocial attachment. It casts light on the social construction of "homosexuality," the connection between gender identity and authorship, and the generation of male authority in a patriarchal culture.

"Byron and Male Love: The Classical Tradition" explores how

Lord Byron adapted different aspects of the classical tradition to poems that expressed his personal feelings for his young male lovers at different stages of his life. Facing the taboo that his society placed on same-sex love, Byron had to look far afield for literary models for expression of such feelings. He found these in the poetry and history of ancient Greece and Rome. But this literature perceived the love of younger males from two different points of view. In the one case, the boy was a love object similar to a girl or woman; in the other, he was undergoing an apprenticeship to a heroic comrade who would initiate him into the male role appropriate to a warrior society. The essay examines variations in homoerotic forms of homosociality.

12
Rereading American Literature from a Men's Studies Perspective: Some Implications

James D. Riemer

What possible implications could a men's studies perspective have for the way we read American literature? After all, haven't feminist critics been telling us for years that literary criticism has been the carefully patrolled province of male critics discussing works about male characters sprung from the imaginations of male authors? True. But to equate a men's studies approach to literature with traditional criticism by males about males created by males would be as unsound as equating feminist literary criticism with criticism that is about female characters or the works of female authors or that is argued by female scholars. Attitude and ideological approach, not the sex of characters, authors, or critics, delineate the men's studies perspective in the same manner that they distinguish feminist literary criticism from other critical approaches.

Just as the erroneous belief that male experience equals human experience affected literary criticism's treatment of women as characters and authors, so has it restricted our perceptions about men in literature. But as feminist literary criticism and theory have brought about changes in the way we perceive women—as characters, writers, and critics—so can a men's studies approach affect and broaden the way we view men in American literature. In the past 10 to 15 years, men's studies has examined our culturally defined ideals of masculinity and how they have affected men's lives, transforming human experiences into ones that are distinctly masculine. Approaching American literature in the light of the concerns and attitude of these studies can change not only our perceptions of male characters and manly ideals but the focus of literary criticism as well.

One major implication of rereading American literature from a men's studies perspective, and one from which some literary critics may instinctively recoil, is the important role literary works can play in enlarging the

base of men's studies knowledge through the possibility of viewing a significant portion of American literature, both popular and "mainstream"
works, as social documents reflecting our society's ideals of masculinity. In
particular, such studies would reinforce the notions that there exists a
multiplicity of ideals of American manhood, some of which at times conflict with one another, and that our society's predominant ideals of masculinity have changed over the past two centuries. One need only examine
the ideals of manliness presented in James Fenimore Cooper's *The Deer-
slayer,* Louisa May Alcott's *Little Men,* and Ernest Hemingway's *The Sun
Also Rises* to perceive how American ideals of masculinity have changed in
a period of less than 100 years. For Cooper, the manly ideal is embodied in
the frontiersman Natty Bumpo, who is self-reliant, a man of few words, in
harmony with nature, instinctual rather than intellectual, morally and
sexually pure, uncontaminated by civilization. Written 30 years later, *Little Men* reveals the later-nineteenth-century's manly ideals, which began to
adapt manly virtues to the civilized commercial setting. Jo's boys are
taught business principles and mannerliness, as well as morality. The important role the little girls in the story play in civilizing the boys reflects the
feminization of American culture taking place and the increasingly significant role of women in the upbringing of males in a culture in which the
father was increasingly less present as an influence in the home. Hemingway's novel reveals a reshaping of the manly ideal in response to the crisis
of masculinity that resulted from World War I. Left with a world in which
it seemed men could no longer validate their masculinity by controlling
their environment, as had the frontiersman and the business mogul, Jake
Barnes embodies the new manly ideal by which men confronted the meaningless and uncontrollable world and the suffering it dealt out by creating
their own codes and rituals of manhood to replace those that had been
swept away.

In their individual studies of American masculinity, the social historians
Joe Dubbert and Peter Gabriel Filene have already made such a sociological use of American literature, albeit on a limited scale.[1] Drawing on a
breadth of materials, Dubbert and Filene also make frequent references to
a range of popular and "serious" literature, both as source and illustration
for their observations on the evolution of the male role and masculine ideal
during the nineteenth and twentieth centuries. The inevitable brevity of
their discussions can but suggest the value of more detailed examination of
individual literary works.

The Dubbert and Filene studies also share a second limitation charac-

---

1. Joe L. Dubbert, *A Man's Place: Masculinity in Transition* (Englewood Cliffs, N.J.: Prentice-Hall, 1979); and Peter Gabriel Filene, *Him / Her / Self: Sex Roles in Modern America* (New
York: New American Library, 1974).

teristic of a majority of the research and scholarship in men's studies in their focus on the values and ideals of the white middle class. By devoting attention to literary works that depict men's lives beyond the bourgeois experience and approaching them from a men's studies perspective, we could add to our understanding of whether or how concepts of the male role, the manly ideal, and acceptable means for validating masculine identity may vary in relation to a man's social, economic and racial–ethnic environment. In addition, we could perhaps gain insight as to how these environments have created or influenced those ideals. For instance, through studies of works such as Henry Roth's *Call It Sleep* and Pietro Di Donato's *Christ in Concrete*,[2] we could gain insight into how masculine roles and ideals from various ethnic backgrounds and the ability to achieve a sense of masculine identity were affected by the immigrant experience. Similarly, reading Jewish-American novels from a men's studies point of view might reveal how notions of masculinity fostered by the Jewish tradition interact with popular ideals of American manhood. Of course, such literary studies cannot be expected to give the whole "truth" about manhood in relation to a particular social, economic, racial–ethnic environment, but they can offer valuable insights into areas for further, potentially corroborating research by sociologists, psychologists, and social anthropologists.

As a case in point, a reading of works by Ernest Gaines from a men's studies perspective could suggest some of the notions of manhood and masculinity that exist among southern rural blacks, a group which has been afforded little attention from sociologists and psychologists.[3] While recent research has added to, modified, and challenged previous studies on black men, such research has for the large part been focused on lower-class, urban black males.[4] Gaines's stories reveal black men who are not concerned with either the material or work-related indexes of manhood, which have been traditionally denied them through social and institutional racism. The ideal of masculinity that appears to be valued by Gaines's black men is not a reaction against the system that excludes them from traditional male goals of power or wealth. The ideal is associated neither with exaggerated expressions of those traditional masculine qualities that remain accessible, such as sexuality and physical prowess, nor with alterna-

2. Henry Roth, *Call It Sleep* (1934; New York: Cooper Square, 1970); and Pietro Di Donato, *Christ in Concrete* (New York: Bobbs-Merrill, 1939).

3. Ernest J. Gaines, *Bloodline* (New York: Dial, 1968); and Ernest J. Gaines, *A Gathering of Old Men* (New York: Knopf, 1983).

4. See Lawrence Gary, ed., *Black Men* (Beverly Hills, Calif.: Sage, 1981); and Doris Y. Wilkinson and Ronald L. Taylor, eds. *The Black Male in America: Perspectives on His Status in Contemporary Society* (Chicago: Nelson-Hall, 1977).

tive forms of intraracial competitiveness. As a character in Gaines's "Three Men" remarks, " . . . face don't make a man . . . and fucking don't make him and fighting don't make him—neither killing. None of this prove you a man. 'Cause animals can fuck, can kill, can fight—you know that?"[5] In Gaines's stories, manhood is more strongly related to a man's inner sense of dignity and self-respect, an idea summed up in "The Sky Is Gray" in the mother's remarks to her son when he turns up the collar of his coat to keep warm. Telling him to turn it back down, she explains, "You not a bum. . . . You a man."[6] Earlier she rejects a charitable offer of food and insists that her son work for it by moving a white woman's garbage. In "Three Men," charity is seen as part of the white culture's process of subjugating and controlling the lives of black men, of sucking away their manly dignity by placing them in a dehumanized position of indebtedness and subservience. At first, certain that Medlow, a white plantation owner, will get him released, the narrator turns himself in for killing another black man. Eventually, however, the narrator recognizes the humiliation he would have to endure if he allows Medlow to free him: "He'd have me by the nuts and he'd know it; and I'd have to kiss his ass if he told me to."[7]

Manhood for the black men in Gaines's fiction is to be found, not in wielding power over others, but in a man's response to the attempts of others to wield power over him. If a man does not accept charity, neither does he allow others to humiliate or subjugate himself or others for whom he is responsible. In *A Gathering of Old Men,* a group of elderly black men come together, each to lay claim to having murdered the son of a plantation owner. By standing together the men momentarily thwart the workings of the white power structure, but more important, by being willing to accept the consequences for the murder and for their defiance of the sheriff, each man hopes to redeem himself for previous unmanly behavior when he failed to stand up for the human dignity of himself or others. It is not important that their defiance culminate in a fight, for as Mathu, the only one among them who has always been respected as a "man," explains, "There ain't no more to prove. . . . You already done proved it."[8] Most important, they have proven their manhood to themselves. The willingess to accept responsibility for one's actions, regardless of consequences, is also seen at the end of the novel when Charlie, the 50-year-old black man who is actually responsible for the white man's death, returns to turn himself in. Insisting that he now be addressed as Mr. Biggs, he explains, "I

5. Ernest J. Gaines, "Three Men," in Gaines, *Bloodline,* p. 138.
6. Ernest J. Gaines, "The Sky Is Gray," in Gaines, *Bloodline,* p. 117.
7. Ibid., p. 145.
8. Gaines, *Gathering of Old Men,* p. 181.

ain't Big Charlie, nigger boy, no more, I'm a man. Y'all hear me? . . . A nigger boy run and run. But a man come back. I'm a man."[9] In "Three Men," the only way for the narrator to break out of the cycle in which the white culture incarcerates the black man for his "brutish" expression of manhood, then frees him to perpetuate that behavior, is to reject the freedom offered to him by the plantation owner. In choosing to go to the "pen," the narrator can stand as a man, for he not only accepts responsibility for his past actions (the killing) but accepts responsibility for his own fate rather than allow others to exploit him to their own ends, to validate their own sense of manliness.

The relationship between literary studies from a men's studies perspective and the larger field of men's studies as a whole is a reciprocal one. For as rereading American literature for what it reveals about our society's manly ideals broadens the base of men's studies knowledge, observations and insights gathered from other fields, such as sociology, psychology, and anthropology, can provide a context that can illuminate our rereading of American literature in new and meaningful ways by affecting the nature of literary criticism itself. If patriarchal values have excluded women writers from the canon and affected literary criticism's treatment of female characters, it is no less true that traditional male values have affected the way criticism has dealt with males in literature. By ignoring elements of a work or character that do not coincide with traditional male interests, literary criticism has been a lot like male conversations. Big on ideas, but safely impersonal. As a result, traditionally, literary criticism by males has viewed the dilemmas of male characters on an abstract, moral, aesthetic, or intellectual level rather than in simply human terms. In particular, the nature and quality of human relationships for the male and the manner in which these are affected by masculine ideals are generally neglected.

This traditionally male focus on the impersonal rather than the personal can be seen, for instance, in the criticism on Sam Shepard's *True West*.[10] Although the play is generally placed among Shepard's three or four "realistic" plays, critical analysis has repeatedly reduced the shifting relationship between the play's two brothers to a metaphor for the relationship between such abstract qualities as creativity and craft, community and individualism, intellect and instinct. Such readings are valuable, but they are offered at the expense or dismissal of more personal concerns. Surely brothers in literature exist as more than vehicles for discourse on abstractions, even in a Sam Shepard play. Or rather, especially this Shepard play. It is precisely viewing the two men as brothers that raises signifi-

9. (Ibid., p. 187.
10. Sam Shepard, *True West*, in his *Seven Plays* (New York: Bantam, 1984).

cant issues on a more personal, less traditionally masculine plane. For instance, what does the relationship between the two men reveal about the role a brother plays in a man's self-definition? How do cultural ideals, especially ideals of masculinity, affect interaction between brothers, or among men in general? How do conflicting ideals of masculinity stifle or complicate the integration of the individual male's psyche? Such questions shift the focus of criticism from the manner in which men's lives reflect universal concerns or dilemmas to a more intimate, personal concern with how cultural values, particularly those connected with ideals of masculinity, affect the lives of men on a personal, human level, often creating dilemmas for the individual male.

By focusing on this personal level with an awareness of manly ideals and their effects on men's lives, men's studies can help us understand the behaviors of male characters in a new light. For instance, an understanding of the crisis of masculinity that occured at the end of the nineteenth and the beginning of the twentieth centuries often can help us perceive male characters' behaviors as attempts to redefine and rechannel the expression of a distinctly masculine identity in a culture where the alternatives for such expression were also being altered and limited by changes in the culture. By the end of the nineteenth century, when the frontier and the battlefield no longer provided readily viable proving grounds for American manhood, men were finding their sense of masculinity threatened on a variety of fronts. At a time when men were becoming increasingly concerned over the feminization of American culture that had taken place, and women were beginning to make inroads into traditionally male territories, the American male found himself striving to achieve a sense of manliness in a commercial, urban world of diminishing opportunities.

Rereading Sinclair Lewis's *Babbitt* in the context of this crisis of masculine identity, we can understand many of Babbitt's behaviors as attempts by a middle-class male to redefine and reaffirm a sense of manliness in a changing social and economic environment.[11] In part, men like Babbitt tried to locate a sense of manly identity by adapting frontier ideals to the world of commerce. But in a culture in which the Victorian concept of manly character was being replaced by monetary wealth as the measure of the masculine ideal, conspicuous consumption became the primary means of validating masculinity for Babbitt and men in his class. At the same time, Babbitt attempts to reaffirm his flagging sense of manliness by recasting his daily experiences in a more manly light, perceiving his real estate deals as manly battles and his drive in his car as a romantic adventure. His discontent and eventual rebellion can be seen as a response to the failure of these

11. Sinclair Lewis, *Babbitt* (New York: Harcourt, Brace, 1922).

redefinitions and adaptations of masculine ideals to reaffirm and validate his sense of manliness in a manner comparable to that offered by earlier ideals of manhood, especially those associated with the frontier experience.

Just as psychologists and sociologists throughout the 1970s and the first half of the 1980s have increasingly brought to our attention the limitations and frequently self-destructive nature of many of our ideals of manliness, so can a men's studies approach to American literature, with its concentration on the personal, reveal the ways in which manly ideals can restrict and complicate men's lives, often interfering with the satisfaction of their basic human needs. For instance, in James T. Farrell's *Young Manhood of Studs Lonigan*, while the undesirable, destructive aspects of Studs's expression of manhood are quite evident, the negative effects that ideals of manhood have on Studs himself are less apparent.[12] Studs's moral degeneration, which is at the heart of the novel, is not simply the result of a weak character or a reflection, in the naturalistic sense, of humankind's baser nature. In some ways it is the outgrowth of confusion and frustration of conflicting ideals of manhood and his economic, social situation. Born too late to prove his manhood on the battlefield of World War I, Studs has few ways of proving his manly qualities of daring, strength, and bravery. At the same time, his social and economic circumstances prevent him from pursuing his society's predominant proof of manhood, conspicuous consumption in the "Babbitt" mode. Nor can his work provide him with the sense of manly accomplishment, which his ideals have taught him to expect or desire. As a result, Studs, as did many men of his class, redirects his intensely physical sense of masculinity into sports, fighting, drinking, and sex. In many ways his proofs of masculinity are acts of rebellion against the moral standards of the middle class, from whose manly ideals he has been excluded.

Studs's life is also complicated by the incompatible demands of conflicting ideals of manhood. Caught between the demands of physical and moral purity associated with earlier ideals of manhood and the demands of the manly ideals of his peers, Studs often appears as weak-willed and self-contradictory. One moment he pledges himself to moral or physical improvement, then soon lapses into his habits of drinking, playing pool, and putting on weight around his middle. Sex, which is a major factor in Studs's sense of manliness, is also often the cause of his greatest confusion because his ideals of male behavior, based on viewing women as either paragons of purity or sexual conveniences, prove incapable of coping with society's

12. James T. Farrell, *Young Manhood of Studs Lonigan*, in *Studs Lonigan: A Trilogy* (New York: Modern Library, 1935).

changing views of female sexuality. Confused and frustrated by the breakdown of the simple dichotomy between good woman and temptress,
Studs's chauvinistic desires to protect and to violate often are directed
toward the same woman. Yet because his friends are also the judges of his
manhood, Studs cannot share his confusion and uncertainty with them,
just as he has learned not to reveal his emotional, sentimental thoughts
about Lucy.

Just as feminist literary criticism has revealed how men have shaped the
lives and identities of women, a close look at male–female relationships in
fiction from a men's studies point of view can disclose the central role that
women play in developing the male's sense of masculinity, not only by
being passive objects through which men validate various self-created
ideals of manhood, as is evident with Studs Lonigan, but also by actively
defining and reinforcing ideals of manly behavior and shaping the way
men perceive themselves. Two stories by Ernest Gaines can offer examples
of the major force women can exert in reinforcing particular ideals of
manhood. In "The Sky Is Gray," Gaines depicts a woman whose husband
has joined the army and who takes responsibility for instilling manly behavior in her young son. She strongly forbids such "crybaby stuff" as
crying, being scared, or his openly expressing love for her. In one instance,
in spite of his pleas, she hits him until he kills a redbird with a fork, picks off
its feathers, cleans it, and cooks it so that everybody has "a little bitty
piece."[13] Although the qualities the mother teaches the boy may have
drawbacks, as when he hides the pain of his toothache until he can no
longer bear it, the behaviors she encourages are those that she presumably
believes are necessary to cope with the harsh realities of their existence and
to prepare him for the manly role of looking after the family if she should
have to go away, as did his father. The idea of a woman enforcing manly
responsibility to one's family is also evident in "A Long Day in November."[14] Tired of her husband's neglect of his family because of his
preoccupation with his car, Mama forces Daddy to burn his automobile, a
stereotypical external proof of masculinity, in order that he devote himself
to a less materially oriented masculine role in his family, a role in which he
is expected not only to be provider but to be an attentive father and
husband as well. For Mama makes clear that, from now on, Daddy will
alternate with her in helping Sonny with his lessons, and he will be the
parent who goes to school to meet Sonny's teacher for a requested meeting. In forcing Daddy to accept his adult masculine role, Mama has risked
compromising Daddy's public image of manly control over his family, so

13. Gaines, "Sky Is Gray," p. 90.
14. Ernest J. Gaines, "A Long Day in November," in Gaines, *Bloodline*.

she makes him whip her with a switch until she cries so that he won't be the "laughingstock of the plantation."[15] In both stories, the women actively shape and enforce ideas of acceptable manly behavior.

Approaching literature from a men's studies perspective is especially valuable in rereading works by authors who have been most closely associated with defining and perpetuating manly ideas. Such a reading not only allows us to examine the effect of these ideals on men's lives, making us more perceptive about possible limitations and negative consequences of the ideals, but it highlights an important implication of the men's studies perspective for the practice of literary criticism. For as male characters' lives are often restricted by ideals of manhood, so does the acceptance of traditional patriarchal values influence and limit the ways criticism has approached the works of writers strongly identified with manly ideals.

Rereading *The Sun Also Rises* from a men's studies point of view draws into focus the degree to which criticism founded on a fundamental acceptance of patriarchal values can influence the interpretation of a text in which ideals of manhood are a central concern.[16] Mark Spilka's essay on *The Sun Also Rises* can serve as an example of the impact patriarchal values have had on Hemingway criticism.[17] Spilka's interpretation of Jake Barnes's relationship to the Hemingway ideal of manliness, embodied in his Code hero, Pedro Romero, is typical in its view of Romero as "an image of integrity against which Barnes and his generation are weighed and found wanting."[18] In delivering Romero into the hands, or rather, bed, of Brett, Jake has betrayed the manly code; he has failed the test of manhood. Underlying this interpretation, as well as much other criticism on the novel, is the tacit, unquestioned acceptance of the values of the Hemingway Code of manhood that Jake has betrayed. Yet rereading the text from a men's studies perspective, it appears that it is not Jake who fails the ideal, but the Code and other manly ideals that have failed the man.

Ideals of manhood are the source of Jake's problem and often the reason he is unable to deal with it in any manner but escape. He is physically unmanned by that most manly of all endeavors, war. Psychologically he is wounded because he places his sense of masculine identity primarily in sexual potency and confuses the possibility of love with the capability of sex. Other manly ideals prevent Jake from dealing with his wounds in a way that would help them heal. While public suffering like Robert Cohn's may not be desirable, its opposite, public stoicism, realistically can only add to

15. Ibid., p. 75.
16. Ernest Hemingway, *The Sun Also Rises* (New York: Scribner's, 1926).
17. Mark Spilka, "The Death of Love in *The Sun Also Rises*," in *Studies in The Sun Also Rises*, comp. William White (Columbus, Ohio: Merrill: 1969).
18. Ibid., p. 85.

the psychological strain. The ideals of male friendship that guide Jake and Bill's relationship keep them from the supportive discussion that could help Jake cope with his pain. More important, perhaps, is the effect that fundamental acceptance of masculine ideals has on the view of Hemingway's Code, which Spilka and others accept as desirable without hesitation. Yet, even by the standards Spilka uses to condemn Cohn's romantic notions, the manly code of Romero would fail to meet the needs of wounded Jake, who must live in the world as it is, not in a bullring in Pamplona or by a stream in Brugete. If manhood resides in creating one's own moral standards and confronting death when one chooses, what use can that be in a world where one's wounds, as Spilka notes, come from senseless and impersonal violence? Being manly when one has set the rules and can see the bull coming is one thing, but can such an ideal get Jake through the night? The ideal of manhood that Romero represents is as impractical in the world as Cohn's discredited Victorian ideals of manhood, and can exist only beyond where one actually lives, much like Cohn's Purple Land. If, as Spilka describes it, Jake's world is "a society which has little use for manliness,"[19] it may well be that manliness as it exists is of little use in meeting the human needs of the individual male.

To borrow a term from feminist criticism, the aim of a men's studies approach to American literature is re-vision: a revision of the way we read literature and a revision of the way we perceive men and manly ideals. It is a revision that seeks to understand how culturally defined ideals of manhood have shaped the lives of men, frequently limiting their growth or frustrating their basic needs. Ultimately, men's studies seeks to revise the way men live their lives so that they are free to guide their lives by human ideals rather than restrict them with purely manly ones. But to change men's lives in such a fashion needs more than recognition of the limitations and negative effects of our present ideals of manhood. There also must be a recognition and reinforcement of positive alternatives to traditional masculine ideals and behaviors.

Unfortunately, a review of American literature, both popular and "serious," will disclose the astonishing infrequency with which such alternative images occur. The American literary tradition has presented us with men who embody any number of manly ideals and men who struggle, often unwittingly, under the burden and limitations of those ideals. But seldom are we given positive depictions of men who represent alternatives to those traditional ideals. A men's studies awareness can make us more sensitive to identifying instances when male characters do break out of the confines of stereotypical masculine behavior, as do the men in John Steinbeck's *Can-*

19. Ibid., p. 83.

nery Row and *Tortilla Flat,* who, through their indifference to traditional indexes of masculinity such as work, material success, and omnipresent competitiveness, are able to develop male friendships that are atypically nurturing, supportive, generous, and noncompetitive. A men's studies approach can draw our attention to popular genre writers such as Robert Parker and Joseph Hansen, in the hard-boiled detective field, and any number of contemporary science fiction and fantasy authors, who are developing positive images of men who depart in significant ways from stereotypical masculine behaviors and ideals. Making us aware of literary works in which men who embody alternatives to traditional manly ideals and behaviors are depicted in a positive light may be one of the more important contributions a men's studies approach to American literature can make. For, in the end, it will be easier for men to revise the way they live their lives if we can help them recognize the possibilities of what they might become.

13

Howells, Stoddard, and Male Homosocial Attachment in Victorian America

John W. Crowley

*In Memory of
Roger Austen
(1935–1984)*

HOMOSEXUALITY

The term was invented a century ago, when the clinical gaze of psychiatry was beginning to fix itself on what one investigator preferred to label "inversion."[1] Scientific study is usually dated from Carl Westphal's paper in 1870 on "contrary sexual feeling" in a female patient.[2] The (ab)normalizing theories subsequently developed by Havelock Ellis, Richard von Krafft-Ebing, Cesare Lombroso, Albert Moll, Sigmund Freud, and others had the effect of bringing homosexuality and all the other "perversions" within the hegemony of the social discourse on sex. As Michel Foucault points out, "The nineteenth-century homosexual became a personage, a past, a case history, and a childhood, in addition to being a type of life, a life form, and a morphology, with an indiscreet anatomy and possibly a mysterious physiology."[3] Formerly an "abomination," homosexuality became a

1. Havelock Ellis, *Sexual Inversion* (1897; New York: Arno Press, 1975). This book began as a collaboration between Ellis and John Addington Symonds, whose name appears as coauthor on the title page but whose fragmentary (and posthumous) contributions to it are placed in an appendix. On the first page, Ellis felt obliged to explain his aversion to the term *homosexual*—a "barbarously hybrid word" for which he claimed "no responsibility." "It is, however, convenient and now widely used."
2. "Die conträre Sexualempfindung," *Archiv für Psychiatrie*, 2 (1870):73–108. See also Henri F. Ellenberger, *The Discovery of the Unconscious: The History and Evolution of Dynamic Psychiatry* (New York: Basic Books, 1970), p. 297.
3. Michel Foucault, *The History of Sexuality*, vol. 1, *An Introduction*, trans. Robert Hurley (New York: Pantheon, 1978), p. 43.

"disease."[4] *Scientia Sexualis* did not, however, gain much currency until the turn of the century; most bourgeois Victorians were far less inclined than the sexologists to discriminate homosexual from other relationships. As Edward Carpenter asserted, as late as 1908, "no hard and fast line can at any point be drawn effectively separating the different kinds of attachment."[5]

Feminist scholars have demonstrated that same-sex attachments between women, as long as they were perceived to be within the "feminine sphere," were unexceptionable in Victorian society. What was called "romantic friendship" or "the love of kindred spirits" or "Boston marriage" was recognized "as a socially viable form of human contact — and, as such, acceptable throughout a woman's life."[6] A woman "could share sentiment, her heart — all emotions" with another woman. "And regardless of the intensity of the feeling that might develop between them, they need not attribute it to the demon, sexuality, since women supposedly had none. They could safely see it as an effusion of the spirit."[7] It seems that "lesbianism," even in the "pathological" cases presented by the sexologists, was preponderantly nongenital.

Some clarity is gained, therefore, by following the example of those feminist critics who distinguish between *homosocial,* referring to the entire range of same-sex bonds, and *homosexual,* referring to the part of the homosocial continuum marked by genital sexuality. Although the homosocial – homosexual distinction is problematical at best, it has a useful, if limited, descriptive value.[8] Until recently, the nature of homosocial

---

4. "From Abomination to Disease" is a chapter title in Ronald Bayer, *Homosexuality and American Psychiatry: The Politics of Diagnosis* (New York: Basic Books, 1981). On the sexologists, see also Frank J. Sulloway, *Freud, Biologist of the Mind: Beyond the Psychoanalytic Legend* (New York: Basic Books, 1979), pp. 277 – 319; and George Chauncey, Jr., "From Sexual Inversion to Homosexuality: Medicine and the Changing Conceptualization of Female Deviance," *Salmagundi,* nos. 58/59(Fall 1982/Winter 1983):114 – 146.

5. Edward Carpenter, *The Intermediate Sex: A Study of Some Transitional Types of Men and Women* (1908; New York: Mitchell Kennerley, 1912), p. 18.

6. Carroll Smith-Rosenberg, "The Female World of Love and Ritual: Relations between Women in Nineteenth-Century America," in *Disorderly Conduct: Visions of Gender in Victorian America* (New York: Oxford University Press, 1986), p. 74. See also, in the same volume, "The New Woman as Androgyne: Social Disorder and Gender Crisis, 1870 – 1936."

7. Lillian Faderman, *Surpassing the Love of Men: Romantic Friendship and Love between Women from the Renaissance to the Present* (New York: Morrow, 1981), p. 159. See also Martha Vicinus, "Distance and Desire: English Boarding-School Friendships," *Signs* 9(Summer 1984):600 – 622.

8. On the problems of terminology, see Smith-Rosenberg, *Disorderly Conduct,* pp. 30 – 52; Eve Kosofsky Sedgwick, *Between Men: English Literature and Male Homosocial Desire* (New York: Columbia University Press, 1985), pp. 1 – 20; Sharon O'Brien, "'The Thing Not Named': Willa Cather as a Lesbian Writer," *Signs* 9(Summer 1984):577 – 580. Robert K.

attachment between Victorian *men* has been relatively neglected, even though, as Lillian Faderman suggests, men as well as women were encouraged to form intense same-sex friendships. One such relationship was that between W. D. Howells and Charles Warren Stoddard.

Stoddard is a writer currently without literary reputation who is recognized, even by name, only by scholarly specialists. Even among his contemporaries, he was admired more for his geniality and social gifts than for his modest talent; but at the time of his death in 1909, Stoddard was still fondly remembered as the author of *South-Sea Idyls* and other accounts of his exotic travels. W. D. Howells, in contrast, was probably the most powerful literary man in Victorian America: author of over a hundred widely read volumes of fiction, poetry, drama, reminiscence, travel, and criticism; a prominent editor and arbiter of taste, whose crusade for literary realism did much to advance the careers of Henry James, Mark Twain, Stephen Crane, and many others; an anatomist of American social ills and a disseminator of European art and ideas. One measure of Howells's importance is the vehemence with which a younger generation of writers, including Van Wyck Brooks, H. L. Mencken, and Sinclair Lewis, attacked him after his death in 1920, when he was vilified as the "Dean" of genteel American letters. Since the 1920s, Howells's reputation has never fully recovered from this obloquy. At present, as one critic accurately states, his work "has been given an increasingly respectful attention from academic scholars, and a handful of his novels are being kept before a wider audience in cheap reprints, largely . . . read by college students in American literature classes."[9] For my purposes, Howells may be regarded as a central cultural figure whose relationship with a marginal figure, Stoddard, casts light on the conception of *homosexuality* in the nineteenth century, on the links between gender identity and authorship, and on the generation of male authority in a patriarchal culture.

I

According to Faderman, "Thoreau was speaking for his time when he observed in his mid-nineteenth-century essay, *Friendship*, that intimacy was much more possible 'between two of the same sex' than 'between the

---

Martin argues that the term *homosocial* is "a linguistic monster" and that it is "best reserved, if at all, for institutions and situations. Thus prisons may be said to be homosocial institutions, but prisoners remain heterosexual or homosexual, according to their principal sexual orientation, regardless of the sexual activity they may engage in while in a homosocial environment." Martin, *Hero, Captain, and Stranger: Male Friendship, Social Critique, and Literary Form in the Sea Novels of Herman Melville* (Chapel Hill: University of North Carolina Press, 1986), p. 13. My usage of *homosocial* is consistent with Martin's suggestion.

9. Kenneth B. Eble, *William Dean Howells* (Boston: Twayne, 1982), p. 182.

sexes.'"[10] Nevertheless, no such intimacy seemed possible between Thoreau and Howells when the young journalist from Ohio paid a visit in 1860, during his pilgrimage to the East. As Howells recalled 40 years later, he had sought out his literary idols and, in most cases, had received from them an approbation beyond his wildest imaginings. At the Parker House in Boston, the votary broke bread with James Russell Lowell, Oliver Wendell Holmes, and their publisher, James T. Fields. "'Well, James,'" averred the Autocrat, with a benevolent glance at Howells, "'this is something like the apostolic succession; this is the laying on of hands.'"[11] The ritual of Howells's investiture into the New England clerisy continued over several days of private interviews, including an audience with Hawthorne, who found "this young man worthy" in a note of introduction to Emerson. Of all these meetings, only the one with Thoreau was disastrous:

> He tried to place me geographically after he had given me a chair not quite so far off as Ohio, though still across the whole room, for he sat against one wall, and I against the other; but apparently he failed to pull himself out of his revery by the effort, for he remained in a dreamy muse, which all my attempts to say something fit about John Brown and Walden Pond seemed only to deepen upon him.[12]

Although Howells apparently preferred the intimacy of hands laid on to Thoreau's hands-off remoteness, he observed certain limits in his contact with men. He recalled that "when [H. H.] Boyesen told me that among the Norwegians men never kissed each other, as the Germans, and the Frenchmen, and the Italians do, I perceived that we stood upon common ground"[13] — although not so narrow ground as Lowell, who "stupefied" Howells early in their acquaintance by saying, "'I like you because you don't put your hands on me,'" and who was said to have attended a reception in his later years only on the condition that "'they won't shake hands.'"[14] Not himself a toucher but not so chary as Lowell, Howells enjoyed the affection of demonstrative westerners like Ralph Keeler, Bret Harte, Charles Warren Stoddard, and Samuel Clemens.

Howells was especially fond of Keeler, whom he remembered as "too vivid a presence in every way not to have left a most distinct impression of himself in the minds of all his acquaintance." Keeler, who once had played a *danseuse* in a burnt-cork company and who lived with "a suave old actor," had hands of "almost womanish littleness" that he sometimes "gayly

10. Faderman, *Surpassing the Love of Men*, p. 159.
11. David F. Hiatt and Edwin H. Cady, eds., *Literary Friends and Acquaintance: A Personal Retrospect of American Authorship* (1900) (Bloomington: Indiana University Press, 1968), p. 36.
12. Ibid., p. 54.
13. Ibid., p. 220.
14. Ibid., p. 208.

flirted" in the air; and he held a *carpe diem* philosophy "which he liked to impress with a vivid touch on his listener's shoulder." Howells wondered whether Keeler's "mind about women was not so Chinese as somewhat to infect his manner"; and he was "framed rather for men's liking." Although Howells realized after Keeler's early death (in 1874) that he had "loved" him, he had done "as little to show it as men commonly do."[15]

Howells's adult love for Keeler during the 1870s was somewhat more constrained than the homosocial attachments of his youth. In the 1840s, in frontier Hamilton, Ohio, he had known a hundred boys but loved just one: a hooky-playing, Huck Finnish pariah. In *A Boy's Town* (1890), Howells recalled their camaraderie as not only "more innocent" than any other friendship he had experienced but "wholly innocent": the boys had "loved each other, and that was all. . . . and if I could find a man of the make of that boy I am sure I should love him."[16] Some years later, after his "nervous prostration" at the age of 17, Howells had enjoyed a more enduring special comradeship with Jim Williams, a compositor in his father's print-shop.[17] The two felt a common enthusiasm for songs and literature, especially Cervantes and Shakespeare, whom they read to each other during excursions in the forest. Howells had also been drawn to a man of nearly three times his age: an eccentric English organ builder with whom he shared a rapture in reading Dickens. As with Jim Williams, Howells's friendship with the organist became inseparable from what he called "literary passion."

In *My Literary Passions* (1895), the title of which establishes a sexual trope that informs the book, Howells asserted that every young (male) writer must "form himself from time to time upon the different authors he is in love with," and his adoration will be "truly a passion passing the love of women."[18] His greatest passions were expressed in fantasies of spellbound submission to a powerful seducer. When reading Thackeray, for instance, young Howells had been "effectively his alone, as I have been the helpless and, as it were, hypnotized devotee of three or four others of the very great."[19] One of these was Heine, whose "peculiar genius" had provided a liberating domination; "for if he chained me to himself he freed me from all other bondage."[20] Long after he had ceased to idolize him, Howells still

15. "Ralph Keeler," *Atlantic Monthly* 33(March 1874):366–367; *Literary Friends and Acquaintance*, pp. 232–234.

16. *A Boy's Town: Described for "Harper's Young People"* (New York: Harper, 1890), p. 192.

17. On Howells's neuroticism, see John W. Crowley, *The Black Heart's Truth: The Early Career of W. D. Howells* (Chapel Hill: University of North Carolina Press, 1985).

18. *My Literary Passions* (1895), in *My Literary Passions / Criticism and Fiction*, Library ed. (New York: Harper, 1911), p. 16.

19. Ibid., p. 102.

20. Ibid., p. 128.

felt a tenderness for Heine that was "not a reasoned love, I must own; but, as I am always asking, when was love ever reasoned?"[21]

What may seem unreasoned at first about *My Literary Passions* is that Howells's rhetoric of desire, expressed in sexually charged metaphors, coexists with a rhetoric of disgust, expressed in vividly excremental imagery. But desire and disgust were the Janus faces of Howells's ambivalence toward the (homo)erotics of his reading: what gave him so much pleasure could also inspire much guilt.

When he was an adolescent, as Howells recalled, his father had once brought him a copy of Chaucer's poems from the Ohio state library, along with the librarian's "question as to whether he thought he ought to put an unexpurgated edition in the hands of a boy, and his own answer that he did not believe it would hurt me." As Howells explained, his father, "without due reflection," had probably "reasoned that with my greed for all manner of literature the bad would become known to me along with the good at any rate, and I had better know that he knew it."[22] Try as he undoubtedly did, the boy could not escape altogether the tainting titillation of "bad" literature: "I am not ready to say that the harm from it is positive, but you do get smeared with it, and the filthy thought lives with the filthy rhyme in the ear, even when it does not corrupt the heart or make it seem a light thing for the reader's tongue and pen to sin in kind."[23] Howells prophesied that in a more civilized future, when the "beast-man will be so far subdued and tamed in us that the memory of him in literature shall be left to perish," then the "noxious and noisome channels" of filth, which sometimes make literary history seem "little better than an open sewer," will have ceased to flow.[24]

For his favorite brother, Johnny, when he reached adolescence, Howells tried to fill the censorial role he felt their father had wrongfully abdicated. "I can't tell you how sick at heart and stomach it made me — the other day, to look over some bad poems of Byron that I admired at sixteen," he wrote in a confidential letter to Johnny in 1863. "If such things don't spoil you, they'll make you ashamed and remorseful, some day." In the same letter, Howells warned his brother, who was soon to attend boarding school: "About this time, you'll form some friendship, I suppose, that will have more influence upon your life than you can know, at once. A young fellow must have some friend; but you'll do better not to have any

21. Ibid., p. 141.
22. Ibid., p. 83.
23. Ibid., pp. 83–84.
24. Ibid., pp. 43, 83.

than to be taken with one who is a funny chap, and at the same time a blackguard."[25]

In this letter there is a telling conjunction of literary disgust with homophobia. Funny chaps, like Bryon's filthy poems, lead to shame and remorse, if not to actual harm. A young man is vulnerable to dangerous attachments that an adult has learned to avoid. The passions of youth, literary or otherwise, are deceiving; the true worthlessness of their object is concealed. For young Howells, the explicitly erotic power of "bad" books had activated a counterforce of repression. "Literary passions" had been possible for him to indulge only because their sexual impetus had been sublimated into imaginary "romantic friendships." For the adult Howells, except in reminiscences of his youthful reading, the pleasures of the text had long since been renounced, including those pleasures that had passed the love of women. Yet in projecting his own experience upon Johnny's, Howells acknowledged the likelihood of *youthful* homoerotic attachments.

Ten years after Howells completed *My Literary Passions*, Freud formulated his theory of psychosexual development, which may be used intertextually as a contemporaneous gloss on Howells's experience. One key Freudian idea was that every boy's "Oedipal complex" involves his desire for *both* parents. Indeed, as Richard Klein paraphrases it, "In the normal development of the little boy's progress towards heterosexuality, he must pass . . . through the stage of the 'positive" Oedipus, a homoerotic identification with his father, a position of effeminized subordination to the father, as a condition of finding a model for his own heterosexual role."[26] Furthermore, as Freud stressed in his case study of Dr. Schreber,

> After the stage of heterosexual object-choice has been reached, the homosexual tendencies are not, as might be supposed, done away with or brought to a stop; they are merely deflected from their sexual aim and applied to fresh uses. They . . . help to constitute the social instincts, thus contributing an erotic factor to friendship and comradeship, to *esprit de corps* and to the love of mankind in general.[27]

That is, in Freud's view, the entire range of what may be called male "homosocial" relations is seen to be more or less eroticized, even if the term homosexual is applied only to genital practices.

25. *Selected Letters of W. D. Howells*, ed. George Arms, Christoph K. Lohmann, *et al.*, 6 vols. (Boston: Twayne, 1979–1983), 1:152. Hereafter cited as *SL*.

26. Quoted in Sedgwick, *Between Men*, p. 23.

27. "Psycho-analytic Notes upon an Autobiographical Account of a Case of Paranoia" (1911) in *Collected Papers*, ed. Alix and James Strachey (New York: Basic Books, 1959), 3:446–447.

There is no evidence that Howells was homosexual in this restricted sense. What might be expected by the logic of Freud's theory, however, is that Howells's repressed and renounced "homosexual tendencies" would be "an erotic factor" most powerfully in those male relationships that reconfigured the "Oedipal" situation: Placed again in the position of a child, he would be inclined to regress, if only symbolically, to the "position of effeminized subordination to the father." In boyhood, Howells was the "effeminized" lover of the literary "fathers" who had engendered the line to which he himself wished to belong; as a young man, he submitted to the laying on of hands by the New England "fathers" of American literature. But this "childish" position, which reactivated a good deal of psychological ambivalence in Howells, was merely a stage toward his becoming a literary "father" himself. His ultimate goal, as for the boy in the Freudian scheme, was to attain (in literary terms) a "heterosexual" majority. As Eve Kosofsky Sedgwick says, "Any male-centered literary text [and I would include here the Oedipalized "text" of a male author's career] is likely to be about homosocial/homosexual as well as heterosexual object choices, and in this way about relations to patriarchal power."[28]

In Freudian terms, an adult "homosexual" would be a man arrested in his subordination to the father; that is, one rendered permanently powerless within the patriarchal order by his "effeminization" and also, since the "effeminized" position is a phase of boyhood development, by his juvenility. To Howells, such a man was Charles Warren Stoddard.

II

Throughout his 15 years with the prestigious *Atlantic Monthly*, 10 of them as editor-in-chief, Howells was determined to broaden the New England base of the magazine and of American writing in general; and he took pride in fostering new talent from the South and West. It was Howells's turn to lay hands on whomever he deemed worthy of his patronage, and Stoddard was just one of many protégés. Howells discovered Stoddard through his poems in the late 1860s, and he soon learned more about him from their mutual friends among the California writers: Harte, Keeler, and Clemens. But Howells did not meet Stoddard face to face until 1888. Thus for nearly 20 years their dealings, mostly on literary business, were only by correspondence.

28. Eve Kosofsky Sedgwick, "Homophobia, Misogyny, and Capital: The Example of *Our Mutual Friend*," *Raritan* 2(Winter 1983):131.

The earliest letter, from 1870, conveys the assistant editor's friendly rejection of some Stoddard poems. Two years later, after he had taken charge of the *Atlantic*, Howells was pleased to accept the prose sketch "A Prodigal in Tahiti," which he judged "the very *bouquet* of vagabond romance—it was infinitely the best thing of the kind that I ever read." Stoddard was urged to pursue this success with a series of recollections of his theatrical experiences. "You are the man," Howells assured him, "to give us the pathetic humor and the quaint poetry of the life."[29] From the start, Howells regarded Stoddard as the most lyrical of the so-called California humorists: more delicate and polished a stylist than either Harte or Mark Twain, but equally comic and easygoing. When one of the theatrical sketches did not turn out as well as Howells had hoped, he blamed the result on "a certain pressure and anxiety in it, which seemed quite foreign to you."[30]

In truth, however, anxiety was native to the real Stoddard, if not to his comical literary persona. His life before the 1870s had been emotionally turbulent, at least in part because of his emergent homosexuality.[31] Having felt intense but unrequited attraction to fellow schoolboys, Stoddard was still sexually uninitiated when, at the age of 21, he sailed to the Sandwich Islands in 1864 and fell passionately in live with a young native. On his return to California he immersed himself in a bohemian life that, as his autobiographical novel suggests, included love affairs with magnetic young men. Longing for pleasures not complicated by civilized mores, he returned to Hawaii in 1868 as a roving reporter for a San Francisco newspaper, and 2 years later he embarked for Tahiti. For his sketches of these journeys, which began to appear in the *Overland Monthly* in 1869, Stoddard drew on his amorous experiences in the islands. As Franklin Walker demurely observes, Stoddard's emphasis was "not on the customary brown maidens with firm breasts, lithe limbs, and generous impulses, but on the strong-backed youths, human porpoises who drive their canoes through the mists of the storm and share their joy and sorrows with the prodigal from California."[32] In one sketch, for example, sharing joy meant sleeping with an affectionate native boy in a fourposter bed.

Although the sketch accepted for the *Atlantic* contained relatively little

29. *SL*, 1:407.

30. *SL*, 2:21. Perhaps to give Howells a better idea of himself, Stoddard sent him a portrait photograph soon after receiving this letter, and Howells reciprocated with one of himself.

31. For information about Stoddard, I am greatly indebted to the late Roger Austen's unpublished biography, "Genteel Pagan: The Double Life of Charles Warren Stoddard," which supersedes all published sources. An earlier biography of Stoddard, also unpublished, is Carl G. Stroven's dissertation (Duke, 1932), "A Life of Charles Warren Stoddard."

32. Franklin Walker, *San Francisco's Literary Frontier* (New York: Knopf, 1939), p. 273.

such material, it could not easily have passed notice in Stoddard's *South-Sea Idyls* (1873), which Howells himself helped to guide into print through his influence with the publisher James R. Osgood.[33] But if Howells found anything untoward in Stoddard's rapture for the strong-backed youths, there was no such indication in his long and favorable review, in which he concluded by welcoming *South-Sea Idyls* "as a real addition to the stock of refined pleasures, and a contribution to our literature without which it would be sensibly poorer."[34] When an illustrated English edition appeared later, Howells was indignant that the "delicate and charming text" had been "defamed" by drawings "so vulgar and repulsive that I do not think anyone could have looked twice inside the abominable cover."[35] He believed that Stoddard too was "scandalized" by an illustration for "Chumming with a Savage," in which the artist had "grossly misrepresented the nature of the harmless story" — what Howells had characterized in his review as "the history of the author's romantic friendship with a Tahitan boy."[36] Although Stoddard's relationship with the islander had almost certainly been genital, the fictional version in "Chumming with a Savage" draped all hints of homosexuality in a chastely voluptuous prose style that left the reader free to imagine only an ennoblingly spiritual passion.[37]

As we have seen, "romantic friendship," including physical (but not genital) intimacy, was a common mode of homosocial attachment among Victorian women. Howells, who had enjoyed such relationships in his youth, could easily extend the concept to Stoddard and his native boys. In his fiction of the 1870s, in fact, Howells himself often portrayed male camaraderie; and at least two pairs of his characters — Gilbert and Easton in "Private Theatricals" (serialized, 1875 – 1876), Ford and Phillips in *The Undiscovered Country* (1880) — seem to be joined in "romantic friendship."

Of these characters, Phillips has the closest resemblance to Stoddard. A colorful and humorous Bostonian dandy, Phillips is deeply self-conscious

---

33. "Send on the copy of your book. I have spoken to Osgood about it, and I know that it will have a fair and favorable chance." *SL*, 2:21n.

34. "Recent Literature," *Atlantic Monthly* 32(December 1873):746. As Austen points out, none of the reviewers — either of the 1873 or the 1892 edition — remarked any breach of sexual decorum. But the *Nation* did note that "life in the Southern Seas is such a peculiarly non-moral life, that we cannot recommend 'South-Sea Idyls' as a book of an invigorating and purifying tone. The Southern Seas — as it used to be said of Paris — are not a good place for deacons." *Nation* 17(December 18, 1873):411.

35. "Introductory Letter" to *South-Sea Idyls* (New York: Scribner's, 1892), p. vi.

36. "Editor's Easy Chair," *Harper's Monthly* 136(December 1917):149; *Atlantic Monthly* 32(December 1873):743. See also John W. Crowley "Howells, Stoddard, and the Illustrations for *Summer Cruising in the South Seas*," *Gay Studies Newsletter* 13(November 1986).

37. On Stoddard's stylistic obfuscation, see Roger Austen, "Stoddard's Little Tricks in *South Sea Idyls*," *Journal of Homosexuality* 8(Spring/Summer 1983):73 – 81.

of his interest in Ford. In a passage that Howells deleted from the manuscript of the novel before its publication, Phillips speaks of the "fascination of such characters" as Ford's:

> "And, — I'm fascinating?" asked Ford.
> "O yes, — to women, and to undecided men like myself. Didn't you know it?" . . .
> "Now you *are* flattering me," said Ford, with an ironical smile. "Be frank: you don't mean it."
> "I'm doing you simple justice," returned Phillips.
> "And can't you see what an irresistible attraction you must naturally have for a man like me?"
> "I've never been at the pains to formulate you," said Ford[.] "I don't know what sort of man is like you."[38]

Even if he had taken more pains than Ford, Howells himself could not easily have formulated what sort of man was like Phillips; for no clear formula existed for such "undecided men" — at least for those in the American middle class.

Sedgwick has constructed "rough categories according to class" in order to distinguish among English homosocial – homosexual "styles" in the nineteenth century. In the first are aristocrats and their bohemian companions, for whom "a distinct homosexual role and culture seem already to have been in existence in England for several centuries," a culture whose strongest associations are "with effeminacy, transvestitism, promiscuity, prostitution, continental European culture, and the arts." For classes below the nobility, however, Sedgwick finds no consistent "association of a particular personal style with the genital activities now thought of as 'homosexual.'" Men of the educated middle class, whose writings and careers have shaped our conception of the Victorian age, "operated sexually in what seems to have been startlingly close to a cognitive vacuum" — without "easy access to the alternative subculture, the stylized discourse, or the sense of immunity of the aristocratic/bohemian sexual minority."[39]

Such categories have only limited application to nineteenth-century America, where neither an aristocratic class nor an aristocratic – bohemian subculture was so well established as in Europe. Of course, there were men

38. I am quoting from the draft "Emendations List" for *The Undiscovered Country*, forthcoming in *A Selected Edition of W. D. Howells* (Bloomington: Indiana University Press). For providing me with a copy of this list, I am grateful to David J. Nordloh.

39. Sedgwick, *Between Men*, pp. 172–173.

from the American social elite who, whether at home or abroad, identified themselves with the style of the English "decadents." But most American men resembled those English bourgeois gentlemen whose sexuality was, as Sedgwick says, "silent, tentative, protean, and relatively divorced from expectations of genre, though not of gender."[40] Even among those like Stoddard, whose same-sex preferences were consistently expressed in genital practices, there was no prevailing homosexual "style."

In England, as Sedgwick remarks, a subcultural gulf existed between aristocratic and middleclass homosexuals. Lord Alfred Douglas, for example, would have had much stronger "stylistic links" to a heterosexual Regency rake than to contemporary middle-class men like J. A. Symonds, the Housmans, or Edward Carpenter, "who, relatively untouched by this aristocratic tradition, turned toward a homosexual role that would emphasize the virile over the effeminate, the classical over the continental." Only after the sensational trials of Oscar Wilde in the 1890s did the "effeminate" aristocratic role "become the dominant one available for homosexual men of both the upper and middle classes."[41]

In America, some middle-class men, such as Stoddard, were attracted, like their English counterparts Symonds and Carpenter, to the "virile" example of Walt Whitman. But Whitman himself was uncertain about his own sexuality, and he was no more receptive to Symonds's homoerotic interpretation of the "Calamus" poems than he had been to Stoddard's "semi-love letters."[42]

As an American of petit bourgeois background, who had come of age long before the turn of the century, Stoddard was caught in the cultural cross-currents. Like his fictional alter ego, Paul Clitheroe, he perceived himself to be "a contradiction": a man of sentiment with a "hyperpoetic" temperament and a love of the fine arts, but also a man of earthy humor with a desire to counter any impression of his being "silly or soft" by cutting "a metaphorical pigeon-wing" in the midst of his own "lofty flight" and turning "everything into ridicule." Possessed of "a kind of feminine shyness, born of delicate pride," Clitheroe/Stoddard also "delighted to

40. Ibid., p. 174.
41. Ibid., pp. 93–94.
42. In 1867, having felt a shock of recognition in reading "Calamus," Stoddard sent a volume of his own poems to Whitman, who did not reply. When Stoddard wrote again in 1869, however, he did receive a cordial answer. See Horace Traubel, *With Walt Whitman in Camden* (Philadelphia: University of Pennsylvania Press, 1953), 4:267–269. "Semi-love letters" is Gay Wilson Allen's characterization of Stoddard's missives; see *The Solitary Singer: A Critical Biography of Walt Whitman* (New York: Macmillan, 1955), p. 467. Allen also discusses Whitman's somewhat evasive dealings with Carpenter and Symonds. On the latter's probing inquiries about "Calamus," see also Ellis, *Sexual Inversion*, pp. 19–21.

think himself a savage; to declaim against the demoralizing influences of civilization." He yearned "to overthrow conventionality with a brave sweep of the hand, and yet he was the final result of a long system of over-education, over-refinement, and over-religious zeal."[43]

Believing he was trapped in a nature past changing, he lived out the "harmonious incongruity" of being an "unheroic-hero," a "pantheistic-devotee," a "heathenized-christian," and a "half-happy-go-lucky aesthetic Bohemian."[44] Stoddard emulated, as much as was possible in America and as much as his intermittent earnings allowed, the bohemian style of the English "decadents"; simultaneously he clung to a self-image of middle-class probity and respectability. As a prominent convert to Roman Catholicism (in 1867), who professed his faith in a religious tract and was later rewarded by academic appointments to Notre Dame and Catholic University, Stoddard felt a particularly acute tension between his public reputation as a virtuous gentleman of letters and his private activities as a quasi-bohemian homosexual. There was always the danger of scandal, and indeed he left Notre Dame under a cloud of suspicion, and he was subsequently fired from Catholic University, again partly on account of damaging rumors.[45]

Whatever he knew of Stoddard's private life, Howells preferred to take him at his public face value. But it is also clear that Howells recognized Stoddard as one of those "undecided men" — insofar as he regarded him as a man at all. Sedgwick suggests that one way in which middle-class Victorians could fill the "cognitive vacuum" of their thinking about sexuality was to "associate the erotic end of the homosocial spectrum, not with dissipation, not with viciousness or violence, but with childishness, as an infantile need, a mark of powerlessness, which, while it may be viewed with shame or scorn or denial, is unlikely to provoke the virulent, accusatory projection that characterizes twentieth-century homophobia."[46] This idea

---

43. *For the Pleasure of His Company: An Affair of the Misty City: Thrice Told* (San Francisco: A. M. Robertson, 1903), pp. 220–221.

44. Ibid., pp. 8, 10.

45. Stoddard taught English literature at Notre Dame from 1885 to 1886, and at Catholic University from 1892 to 1903. Never happy at South Bend, Stoddard was embroiled throughout his tenure there in controversy with the clerical faculty over the private and academic affairs of an undergraduate, one of his innumerable "Kids," as Stoddard called his youthful companions and lovers. His later dismissal from Catholic University ostensibly resulted from economic retrenchment at a time when enrollment in his classes was dwindling. But other factors may well have been the rivalry of Stoddard's colleague, Maurice Egan, and the impropriety of Stoddard's off-campus living arrangements with Kenneth O'Connor.

46. Sedgwick, *Between Men*, p. 177.

goes far toward explaining the subtle dynamics of the Howells–Stoddard relationship, for Howells always shared his friend Samuel Clemens's assessment of "poor, sweet, pure-hearted, good-intentioned, impotent Stoddard" as a man without "worldly sense": in short, as a child.[47]

Clemens had occasion to observe Stoddard at close range, in London during the winter of 1873–1874, when he hired him as a secretary–companion whose chief duty was "to sit up nights with me & dissipate."[48] Two years later, when he was languishing as a freelance writer in Italy, Stoddard asked Clemens for help, and Clemens turned immediately to Howells. The idea was to arrange a diplomatic sinecure through Rutherford B. Hayes, Howells's cousin by marriage, who was expected to win the upcoming presidential election. As one of the "stainless literary incapables," Stoddard impressed Clemens as having "just the stuff for a consul." Howells agreed, and he promised to "leg like a centipede for C. W. Stoddard, whose virtue-ward-leaning frailties I love and admire."[49]

Beneath the jocularity of Clemens's and Howells's remarks about Stoddard runs an undercurrent of scorn for his "impotence" and, implicitly, for his *un*virtue-ward-leaning "frailties." He was charming, to be sure, but helpless; talented but, alas, incompetent to manage his affairs, to make his own way in the manly worlds of literature and life. This view of Stoddard tallies with his own portrait of Paul Clitheroe, who has "never outgrown a certain childlike ingenuousness and he was not likely to outgrow it."[50] His "unpracticability, his want of application, his vagaries, were freely commented on. They, the critical friends, were ready to wash their hands of him; it were vain to imagine anything could be done for, or with, such a dreamer as he."[51] Like Stoddard's, Clitheroe's literary career has been erratic and largely unrewarded; his lack of economic success has been held against him. "'A shirker of responsibility; one willing to live upon his friends' — alas, this was the unenviable reputation he had innocently and unconsciously achieved."[52] In Howells's view, Stoddard never earned the right to be treated like a man because he never outgrew such childish dependency.

47. *Mark Twain — Howells Letters: The Correspondence of Samuel L. Clemens and William D. Howells, 1872–1910*, ed. Henry Nash Smith, William M. Gibson, and Frederick Anderson (Cambridge: Harvard University Press, 1960), p. 154. Hereafter cited as *MT–HL*.

48. *MT–HL*, p. 154.

49. *MT–HL*, pp. 153–155. Nothing came of Howells's efforts in 1876 (and again in 1879) to arrange a consulship for Stoddard.

50. *For the Pleasure of His Company*, p. 28.

51. Ibid., p. 88.

52. Ibid., p. 221.

III

The relationship between Howells and Stoddard became more intimate only after the latter paid a long-delayed social call in August 1888.[53] Howells was living then at Little Nahant, Massachusetts, where he hoped his ailing daughter Winifred would take strength from the bracing sea winds. It was a gloomy time in his life — caring for Winifred, who was to die less than a year later, was a fretting task — and the amiable guest offered an especially welcome diversion. In his later remembrance of their first meeting, Howells cherished Stoddard's drollery, vitality, and social genius — his "utter lovableness."[54]

Their meeting in Nahant evidently kindled deep affection between the men. But Stoddard also struck up a friendship with Howells's daughter Mildred, and throughout the 1890s there were occasional visits and frequent expressions of ardor all around. In 1892 Stoddard begged Mildred and Howells to autograph his precious copy of *A Little Girl Among the Old Masters*, a book of her childish sketches that her doting father had edited 8 years before. Stoddard added, effusively, how much he wished he could be with them. Howells replied in kind: "We want you dreadfully, for we all love you dearly. I hope that in some world that is worthier of us than this is, you will be our next neighbor."[55] Also in 1892, Howells wrote a glowing prefatory letter to the new (Scribner's) edition of *South-Sea Idyls,* and Stoddard thankfully proffered his "heart" (a cloth cutout surmounted by a cross) as well as an affectionate poem. At Christmas he was repaid with the "heart" of the Howells family, as designed by Mildred. Likewise in 1894, when Stoddard was unanimously chosen to be the Howells family's Valentine, Mildred sent him a commemorative drawing. In expressing his "love" for Stoddard, Howells always put it in the context of a collective

53. As early as 1873, Howells had expressed a desire to meet Stoddard whenever he came east, but they missed connections at that time. Stoddard, who was an inveterate traveler, lived abroad during many of the years between 1873 and 1888.

54. *Harper's Monthly* 136(December 1917):148. Howells remarked that Stoddard was so widely esteemed for his delightful company "that, as he complained once, he was being perpetually passed round on a plate, and there were none of his hosts who did not wish to add some special garniture to the dish." Out of some such motive, perhaps, Howells urged a pair of his own slippers on his guest. Stoddard later joked to a friend that he had stepped into Howells's shoes and was henceforth obliged to be "realistic." This was the sort of wit that had enchanted Howells on Stoddard's arrival at Nahant. Seeing that his middle-aged guest no longer matched his image in the old photograph he had sent in 1873, Howells had exclaimed, "'Stoddard, I thought you were young and flowing.'" With a "deep sigh of humorous sense," Stoddard had quipped, "'I used to flow.'"

55. *SL,* 4:30.

feeling — as if to remind Stoddard (and himself) that anything approaching a "romantic friendship" between them was something to be shared with Howells's family.

In 1901 Stoddard wrote in praise of *Literary Friends and Acquaintance* (in which he had not been mentioned); and Howells, forgetting that he had already replied in July, made up for his imagined oversight in a second acknowledgment in September: "When your dearest and sweetest letter came in June I read it aloud to my daughter, and we both said once more that you were the loveliest soul unhung. . . . Why do you never come to New York, any more? You would relieve that vile place of a part of its reproach, and you would be fallen on the neck by the whole Howells family." On this occasion, Howells also enclosed a poem as testimony to what he had called in his earlier letter "the irrefragable amity between us":

> *If you are not in this book,*
> *My dear Stoddard, turn and look*
> *In the author's heart, and there,*
> *Lightening, sweetening all its care,*
> *Mirrored in its most sacred place,*
> *You shall see your own dear face.*[56]

This was the last in a series of 21 letters that Howells wrote to Stoddard after their meeting in 1888.[57] Nearly all were addressed simply to "My dear Stoddard" or "My dear friend." There were also, however, some curiously affectionate salutations, to which Kermit Vanderbilt has called attention.[58] But all these letters closed perfunctorily, and they were less

56. *SL*, 4:271. Stoddard was "not in this book" because Howells left off his literary reminiscences at a point before he had known him; the omission was without prejudice.

57. Like his character Paul Clitheroe, who writes "scores and scores" of letters to "all sorts of people" and who loves to receive replies "from the four quarters of the globe" (*For the Pleasure of His Company*, p. 166), Stoddard had virtually a fetish about his correspondence. It appears that he saved every scrap he ever received from Howells and his family: 34 items in all (Huntington Library, San Marino, California). On the other hand, Howells (or Mildred, who sorted his papers) saved only 14 of Stoddard's letters, including 3 addressed to Mildred (Houghton Library, Harvard University). As a result, there are some obvious gaps in the Stoddard-to-Howells side of the written record.

58. See Kermit Vanderbilt, "19th-Century Literature," in *American Literary Scholarship: An Annual / 1979*, ed. James Woodress (Durham: Duke University Press, 1981), p. 213. Vanderbilt asks rhetorically if such "troublesome" evidence should be "whispered and then skittishly evaded and dismissed?" Rather, scholars must "pull back the curtains of prudery" and seek "a larger understanding of the private and creative ordeal of Howells and his friends." Vanderbilt is referring to Howells's letters of October 32, [sic] 1893, December 20, 1893, April 8, 1896, June 18, 1896, and November 30, 1897 — all in the Huntington Library.

personal in content than some of Howells's letters with conventional salutations. The great majority of Howells's letters to Stoddard, in fact, were on business, either literary or social, and they were as matter-of-fact in tone as they were in substance.

It would seem, then, that Howells's occasional use of affectionate salutations was not intended too seriously. Likely, this was a gentle parody of Stoddard's own perfervid epistolary style: Howells was joining in the spirit of what he took to be "California humor," of the sort he had always relished in Stoddard's sketches. There is nothing to indicate that Howells and Stoddard were engaging in a "homosexual" flirtation. Howells was repelled by the idea of same-sex genitality.[59] And Stoddard, who was not, was otherwise engaged: with his latest "Kid," Kenneth O'Connor, with whom he moved into his Washington "Bungalow" in 1895.[60]

All the same, Stoddard was something more than an acquaintance to Howells, and there was a subtly erotic factor in their homosocial attachment. To parody Stoddard's style was also for Howells to entertain (and simultaneously to dismiss) the sexual overtones of such language. From the "safe" position of his heterosexuality — which Howells constantly emphasized by invoking his whole family's devotion to Stoddard — he could enjoy a vicarious literary passion. As I have suggested, the kind of literary passion that Howells had indulged in his youth was incompatible with his adult gender identity; incompatible, that is, with the Victorian code, as also inscribed in Freud's psychosexual theory, by which "homosexuality" was regarded as a boyhood phase that a man must outgrow in order to reach a position of dominance in the patriarchal power structure. For a man like Howells, "romantic friendship" could be experienced *only* in parodic form, once he had become a man. It was different for the "childish" Stoddard, who represented to Howells a forsaken part of his own emotional life. And just as Howells's youthful (homo) eroticism had been marked by both desire and disgust, so his adult feelings toward Stoddard were ambivalent: wistful envy and compensatory contempt. This emotional dialectic is seen most strikingly in the two climactic episodes of the Howells–Stoddard relationship.

59. Howells expressed a literally nightmarish dread of (apparently homosexual) attacks by his brain-damaged brother, Henry, who lived with Howells's father and who was locked in a barred room during his periodic fits of a violent and sometimes of a sexual nature. Howells wrote to his father on February 13, 1887: "I dreamed of Henry last night as I have several times, and he attacked me in that odious way; he does it in all my dreams of him." A week later he reported "a pleasanter dream of Henry; he forebore to 'jounce' me." *SL*, 3:183n, 182.

60. Stoddard was given to gushing about his beloved "Kid," whom he was eager to bring to New York to meet Howells, who must have suspected, if he did not know certainly, that Stoddard's relationship to O'Connor was sexual. When no such meeting could be arranged, Stoddard instead invited Howells to Washington, but Howells demurred.

On November 23, 1892, 3 months after Stoddard visited Howells's summer home in Maine, the latter remembered "with envy and regret the hours we passed together in good Acton Taylor's front yard; I wish I had spent all the summer there." Having reaching his deepest point of intimacy with Stoddard, Howells was emboldened to ask some provocative questions: "Whenever we feel gay or sad, we say, we wish Stoddard were here. Does everybody like you, and does it make you feel badly? Are you sure that you are worthy of our affection? If you have some secret sins or demerits, don't you think you ought to let us know them, so that we could love you less?"[61] Howells seemed to be joking here, but as in his affectionate salutations there was more than simple playfulness. He was both inviting confidences and defending himself against receiving them, both expressing a personal interest and checking the impulse toward such intimacy. Stoddard seized on these curiously teasing queries as an opportunity to divulge, obliquely but unmistakably, more of his homoeroticism than he had ever revealed before in his letters to Howells. Stoddard offered as "one of the reasons why I should be despised and rejected" a riddling tale, titled "The Spellbinder," in which he embroidered on what may have been a real adolescent experience — of the sort that Howells had warned his brother against in 1863.

As a schoolboy in California, Stoddard had been infatuated with a godlike youth who, as he told Howells, "had scorn of everybody and everything — save only himself."

> Me he ignored utterly even while I worshiped [sic] silently in his presence and secretly wished that I might die for his sake; for his briefest pleasure I felt that I would joyfully return to dust. Such is the heart of youth when it has been touched by the spirit of romance!
>
> At the close of his first term at school he, one day, wanted a match: we were all in the campus in Holiday attire; all in high spirits and most of the fellows were at his feet. I worship silently and apart — as was my wont.
>
> O Blessed Day! It chanced that there wasn't a match in the crowd; But I was not in the crowd; I was never in the crowd; I had a match. Having become desperate in his fruitless search for a match he, at the last moment, discovered me. I thought I heard a voice from heaven crying for a match. Kismet! My hour had come! He asked me in the doubtfullest way if I had a match and I produced one. It was the proudest moment of my life. The dews of joy were damp upon my brow; my heart turned over with delight. I wished I were a match that he might strike my head against something and consume me at the tip of his cigarette.
>
> He condescended to take my trembling match and turned away without uttering one syllable of thanks. Had I been a paper matchbox he could not have treated me with less indifference.

61. *SL*, 4:30.

My admiration of his haughtiness was boundless. I felt that I had not lived in vain. The one word, the one moment had attoned *[sic]* for the draining of a cup of bitterness that was forever brimming over. Once more I searced *[sic]* to obscure his vission *[sic]* for a moment. It was, apparently, as if I had never been born.

A second term was drawing to a close. I was still unnoticed; yet all this time I would have dragged myself at the wheels of his chariot—had he only given me the chance. In the last pathetic moments of commencement-day—when every heart was in its unaccustomed throat — suddenly the Match-King turned upon me—upon *me*, his abject slave—and protested love of me; and would have me pass my vacation at his Palace; and sit upon his right hand, that he might make mine enemies my footstool; other unspeakable attractions were offered too numerous to mention.

What did thy servant? With one momentary, far away glance that did not admit him or the likes of him within its range, I dismissed his overtures with a wave of my hand as something impossibly presumptuous, and soared away.

The spell was broken. My hour of deliverance had come. At that moment moment *[sic]* he crumbled before me—a creature of the commonest clay—and on the hights *[sic]* of Olympus there was loud laughter among the Gods.

Moral: We are ever human even if we seem divine.[62]

Howells replied with his accustomed half-seriousness, assuring Stoddard that he was duly "hated" but loved all the more for this revelation of his human frailty. Howells added that he could comprehend why Stoddard had finally spurned the Match-King; for an idol has no business to forget himself: One so exalted should remember to be consistently regal.

The "moral" of "The Spellbinder" would seem to apply both to the idol (who proved himself to be less "divinely" indifferent, and thus more "humanly" vulnerable, than his worshipper had supposed) and to the idolater (whose "human" impulse to retaliate proved him to be less than "divinely" forgiving). Freud no doubt would have interpreted "The Spellbinder" as a "homosexual fantasy"; he would also have discounted its "moral" and fixed instead on its insistently sexual imagery and its theme of "masochism" and compensatory "sadism." Howells, who would explore "sado-masochism" in some of his late fiction,[63] intuitively grasped the psycho-

62. Letter of November 30, 1892; copy in Stoddard's 1904 notebook, Bancroft Library, University of California, Berkeley. Quoted with permission. The original of this letter is not extant.

63. See *The Son of Royal Langbrith* (New York: Harper, 1904); *Miss Bellard's Inspiration* (New York: Harper, 1905). In both novels Howells depicted marriage partners bound together by deep desires to abuse and be abused. See also John W. Crowley, "Howells and the Sins of the Father: *The Son of Royal Langbrith*," *The Old Northwest* 7(Summer 1981):79–94.

logic of "The Spellbinder." That is, Howells understood the psychodynamics of a master–slave relationship: that the idol's authority depends on the repression of passion; that the idolater's passion depends on abjection. But he who worships possesses a hidden strength that is the mate to the hidden weakness of he who is worshipped. The master's position is precarious; his authority is vulnerable to a sudden reversal of polarity in the field of power that would render him a slave.

Here once again is the binary of powerful–powerless, as inscribed in the Victorian gender code of patriarchal dominance–effeminate submission. These were the unconscious terms of Howells's relationship to Stoddard: He was his friend's "idol," his master in the literary world, and the grammarian of their interpersonal discourse. Although it seems that Stoddard wished to be frank about his homosexual life, the limits of candor were set implicitly by Howells, whose reticence bounded their intimacy and enforced an inequality between them. As far as Howells *did* encourage Stoddard's confessional impulses — as in asking the kind of questions that had elicited the Spellbinder letter — he was, like the Match-King, forgetting himself and jeopardizing his own dominance.

It is not surprising, then, that Howells proved to be reticent — at least to Stoddard himself — about the latter's autobiographical novel, *For the Pleasure of His Company,* which was completed during the 1890s.[64] After reading a draft in 1896, Howells complained to Louise Imogen Guiney:

> I never saw good material so slightly and inconclusively treated by so charming a master as in his story. There was the potentiality of three or four beautiful stories in his strange performance; but they seemed not to arrive at any common destination. I have not been well enough to criticise the book distinctly to him; but I felt, as you did, the pathetic nervelessness of it. . . . I doubt if the book ever finds a publisher, or if it does, a public.[65]

Certainly, Howells had aesthetic grounds for criticizing this "strange performance"; by his own canons for "realism," the novel could only be judged a complete failure.[66] But when Howells referred to its "pathetic nervelessness," he may have been thinking of its "decadent" atmosphere; for Stoddard's homoeroticism was far more overt here than in his earlier

64. Although Stoddard kept Howells informed (sometimes through Mildred) of his progress, he received his strongest editorial support from Rudyard Kipling, who suggested the title of the novel and took a proprietary interest in it.

65. *SL*, 4:137–138.

66. On the level of plot, for example, the novel is disjunctively episodic, and the chronology of Paul Clitheroe's life is so scrambled that it is nearly impossible to follow. Furthermore, in his vaguely Browningesque attempt to present a "thrice-told" tale from conflicting points of view, Stoddard seems to have lost narrative focus altogether.

fiction. In any case, Howells was soon to lose all pleasure of Stoddard's company.

IV

In November 1902, when he was feeling more than usually impoverished, Stoddard wrote to both Clemens and Howells to complain that Fred Harriott, his literary agent, had pocketed an advance of $400 from the publisher of *Exits and Entrances* (1903). These loyal friends sprang into action: Howells explored ways to pressure the agent through publishing channels; Clemens drafted a vitriolic letter to the malefactor; Howells toned it down in the belief that diplomacy, not force, would prevail. It did and didn't. On December 14, Stoddard informed Clemens that Harriott had now paid him $250. Unfortunately, however, he had withheld the balance and insinuated a threat "to reveal certain supposedly discreditable incidents in Stoddard's career."[67] Clemens clamored for even stronger action against Harriott, but the illness of his daughter Jean forced him to put the matter entirely into Howells's hands. He prepared another letter, sterner than the first, but still calculatedly composed. "H[arriott] seems now disposed to make a stand," Howells told Clemens, "and as what we want is merely to get the money for S. and leave H. to his bad dreams, we had better not to use the whip till we have tried chucking a little more."[68]

So preoccupied was Howells with Stoddard's affairs that Stoddard popped up in one of his own bad dreams, and soon thereafter Howells became exasperated.[69] In December he had complained to Clemens of

67. *MT–HL*, p. 755n. The quoted passage is the editor's paraphrase of Stoddard's letter to Clemens of December 14, 1902. It may be that Harriott was attempting to blackmail Stoddard for homosexual indiscretions.

68. *MT–HL*, p. 759.

69. Howells treated the dream as a joke, telling Clemens that he "must really complain to you of the behavior of your man Sam. I called last night at your place with our old friend Stoddard, and found that to reach the house, I had to climb a plowed field, at the top of which Sam was planting potatoes. . . . [W]hen we came in easy hail of Sam, he called very rudely to us, and asked us what we wanted. I said we wanted to see you, and he said, 'Well, you can't do it,' and no persuasion that I could use had the least effect with him. He said that nobody could see you, and when I gave him my card, and promised him that he would not have a pleasant time with you, when you found out whom he had turned away, he sneered and said he would not give you the card. To avoid mortifying inquiries from the people we had left at the foot of the hill, we came down another way. . . . I cannot remember that Stoddard said anything, but I felt he was as much annoyed as myself." "Bet Howells is drunk yet," Clemens wrote on the envelope and then composed a rollicking sequel to the dream (*MT–HL*, 763–766). All very amusing. But the emotional coloration of the dream—its concern with a servant's annoying rebuke to authority, with Howells's mortification and humiliation—and Stoddard's silent presence in it might be interpreted as a revelation of Howells's unconscious attitude toward the Harriott affair, and also as a foreshadowing of his angry refusal to involve himself further, which occurred just 2 weeks later.

Stoddard's ingratitude: "Under the circumstances, I think a plain 'Thankee!' would have become him. The way of the benefactor is hard."[70] Four days later, he told Clemens that he had returned one of Stoddard's stories, calling it, with unwonted severity, "rubbish of the sort that would appeal to a lovesick chambermaid."[71] His simmering resentment boiled over on February 28, 1903, when he denied Clemens's appeal for yet another assault on the recalcitrant agent: "No, my dearest Clemens, I wont. I was rather anxious to help Stoddard than to do justice on Harriott, and since Stoddard has not breathed one grateful blessing on our efforts, Harriott may go milk all the millionaires, for all me, of the last drop of human kindness in their iron dugs, before I will ask him to put the pail to the lips of that veteran babe and suckling."[72] Clemens scribbled on the envelope of this letter, which he may have forwarded to Stoddard, "Howells won't do any more — & he is right."[73]

Howells did not formally break with Stoddard in 1903, but their correspondence lapsed and their former intimacy turned bittersweet. That summer, *For the Pleasure of His Company* was finally published, but Howells was not moved to lift a finger to help the novel. He never reviewed it, and he apparently kept his silence about it to Stoddard. In December 1903, he did review *Exits and Entrances*, which had been the occasion of the Harriott affair. Howells praised the book in an ambiguous and backhanded way, remarking that the volume — as if it were a personification of Stoddard — had lain before the reviewer all summer, "softly beguiling, gently reproaching him to some recognition of its rare virtues of whimsical humor, frank confidence, capricious reserve, graphic portraiture of persons and places, and a heart of poetry pulsing through all." Stoddard was grouped once again with the California humorists and credited with "that airy grace which is altogether personal to him." But in contrast to the expansive review of *South-Sea Idyls,* this one was notably constrained. In fact, as Howells bluntly admitted, he was using his brief notice of Stoddard as a pretext for his own lengthy essay on Bret Harte: "But above all we believe we prefer among the desultory sketches of his [Stoddard's] latest book his 'Early Recollections of Bret Harte,' or, if we do not, we at any rate find it the most convenient for positing our own recollections of that charming personality."[74]

The next time he received a book from Stoddard, Howells did not even bother to acknowledge it, thus repaying Stoddard's earlier ungrateful

70. *MT–HL,* p. 754.
71. *MT–HL,* p. 754.
72. *MT–HL,* p. 766.
73. *MT–HL,,* p. 766n.
74. "Editor's Easy Chair," *Harper's Monthly* 108(December 1903):153.

silence tit for tat. As he guiltily confessed 2 months after Stoddard's death in 1909, he had just then come around to reading "a very amusing book about traveling in Greece, Turkey, Palestine and Egypt—a Californian's, who sent it me [sic] three years ago, and never got a word of thanks from me. Now he is probably dead from my ingratitude, which I shall try to atone for too late."[75] This atonement was eventually to take the form of the fond recollection of Stoddard that Howells published in 1917, in which neither Harriott nor *For the Pleasure of His Company* was mentioned. But a year after worrying that he had killed Stoddard with unkindness, Howells did not hesitate to assassinate his character in the account of the Harriott affair he wrote for *My Mark Twain* (1910).

There he did not take posthumous revenge on Stoddard by name, referring to him instead as "one of the most helpless and one of the most helped of our literary brethren." He also foreshortened the actual sequence of events, with the effect of scanting his own involvement. The "hapless brother," he recalled, had presented the fact of Harriott's embezzlement but had not asked directly for help, "probably because he knew he need not ask." Nearly 8 years later, Howells was still furious that his partisanship had been taken so ungratefully for granted. He noted that after receiving partial payment, "the helpless man who was so used to being helped did not answer with the gladness I, at least, expected of him":

> At this point I proposed to Clemens that we should let the nonchalant victim collect the remnant himself. Clouds of sorrow had gathered about the bowed head of the delinquent since we began on him, and my fickle sympathies were turning his way from the victim, who was really to blame for leaving his affairs so unguardedly to him in the first place. Clemens made some sort of grim assent, and we dropped the matter. He was more used to ingratitude from those he helped than I was, who found being lain down upon not so amusing as he found my revolt. He reckoned I was right, he said, and after that I think we never recurred to the incident. It was not ingratitude that he ever minded; it was treachery that really maddened him past forgiveness.[76]

For Howells, if not for Clemens, Stoddard's "ingratitude" had been tantamount to "treachery." It was a maddening betrayal of the unspoken assumptions that had governed their entire relationship: that Stoddard the child would submit to Howells's parental authority without ever acting the spoiled brat. The way of the benefactor had become hard indeed when the

75. *SL*, 5:279.
76. *Literary Friends and Acquaintance*, pp. 312–313.

"veteran babe and suckling," whose infantile helplessness seemed to be responsible for the trouble from which his dependency was meant to protect him, failed to appreciate duly the milk of his protector's human kindness.

Although Howells used such imagery of "feminine" nurturance, it was in the context of a rage against Stoddard that was clearly patriarchal. In seeking to nurture Stoddard, Howells had, like the idol in "The Spellbinder," forgotten himself. He had become "effeminately" vulnerable to Stoddard's neglect (which he read as rejection), and he had been left childishly wanting—an abject supplicant to an "undecided man"—thirsting for a drop of his gratitude. Far better had his dugs been iron like the millionaires's; *they* knew how to deal with the likes of Stoddard. When the manly pride of laying on hands had suddenly switched to the unmanly humiliation of being "lain down upon," Howells revolted fiercely. But he could never regain his former ascendancy over Stoddard.

In 1920, the year of his own death, Howells published his anthology of *The Great American Short Stories,* in which "A Prodigal in Tahiti"—the first sketch he had ever accepted from Stoddard—was conspicuously included, despite its being "a bit of autobiography and not a dramatic invention." Howells fancied that the situation would have amused his erstwhile protégé: "if there are smiles in heaven, where he has been these half dozen years, he must be looking down with a characteristic pleasure in the dilemma of the earliest editor of a study which refused to be quite a story."[77] After nearly 50 years, in Howells's last figuration of his relationship to Stoddard, it seemed to have come full circle. But Stoddard, after all, had eluded Howells's grasp. As in "The Spellbinder," when the hour of deliverance had arrived for the idolater, a last laugh was heard from the heavens.

---

77. "A Reminiscent Introduction," *The Great American Short Stories: An Anthology* (New York: Boni & Liveright, 1920), p. ix.

14

Byron and Male Love:
The Classical Tradition

Louis Crompton

The facts about Lord Byron's bisexuality have been well known for a generation. They are amply documented in the writings of his two most important modern biographers, Leslie A. Marchand and Doris Langley Moore. Before these scholars published their unbowdlerized versions of crucial letters, journal entries, and contemporary memoranda, speculations on this subject had existed, notably in the studies by Peter Quennell and G. Wilson Knight. But Marchand and Moore were the first to place several crucial facts beyond doubt.[1] As a teenager at Cambridge, Byron fell seriously in love with another boy, John Edleston, 2 years his junior. Later he looked forward to his first journey to Greece because it might provide opportunities for homosexual experiences (which were still capital offenses in early-nineteenth-century Britain), and indeed did have such experiences during his sojourn in Athens. Finally, we now also know that at the end of his life, when he returned to Greece as a leader in the movement for Greek independence, Byron fell desperately in love with another Greek boy and wrote about his affair in his last three poems.

My present aim is not to review these facts[2] but to illuminate how Byron's reading of Greek and Latin literature and his knowledge of classical history gave him a conceptual framework for understanding his feelings, unacceptable as they were to his fellow countrymen, and a mode for

1. Peter Quennell, *Byron: The Years of Fame* (New York: Viking Press, 1935); G. Wilson Knight, *Lord Byron's Marriage* (New York: Macmillan, 1957); Leslie A. Marchand, *Byron: A Biography*, 3 vols. (New York: Alfred A. Knopf, 1957); Doris Langley Moore, *The Late Lord Byron* (London: John Murray, 1961) and Appendix II ("Byron's Sexual Ambivalence") in *Lord Byron: Accounts Rendered* (London: John Murray, 1974).

2. I attempt to do this in my book *Byron and Greek Love: Homophobia in 19th-Century England* (Berkeley: University of California Press, 1985).

expressing them in a poetic form where gender was often ambiguous or disguised. But in order to do this we must first understand how these ancient traditions, so different from ours and so ambivalently regarded by English society in Byron's day, perceived the links between love and gender, and specifically how they perceived homoerotic relations between males. Although the two cultures shared important common assumptions about such matters, it may be useful to contrast what we may call the heroic Greek tradition with the Latin or Horatian mode.

The Greek ideal received its most notable expression in the speech of Phaedrus in Plato's *Symposium*. In this dialogue, the most famous discussion of love in classical antiquity, perhaps of all time, the guests at Agathon's banquet are invited to deliver panegyrics on the subject of *eros*. They assume as a matter of course that love as a bond between individuals means primarily love between men, inspired by youthful male beauty, and proving itself through heroic actions:

> For I know not [Phaedrus declares in the speech that opens the dialogue] any greater blessing to a young man who is beginning life than a virtuous lover, or to the lover, than a beloved youth. For the principle which ought to be the guide of men who would live nobly — that principle, I say, neither kindred nor honor, nor wealth, nor any other influence is able to implant so well as love. . . . And if there were only some way of contriving that a state or army should be made up of lovers and their loves they would be the very best governors of their own city, abstaining from all dishonor, and . . . when fighting at each other's side, although a mere handful, they would overcome the world.[3]

The most celebrated instance of this love in Greek literature was the love of Achilles for Patroclus, which, whatever its nature in Homer, Aeschylus made explicitly sexual in a famous tragedy entitled *The Myrmidons,* known to us now only through fragments. In Athens its archetypal instance was the love of Aristogiton and Harmodius, the tyrannicide heroes whose statues stood in the place of honor at the center of the city, as martyrs to, and patrons of, Athenian democracy. In the history of Greece its most famous realization was the so-called Sacred Band of Thebes, a regiment of 300 lovers who fought side by side, which existed for 50 years until its annihilation at Cheronea by the forces of Philip and Alexander.[4]

3. *The Dialogues of Plato,* trans. Benjamin Jowett, 4th ed. (Oxford: Clarendon Press, 1953), 1:510.

4. Sir Kenneth Dover's *Greek Homosexuality* (London: Duckworth, 1978) is an impressive recent treatment of the subject, but rather narrow in its approach. Félix Buffière's *Eros adolescent: la pédérastie dans la Grèce antique* (Paris: Société d' Édition "Les Belles Lettres," 1980) is much more comprehensive in its treatment of historical and literary sources.

In Western civilization, love first took on social value in a warrior society. It was esteemed as a source of military morale and was regarded as noble because it inspired self-sacrifice. Women might achieve it, as in the case of Alcestis who died for her husband, but this was a rare exception. Primarily it was a form of male bonding, in which an older lover, or *erastes*, devoted himself to a younger *eromenos*, or beloved.

Byron has left ample evidence that he was familiar with the literary and historic traditions of Greek male love. He gives no sign that he knew the *Symposium* (which was largely ignored or bowdlerized in his day), but he does celebrate Harmodius' heroism in Canto III of *Childe Harold*, and, in a catalogue of romantic friendships that he includes in a letter to his friend Elizabeth Pigot, he mentions Orestes and Pylades, who are identified as heroic lovers in the pseudo-Lucianic dialogue *On Love*. And we know from a letter written in Greece that he visited Mantinea where Epaminondas died leading the Sacred Band and was buried with his lover Cephisodorus, who also fell in the battle.[5]

Byron was most conscious of this Greek tradition in its Latinized form. There are very few examples of heroic love in Latin, but Virgil in the ninth book of the *Aeneid* tells a story obviously inspired by Achilles and Patroclus, the episode of Nisus and Euryalus, a tale that early gripped Byron's imagination. Not only did he include Nisus and Euryalus in the Pigot catalogue, he also wrote a narrative poem which was, as he put it, "paraphrased" from Virgil. Nisus is the older youth, Euryalus the beautiful younger boy for whom Nisus dies when he tries to rescue him from their foes. Byron in his couplets describes him as a "rose," a "crimson poppy," and a "fading flower." The "celestial pair" die in each other's arms in a kind of Byronic *Liebestod*. Another story of heroic sacrifice in classical antiquity that appealed to Byron was the legend of Antinous. Byron had earlier translated Hadrian's famous address to his soul in the *Hours of Idleness*. In his notes to *Childe Harold*, Canto II, Byron refers to Antinous' "noble" death, purportedly a sacrifice he voluntarily made to further the success of his imperial lover, a death that Hadrian commemorated by founding a city named after his *eromenos* and inaugurating a religious cult in his honor.[6]

But Hadrian was the most hellenized of the Roman emperors, and his love for Antinous, whom he deified after his drowning, was unique, to my knowledge, in the annals of Latin biography, where homosexual affairs usually figure simply as titillating gossip. Suetonius' *Lives* of the first 12

---

5. *Byron's Letters and Journals*, ed. Leslie A. Marchand (Cambridge: Harvard University Press, 1973), 1:127, 2:16.

6. The historical background for this relationship has recently been documented in an interesting book by Royston Lambert, *Beloved and God* (New York: Viking, 1984).

328   Louis Crompton

Caesars is a good example of this denigrating tendency. Indeed, Latin literature on the theme of male love, taken as a whole, contrasts strikingly with Greek literature. No philosophical discourses or tragic dramas celebrate homosexuality as a source of courage or wisdom or civic virtue. The Greeks saw a boy's relation with an older man as an initiation into the world of male valor and power and privilege, and therefore as a social institution. This is especially evident in the poetry of Theognis and in the so-called Cretan rapes described by Strabo, which were pseudo marriages transmitting the values of a military aristocracy. Latin poetry, by contrast, regularly presents boys and women alike simply as objects of affection or desire. Here the two genders are assimilated to each other, the boy playing essentially a feminine role. In a well-known passage on love in Book IV of *De Rerum Natura*, Lucretius speaks of Venus launching her shafts either through the power of a woman or "a boy with girlish limbs." Even the poet Ovid, who is almost an anomaly in the Augustan age in addressing no poems to boys, still recognizes the literary convention. At the beginning of his *Amores* he complains, "I have no boy I can sing of, or long-haired girl."

This tradition was not, of course, unknown to Greek literature. Many of the poems of Book XII of the *Greek Anthology*, which collects about 300 brief lyrics on the subject of the love of boys, could as easily have been written to or about women or girls. But in Latin literature, this feminizing tendency almost entirely holds the field. The love poems written by Catullus to Juventius, by Tibullus to Marathus, and by Horace to Ligurinus, for example, are remarkably similar to the poems these poets address to women. One of Catullus' most famous love poems to Lesbia tells her how many kisses he desires. It is closely parallel to a poem to Juventius which begins:

> *If I could go on kissing your honeyed eyes,*
> *Juventius, then I would kiss each of them*
> *Three hundred thousand times and not be sated.*[7]

Byron was very familiar with this poem. He translated it on November 16, 1806, and published it a year later with the acknowledgment, "Imitated from Catullus." But since poetry addressed to one's own gender was taboo in his age he added a legitimating subtitle, "To Ellen."

Byron made this translation at age 18, at the height of his emotional involvement with the Cambridge choir boy John Edleston, which had begun about a year earlier. Catullus may have been the inspiration for this poem in two different ways. For as Byron changed the addressee of his

---

7. Carmen 48, trans. James Michie, *The Penguin Book of Homosexual Verse*, ed. Stephen Coote (New York: Penguin, 1983), p. 80.

translation from male to female, so Catullus changed the gender of the speaker in his Latin translation of Sappho's famous ode, making the poem an expression of his love for Lesbia. On the one hand, Catullus used a heterosexualized lesbian poem as a vehicle for his own heterosexual emotion; Byron, by contrast, used a heterosexualized homoerotic poem to disguise his homoerotic feelings. In Georgian England, such a strategy was essential. A mistake about gender, if publicly detected, could lead to ostracism and exile. Thus the newspaper paragraph that in 1784 cut off Byron's older contemporary and fellow author William Beckford from English society for the remaining 60 years of his life read as follows: "The rumor concerning a *Grammatical mistake* of Mr. B—[William Beckford] and the Hon. Mr. C—[William Courtenay] in regard to the genders, we hope for the honour of Nature originates in *Calumny!*"[8]

But the poem that became a byword for bisexual amorousness in Byron's circle was another Latin classic, Horace's celebrated "Ode to Venus" from Book 4 of the *Odes*. In these lines Horace confesses his passion for Ligurinus, and laments that, at 50, he is far too old for such an infatuation; he tells us that he "takes no joy in the naive hope of mutual love of woman or boy." Byron repeatedly quotes Horace's phrase *"nec femina nec puer"* in his letters as a code reference to his homosexual experiences in Greece. In his humorous "Petition to J. C. H. [John Cam Hobhouse]" in which he bids him salute their common friend Charles Skinner Matthews, who shared Byron's homoerotic interests, the expression "Horatian way" is used as a synonym for bisexuality.

Byron's own psychological development reveals that, first as a boy and then as a young man, he turned at one moment to women, at another to his own sex. Seduced by his Scottish nurse at the age of 9, he eventually complained of her behavior to the family lawyer. The one oblique reference to the relation he makes in his journals shows neither ill will nor indignation; he does, however, coolly assess its effect as negative. Some of his melancholia he thinks may be traced to his precocious sexual initiation. A far more sensitive point was his deformed foot. When a sympathetic nurse ill-advisedly commiserated him on his disability, he is reported to have struck her with his child's whip and to have lashed out in his boyish Scots dialect: "Didna speak of it." His mother's comments must have been even harder to bear. Proud, foolish, doting, irascible Mrs. Byron called him a "lame brat" when he exasperated her. Later (quite unfairly) he blamed his deformity on her prudery for not having proper medical attendance at his birth. His bitterness must have been intensified when he fell violently in love with Mary Chaworth at the age of 15, only to have her reject him as "that lame boy."

8. Noel I. Garde, *Jonathan to Gide* (New York: Vantage Press, 1964), p. 501.

About Byron's relations with boys at Harrow, there is a degree of mystery. We know he took a protective attitude there to several younger boys, including William Harness, who was also lame, to whom he wrote poems and with whom he began a faintly amorous correspondence after his return from Greece. Numerous verses celebrating romantic friendships were inspired by other schoolmates. In "Childish Recollections," the most elaborate of these poems, he tells us the intensity of these attachments puzzled him; he ascribed their force to his lack of close family ties. Several years later, Lady Caroline Lamb reported to Lady Byron that Byron had confessed to having "corrupted" three of his school fellows. (We do not know if the expression was Byron's, adopted to shock her, or whether Lady Caroline herself chose the word.) Whatever components of affection and lust mingled in Byron's Harrow friendships, it appears that none of them matured into an intensely reciprocated love affair.

Such a development came in Byron's first year at Cambridge when he fell in love with John Edleston. What seems to have made this relation different from Byron's earlier emotional entanglements was Byron's conviction that, for the first time, he was loved in return. He describes the experience in two revealing poems, "The Cornelian" and "Pignus Amoris." John, whom Byron had presumably showered with gifts, tried to reciprocate by giving him a cornelian heart. His anxiety that Byron might despise so cheap a present caused him to burst into tears. Byron, assured for the first time that someone could indeed love him, burst into tears himself. Byron included "The Cornelian," which gives some details of this episode, in his first book of privately printed poems and then suppressed it. "Pignus Amoris," which recounts the story more fully, remained in manuscript until 1898. In both poems, Edleston's sex is male, and he is described simply as a "friend." But when he next ventured into print, Byron was more cautious. Edleston has become abstract — he is a "Form," a "Voice," a "Face," a "Bosom," etc — but Byron describes a physical closeness expressed by kisses and embraces. For this reason, Byron changed Edleston's gender by calling the poem "Stanzas to Jessy" when he published his quatrains in *Monthly Literary Recollections*. After Edleston's death, Byron employed the same device in the elegies which transformed Edleston into Thyrza, this time going a step further by referring to his beloved as "her" in one of this lyrics. In "To Thyrza" he speaks not only of kisses but a "passion" that might conceivably have asked "for more" than these, thus implying a definite undercurrent of erotic feeling. The poems, of course, created much curiosity, not least among Byron's female readers. A decade later, after their separation, Lady Byron, who shared the general puzzlement about Thyrza's identity, recorded a conversation Byron had with her about Thyrza. Byron, she wrote, "described *her* beauty as he has described beauty in the abstract" — obviously he was concerned not to give away the truth about Edleston's gender.[9] Lady Byron added further details about the intensity of the feelings Byron had experienced: He "told me of the emotion with which he used to expect the hour of meeting, when he would walk up and down till he almost fainted, and said he was sure that such a state of excitation, if circumstances had not put an end to it, must have destroyed him."[10] There is no reason to believe that Byron, in this voluntary confession, was exaggerating his responses, which by English standards would have been quite unacceptable as inspired by another male.

On the same day he wrote "To Thyrza," Byron wrote a much stranger poem, the "Epistle" to Francis Hodgson. There, in a mood prophetic of the "Byronic hero" of his later dramas and tales, he envisages himself becoming one of the "worst anarchs" of his age in a kind of bloody civil war. The poem was written as an exasperated response to an effort by Hodgson to raise Byron's spirits after he had heard of Edleston's death. It contains only one oblique reference to Edleston — "all I loved is changed or gone" — where the second loss presumably refers to John and the first ("the change") to Mary Chaworth, who by this time had married someone else. This poem suggests that her rejection of Byron was curiously interwoven with his feelings about Eldeston, whose love must have appeared as a kind of reassurance.

The last three poems Byron wrote in Greece, shortly before his death in 1824, contrast with the Edleston poems by being conceived, like "Nisus and Euryalus," in the heroic tradition. But this time the heroic circumstances derive from Byron's own life and situation. Lukas Chalandritsanos, the handsome 15-year-old Greek boy Byron fell in love with, was a "freedom fighter" in the war of Greek independence who was given a minor military command by Byron at the Greek headquarters in Missolonghi. In the famous poem completed on his thirty-sixth birthday, Byron decries his infatuation as a distraction from his duty as a political and military leader:

> *Tread those reviving passions down*
> *Unworthy Manhood;— unto thee [i.e., Byron]*
> *Indifferent should the smile or frown*
> *Of Beauty be.*

Indeed, Byron read the poem publicly to his friends on his birthday as a kind of statement of recommitment to the Greek cause, which he was ready to die for in battle. But Byron had underestimated the strength of his "maddening fascination," as he called it in the second of the three last poems. His final poem ("Love and Death") is an impassioned declaration of love in which he enumerates the occasions in which he has shown his

---

9. Malcolm Elwin, *Lord Byron's Wife* (New York: Harcourt, Brace and World, 1962), p. 283.

10. Ibid.

devotion to Lukas. He had been willing to fight the Turks hand-to-hand to save him if they had been captured during the sea voyage to the Greek mainland. He was anxious about his safety when shipwreck threatened. He nursed him through a fever and was obsessed with thoughts of him when he himself was at the point of death after a convulsive fit a few days later. Though all these events were real episodes in Byron's life, they are strikingly close to the signs of devotion a Greek *erastes* was traditionally expected to show towards his *eromenos,* as set forth, for instance in the pseudo-Lucianic dialogue on love. Byron's own life thus ended by affirming two kinds of ancient Greek heroism: first the willingness to fight to the death for Greek liberty, and to put love aside to do this, and second, when the renunciation of love proved impossible, to play the protective role of the heroic *erastes,* even though he knows Lukas does not and cannot return his love:

> *Thus much and more—and yet thou lov'st me not,*
> *And never wilt—Love dwells not in our will,*
> *Nor can I blame thee—though it be my lot*
> *To strongly—wrongly—vainly—love thee still.*

The affair ended in an impasse and Byron died a few weeks later, the victim of fever, kidney failure, and the ineptitude of the physicians who attended him. His poem "On This Day I Complete My Thirty-Six Year" was published a few months after his death. "Love and Death" did not appear until more than 60 years later. When it was printed in *Murray's Magazine* in 1887, the editor added the following comment, which had the effect of obscuring its real origin: "A note attached to these verses by Lord Byron states that they were addressed to no one in particular, and were a mere poetical Scherzo."

Whether Byron actually appended such a note or whether it was concocted by his friend John Cam Hobhouse (who apparently destroyed the original) to disguise the facts is unclear. "Love and Death," which addresses Lukas in the second person throughout, is genderless, though the military context certainly suggests a male object. It was not until the 1950s that Byron's biographers established its significance as a personal confession. But if we now look at it in its true context, we see that it not only expresses a deeply felt and painfully frustrated love but assimilates this love to the male roles deemed appropriate in classical Greek culture. Byron used an ancient tradition to frame and justify a passion that his contemporaries would have found incomprehensible.

AUTHOR'S NOTE: This essay is a revised version of a paper delivered at a seminar on Byron and the Question of Gender, sponsored by the Byron Society, at the annual meeting of the Modern Language Association, Chicago, December 27, 1985.

About the Contributors

Harry Brod has held a joint appointment in the Program for the Study of Women and Men in Society and the Department of Philosophy at the University of Southern California from 1982 to 1987. For 1987–1988, he is a Fellow in Law and Philosophy at the Harvard Law School, where he is working on men's reproductive rights. He has edited special issues of several scholarly journals on various aspects of men's studies. His articles on men's studies and feminism have appeared in numerous academic, professional, and popular publications. He is a frequent lecturer and men's movement activist, and is currently the National Spokesperson for the National Organization for Changing Men. He has published on social and political theory, Hegel, applied ethics, and critical thinking, and is writing a book on male feminism.

Tim Carrigan teaches sociology at Macquarie University, New South Wales, Australia.

Bob Connell is foundation professor of sociology at Macquarie University in Sydney (NSW 2113, Australia). His books include *Making the Difference; Teachers' Work; Class Structure in Australian History;* and *Which Way Is Up?* In press is a book setting out a general social theory of gender. He is currently involved in a life-history study of changes in masculinity, a survey on gay sexuality and the prevention of AIDS, an analysis of the state in sexual politics, theoretical work on the relations between structure and practice, and sharing the care of a 2-year-old daughter.

Louis Crompton is professor of English at the University of Nebraska at Lincoln. He is the author of *Byron and Greek Love: Homophobia in 19th-Cen-*

tury England and teaches a course in sex roles in literature. He is at work on a book on *Homosexuality and Civilization.*

John W. Crowley received his B.A. from Yale University (B.A.) and his M.A. and Ph.D. from Indiana University. Since 1970, he has taught at Syracuse University, where he is professor of English and director of the Humanities doctoral program. Author of numerous articles on W. D. Howells and other American writers, he has written two books and edited several others. His most recent work is *The Black Heart's Truth: The Early Career of W. D. Howells* (University of North Carolina Press, 1985). At present, Crowley is serving as guest editor for the Howells sesquicentennial issue of *American Literary Realism,* and he is preparing for publication Roger Austen's biography of Charles Warren Stoddard.

Peter Filene has been teaching a variety of courses at the University of North Carolina, Chapel Hill for the past 20 years. His current research focuses on biographical and fictional narrative. He has been learning, meanwhile, from a men's group every Monday and a writing group every Thursday. His latest books are *Men in the Middle: Work and Family in the Lives of Middle-Aged Men* (1981) and a revised edition of *Him / Her / Self: Sex Roles in Modern America* (1986).

Clyde W. Franklin II is a professor of Sociology at The Ohio State University, Columbus. He specializes in social psychology and gender. His recent publications include *The Changing Definition of Masculinity; Black Male— Black Female Conflict: Individually Caused and Culturally Nurtured;* and, *The Black Male Barbershop as a Sex Role Socialization Setting.* Currently, he is finishing a fourth book entitled *Men and Society* and doing research on suburban black male youth socialization.

Dorothy Hammond and Alta Jablow received their doctorates in cultural anthropology from Columbia University in 1963. They are, presently, Professors Emeritae in the Department of Anthropology, Brooklyn College, CUNY, having retired in 1986. They have collaborated in the writing of *The Africa That Never Was* (1970), reissued as the *Myth of Africa* (1977). They have written several modules on the role of women and *Women in Cultures of the World* (1976). Separately, Hammond's interests and writing have been on associations and magic; Jablow on folklore, particularly the trickster figure. They are currently engaged in research for a book on the nature and role of friendship in society.

Michael S. Kimmel is assistant professor of sociology at Rutgers University, where he teaches courses on social movements, comparative historical sociology, social theory, and the sociology of the male experience. He is the author of *Absolutism and Its Discontents: State and Society in 17th Century France and England* (forthcoming 1988) and *Revolution in the Sociological Imagination* (forthcoming 1988). He edited a special issue of *American Behavioral Scientist* on Men's Roles (May/June 1986) and is also the editor of *Changing Men: New Directions in Research on Men and Masculinity* (1987). His current research includes a study of the "engendering" of sexual desire (with John Gagnon) and a book-length study of men's responses to feminism in late nineteenth- and early twentieth-century United States. He also writes regularly on sexuality and gender for major magazines and newspapers, has served on the National Council of the National Organization for Changing Men, and is the book review editor of *Society* and *Changing Men*.

John Lee is researching the history of homosexual subcultures in Australia.

Michael Messner is a lecturer in the Department of Sociology and Social Services and a member of the Center for Family and Community Studies at California State University, Hayward. He is an associate editor of *Changing Men: Issues in Gender, Sex, and Politics* and was the guest editor of a special issue of *Arena Review 9* (2), Winter 1985, on sport, men, and masculinity. Current research interests include organized sport and the ideology of male superiority, and the political economy of male participation in parenting.

Richard L. Ochberg is a clinical psychologist in New Haven, Connecticut. He is interested in the interplay between psychodynamic and cultural influences on the conduct of adult lives, and especially, careers. His recent book, *Middle-aged Sons and the Meaning of Work* explores the symbolic relationship between men's careers and their largely unconscious attempts to come to terms with their fathers. He has also done research on gender differences in mentoring. He is currently co-editing a special edition of the *Journal of Personality* on psychobiography and life narratives.

Joseph H. Pleck is the Henry R. Luce Professor of Families, Change, and Society at Wheaton College (Massachusetts). He is the author of *Working Wives, Working Husbands* (1985) and *The Myth of Masculinity* (1981). His current research focuses on paternity leave and on adolescent male contraceptive behavior.

James D. Riemer is assistant professor at Marshall University. He has most recently published essays in *The Southern Quarterly* and *Erotic Universe:*

Sexuality in Fantastic Literature. In addition to pursuing his research interests involving the plays of Sam Shepard and approaching American literature from a men's studies perspective, he is currently completing a book-length study on the fantasy novels of James Branch Cabell.

Drury Sherrod is a social psychologist, associated with the Claremont Colleges in Claremont, California, where he has served on the faculties of Pitzer College, Scrips College, and the Claremont Graduate School. He has published a textbook on social psychology and numerous articles on environmental stress, self-perception and social behavior. His current research focuses on social support and friendship, and his most recent publication is entitled "Social Skills and the Stress-Protective Role of Social Support," with S. Cohen and M. Clark in the *Journal of Personality and Social Psychology,* (May, 1986). He is currently writing a book on gender differences in friendship and is researching friendship patterns in adult men and women.

Catharine R. Stimpson is professor of English and dean of the Graduate School at Rutgers University, the State University of New Jersey. Now the editor of a book series for the University of Chicago Press, from 1974 to 1980 she was the founding editor of *Signs: Journal of Women in Culture and Society.* The author of a novel, *Class Notes* (1979); the editor of six books, she has also published over 80 monographs, short stories, essays, and reviews. Her book on Gertrude Stein and cultural change is under contract for publication.

Perry Treadwell has pursued studies at the U.C.L.A. Brain Research Institute, the University of Minnesota and the Salk Institute. He retired from Emory University Medical School in 1974 to devote full time to consulting. He is the author of several publications in popular literature on men's issues including *Voices* and *Men Freeing Men,* cofounder of The Men's Experience, a men's support organization, in 1977 and the Southern Institute of Gender Studies in 1985. Presently Treadwell is building a Men's Studies Bibliography Data Base and is leading workshops called "Making the Male Connection: Intimate Friendships," exploring friendships between men and between men and women.

Index